I0234603

ODYSSEY OF MY LIFE

ODYSSEY OF MY LIFE

SHIVRAJ V. PATIL

RUPA

Published by
Rupa Publications India Pvt. Ltd 2014
7/16, Ansari Road, Daryaganj
New Delhi 110002

Sales centres:
Allahabad Bengaluru Chennai
Hyderabad Jaipur Kathmandu
Kolkata Mumbai

Copyright © Shivraj V. Patil 2014

Photographs courtesy Shivraj V. Patil

All rights reserved.
No part of this publication may be reproduced, transmitted,
or stored in a retrieval system, in any form or by any means, electronic,
mechanical, photocopying, recording or otherwise, without the prior
permission of the publisher.

ISBN: 978-81-291-3001-3

First impression 2014

10 9 8 7 6 5 4 3 2 1

The moral right of the author has been asserted.

This book is sold subject to the condition that it shall not, by way
of trade or otherwise, be lent, resold, hired out, or otherwise circulated,
without the publisher's prior consent, in any form of binding or cover
other than that in which it is published.

*This book is
dedicated to the
spirit and the
memory of spirituality
of Sri Sathya Sai Baba*

CONTENTS

Preface ix

1. My Village 1
2. Family Members 9
3. My School and College Years 23
4. Lecturer and Lawyer 42
5. Member and President of Latur Municipality 63
6. Member of the Maharashtra Legislative Assembly 89
7. Deputy Minister of Law and Judiciary, Irrigation and Protocol 111
8. Presiding over the Maharashtra Legislative Assembly 122
9. Member of Lok Sabha 141
10. Visits to Vietnam, Cambodia, Laos and North Korea 156
11. Union Minister of State for Defence 167
12. Foreign Trade Minister of State with Independent Charge 180
13. Union Minister of State in the Textile Ministry with Independent Charge 201
14. Minister of State in the Ministry of Science and Technology, Nuclear Science and Technology, Space, Electronics, Ocean Development, Genetic, Non-Conventional Energy 209
15. Minister of State in the Defence Ministry for Defence Production and Supplies 230

16. Union Minister of State for Civil Aviation with Independent Charge	239
17. Union Minister of State for Tourism with Independent Charge	248
18. Deputy Speaker, Lok Sabha	251
19. Speaker, Lok Sabha	254
20. Sitting on the Opposition Benches	312
21. Deputy Opposition Leader of the Congress Party in the Lok Sabha	319
22. Home Minister	333
Biodata	403
Acknowledgements	409
Index	411

PREFACE

This book contains information about my personal life, family members, friends, political colleagues and leaders who helped me in my political journey. It also talks about my innings in a municipality, as its member and president; my innings at the state and Union level legislatures and executive; my journeys to foreign countries and international conferences; about the past, the present and future situations relating to the systems; and issues and problems and their solutions.

This book does not say that I did this or did not do that, or that I was responsible for good things and not for the unfortunate mistakes and defects found in the working of the institutions, organizations and governments. It does not praise or criticize anybody and does not have any spicy material.

What is written about my personal life, family members and friends is very brief. What is written about the situations, issues and solutions finds more space in the pages of this book. The systems, issues and problems that may occur in the future and the solutions that may be found to overcome these difficulties occupy more pages of this book.

The book is written not to entertain the readers. It is meant to leave back the account of the situations that were faced and handled in the past, and that may be required to be handled in the future.

The readers who have knowledge about the situations, organizations and governments may find reading it less cumbersome and more useful.

Let us wait and see how it would be judged by them.

1

MY VILLAGE

A huge horse loomed above me, looking all the more frightening because it refused to stand still, shifting menacingly from side to side and stamping its hooves on the road. I stood petrified as my grandfather tried to control it, pulling its reins hard. He wanted me to climb on the back of this horse. When I expressed my fear, saying that it could throw me on to the ground, he got quite angry with me and lifted his hand as if to hit me. He restrained himself, then picked me up and threw me on the back of the horse. It became more restless and began to raise its front legs alarmingly. Grabbing the saddle and rein, I tried to keep myself on its back. At that moment, a drum-beater who was going to attend a marriage ceremony in the neighbourhood passed by. My grandfather stopped him and made him beat his drum to make the horse dance vigorously, in tune with the rhythm of the drumbeats. When the horse was fully controlled and I became a little steadier in the saddle, he pulled me off its back, put me on the ground and said, 'Now, run back to the house. This is not for you—you are too timid.' I followed his instructions. While returning to the house, I realized that it was not very difficult to ride a horse. I could do it with a little training. I decided to learn horse-riding with the help of family assistants. Within a few days, I did learn to ride without difficulty.

My earliest memories are of my grandfather, Veer Bhagwantrao

Patil. He loved horses, camels, bullocks and cows. He wanted all his family members to learn and master the art of horse-riding, and all his sons did so. Even the small children of his family were made to learn horse-riding in the early years of their lives. The fact that I had mastered horse-riding well was proved one day when our family members, including my grandfather, father, uncles and aunts, were returning to our village after attending the wedding of a close relative's son. As we passed through a rocky, forested area, it started raining. Some young members of the family were riding horses, while the others were sitting in bullock carts, well covered to protect the occupants from the sun, wind or rain. One of our assistants gave me an umbrella to protect myself from the rain. When I opened the umbrella, the animal got scared and began to jump wildly. My grandfather leapt out of his bullock cart, rushed to it, caught hold of its reins and tried to control it. But the horse was too big and strong. It tossed him from one side to the other. Fearing that my grandfather could be thrown to the ground and trampled upon by the scared horse, I asked him to give up the reins and withdraw, and leave the animal to be controlled by me. My grandfather was reluctant to leave the horse, but when I kept entreating him, he gave up the reins. I allowed the horse to run for a distance, and then tried to control it. The horse, too, perhaps realized that the umbrella was not a dangerous object and quietened down, allowing me to ride it. I brought it back to the place where the bullock carts had stopped. My grandfather patted the horse on its neck and me on my thigh, and said, 'Now I know you can ride any horse. I am happy. This, you should know, is the result of my throwing you on the back of my horse that day. You should remember it. Good. Very good.' Everyone who had seen what had happened was happy to hear my grandfather's words.

Girijabai, my grandmother, was the favourite of her paternal family, who gave her great importance and allowed her to take decisions in many family matters, which could have been taken by her father. In her husband's family, she was given even more importance. She was not educated but had common sense, which she used to manage the affairs of the family in the best possible manner. That was why her husband approved and agreed to whatever she did or decided, without questioning her. She had learnt the art of treating many ailments. Patients belonging to all castes, religions and sections of society, especially those who were poor, sought her medical help. In those days, the society was not as advanced as it is today. Untouchability and caste discrimination were practised, and those who violated the customs were looked down upon and also treated as untouchables—but this did not bother my grandmother in the least. Her husband, all her sons and most of our family members appreciated and supported what she did. In fact, in the family, nobody had the guts to oppose her views and actions, which were always correct, considerate and helpful to others.

She loved her grandchildren more than her own children. My cousin Hanumantrao and I were her most favoured grandsons. She loved me more than my mother could have.

We lived together in a big village called Chakur in Latur district, Maharashtra. Before the reorganization of states, it was in the Bidar district of Hyderabad state, then a rich and powerful monarchy ruled by the nizams of the Asaf Jahi dynasty. Now, Bidar district is in Karnataka. Chakur has become a taluka (subdivision of the district), and is growing in size and importance with great speed.

My grandfather was the head of the village. Most of the inhabitants of Chakur were landless labourers and farmers, while a few were traders. There were a few government and private hospitals manned by doctors and nurses, as well as educational institutions where teachers from all parts of the district and the state were employed. The villagers were a contented lot. They worked hard to earn their subsistence and lived on their modest income.

At the centre of the village stood a structure which looked like a small fort, and was called a 'gadi'. The gadi had tall and strong walls, supported and held by roundish structures called 'buruj'. On top of it were five houses, occupied by the families of my grandfather and his cousins. Only one road allowed the inhabitants of the gadi to reach their houses. This road could be closed by shutting the big gates, when required, to provide safety to the structure and its occupants. In the olden days, the gadi provided shelter to its occupants and the villagers when attacked by dacoits or by forces from other states. It was surrounded by a ring road from which a few roads went out of the village. A few roads had some big houses and small shops, where traders lived and did their business, on both sides of them. These traders purchased farm produce and sold goods, clothes, medicines and other such items to the villagers.

The house occupied by my grandfather's family was quite big and could accommodate a large number of persons. It was built by him and my father during the period in which my brother and I were born. My grandfather, grandmother and my father lived there all their lives. In the latter part of their lives, my uncles and their families moved out to live separately in other houses.

The house was very comfortable to live in, and is intact even today. But now, no one lives there or in the other houses on the gadi. All the former inhabitants have built houses in other parts of the village.

The houses on the gadi were built with stones, mortar, mud and wooden rafters, in the style of olden-day houses. At the centres of the houses there were open spaces, which allowed ample sunlight and air, cooling the interiors in summer and keeping them warm in winter.

■

Chakur is connected to other villages, towns, and cities in three states—Andhra, Karnataka and Maharashtra—by road and rail. Because of this, it is visited by many villagers from the area. Now, it has many government offices.

At a distance of two kilometres from the village is a lovely hillock, known as the 'hillock of Haquani Baba'. It might have been a volcano earlier. On the top is the tomb of Haquani Baba, from where the view is breathtakingly panoramic. I used to go to the tomb on horseback nearly every day during my school and college holidays. My family members visited it at least once or twice a year to offer their prayers, joining people of all religions from the area. The hillock is surrounded by land, which does not have many trees but has a waterbody that provides water to people visiting the tomb.

Near the hillock is a railway station, the Latur Road railway station, on the railway line which goes from Hyderabad to Parli. Chakur is connected by road to Latur, a big town, which has become a district headquarter and is one of the well-known marketing and trading centres of the area. Latur has become an educational and medical centre, where needy persons go for their children's education and for medical assistance for ailing family members. This is the town where I completed my secondary education, began my legal profession, joined political activities and contested eleven elections, one to the local body and ten to the legislatures.

My grandparents had three sons and one daughter. Their daughter died young. Vishwanath aka Sambhaji Patil, Gurunath aka Bhavurao Patil and Madhavrao Patil, their three sons, the sons' wives and children lived with their parents in the houses on the gadi for many years after they were married. Even though the three brothers later lived separately, they and their families had very cordial relations with one another. They shared joys and sorrows, and celebrated all festivals together without fail. In this my father, the eldest brother, always took the lead.

My family owned land in three villages, which were divided between the three brothers after they started living separately. While they still lived together, the land was looked after by my grandfather, and the three brothers helped in the supervision.

The lands were fertile and yielded a sizeable income, which was used by Veer Bhagwantrao Patil to meet the family expenses and to provide funds to satisfy the demands made on him as the head of the village. The income from the land was enough to meet the family expenditure, but not to meet all the personal and social obligations every year. For some years, therefore, my grandfather had to borrow from moneylenders. During this period, he faced difficulties in making ends meet.

My grandfather treated the villagers as his family members. He did not attach importance to moneymaking, but believed in keeping the people around him happy and satisfied. He would help the villagers to get their children married, their family members treated in hospitals, and made sure that festivals of all religions were celebrated in the village. He treated the servants in the family with understanding, consideration and kindness. They, in turn, loved and respected him.

In the last days of his life, he did not see eye to eye with my father. At that time, he was a widower. Instead of living in his house, he began to live in his farmhouse away from the village. His sons and other relatives tried their best to persuade him to stay with the family, but he paid no heed to their entreaties. I was asked to try to bring him back to the house. When I tried to persuade him to accept the requests of the family members, he became angry, but finally agreed to go to the family house with me. I asked him, 'Do you want to go to the house in a bullock cart or on horseback?' and he replied, 'I prefer to walk.'

So he, a few assistants and I came to the village walking. At one place on the main road, from the opposite direction, a Moharrum procession was going out of the village. On seeing the procession, he stood in the middle of the road, in front of the men carrying the tazias. Then he grabbed a tazia, as well as the person carrying it, and shook them vigorously. Tears began to roll down his face as he asked agitatedly, 'Why? Why are you treating me like this? What wrong have I done in my life? You are not giving me the life I deserve in the last days of my existence. Why?' Everyone who saw the scene and heard him shouting loudly was bewildered. I was also confused and worried. Slowly, I went close to him and said, 'Let the procession go. Let us go to our house.' For a few moments, he stared at me, and then he moved towards the house. When we entered the house, he looked very tired. He sat on his cot, then lay down. That scene is one I carry in my mind very vividly even today.

I was my grandfather's favourite. He would give me whatever I asked for. He once got a beautiful horse, for my use only, and even constructed a wrestling house for me and the other children. Everybody knew that he would not refuse me anything, so all the family members and assistants also did not dare to say no to me.

He taught my brother and me to swim by adopting a method similar to the one he had used to teach me horse-riding. In villages, there are no swimming pools; villagers use the wells in their farms to learn swimming. My brother and I were asked to do so in the well of one of our family farms close to the village. Other boys had also learned to swim in that well. But we used to go there, take off our clothes and sit on the edge of the well, watching other boys swimming without getting into the water ourselves. For a few days, our grandfather watched us doing that. Then one day, he crept up silently behind us and pushed us into the well. As we fell into the water, we were terrified. He did not allow the other boys to help us. We flailed our hands and legs and somehow kept ourselves floating, then came out of the water. This way he conveyed to us that keeping afloat and swimming in water was not very difficult, and we learnt how to swim within a few days.

Fearlessness was an important feature of his character. Nothing frightened him. At the same time, he frightened nobody. He was tender and considerate to all the people around him.

When he breathed his last, I was in Mumbai studying for my LLM degree. On receiving the sad news, I went to my village, travelling for fifteen hours by train and bus. After I reached the village, I found a large number of mourners, collected in and around the family house, waiting for me. I offered flowers in front of his body. There were no tears in my eyes, but my heart was weeping. I felt it was bleeding. But I controlled myself and did not lose my composure. Those who were there could understand my feelings and sympathized with me.

My grandfather's funeral procession took two hours to reach the burial ground. People in the gathering sang bhajans, religious songs, to the accompaniment of musical instruments. One person sang only two lines of a Marathi bhajan repeatedly for two hours:

'Ahmi Jatu Amuchaya gava.
Amucha Ram Ram ghyava.'
(I am proceeding to my village.
Please accept my salutation.)

The number of people who had joined together to take him on his final journey showed how much he was loved and respected by the villagers and others from the area. On his death, my father was the most affected person.

2

FAMILY MEMBERS

My mother had gone to Chincholi, to her father's house, to deliver me, her first child on 12 October 1935. After my birth, due to post-delivery complications, she breathed her last. In the same village, one day after I was born, a baby boy was born to a lady named Kulsumbi. That baby died within five days of his birth. My maternal grandfather approached Kulsumbi to find out if she would take care of me for a few days. She was grieving for her son, but was kind enough to agree. Her husband and other members of her family also did not object. She took care of me not just for a few days but for one year. For six months, she lived in Chincholi, and for the next six months, she lived in Chakur with me, and then put me in the custody of my grandmother. She could have looked after me for more than a year, had she been asked to do so, but my grandmother thought that she would be able to bring me up without Kulsumbi's help, and told her she could return to her village.

My cousin Hanumantrao also lost his mother at the age of five. So first, my grandmother took care of me, and after ten years, she took care of my cousin as well. My cousin and I were, therefore, very close to her, and she showered her love and affection on us as if we were her own sons.

∎

After my half-brother and I completed our primary education in Chakur, my father wanted to send us to a big city for higher studies. My grandmother was reluctant to allow us to leave her and our village. She argued that the family had lands, which could help the children to support themselves in their future splendidly, and that it was not necessary for us to be educated and join service of any kind, requiring us to work under the control and command of others. She was of the view that for an understanding of life and society, the upbringing of the children in her family under her and other family members' supervision was better than what would be taught in educational institutions. However, my father was determined to educate us. He persuaded his mother to agree to his plan, so she finally conceded. But in her heart of hearts, she was so saddened when we went away that it affected her health, and maybe even led to her death. She died when I was in Latur, studying in the high school. Her death affected me tremendously. With her death, I felt that I had become an orphan. No other person in the family could take her place in my life.

■

My father Vishwanath Patil, also known as Sambhaji Patil, was a pragmatic, liberal person who believed in conducting his own life in a disciplined, correct and just manner, and expected all his family members to be the same. When he grew up, he helped his father in discharging family and social duties, looked after the lands, collected taxes and helped in maintaining law and order in the villages of which my grandfather was the head. In his relationship with his parents, he was very respectful, and in dealing with his brothers, he was very helpful and affectionate. He was considerate to the ladies of the house, and in dealing with his children, he was very strict. With his brothers' children, he was friendly and affectionate. With the family assistants, he was correct and strict.

The villagers and his relatives respected my father but loved him less than his father. My grandfather was more generous when it came to helping all those who approached him for succour. He did not always have enough funds to meet his personal and social obligations, but because of my father's careful attitude towards money matters, he was never short of funds to meet any of the legitimate demands made on him by his family members or the villagers. Because of my father's insistence, all things were done in time and in a disciplined manner. Nobody could take him lightly. That made him capable of getting things done correctly, and earned him the reputation of being a hard taskmaster. What he expected from others, he expected from himself; what he got from others, he got from himself too. So he was respected and at times, feared as well.

My half-brother Rajeshwar and I were given whatever we needed. But we could never summon up the courage to ask my father directly for anything—it was always through our grandmother or through the assistants of the family. Whenever we were asked to meet him, we used to pray to God that he should not find fault with us and that he should not be angry with us. We found it difficult to talk to him.

Once, my father saw me quarrelling with Rajeshwar and being a little rough with him. Since my brother was not physically as strong as I was, my father felt that I was being unjust to him. As a punishment, he ordered me to sit in a big pot, which was kept in a corner, until the time he returned home from the fields. I had no option but to obey him. I got into the pot and kept sitting in it. My grandmother and the other ladies of the house were amused to see me sitting quietly in the pot. However, after half an hour, they asked me to come out of it. But I continued to sit in it without heeding their suggestion. Then they dragged me out of the pot, but I went back after sometime. Again they dragged me out. Again I got into it. This was repeated five or six times. Even when my grandmother assured me that she would speak to my father and tell him that they took me out, I was not willing to go by her advice. Then they left me where I was and gave me some food to eat. I ate the food sitting in the pot. After about four to five hours, in the evening, my father returned to the house and asked me to come out, which

I did. My grandmother scolded him, saying he should not treat children so harshly. My father kept smiling. He also must have felt that the punishment given to me was too severe. After that incident, at no time in my life did he punish me or get angry with me. On my part, I did not give any opportunity to him to be cross with me. But the fear of his anger that I had developed never left me.

Another time, I jumped from the branch of a big mango tree while playing a game called 'dup' in my village and fell on the left side of my body, fracturing my hand. When the other players saw what had happened to me, they were worried, thinking that we would be taken to task by my father. At that time, my father was in the adjacent farm. They decided to inform him about the accident; otherwise they thought he would become even angrier with us. One of them was persuaded to go and tell him what had happened. When my friend broke the news to him, he was surprised to see that my father was not angry or perturbed. He only asked if I could walk or not and when he was told that I could, he asked the boy to take me to my house. My friends did so. I was under the impression that in the evening, he would give me a piece of his mind.

When we met in the evening, he asked me, 'Is it paining?'

I answered, 'No.'

I was waiting for him to explode with rage.

Instead, he said, 'Okay, go to the doctor tomorrow, and get your hand fully examined and properly treated. Take Shamsher Mamu with you.'

I was still afraid that he would scold me, so I kept looking down at the floor and avoided his gaze.

He guessed that I was afraid of his anger. To put me at ease he said, 'Well, children should not worry about such small things. They should be bold and brave enough to take risks. Now you can go and rest until dinner-time.'

My relief knew no bounds.

My father surprised me some years later for the second time, when I again met with an accident while riding a motorbike. After I had passed my matriculation examination, as promised, he had given me a new BSA motorbike. One day, I had gone to the Latur Road railway station on my new motorbike with Mahadev Swami, a friend of mine. There, I saw one of my uncles on his old motorcycle. He left the railway station a few minutes before me. When I found that he was driving fast and getting ahead of me on his old machine, I tried to overtake him, but I had very little experience of driving a bike. As I increased the speed and tried to cut the distance between us, I faced a sharp turn I could not negotiate properly. My machine went off the road straight into a ditch filled with mud and water, and I fell right into it along with my friend. I was also thrown from the driver's seat and became unconscious. Swami got up, pulled me out of the ditch, sprinkled muddy water on my face and brought me back to consciousness. He switched off the bike's engine. Luckily, the bike was not damaged. My uncle had seen the accident, but instead of coming to my rescue, he sped off to inform my father and grandfather.

My grandfather came to the accident site on horseback, followed by my youngest uncle, Madhavrao Patil, and other villagers and young boys. My uncle took Swami back to the village on the motorbike. I was asked to ride on the horse, which I did very reluctantly because I was quite embarrassed. As we rode back to the village, people came out in large numbers to see us. I reached my house on horseback, followed by many young boys and villagers.

At home, all the members of the family, including my father, had collected at one place. When they saw Swami unhurt and when they learnt that I was also not injured, they began to poke fun at him. When I reached the house, the mood of the gathering was not morose but quite cheerful. I was worried because I did not know if this time my father would be as understanding and considerate as he was when I had met with the accident while playing 'dup'. I kept looking away from everyone. My father was composed as he always was, but I tried to avoid looking at him. This time also he understood what was going on in my mind and repeated the words he had used the first time I had met with an accident.

He went up to Swami and said, 'Bold boy. Brave boy. You should be like this always. All young ones should be like this, always ready to take risks and afraid of nothing. You should conquer fear and should not be afraid of anything.'

In fact, those words were uttered for me too. They made me feel relaxed and removed the burden of fear of my father's anger from my mind.

These two accidents, my father's reactions to them, and the words he used to reduce the apprehensions in my mind helped me a lot in the future to face difficult situations and take risks when the occasion arose.

My father looked serious and tough, although he could be playful and considerate too. But his reputation was that he had an obdurate nature. It was very rare to see the softness in his character, but he revealed this side of him to me and members of our family on three occasions.

We saw it for the first time when my grandmother passed away and the second time when my grandfather died. We saw it for the third time when my betrothal ceremony was taking place.

At the time of my engagement, many guests were present in our house. Before the ceremony started, I was required to take my father's blessings, but I could not see him anywhere. His friend, Panditrao Kulkarni, tried to find where he was. He discovered my father in a room at the back of the house, alone, shedding tears. When he saw his friend, he tried to control himself, but could not stop crying. His friend tried to console him, understanding that my father was perhaps remembering my mother, who had died when I was just five days old, or my grandfather, who had been very keen to see me married in his lifetime—which was not to be. Some relatives of mine, instead of waiting for my father to come to the main part of the house to participate in the ceremony, took me to the room he was sitting in. When he saw me, he tried to wipe the tears from his eyes and be normal. I touched his and his friend's feet. They blessed me. I could see tears in the eyes of both of them.

My father believed in giving incentives and encouragement to those who discharged their duties well. When I passed the examination for the fourth standard, he gave me a watch; when I passed the seventh standard examination, it was a bicycle; and, as mentioned, I got a motorcycle when I passed the matriculation.

He had modern ideas about life and education, and knew how to get things done, how to manage and administer activities. However, he had no liking for politics. He was of the view that politics was very complicated and was not meant for straightforward people. He never appreciated my political activities.

■

In my family, all the male members of the generations previous to mine had been married more than once. Gangabai and my father were married to each other when they were very young. Bhagirtibai, my mother, who was also called Velduda, and my father were married when they were much older.

Gangabai was a very frail, beautiful, soft-spoken and kind human being. She never tried to control others and loved all the members of the family. She cooperated with everyone. Rajeshwar Patil, my brother, was the only child born to her. She loved him and me abundantly.

Bhagirtibai gave birth to me six months before Rajeshwar was born. In photographs of the family, all the members can be seen, except for my mother. All the photographs were taken when my brother and I had become students of the secondary school.

My family told me that I look like my mother. They said that she was tall and fair. Although illiterate, she was capable of tackling all situations and problems. She was very affectionate towards children, and helpful to the villagers. They did not talk much about her to me, sensitive to the fact that she died when I was only five days old.

Gurunath, also called Bhavurao, my eldest uncle, was frail in body, but studious and blessed with a brilliant brain. He wanted to study at a university, but the family elders did not let him have his way, since they felt that members of the family did not need to study or join any service or profession to earn their subsistence. He was a reclusive person and died young. The children in the family admired his scholarly nature, and I was one of those who loved and respected him the most. He tried to encourage me to study and continue my university education, more than most of the other members of the clan.

Madhavrao Patil, my second uncle, was endowed with a supple, attractive body and handsome facial features. He was not interested in getting educated and lived a long life, all the time enjoying what his status offered him. There was not a very big age difference between him and my brother and me, so he treated us as his friends, helping us out of difficulties of all kinds. In 2012, he breathed his last. His death has deprived me of a friend and a relative who was always there for me in times of need.

My aunts have always been very affectionate and helpful and treated my brother and me as their own sons. In fact, they have been motherly towards me. Haribai Kaku was married to Madhavrao Patil when they were very young. She lived in our family since she was just a child. So she, my brother and I grew up together, and her feelings for us were of a mother and sister. In all my difficult times, she and my uncle gave us succour. When my wife suffered from liver cancer, she looked after her, encouraging both of us to face the deadly disease boldly. She was by her bedside up to my wife's last moments, and I know that no one else could have taken such good care of her as she did. She is a compassionate lady who is learned, broad-minded and wise. She has the capacity to accommodate everybody in the family and to manage family matters. She suffered many ups and downs in her life, but did not allow the equilibrium of her mind to be upset. One can learn many lessons from her life.

Hanumantrao, also called Anandrao or Chandrasekhar Patil, son of my uncle Bhavurao Patil, is educated, methodical in all things he does, careful in money matters, very frugal and not inclined to get involved in anything which does not fall in the area of his activities. He has two sons, who are lawyers practising in the High Court of Maharashtra and other courts, and two daughters who are married. He has been helping me a lot in my family matters.

■

Keshavrao Patil, my maternal grandfather, was the brother of the head of the village of Chincholi in the Latur district of Maharashtra. He had five sons, three daughters, fertile lands and had earned a good reputation in the village and the area in which his village was located. He was respected by his relatives, friends, villagers and the people in the area for his strong common sense, capacity to decide disputes between private parties, and for maintaining tranquillity and peace in and around his village. His lands were very fertile and gave him a good income. In some ways, he was more influential than my paternal grandfather, and the real head of his village, his cousin. He lived a long and meaningful life. His eldest son inherited many of his qualities, and he encouraged him to do whatever he wanted to. Even today, he is remembered with respect by many in the area.

Trimbakrao Patil, my maternal uncle, was a very bold, dynamic and enterprising person from his area. He held no political position, yet, all the persons from his area who were interested in political activities sought his assistance in their political enterprises. He had groups of friends from different villages in the area who were always at his beck and call. He was against exploitation and stood by the side of those who he thought were subjected to injustice and inequality. He was not highly educated, but he was acquainted with all the educated and qualified persons from his area. The poor and the destitute were always inclined to stand by him.

My father was opposed to my participation in politics. But my maternal uncle always encouraged me to be active in the politics of the district, the state and the nation. On several occasions, when I was in difficulties, I found him rushing to my help. He was a great source of inspiration and strength for me. In all my elections, when he was physically hale and hearty, I had no difficulty in winning the votes and support I needed. When he was not well, I was less effective and defeated. Many people supported me in my elections, especially leaders of my party at the national and state levels. The policies of the party helped me. The people supported my party and me for the policies and leaders it had. At the same time, the local leaders and supporters like my maternal uncle helped me to take the policies to the people, and explain how the leaders played their role in getting political freedom, and are trying to attain social, economic and cultural freedom and justice to one and all.

My maternal uncle tried to convince my father that my decision to join political activities did not mean that I was marching in the wrong direction. With his departure from this world, I have become less effective and more vulnerable.

■

Rajeshwar Patil, my brother, is a lawyer now and lives in Latur. He leads an unambitious life, is straightforward and takes part in local, taluka and district politics. He has two sons, Naresh and Vikram, and a daughter, Pankija. They are all married with children. My sister-in-law died of cancer.

■

Vijaya, my wife, came from the Sindagi family of Sholapur, and she lived with us in our village quite happily. She was educated up to matriculation, had very strong common sense, was affectionate towards all family members, and quite undemanding. She was not a degree-holder, but she had the capacity to talk and converse with anybody in a comfortable, correct and dignified manner. She had no difficulty in talking to dignitaries such as the president, prime minister, ministers or any foreign visitors. Her style was to hear what others had to say, speak only when it was absolutely necessary and when she knew the subject and was sure about the correctness of the statement she had to make. She did not believe in contradicting others and never tried to show that she knew more than others. These qualities helped her to move about in the political circles of Delhi, which she was compelled to do because of the protocol that went with my position. She avoided meetings in which her presence was not absolutely necessary or required.

When I faced difficulties in my political activities, she stood by me like a rock in all the ups and downs of my life. Never did she complain about the discomforts she had to face and suffer because of my political activities and public relations. In all situations and positions, good or bad, high or low, she maintained equanimity and balance. Such behaviour would not have been possible even for many politicians of experience.

She loved her relatives, friends and family members. She adored our son and daughter, but her love for our daughter was more poignant as the mother and daughter were very close. Probably, that is true of almost all mothers and daughters. She died of liver cancer. When she was alive, I did not know how important she was for me—I realized her value in my life more acutely after her death, and the void created by her departure cannot be filled. Her memories crowd into my mind when I am alone, although I try to insulate myself from memories of my past life. They do not fully disappear, but keep entering my mind.

Shailesh, my son, has studied fine art, and at present looks after my ancestral property and some business he has set up. He helps all my friends and colleagues in their social, cultural and political activities, but is not interested in getting any position in politics. He has developed a style which suits political activities, and can help in dealing with voters and the general public. He is very straightforward in his behaviour with others. He is married and has two daughters.

He lives in Latur and at times, in Delhi and Mumbai.

Archana, my daughter-in-law, wife of Shailesh, is a medico who is very intelligent, well informed, well behaved and quite capable of discharging any duty given to her. She is interested in politics. She is not practising medicine anymore, but is looking after her daughters who are studying in Delhi, and is in the process of establishing a super-specialty hospital near Udgir, a rural area close to her father's village. The project is quite ambitious and she is trying to complete it with the help of about twenty doctors practising in the area. Her father, Madhavrao Patil Kawalkhedkar, and I lived together when we were doing our college education at Hyderabad. She and my son met during my election and decided to marry. After the death of my wife, she, my son and their children shifted to Delhi to live with me and since then, until the time I shifted to Chandigarh as the governor of the state of Punjab, they lived with me. Now they live in Noida for reasons of their children's education.

Swapna, my daughter, was a brilliant student, very well behaved, intelligent, ambitious and capable of doing any duty entrusted to her. She studied law, married into a family of lawyers, to the son of Shivraj Patil, who was a judge of the Supreme Court. Her husband, Basava Prabhu Patil, is practising in the High Courts and the Supreme Court, and is a brilliant lawyer who is doing very well. Swapna and Basava Prabhu used to live in Bengaluru. She was inclined to join politics if an opportunity was given to her and she had expressed her wish to do so many times.

At the time of the delivery of her son, the child had to be forced out of the womb because it was too big, and in the process, one hand of the child was damaged. It was a shock for Swapna and she kept asking, 'How could this happen to my child? Why did it happen to my child?' In the post-delivery period she suffered from depression, just as she had after the birth of her first child. However, she had overcome the depression the first time with the help of doctors from Latur who had come to Delhi and her mother, who was then alive.

But the second bout of depression was so severe that she ended her life, which was a terrible bolt from the blue for all of us.

Her husband, Basava Prabhu, is a very affectionate and gentle human being who loved his wife. He suffered the most, but bravely put up with the loss. When my daughter died, her son was only twenty-five days old. He had to bring him up and did so with the help of his mother. His daughter was also very young, so he decided not to marry a second time for more than ten years. Now the children are grown up and capable of looking after themselves and he has married a lady who is also a widow and a lawyer, with a daughter. All of them live happily with one another, carrying out their duties in the best possible manner.

Swapna appears before my mind's eye every now and then, when I am alone. It causes me a lot of sorrow. I try to bear it with courage, but it is not always possible to stop grieving. What can be done? I do not know.

Rudrali, my granddaughter and daughter of Archana and Shailesh, is a college student and wants to study law. She is a very studious, brilliant girl and has won many prizes in her school. She says she is interested in politics, and if she gets a chance to enter the national or state legislature, she is bound to do very well. She has legal acumen and the capability to deal with all kinds of situations, is very bold, unafraid to take risks, and understands human nature and political situations at the local, state, national and international levels very correctly. She has a personality which can adjust in the executive, legislature or judiciary.

Rushika, the second daughter of Archana and Shailesh, is equally brilliant, bold, intelligent and hard-working as her elder sister Rudrali. She is less ambitious, more artistic. She is usually quiet, but when she speaks, she makes very pertinent points and gives the impression that her mind is more developed than that of any person of her age. She paints beautifully, and the family encourages her to paint and do artistic things. She has not decided upon the line she wants to take in her future life. She keeps saying that she does not want to be a lawyer or a politician, but she has not yet finally decided what she wants to do. Whatever she decides to do, she will do well.

Arushi, the daughter of Swapna and Basava Prabhu, is also a very healthy, beautiful, brilliant child, who wants to study law and is likely to succeed in the profession which her father and grandfathers had also taken up. At present, she is trying to complete her higher secondary education, like Rudrali is doing. She is also very enterprising, but less ambitious than her mother was. After the death of her mother, she too helped her grandmother to look after her brother. Like Rudrali, she is capable of fulfilling her duty and facing any problem with confidence, and like Rushika, she is a very talented artist. We all encourage both these girls to develop their artistic talents and not to give up the interest they have developed in art. She took care of Achintya, her brother, and tried to discipline him as her mother would have done. The way she has borne responsibilities is likely to help her in her future activities and life.

Achintya, my grandson, is very strong in his body and mind, and enjoys playing cricket and other games. He is brilliant in his studies, and loves computers, the Internet and other electronic gadgets, which help him to be in contact with what is occurring in the world. He has a very strong and logical mind which he uses astutely and very often. The ambience in which he is growing up is helping him to develop his personality in the best possible manner. Since his right hand is affected, he uses his left hand, although at times it appears he regrets that he is not able to use his right hand as others do. However, his hand has now been operated upon quite a few times, which has improved it.

He wants to be a cricketer rather than a lawyer, though he would like to study law. But he would rather try his luck in cricket as a career. And he says that after he retires from cricket, he will practise law.

3

MY SCHOOL AND COLLEGE YEARS

In the nizam's state in the 1930s and '40s, a few big villages had primary schools, there were high schools in talukas, colleges in the divisional headquarters, and Hyderabad, capital of the state, boasted one university run by the government.

Chakur had a primary school and other educational institutions, as it has now. The school ran classes in a big dilapidated building owned by a private person from Chakur, but it had no library, no furniture and no playground. The teachers, who came from the area, took pride in the fact that they were educating the young generation. They aspired to see the state governed by elected representatives of the people, and were sympathetic to the freedom movement run by the Congress party and leaders like Mahatma Gandhi, Pandit Jawaharlal Nehru, Vallabhbhai Patel, Maulana Abdul Kalam Azad and others. They were proud of the culture in which they were brought up, and encouraged the students to adopt a scientific and modern approach in their lives, while remaining true to their own culture. People of the village respected and loved them for teaching the children sincerely.

The government later built a new building for the school, located on the border of the village. The new school building was well furnished, had a library and a big playground. My brother and I attended our classes for four years in the old building, and for one year in the new one.

I was rated as a good student, amongst the top few in the class. There were a few who did better than me, in spite of the fact that they did not have all the facilities and help required for a good education. They belonged to poor and destitute families, but did well because they did not have many distractions and could concentrate better on their studies. However, they could not continue their studies after they completed their primary education, which was very unfortunate. If they had had the opportunity to obtain higher university education, some of them could have reached the top in the areas they had adopted as their careers.

I took part in sports and games regularly in the last year of my primary education and did as well in them as in the classroom. My father kept a watch on my studies, as well as my brother's. He made us write one page in Marathi, one page in Urdu and one page in English every day in our notebooks, and get his signatures on them. My brother and I did the exercise for the last three years of our primary education. We were terrified when we had to take our notebooks for his signature, thinking that he would find mistakes and take us to task. Every day before taking our notebooks to him, we offered our prayers to Lord Ganesha to save us from his anger.

While we were in primary school, we were not given private tuitions. Our uncle had a few magazines and books, other family members had religious books, but there was no library in our house. So we read and studied textbooks, but had no access to any other kind of literature. At times, we read the Ramayana and Mahabharata written in Marathi, but that was all.

In our primary school, the medium of instruction was Marathi. Along with that, we were required to learn Urdu and English.

As in many schools, students formed different groups. These groups, at times, fought pitched battles—either because students belonging to one group teased the students of another group or tried to show that one group was superior to the other. The battles were not fought in the school or within its compound, but in the open fields outside the school, so that the teachers did not know what was happening. The groups did not complain to their teachers, their parents or the police, reserving their right to take revenge against their rivals on their own.

My brother, my cousins, some close friends and I belonged to one group, and we often fought with other groups fiercely, using stones and sticks. One of my cousins was an expert in fighting and the tactics required to defeat the boys of the other group. He was always at the forefront of the battle and made sure that his group could win. If he had gone in for higher education and joined the military, he could have become a very successful high-ranking army officer, but because of his family's financial difficulties, he could not continue his education beyond the primary level, and had to remain in the village helping his parents do small jobs.

I participated in the fray with fervour, but the elders of my family had no idea about these battles.

One of my friends who joined in these fights was Mahadev Swami, the one who was with me during my motorbike accident. His father had died when he was young. He had to bear the responsibility of looking after his mother and sister, as well as the family property. He was active, intelligent and bold. In later years, he was ever ready to take political risks and fight elections, which helped him to become the youngest sarpanch (head) of his gram panchayat. He contested many elections to public bodies, winning some and losing others. In private and public life, he was always with me. My father treated him as my closest friend and tried to convey certain messages to me through him. In almost all the elections I fought, he moved from village to village, canvassing for me. He was a close friend of Trimbakrao Patil, my maternal uncle from Chincholi. The two planned and made designs to see that in almost all the elections, I could win and no disturbances were caused.

■

My father was keen to give us a high-quality education and help us to get university degrees. However, my grandfather and grandmother thought that a university education was unnecessary for us because the family had land and property, which could sustain us and our children in the future. Because of these views, my father and uncles did not acquire university degrees—they were literate, but not fully educated. Their strong common sense and family traditions helped them to cope with the challenges of their lives. On this point, my father differed from his parents. He had made up his mind to ensure that we reaped all the benefits of modern education.

We did learn a great deal from our family and the villagers. We were allowed to express our views freely, except in the presence of our father. We could talk to our grandparents, mothers, uncles, relatives and assistants working in the family and the villagers who visited our house. The only discipline we were expected to follow while talking with others was to speak politely, and after thinking carefully about the issues and matters under discussion.

Our grandfather and father were invited to numerous marriage ceremonies and religious and cultural functions, but could not attend all of them. My brother and I were often asked to deputize for them at such functions and ceremonies. For children of our age, this duty was not very easy to perform. The assistants in the family guided us and gave us instructions about how to behave. We were not expected to talk more or less than was required. We had to behave respectfully towards our elders. These contacts with the villagers helped us to develop self-confidence in ourselves and taught us the correct kind of protocol to be followed. The villagers not only gave us honour and respect, but their love and affection also. We learnt to be respectful to all the assistants and servants in the family. We learnt how other people lived, what their problems were and to share their joys and sorrows. We learnt to do things in the proper manner. Thus, the education we acquired in the early years of our lives was very useful and valuable, and helped us in many ways in the future.

■

Udgir is a taluka (subdivision) of the district of Latur, close to Chakur. It had a government secondary school known for its high educational standards. It was connected to my village by train. That was why my father wanted my brother and me to join the high school in Udgir. However, the headmaster of the school refused to admit us, on the grounds that we were students who had studied in a rural primary school. He thought that we would not be able to cope with the standards of his high school. We were very disappointed.

Latur was a taluka at that time, but now it is a district. In the 1930s and '40s, it had two high schools, one of them run by a private trust and the other one by the government. We tried our luck in getting admission to the government high school in Latur and were fortunate to get seats because the school catered to students from rural areas. The other private high school admitted students from urban areas, and had a good reputation for its standard of education.

One of the teachers in the government high school, who was also from Chakur, was a friend of my father and helped us to get admitted in his school without any difficulty. For one month we stayed at his residence, and then shifted to the hostel run by the high school and lived there for nearly one year, until the time our parents shifted to Latur to provide better facilities for our education. On the death of my grandmother, our parents returned to Chakur to be with my grandfather. So for the last two years of my stay in Latur, I lived with our friends in rented rooms and ate in hotels.

For about four months in that period, after getting admission in the high school, our family members called us back to Chakur because turmoil had erupted in all parts of the state. The disturbance was generated by the extremists in the nizam's state who wanted the Hyderabad state to remain separate from the Union of India after India got its independence from British rule and the princely states merged with either India or Pakistan. The troublemakers used the religious card to disturb the peaceful atmosphere. Eventually, the government of India took 'police action' against the regime and

Hyderabad became part of the Union of India. That was what the people in the nizam's state had wanted.

Before and during the police action, the people in the state suffered damage to their properties and some lost their lives. Because of the police action, the disturbances were controlled in a short time and damages were reduced to the minimum. The wise, broad-minded people in the state, who belonged to all sections of the society and whose number far exceeded the number of the troublemakers, also helped the state to handle the situation in an effective manner and reduce the extent of losses. Those who contributed to creating and retaining the ambience of peace and understanding should be congratulated wholeheartedly by all broad-minded people in the state and the country, and should be mentioned in the history of that period.

When the police action took place, we were in Chakur. We watched the movement of the nizam's army in the vicinity of our village. In fact, many of these armed people exchanged their clothes and weapons for civilian clothes and food while escaping from the place where they were stationed. This happened while an aeroplane flew over Latur Road where they were stationed, and over the hillock of Haquani Baba and our gadi.

After the police action was completed, we were sent back to Latur to continue our education. Before the police action, the medium of education in the high school was Urdu. When the state joined the Union, it had three parts, and used three languages—Telegu, Kannada and Marathi—in their regions. Latur had been a part of Marathwada. In schools in Marathwada, Marathi was used as a medium of instruction.

In high school, I did well in studies and games, just as I had done in primary school. My teachers encouraged me to study science subjects. In my high school days, I also learned drawing and painting, which helped me a lot when I became a teacher and turned me into a lover of art.

In Latur, the students of the two high schools competed with each other in studies, in games and sports. The competitions made them mentally and physically competent and strong, but also incited them to quarrel with one another. When on occasions fights broke out, they were controlled by teachers, police and elders in the town. In studies, as well as in games, the private high school students did better than their counterparts in the government high school. I did not participate in the school fights at Latur in the way I had done in Chakur. In Latur, I played the role of peacemaker which was of a reconciliatory nature.

I learnt many things on the playground, in the company of my roommates and friends by visiting their houses and villages and coming in contact with their family members and villagers. During vacations, we travelled to our villages, swam in the wells in agricultural fields, and discussed many issues of common interest.

My father did not ask me to pass the matriculation examination with first-class marks, because at that time people did not expect boys from villages even to pass that examination. But now, it is not so. Students from the rural areas are proving equal to the students from urban areas in getting good marks in examinations and in wining gold medals.

■

Osmania University in Hyderabad is well known in the country. Subjects taught there include humanities, sciences, law, medicine and engineering and other old and new subjects. In the 1950s, its campus fell outside the borders of the city, in a boulder-studded area with only a few trees, some houses and thatched sheds. The buildings of the university are magnificent, and the hostels of the university are palatial and provide very good facilities. The city of Hyderabad had a few colleges which also had magnificent buildings and very good educational faculty and standards.

I had decided to study science and joined the city college which was located on the banks of the Musi river, by the side of the High Court of Hyderabad, now Andhra Pradesh. On the opposite bank of the river stood the Osmania hospital. These three buildings, in the old city of Hyderabad and close to the famous Charminar, are very imposing and impressive.

My friends and I had submitted forms for admission in many colleges in the city. My friends wanted to study commerce and arts. They got admission in different colleges. I got the opportunity to study in the college of my choice, for which I was very happy.

In the intermediate year, I studied physics, chemistry, biology, English and Marathi. Overconfident because of my success in earlier examinations, I thought that it would be very easy for me to study any subject and pass in all examinations. So I decided to do bodybuilding and paid little attention to my studies. I had read that Bal Gangadhar Tilak was very weak when he passed his matriculation examination, and it was only after he paid more attention to bodybuilding in the first year of his college that he became physically strong. I wanted to emulate him and I devoted my time to bodybuilding activities, consumed large quantities of food and rested for hours even during the daytime. In bodybuilding I achieved what I wanted to achieve, but in my studies, I slipped down from the level at which I always used to be in the previous years of my student life. This was noticed by friends who lived with me and by the mother of one of my friends who cooked food for us all. Soon, my father got to know about it and was certainly not very happy with it. He was of the opinion that the glamour of city life and the liberal monthly allowances given to me had diverted my attention from studies. He had also learnt that I had sold the gold ring given to me to purchase a few books written by Pandit Jawaharlal Nehru for my general reading. He felt that instead of selling the ring, I could have asked him for extra money. So he reduced my monthly allowances drastically. Luckily, in the first year of my college, my grandfather came to meet me, and was very happy to see that I looked healthy and strong, and gave me plenty of money which I could use to buy anything I wanted, all the equipment required for bodybuilding, and to enjoy life in the city.

Later, I realized that the money that he had given could not raise my educational standard in my class. On realizing that I was not doing well in my college education, I changed my lifestyle. I began to study for nearly fifteen hours every day and gave up bodybuilding, games and sports. This was communicated to my father. But he had decided to discipline me. So, he did not increase my monthly allowance and raise it to the original level. I too decided not to ask for more money and manage my life with the amount given to me. That made me live a very frugal life.

What I did made me capable of facing and overcoming difficulties that occurred in my life. I learnt to use time in the most appropriate and correct manner. What I learnt then remained with me throughout my life and proved to be a very valuable boon. Adversity taught me a lot and became my great guru.

I did not regret going through that kind of rigorous life. I passed the intermediate examination and became qualified to do my graduation in zoology, botany, chemistry, English and Marathi.

▪

I passed the BSc examination conducted by Osmania University with ease and comfort. While studying for my BSc, I lived in the 'C' hostel of the university, which had rooms in each of which only one student could live. The facilities that were provided to the students were as good as the facilities provided to students who lived in the 'A' and 'B' hostels.

In the university, I joined the National Cadet Corps (NCC). I took great interest in the NCC parade, shooting exercises and attending the camps. The NCC officers were happy to see that I did well in all its activities and encouraged me in every respect. I liked the discipline the NCC tried to inculcate in its cadets, and the frankness with which the cadets were asked to express their views. The values I imbibed as an NCC cadet helped me a great deal in my future life. I took part in other extra-curricular activities. Two years of my life on the campus of the university were spent fruitfully and I developed the confidence to face all kinds of future challenges.

■

I left the campus to pursue the LLB course in Chadarghat College, which was located in the heart of the city, and attended morning classes for three hours every working day. That gave me many hours of the day to do anything else I liked. Since I wanted to utilize the time available to earn some money, I joined the Agarwal High School as a science teacher. I taught biology to classes 10, 11 and 12 and general science to classes 5, 6 and 7. The medium of instruction in the school was Hindi. To teach the students, I used my knowledge and skills of drawing and painting. I prepared charts and drew diagrams on the board to make the subjects easier to understand. That was how teachers were expected to teach their students, and it earned me the approval of the headmaster and school management.

One of my friends wanted me to tutor his relatives as well. I accepted the offer and taught them after school hours. After 4 p.m., I could play badminton with the students of higher classes and other teachers.

The department of education at the state level had planned to make science lessons more easy and interesting by holding science exhibitions. I organized many science exhibitions too, which were appreciated by the students of Agarwal High School and other schools and colleges.

In the Agarwal High School, there were two other teachers, Rajabhahu Udgirkar and Brijmohan Agarwal, who came from Latur and who taught the students of higher classes commerce and English. We became good friends. They treated me as their family member. They were married, and on several occasions, they invited and compelled me to have lunches and dinners with them. Both my friends and I returned to Latur to take up new jobs. They were brilliant and hard-working, but died young.

I was attending the LLB classes, teaching students in and outside the school, playing games regularly, and attending social and cultural functions. All that required careful time management which I learnt in that period of two years. This helped me to pass my LLB examination, and see that my students did well in their examinations.

■

My grandfather was very keen that my brother and I get married during his lifetime. He insisted that his wish be fulfilled. My father had decided not to take any steps to marry off his sons while they were completing their education. It was only when we were about to finish our studies that he agreed to arrange our marriages.

In 1960, my brother and I were to be married. But matters did not turn out quite that way, because a few days before the wedding date, the parents of the girl I was to marry broke off the alliance. It caused a lot of embarrassment to my family members and my grandfather was very angry and upset. My father felt confused. However, the situation was a blessing in disguise for me for I was in no hurry to get married, because I was keen to continue my studies and do post graduation in law, either in India or abroad. However, I did not let my sense of relief show—I merely appeared less disturbed than other members of the family.

Thinking that I would be feeling unhappy because of my marriage not taking place as it was decided to take place, my father allowed me to study for an LLM degree in Bombay so I proceeded there. Not getting married helped me to continue my studies for two more years, and do my LLM.

The school authorities were unwilling to allow me to leave my job, but when I explained that I had planned to practise law, they reluctantly accepted my resignation and with a good send-off allowed me to leave. I had put my heart into teaching the students, which gave me great satisfaction. What I did in the school for the students was karma yoga for me. I realized this after completing my education and on embarking on my practical life. For me, the pleasure of doing a job well was a more valuable remuneration than the salary I received.

■

Mumbai University did not recognize the LLB degree of Osmania University, and Osmania University did not recognize the LLB degree of Mumbai University. Initially, Mumbai University did not grant me admission on this ground, but later it admitted me on the basis that the LLB degree of Osmania University was equivalent to that of Mumbai University. The rules that were followed to admit the students in Mumbai University provided that admission could be given to a student if the degree obtained by him was recognized or was equivalent to that of its degree. Professor Irani, the dean of law of Mumbai University, helped me. When I approached him and explained my predicament and why I wanted to study in his university, he took my matter to the senate, got its approval and allowed me to attend the LLM classes.

Before the states' reorganization, the Marathwada region, in which my district and village were located, was in Andhra Pradesh. After the reorganization, it became part of the state of Maharashtra. The cases in the High Court of Andhra Pradesh, which were filed by clients from Marathwada, were transferred to the High Court of Mumbai. So the lawyers from Marathwada shifted their offices from Hyderabad to Mumbai. That was why my father had suggested that I should do my LLM not from Hyderabad but from Mumbai, and I accepted his advice. Professor Irani who helped me out did not know me. What he did emanated from his desire to help students keen to study in his department, and because in the reorganization, Marathwada had become a part of Maharashtra.

Professor Irani was a well-known lawyer who conducted cases filed in courts under the private or public international law in the High Court or the Supreme Court. He taught the students who had joined branch one. In branch one, jurisprudence, constitutional law, private and public international laws, the United Nations and legal history were taught.

His style and method of teaching were different from the style and method of other law professors. He did not sit on a chair or make use of the blackboard, but sat on the edge of the table and interacted with the students. The students studying for LLM were mostly senior officers and learned persons, only a few being young or full-timers. He treated them as his friends and asked them about the books, journals and cases studied and read by them, trying to understand the points made in the books and journals and law reports studied by them. He suggested other books and articles for them to study. The atmosphere in the classroom was very friendly and inspiring. As one of the young and full-time students, I did not participate in the interaction. Instead, I kept observing and listening to the dialogue of the students and their professor. However, I not only attended the classes regularly, but remained in the law library of the university every working day from 9 a.m. to 7 p.m., studying, taking notes and writing my views on what I read. Noticing this, the dean was happy to see that I was serious in my studies. In the library, he discussed with me new theories that were developing and enriching jurisprudence and laws. This encouraged me to study my subjects more seriously and helped me to pass the LLM examination with good marks.

Only one road divides the Mumbai High Court from the Mumbai University. This enabled me to attend the High Court at times, in the company of a few lawyer friends. Whenever I received the information that a good lawyer was going to argue an important case, I was present in the courtroom.

My father wanted me to join the office of Ramchanderrao Nandapurkar, who was our family lawyer representing us in a few cases filed in the Hyderabad High Court. He had asked me to find out if he would accept me as his junior in his law office, and as assistant in the courts also. Ramchanderrao was willing to allow me to work with him. However, he said, 'I am of the view that you are not likely to practise in Mumbai. You are likely to practise in Latur, join politics, and come to Mumbai as a legislator who makes laws, and not as a lawyer who interprets the laws. That is my prediction. That does not mean that you are not welcome to work with me while you are studying for your LLM.' I had thought that he was trying to be nice to me, but was not willing to admit me in his office. Later, I found that he was always very helpful, and at no time, whenever I attended his office or the court, did I feel that I was not welcome. He was a reputed lawyer and a very good human being. He had handled many cases of private and public importance from my village, my family and my area.

His prediction proved to be correct to the hilt. I did not establish my law office in Mumbai. I practised for a few years in Latur, joined politics, became a member of the state legislature, and went to Mumbai where I made laws as a legislator and as the law minister. I do not know what had prompted him to make that prediction.

■

My wedding took place in the same year that I did my LLM. After marriage, according to my family custom, the newly married couple is sent to Sangameshwar, where the temple of the family deity is located. My wife, other family members and I were sent to take the darshan of the deity. While returning from Sangameshwar, at Bidar, I saw the LLM results of Mumbai University published in a newspaper. Scrolling down the list of successful students, I did not find my number. I thought that I had failed. However, when I read a note at the end of the list, I learnt that my result was withheld. I was confused and unhappy. I did not find it easy to disclose the news to my family members and my wife. In that gloomy mood, I returned to Chakur. My father then asked me to go to Mumbai to find out why my result was withheld.

In Mumbai, I met the dean. When he saw me, he smiled and

congratulated me. When I told him that my result was withheld, he telephoned the examination branch of the university and the in-charge of the examination branch told him, 'The student had done his LLB from Osmania University and the LLB degree of that university is not recognized by ours. His admission and studying in our university were not in accordance with the rules and were not legal. So his result could not be published.'

The dean explained to him, 'The LLB of Osmania University is equal to the LLB of Mumbai University. The rule under which students from other universities can be given admission in our university provides two criteria. One relates to the recognition of the degree, and the other to the equivalence of the degrees of the university which gives the degree and the university which gives the admission. Moreover, the senate was informed about this case, and the senate had approved the decision taken by the law department. The senate did it because the rule also allowed it.'

After this, the examination branch had no difficulty in publishing my result and informing me that I had passed the LLM examination.

During the days when I was studying, I kept reading books not connected to my subjects, but relating to general issues which were discussed in many other forums. I read books on Indian history, world history, wars, science and technologies as well as biographies of great Indian and world leaders. My general reading helped me in my examinations, especially the LLM one. I had read many books written on the First and Second World Wars, especially those written by Winston Churchill on these topics. While writing the answers to questions relating to international laws, the United Nations and the development of the laws of oceans and space, the books which were not prescribed for the students of LLM and which I had read helped me to write on aspects which were of great importance and of futuristic value.

■

Families teach many things to their children. They teach them how to behave with elders, youngsters and persons of their age group, with family members, with guests, with people from outside their families, in schools, colleges, offices and professions. The children learn the languages they speak from the members of their families. They learn what is important in life, about money, authority, knowledge, boldness, kindness and compassion for others, readiness to face problems as they present themselves, determination to work for their lives, their families and the societies in which they live.

In educational institutions, they learn languages and other subjects, and get to know how vast knowledge is and how complicated societies are, and how hard they have to work to achieve the aims and objectives of their lives. Students spend nearly twenty-four years of their lives in educational institutions. What they learn is very precise and well planned. What they learn makes them strong and capable of doing great deeds. But that is not sufficient. Much more has to be learnt by human beings—they have to continue learning from the day they start understanding the things around them until the time of their departure from the world. They, in fact, have to keep learning throughout their lives. Education has to continue from birth to death.

Outside schools, colleges and other kinds of educational institutions, human beings have to educate themselves, in their families, outside their families, in the societies in which they live. Their lives and societies are bigger than their educational institutions, and their minds should be receptive, analytical and able to draw correct conclusions. If these qualities are developed, human beings can become capable of achieving great heights.

It is said that the mind of man has a tremendous capacity to learn, to think, and discover new realities existing in the cosmos. If it is developed fully, it can extend knowledge acquired by humanity. It can understand the present and see into the future, and what can happen to matter, energy, knowledge, time and space, not only on our planet but in the totality of the universe.

Aurobindo Ghosh says all this in *Life Divine*, his principal philosophical work. And what is said by him and other wise people cannot be brushed aside as unreliable and hypothetical.

What I learnt in my educational institutions was greatly helpful. What I learnt outside of them was also of much use. The most important thing I understood from all the sources of education, the offices in which I worked, the society, and in my travels to different countries, and through my reading of a wide range of books was that no amount of learning can be compared to what remains to be learnt, the real, ultimate knowledge. And I think this is the most important lesson I developed through my entire education.

In the new education policy made in 1986, it was said that citizens need be educated throughout their lives. The population of India is 1.2 billion, but the number of schools is not enough to educate all the children who have been given the fundamental right to education. We do not have the methods to keep educating citizens throughout their lives. Other questions discussed are what kind of education should be given to the students, what should be done to make citizens able to discover new knowledge and develop new sciences and technologies, and where that should be done. Knowledge, sciences and technologies are more important than labour, capital, management and markets, to increase productivity and production and develop new machines and tools of production. At present, knowledge is more expensive than most of the objects. In the future, it is going to dominate all fields of human activities and existence.

To see that the fundamental right to education given to students is made a reality, a large number of schools and educational institutions should be established by the government or by private organizations and individuals.

To educate the citizens, new methods should be developed. Electronics can help in this respect. Dedicated channels, transponders and satellites can be provided for educating one and all. Through them, citizens can be enlightened. The new systems of the print and electronic media can help. In olden days, through discourses, citizens were taught how politics was practised, how the economy was developed, how social harmony was maintained, how prosperity and happiness were achieved, and how meaningful lives were lived. The same can be done now by using new tools available in the present times. Education through these kinds of tools can reach the doorsteps of citizens.

Education should make a human being capable of supporting himself and earning his bread and butter. It should make him skilful and able to use new tools and technologies. It should teach him the purpose of life, make him broad-minded and considerate towards his fellow beings and other creatures and plants and non-living substances. It should help him to raise his standard of morality and capability to cope with situations of all kinds. Education which helps in making man able in only one aspect of life is not really helpful. It should be holistic and all comprehensive.

Education is not about learning something from others or books only. Knowledge acquired in this manner is borrowed knowledge. In the initial stages, it is necessary to know what others have done and what they think. But to be truly educated and wise, man needs to discover new knowledge, new sciences, new technologies, to do research and development, and add to the store of knowledge already acquired and achieved. For this purpose, there should be institutions to carry out research and development. Man should be trained to think in a manner which can discover new realities.

To raise the standard of education, families, educational institutions and societies must use conventional and non-conventional methods, new tools and technologies, electronics, informatics and communication systems, for twenty-four hours of the day and 365 days of the year.

For these purposes, colleges, universities, research laboratories and educational institutions should be established by the governments and private bodies and individuals. Private bodies should be allowed to raise the funds they need to establish and run them. They may be compelled to admit in their institutions at least 30 per cent of students from poor families on fees paid by the students in government educational institutions.

These institutions should be established away from big cities, on land purchased by private bodies, not given by the governments. Governments should give these institutions water, electricity and transport facilities, and the freedom to decide what kind of education should be imparted to learners, within the broad outlines drawn by the governments.

If these steps are taken, the right type of objectives of education can be achieved in shorter and acceptable time frames.

4

LECTURER AND LAWYER

After completing post graduation, my plan was to settle in Mumbai and practise in the High Court. My father wanted me to practise in Latur, look after the family property, and support him in family matters. I whiled away my time for some months, visiting different cities, trying to come to a decision. I went to Delhi, Bengaluru, Hyderabad, Chennai and Aurangabad. In Aurangabad, a few friends of mine were studying for an LLB degree in the Manikchand Pahade (MP) Law College. Because of financial difficulties after completing graduation, they had discontinued their education to earn money to help their families, and to save money to complete their education by obtaining law degrees.

When I met them at the MP Law College, they introduced me to the principal, and told him that I had done my LLM from Mumbai University. One of the law lecturers of the college had gone to Delhi on leave for one year of study, in All India Institute of Law, and the principal was trying to get someone to take his place. He asked me if I would join the college as a lecturer if that post was offered to me for one year. I thought, until the time I take a final decision about the place where I could practise, I could do the job. So I accepted the offer. He asked me to visit the college the next day and lecture the students for one hour on any legal matter, so that he could assess whether I was capable to conduct classes and teach the students or not.

Next day, for forty-five minutes, I lectured the students on jurisprudence. The principal was convinced that I would have no difficulty in teaching the students. On the same day, he gave me the appointment order and asked me to join the college in the shortest possible time.

I had not thought I would get the offer and was happy to receive it. My friends were also glad that I was joining their college. After returning to Chakur from Aurangabad, I disclosed the news to my family members. My father did not comment on receiving the news, but I felt that he was not opposed to what I had decided. He might have thought that I accepted the lecturer's post to avoid practising law in Latur. Later, he said that I could practise in Latur for a few years, and then go to Mumbai.

My wife wanted to know if she could go to Aurangabad and stay with me. I told her that I would take her to Aurangabad once I found rented accommodation and until then she could stay at Chakur, where my sisters and sisters-in-law had become her friends and did not allow her to feel too lonely.

■

Aurangabad is an ancient city established by the Mughal Emperor Aurangzeb when he was the governor of the southern part of the Mughal empire. It has an old underground water supply system connected by pipelines made of clay. At present, it is a centre of learning, culture and also of industry. The people were peace-loving and the ambience of the city made me feel happy and comfortable. I enjoyed staying there for a few months.

Apart from civil and criminal courts, it has revenue appellate courts as well. Many lawyers from Latur, and also from other districts and talukas, filed and conducted revenue appeals in the revenue appellate courts.

In MP Law College, I lectured the students on jurisprudence, international law and legal history, the subjects I had studied for my LLM and also what the lecturer on leave used to teach.

I had no difficulty in preparing the lectures. In fact, the lectures were more elaborate than was needed by the students, which made them interesting and I enjoyed delivering them. That made my stay in the college very delightful. Other lecturers, some of whom were practising lawyers, and the principal and trustees were happy to have me in their college. Some of them became my lifelong friends.

I worked for three hours in the morning and three hours in the evening, sometimes taking two periods in the morning and one period in the evening or vice versa. I had enough time to attend hearings at the courts, as and when I felt like listening to the arguments in the cases conducted by my lawyer friends, to follow interesting law points.

One of my distant maternal uncles, who was also a lawyer and older than me by only a few years, was very friendly with me. His name was also Shivraj Patil. He used to come to Aurangabad to conduct revenue appeals and meet me. He was of the view that if I had decided to practise law, I was committing a mistake in spending time doing the job of a lecturer. He used to tell me that the time thus spent was wasted and that the sooner I started the practice, the better it would be for me.

I was sceptical about being able to start earning money within a short time after starting my practice, so I asked him how I would fare in Latur. His reply was that I would do well, certainly better than I would be able to do if I began my practice in Mumbai. As a senior lawyer, he and his friends and seniors would be there to help and guide me. Moreover, he felt that I, too, would be able to collect a good number of briefs. What he was in the habit of saying every time he met me convinced me that the sooner I began my legal profession, the better it would be for me. As I could not start my legal practice in Mumbai, I could begin my practice in Latur, which would please my father too. My uncle's efforts to persuade me had an impact on me and I was inclined to act on his advice. Moreover, the lectureship was only for a year. All these aspects went in favour of my shifting from lectureship to the legal profession.

I would spend Saturdays and Sundays in Chakur. Going to Chakur from Aurangabad was not difficult. I could travel by train from Aurangabad to Nanded and by bus from Nanded to Chakur.

On one such visit to Chakur, I was asked by the villagers to receive Yashwantrao Chavan, then the defence minister of India, Vasantrao Naik, then chief minister of Maharashtra, Shankarrao Chavan and Keshavrao Sonawane, then the ministers of irrigation and cooperation respectively, and deliver a welcome speech. Yashwantrao Chavan had come from Delhi by an air force plane to Bidar and from there was going to Dhoki, which was close to the Latur and Osmanabad districts, to inaugurate a sugar factory. All the other high dignitaries had gone to Bidar to receive him and were going from Bidar to Dhoki to attend the inaugural function. At Chakur, a new small cooperative oil industry had recently been established and the people of Chakur wanted it to be inaugurated by Yashwantrao Chavan. Chakur was en route to Dhoki, so the chief guest agreed to the villagers' request.

In the afternoon, the high dignitaries arrived at Chakur and the chief guest inaugurated the factory. He agreed to address the villagers who had gathered there in large numbers. I welcomed the guests and thanked them for obliging the people in the area by breaking their journey at Chakur for an hour and inaugurating the oil mill. In my speech, I explained what could be done in the area to raise the economic standards of the people. My suggestions were that the raw material available in the village should be used, and new methods and technologies should be introduced to ensure that better yields were made available.

Yashwantrao Chavan and other guests liked my brief speech and the points made in it. In his address, Chavan referred to the points made by me and his response was very useful to me in my future political activities, because the political leaders from that area paid more attention to me and offered me work in the party whenever opportunities came. Shankarrao Chavan and Keshavrao Sonawane became more friendly. They encouraged me in political activities in the area. At different levels in other fields also, they helped me, as they would have done to a close relation of theirs and a matured politician. They became and remained my friends, philosophers and guides. They were responsible for me joining politics, even when my father was opposed to it.

Shankarrao Chavan was the president of the municipality of Nanded, a town in the Marathwada region of Maharashtra, the minister of irrigation, agriculture and education, and rose to become the chief minister of Maharashtra. He was the deputy chairman, Planning Commission of India and then the education and home minister at the national level.

He took great interest in encouraging young men and women to join politics at different levels. He helped me in politics at the taluka, state and national levels as my friend, philosopher and guide and I constantly sought his advice.

Keshavrao Sonawane was a lawyer who helped poor litigants in courts without charging any fees, and as the minister for cooperation in the government of Maharashtra, was a leader of the area and the state, well known for his clean politics. He was responsible for including many of my friends and me in active politics and helping us in our political activities. If it were not for him, I probably would have remained a lawyer practising at Latur or Mumbai. He made my friends and me join politics at the local level. The journey started from the Latur municipality and continued through the Maharashtra legislature, up to Parliament. I became president of the municipality because of him and some of his friends. Later, some aberrations in our relations developed, but that did not disrupt the friendship and cordiality between us. He lived a very honest and clean political life, and helped youngsters to join the main stream of practical politics. In a way, he was like a political guide to me. He never expected anything in return for what he did for me.

Keshavrao Sonawane's elder brother, Manikrao Sonawane, was a close friend of my father and a member of a respected family in the area. His father was a friend of my maternal grandfather. Respected and loved, he was the chairman of the Latur market committee for many years and the president of the Latur municipality. He was responsible for making me an honorary lecturer of commercial, industrial and labour laws in Dayanand College, inducting me in the Latur municipality and local politics, and giving me a privileged position in the eyes and hearts of the people by treating me with affection and regard in Latur.

He contested the election to the Lok Sabha in 1979 against me because of the pressure from a new party established under the leadership of Yashwantrao Chavan and Sharad Pawar. In that election, I was preferred by the voters, but that did not affect his relationship with me. He continued to be as affectionate towards me as he was before that election. He will always be remembered for his contributions to the development of trade and the establishment of educational institutions in Latur, among other activities. I shall always respect his memory.

■

In Aurangabad, the police and the NCC had begun to give rifle training to able-bodied citizens. I was interested in the art of firing since my family possessed many firearms. My grandfather and all the others knew how to use them and even the small children were taught to use swords and spears. I had developed a liking for martial arts, and when I joined the NCC, I never missed a chance to attend the training given to cadets to fire different kinds of weapons. So I joined the rifle training started by the police and the NCC and won the first prize in a firing competition.

■

Eventually, I resigned from the lectureship in law and went to Latur to enter the legal profession. The trustees, principal and students of MP Law College wanted me to continue in the college, but I told them that I had completed the course needed to be taught to the students. Moreover, the examinations had taken place and

I had evaluated the papers that were sent to me. The lecturer who had gone to Delhi was also about to return to Aurangabad and resume his duties. I admitted that I had decided to practise law and was not going to change my mind. Moreover, the college had not appointed me permanently.

Close to Latur in Warawanti, my family had land and a 'gadi,' but the 'gadi' was in a dilapidated condition. Instead, I rented a room in a building which was occupied by Harish Chandra Patil, a very well-known lawyer in the area, with whom my distant maternal uncle, Shivraj Patil Mogekar, was practising. Harish Chandra Patil was willing to allow me to work in his office as his junior, although more than half a dozen lawyers already worked with him. Whoever wanted to join his office was welcomed since Harish Chandra Patil did not think that lawyers joining the Latur bar would take away his clients and reduce his practice. He had confidence in himself, and thought that allowing more people to work in his office would make him better known to the people and bring more cases to his office. He was always kind and considerate to his juniors. When he prepared to conduct complicated cases, he discussed them with his juniors. He made them read relevant cases given in law reports and discuss them with him. At the time when the cases were heard, the witnesses were examined or cross-examined or arguments were made, all his juniors and other lawyers were also present. He was always very brief and to the point. Never did he annoy the judge by arguing wrongly and unreasonably, which is why he often won the cases. He went to other districts also to handle complicated criminal cases in sessions courts. His office dealt with all kinds of cases—criminal, civil, matrimonial—but his office was well known for conducting criminal cases.

Politically, he was inclined towards the socialist ideology and opposed to the Congress policies. His political views were not acceptable to many of his juniors, but that did not create any problem for them. Harish Chandra Patil and Shivraj Patil Sulalikar belonged to the socialist party. They never supported me in the elections I contested, but I knew that they had a soft corner in their hearts for me and were not unhappy when I won the elections.

Privately, we did discuss policies of different political parties with one another in a very candid manner. The discussions used to be highly enlightening and helpful to understand complications involved in politics at different levels. In our discussions, we never used words or language that could hurt any one of us. The sincerity and faith in our views were always visible. Even now, we have the same kind of cordial relations which we had developed when we were in Latur, and I have no doubt that this relationship is bound to last up to the end of our lives.

In Harish Chandra Patil's office, there were three lawyers whose names were Shivraj Patil. All of us were related to one another. Some judges, lawyers and clients used to make fun of the fact that in his office there were four Patil lawyers, including himself, and three Shivraj Patils. One Shivraj Patil who conducted criminal cases was called criminal Shivraj Patil; the second Shivraj Patil who handled civil matters was called civil Shivraj Patil. I was the third Shivraj Patil, who had not handled any case in the first few months of my joining office. So, I was called political Shivraj Patil.

I attended all the cases conducted by my senior in courts at Latur and in other districts. In our travels, we discussed legal matters, political issues and other social matters. He treated me as a member of his family. Once, he told me that to develop my independent practice and personality as a lawyer, I should have my own office. Even after I established my own office, I would always be welcome in his office, and could attend and conduct trials and appeals which were entrusted to him and his office, use his library and consult him on any issue. He gave me this assurance and advice in the sincere desire to see that I did not remain a junior lawyer for a long time. I followed his advice and established my own independent office within four to five months after I joined the bar. From the first day at my office, I began to collect law books and reports and files. My office was one of the most well-managed offices in the area, and within a few months, about four junior lawyers joined me and worked for the next three to four years. I had many relatives from the area who sought my advice in legal matters, which I gave very candidly. I was not inclined to just collect cases by giving false promises and wrong advice. In cases they could not win, I always told them to refrain from going to the courts. Sometimes they would not take my advice and consult other lawyers. In such matters they filed the cases and failed, and it was only then that they valued my opinion. My reputation grew when they discussed my suggestions with other clients, who then developed confidence in the advice given by my office.

In the courts, my colleagues and I were very correct, regular and avoided seeking frequent adjournments. In our office, we studied files right up to midnight, and examined and cross-examined the clients and their witnesses to extract facts. In many cases, some of us visited the scenes of offence and disputed places to understand the facts of the case in a better manner. We prepared our arguments anticipating the points which the lawyers conducting the cases against our clients could make, and we were very lucid, brief and well prepared. This way of conducting cases was appreciated by the judges. What my office did in the courts earned the cooperation of all and helped our clients.

As for the fees, we did not higgle and haggle. We accepted whatever fees was given to us by our clients, and sometimes, we did not even charge them. This attitude brought many briefs to our office. The judges, opposition lawyers and senior lawyers were treated in a very polite manner by us. The lawyers in my office were young and it was quite easy and natural for them to be polite with others.

In my office, there were criminal cases, cases relating to matrimonial matters, cases relating to the Workmen's Compensation Act, cases pertaining to the land acquisitions matters, given by my relatives, relatives of other lawyers working in my office, their friends, and a few cases given by those who could not afford to pay the fees of the lawyers. Within a few months, we had a large number of cases collected in my office. In those days, in the 1960s, the government of India and the government of Maharashtra had decided to build minor, medium and major irrigation dams, for which lands were acquired by the government. The compensation given by the Maharashtra government was not adequate, but those who went to court got an enhanced and more satisfactory compensation. The government invariably went to the High Court and the Supreme Court and lost their cases. In some cases, the High Court and Supreme Court increased the compensation given by the lower courts.

A large number of cases which could be tried in the session court and magistrate's court piled up in my office. Generally, with the help of my colleagues, I handled the session's trials. At times, I conducted criminal cases in the lower courts too. Fellow lawyers in my office were very bright, sincere and well prepared, and had the confidence to handle cases in lower courts, as well as higher courts. But at the request of the clients, and to make them feel more confident about success in their cases, I conducted the session's trials more often than my friends did. In almost all cases, it was possible for my office to get favourable judgements. That was because, while accepting the briefs, we were very candid, careful and selective.

I was also invited to conduct cases in the sessions courts in other districts. I remember very vividly one case, which I conducted in the session's court at Parbhani. It concerned Gurunath Bayale, a lawyer who commenced his legal practice at my office. He was not serious about practising law because he had lands and other businesses to look after. His maternal grandfather and uncles lived in a village, in Parbhani district. One night, their house was attacked by dacoits. His grandfather was beaten up by the dacoits. His uncle had a gun. He took his gun and tried to defend his father and attack the dacoits. When the dacoits saw him rushing towards them with the gun, they ran out of the house and the village. The young man chased them and followed them outside the village.

Outside the village he fired at the dacoits. One of the dacoits was hit by the bullet and killed. A murder case was filed by the police against the uncle and he was put behind bars. His elder brother went to the police station and told the police that he, and not his brother, had fired the gun and killed the dacoit. The police freed the younger brother and arrested the elder brother. A chargesheet was filed against him then, and the case was conducted in the Parbhani session's court. I was asked to defend the accused. I accepted the brief and conducted the case.

Outside the village boundary, there was a railway station. The police recorded the statement of a witness who said that he was in the railway station when the gun was fired and the dacoit was killed. In the court, he said that he could identify the accused who had killed the dacoit. The incident had taken place in the darkness of night. Then, it was drizzling. And there was no one else in the area. The police had put up the witness because the accused had admitted that he was responsible for the murder. They thought that having an eyewitness would strengthen their case. During the cross-examination, I got the facts that it was night and drizzling, the eyewitness was from a neighbouring village, he did not know the accused and had seen him only once, and that he was at a distance of nearly 2,000 paces from the accused, on record.

All these facts could have been enough to prove that the witness could not have seen the accused in the dark, and it would be wrong to hold that he could identify him, the case against him was weak and could not be proved beyond a shadow of doubt, so the benefit of doubt deserved to be given to the accused. However, I committed a mistake by asking the witness, 'If it was dark, if it was drizzling, if you had seen him only once, how could you identify him here and now?'

The witness replied, 'There was a light hanging from a pole near the railway station. That's why I could see the accused and now I can identify him.'

The judge held that the evidence of the eyewitness was enough to convict the accused. According to him, the witness had seen him in the light of the lamp on the pole and so it could be held that he was able to identify the accused correctly.

I was very sorry. I had thought that the case was weak and that the accused would be acquitted.

We took the case to the High Court. Rajni Patel, who was a well-known criminal lawyer, was asked to file the appeal and argue the case. When I gave him the file, he asked me why it was necessary for me to ask the witness how he could identify the accused in the dark. However, he said he would do his best. He argued the case only for a few minutes and got the accused acquitted.

In his argument, he pointed out that the distance between the accused and the witness was of 2,000 paces, that is, nearly 2,000 feet. He said that fact was on record and was undisputed. He quoted two to three Supreme Court judgements in which it was held that on a dark night in the streetlight, it was not possible for a witness to see the accused, remember his features and identify him in the court if the distance between them was more than 150 feet. He argued that there were no other eyewitnesses, no other evidence on which reliance could be placed; hence, the accused was entitled to get the benefit of doubt and be acquitted because the distance between him and the witness at the place of incident was about 2,000 feet. The judge accepted the argument and acquitted the accused.

The strangest thing that happened relating to this case was that within three months of the acquittal of my client, his younger brother—who was responsible for the death of the dacoit—met with an accident while riding his tractor and died. Was that providential justice?

■

My office dealt with quite a number of matrimonial cases. Most of them were handled by my lawyer friends in my office, although I did handle a few of them. To conduct matrimonial cases is not very easy. They take a long time to be decided. The Hindu Marriage Act was introduced in Parliament as a part of the Hindu Code Bill in 1952 and passed in 1956. There were many members of Parliament and many others out of Parliament who opposed it tooth and nail. The Hindu Marriage Act, as passed, is the product of compromises, giving more time to the two parties to patch up their differences, compromise and live together. In the first instance, it allows the husband and wife to live separately for two years. If, within the period of two years, they decide to live together, it allows them to do so. If they do not decide to live together, a case has to be filed to get the divorce. A divorce case may take more than eight years to be decided. The case for separation may take two to three years to be decided. After two years, the case for divorce can be filed. It can take two to three years to be decided. Thus, eight to ten years of time has to pass before the divorce is given. This time limit may increase if appeals against the orders of trial courts are filed—and that may take yet another four to five years. The divorce can be given only if the parties agree to get divorced in an acceptable time frame. This is done in order to give them the maximum opportunity to live together, rather than divorce and live separately. In India, marriages were supposed to be sacraments, and not just contracts. The Hindu marriage law followed in India, before the present law came into existence, was one of the most conservative laws, inclined in favour of men and against women. The Christian law of marriage is more liberal than the Hindu law of marriage. The Muslim law of marriage is even more modern and liberal than the Christian law of marriage. Those who wanted to retain the basic nature of the Hindu law of marriage succeeded to a great extent, thinking it necessary to protect the sanctity of marriage and the children born to the married men and women. Towards this aim, what they did was not wrong, but if the husband and wife cannot remain together, not to decide the case in reasonable time and to compel them to live together, is also not very just or correct.

These days, some young men and women live together and

procreate without getting married. Maybe they think that this was the norm in ancient times when men and women were not bound by any laws. Some people think that what they are doing is right. In my view, it may create problems for the children born to them. If there are no ceremonies and rituals followed, in presence of relatives friends and well-wishers, the bond that may keep the husband and the wife together may be weakened.

In my judgement, swinging from one extreme to the other is no good. Therefore, some rules and regulations that are acceptable to people should be followed to see that the relationship between man and woman becomes stronger and not easy to break, according to the whims and fancies of one partner or the other. The marriage laws in all parts of the world have been in existence for thousands of years. They would not have existed if they were of no use and unnecessary.

Some laws have been changed in our countries. Amendments have been made to empower women and give them more powers to retain the right to own and possess property. However, the provisions of laws that are relevant to living together or separately, and divorce are more difficult to amend and change. If a change is needed, it should be carried out after creating a consensus and generating public opinion.

■

The Workmen's Compensation Act protects the interests of workers who suffer injuries while doing the work for which they are employed. It is made applicable to workers in industries, trade, agriculture, transport and other such kinds of activities. It has been in the statute book for many years.

It is used by the workers in industry, but it is not used in the same manner by the workers in trade, transport and agriculture. The reason for this kind of utilization of the act lies in the fact that workers in trade, transport, agriculture and other activities are not aware of the fact that there is a law which can give them relief when they suffer in the course of their employment. Generally, these cases are decided by the courts in favour of the workers. But if the cases are not filed in the courts, the courts cannot help them. The police machinery, NGOs and lawyers can help them. The media can play the role of making them aware of the existence of the law. In the present times, enlightening them in this respect is not very difficult. The print and electronic media do have the capacity to reach every nook and corner of the country.

In my opinion, steps for this purpose should be taken by trade unions, NGOs and the governments. Conducting a few cases in court and helping the workers to get compensation is laudable and necessary. But making the workers aware of this right given to them is more important.

I conducted a few workmen's compensation cases, and successfully got them the relief. I was happy to do that.

■

Laws are made to see that governance is done, not in an arbitrary manner, but according to the laws made by the legislature and rules made by the executive. They protect citizens against the tyranny of the whimsical discretionary powers of those who govern and rule. They also protect the weaker sections of society from getting exploited by the stronger sections. The citizens then know what to do, and what not to do, how to do many things in a proper manner.

To see that the laws are interpreted properly and used correctly and justly, courts are created. In order to see that court decisions are correct and not arbitrary, there are appellate courts created in different parts of the country. The Constitution of India provides that citizens have equal opportunities, and all laws should be made applicable to them in one and the same manner.

However, all citizens are not in the same position to use these principles in the same manner. It is said that all are equal in the eye of the law but not in the court of law. A rich client can have an experienced and expensive lawyer to plead his case. A poor client is not generally in a position to pay the fees of an experienced and expensive lawyer. When a case is presented in the court by an experienced lawyer, and by a less experienced lawyer, chances of the experienced lawyer winning the case for his client is very much there.

There are many clients who cannot afford to go to the courts to get justice. They suffer silently, or they revolt and commit crimes against those responsible for their plight. They cannot pay the court fees of their lawyers. Hence, schemes were made by state governments and the government of India to give legal aid to needy persons in the society. These schemes have provisions enabling the payment of fees of lawyers and court fees by the government. They have given some relief to needy persons, but the amount paid to the lawyers under these schemes is not equal to the fees paid to the lawyers on the opposite side, and that makes the difference.

The existing legal aid schemes need changes, strengthening and improvements. More funds should be given to them. Funds for this purpose can be given by the courts out of fines charged on the erring clients. Citizens need food, shelter, medicine, education, entertainment, equality and justice—economic, social and cultural—given to them by governments and the society. We need to march towards these goals in order to be called just, modern and forward-looking.

■

The Latur bar association was well known in the Marathwada region. In the 1960s, it had nearly 200 lawyers, some of whom were engaged to conduct cases in other districts and the High Court. Now it has about 1,000 lawyers. Some of the lawyers from this place have been elevated to the position of High Court judges. The Latur bar association was not very active, and its members were not senior members practising in the courts. They were elected but did not organize any activities for the association.

Some young lawyers who had completed their legal education

had come to Latur to practise. Amarchand Darda, Brij Mohan Agarwal and I were among the new lawyers who had formed a group, spent leisure time together, and helped each other in cases in the courts. This group decided to contest for the membership of the association, and the old members of the association did not object to our decision. Those who contested the election from this group got elected. That was the first election in Latur which I had contested and won. Then I was elected as the secretary of the association.

Amarchand Darda and I had studied for our LLM degree in the department of law, Mumbai University. After joining the Latur bar, we conducted some cases in cooperation with each other. Amarchand helped me to contest the elections to the bar association of Latur, to the Latur municipality, to the Maharashtra legislative assembly, and finally, to the Lok Sabha. He was bold, intelligent and fearless, always ready to take risks and make his friends do the same. I feel that if he had not been there to inspire and compel me to fight the elections, I probably would not have contested them. He was the only friend who could bluntly tell me where I went wrong, and at times, quarrelled with and opposed me. But in his heart, he never carried any ill will for me.

Brij Mohan Agarwal had studied in the government high school in Latur, worked as a teacher in Agarwal High School in Hyderabad, joined the Latur bar and practised as a lawyer. He was elected to the Latur municipality and became its second president for one year. He was very active in local and district politics, a powerful speaker in Marathi and Hindi, and was in demand by politicians to canvass in their elections. In Hyderabad, while working in Agarwal High School, we became good friends.

Well known for speaking out his mind in favour or against any person or any idea, he seldom followed a middle path. In all my elections and political activities, he stood by me. His calculations and assessments about the mood of the voters and the people was spot-on, and whatever he predicted proved to be accurate and correct. I depended a great deal on his judgement.

His family treated me as a member of their family, showering affection on me. He died young, and a stormy and very effective career came to an end prematurely. In his death, I lost a special and valuable friend.

These two lawyers and I cooperated with one another in court cases, politics and social activities. We, the elected members of the Latur bar association, decided to hold a conference of lawyers from our district and other districts in the region, as well as the lawyers practising in the High Court.

The conference was attended by many lawyers, such as Ramrao Adik, Ramchandrarao Nandpurkar, and other lawyers and judges of the Latur court. In the conference, some very important current legal issues were discussed. Everybody admired the dignity with which the discussions took place. It became a much talked-about topic in all the bar associations of the courts from where the lawyers had attended the conference.

Top of the agenda was whether laws should or should not be changed and amended frequently. According to some lawyers, they should be changed because, with time, they need to be changed while others felt they should not be changed too frequently. We agreed that laws are based on certain principles and philosophies, which are not changeable, or freely changeable.

There were some lawyers who thought that the present laws made by the legislatures balance the interests of different sections of the society. If the balance is correct, the laws become more acceptable and implementable.

■

In the 1967 general elections to the legislative assembly of Maharashtra, Keshavrao Sonawane, who was then the cabinet minister for cooperation in the government of Vasantrao Naik, contested the election from Latur constituency. Bapusaheb Kaldate, who came from Beed district, which is adjacent to Latur district, and who was a member of the Socialist Party and quite an effective speaker in Marathi, was made to contest against Keshavrao, by some of the traders and others from Latur. The parties fought the election by putting all their might in the fray and using all kinds of tactics and methods. The friends and supporters of Keshavrao Sonawane and the Congress party, who held important posts and positions in the taluka and in the district, did speak about the issues, explaining what the government did for the people, what the candidate did for the voters, rebutting charges levelled against them, and the government replied to the criticism hurled at the party, its leaders and supporters. The Congress candidate campaigned in a leisurely manner. He took me and my friends with him to all the meetings he attended. Generally, we travelled in one car and spoke from one platform in the towns and villages. His style of speaking was soft, gentle and responsible. He was not as fiery and aggressive as his opponent.

Invariably, I was asked to speak at all the meetings. I adopted a different method to communicate with the voters. In my speeches, I did not speak about what was done in the taluka and the district, nor did I rebut the points made by opponents, or reply to their criticism. That was done to some extent by the candidate and to a large extent by his supporters holding important posts and positions in the taluka and the district. I spoke to them on political issues, economic policy, social harmony and cultural aspects of the society in Maharashtra and India. I spoke about five year plans, and how agriculture, industry, trade, etc. can be developed in the state and the country. Although the elections were organized to elect members to the state legislature, I explained how India developed its defence and foreign policies. I spoke about the relations between the Union and the states. I used simple, direct and gentle language to make my points. I did not criticize any opposition leader or worker. What I said was different from what the others were saying. The voters appeared to like what I was doing and saying.

The election results did not go in favour of the Congress

candidate. That demoralized many old Congressmen and I, too, was disappointed. However, we young lawyers were less affected than other Congressmen. We continued our routine in the courts.

■

Once, I was called to speak to the students of Dayanand College on the use of the national language in all parts of the country by a friend of mine who was teaching Hindi to his students. I said India has decided to make Hindi the national language. To keep the country united and help people communicate with one another easily, they should develop one language. The language which could be used for this purpose was Hindi, because it was spoken by the largest number of the states and people in the country. India had also decided that English should be used as the official language as the non-Hindi speaking people in the country wanted it to be used. English is an international language. It helps us to communicate with other countries and people in the world, an advantage we should not give up. Other countries of the world are trying to learn English to participate in international activities, and this should be appreciated and understood by us. While Hindi should be learnt by all non-Hindi speaking states and people, it should not be forced upon them. There are many other languages spoken in the different states, which are ancient and rich, that should be protected, developed and enriched. They can be used in the states for all purposes by the governments and people. Thus, India has accepted a three-language formula: Hindi, English and the state language. What is, therefore, needed is an enlightened, long term, holistic international and futuristic attitude to our languages.

Many trustees of the society running the college, lecturers and students attended the lecture and appreciated it. The trustees were happy to meet me. Manikrao Sonawane, an old friend of my father, was told that I had taught law in MP Law College before coming to Latur. Since he was looking for a lecturer to teach commercial, industrial and labour laws to BCom students, he asked me if I would teach them these laws for one hour a day. I had no difficulty in accepting the offer. Within a few days, I became an honorary lecturer and went on to teach the students for nearly ten years. I liked the job I did, and the students were happy with my way of teaching. In the college, I made a number of friends who have remained my friends for life.

Even when I became the president of the Latur municipality in 1967, I did not discontinue teaching. It was only when I became a minister in the council of ministers of Maharashtra that I could not continue my legal profession or teaching, and I had to resign from the honorary lectureship.

In Latur, I conducted cases in courts, attended to my duties as the municipal president, and taught the students of Dayanand College. I could do it because I enjoyed what I did and used my skills to manage my time scientifically, and not waste it on insignificant matters. I was able to do so, also, because of the cooperation rendered to me by all those with whom I had the good fortune to work—the lawyers working in my office, the officers and elected members of the municipality and the college principal and students.

5

MEMBER AND PRESIDENT OF LATUR MUNICIPALITY

In the general elections to the Maharashtra legislative assembly held in 1967, the minister for cooperation of the state, Keshavrao Sonawane was defeated and Bapusaheb Kaldate was elected in Latur constituency. That disappointed the old Congress leaders and its supporters, who thought that the Congress party in the taluka was weakened and would not be able to win other elections to be held a few months after the general elections to the legislature. They withdrew from the public activities of the Congress party. But this did not deter Keshavrao Sonawane, his brother Manikrao Sonawane, Chandrashekhar Bajpai and other leaders, who decided to bring back the glory of their party to the position which it had occupied. They decided to meet the voters and Congress workers, and prepared the party to contest all elections to all bodies in the area, putting up young candidates.

In the general election, my friends and I had campaigned for the Congress party. The people had appreciated the manner in which we had participated in the election, and spoken about the important issues faced by the state and the country. The leadership in the district had also appreciated what we had done. So, they wanted us to be put up as candidates in the municipal elections. They felt that we would be elected, but if we were not elected, it would not affect the prestige of the party because we were not senior

Congress persons. That was why Keshavrao Sonawane, Manikrao Sonawane, Chandra Shekhar Bajpai and some other senior Congress leaders approached my friends and got their consent to contest the municipal elections as Congress candidates. They approached me also. But I was reluctant to accept their suggestion and the offer. My father was opposed to the idea of my joining political activities. He thought that as a lawyer, I was doing well, and that I should not divert my attention from the legal profession and join an activity which was full of uncertainties. He was of the view that I lacked the qualities required to be a successful politician and the ability to deal with tricky situations. I was of the view that within two to three years, I would shift to Mumbai to practise in the High Court. I thought it would not fit well in the design of my future life if I joined municipal and political activities as an elected member or as the president. But then, my friends insisted that I should accept the offer. The leaders also forced me to be the candidate, saying that they would help my friends and me to discharge our duties in the best possible manner. Friends of my father told him not to oppose my entry into politics, and allow my life to be shaped as destiny had decided and designed for me. I agreed to contest—and then, I won the election.

▪

The election was not difficult for me. My opponents knew that I would win it, so they did not concentrate on opposing me. They spent more energy and put in more effort in the constituencies which according to them were possible for them to win. The candidates who opposed me were old, not interested in political activities, and knew that they would not get elected. They had been forced to contest because their parties did not want me to get elected unopposed.

In that election, nearly 80 per cent of Congress candidates were elected. That kind of success restored the confidence of the Congress party leaders and workers in their ability to obtain the approval of the people. It helped me because of the determination and efforts of the leaders of the Congress party at the apex in the district, and because the candidates who were put up were more acceptable than those of the opposition parties. The Congress candidates' style of speaking and dealing with the people got them the votes of the people.

In politics and in life, human beings have to face ups and downs. If they succeed, they should not feel that they are all powerful and should not behave in an arrogant manner. If they fail, they should not lose heart and give up trying to succeed. That was what the district leaders did. After that, for nearly five decades—continuously—the Congress party of the area won almost all the elections. This was the first lesson I learnt in that period.

■

The Congress party selected me to contest the election for the presidentship of the municipality. As the party had a comfortable majority in the council, it was not difficult for it to get its candidate elected. The party had many elected members who could have been good municipal presidents. Some of them wanted to occupy that position for at least one year in their term of five years in the council. Hence, the party decided that at the end of every year, the president should tender his resignation to Keshavrao Sonawane, who could then either continue with the same member or select some other member to be the president of the local body. This arrangement was acceptable to other deserving candidates. The first election to the presidentship was contested by the opposition parties, to prove that the president was not elected unanimously. The candidate who contested against me congratulated me before the voting was begun. My election was in tune with the expectations of the people, the Congress workers and leaders.

I continued as the president for two years. At the end of the first year, I tendered my resignation, as decided by the party. However, I was asked to continue to hold the position for one more year. At the end of the second year, my resignation from the post was accepted and Brij Mohan Agarwal was elected as the president. He was a brilliant member of the council. He knew how administration was done and produced very good results in his tenure. At the end of one year, he tendered his resignation, which was accepted.

In the fourth year of our term in the council, Abubakar Sidiqui was elected as the president. Abubakar Sidiqui was a well-known Urdu poet. He had little experience of working as an administrator. He was loved and respected by the people. It was a great pleasure to hear him reciting his poems. He and I travelled to Mumbai from Latur by car several times, and as I drove, he recited his poems or we discussed issues relevant to municipal administration, state and national politics. His poems reflected his lofty ideas about human nature, the problems of the people, and national and international issues. All his poems deserved to be published in a book form, so that they could be easily available to lovers of Urdu poetry and lofty concepts. But he could not manage this because of his financial condition. He was also reluctant to ask for help from anyone. The literary treasure he had created has remained unknown. I cherished his friendship and liked to be in his company, talking about things which could elevate human beings to a higher level of existence.

He enjoyed the goodwill of the people. So no difficulties were created for him when he was the president. He needed the help of elected members to function as the president in a correct and legal manner, and it was given to him wholeheartedly by former presidents, other councillors and officers of the local body. At the end of the year, he tendered his resignation from the position of the president.

In the fifth year, I was asked to be the president once again. That was the year when the general elections to the legislative assembly of Maharashtra were to take place. The party had felt that with me at the helm of affairs in the municipality, a favourable public opinion would be created, which would help the party to get its candidates from the area elected with ease and comfortably. In my third term as the president, I functioned only for a few months. In

1972, I was given a ticket to contest the election for the legislative assembly of Maharashtra. I won that election. After the result of my election was declared, I resigned from the presidentship of the municipality.

In my place, Ramjibhai Bhatia was elected as the fourth president in the year 1972. He was also a well-known wholesale grain merchant conducting trade and business in Latur and areas around the town. An honest and sincere person, he took pride in the fact that the fattest sum of money was kept in the bank during his presidentship of the local body.

He continued as the president until the time his term came to an end in 1972, and new elections to the council were held.

■

The municipal act of that time provided that subject committees consisting of some members of the council were created to take decisions in some matters. They had chairpersons who could convene, hold and preside over the meetings of the committees. The chairpersons could hold as many meetings as they thought were required. The decisions taken by them were final in many matters, enabling the officers of the municipality to act upon them. This arrangement was done to ensure decentralization of power in the local body. It reduced the burden of duties the council and the president had to perform.

The chairpersons who were elected were all experienced, helpful and just citizens. They behaved in a very responsible manner and cooperated with the officers and me to share our burden in a very admirable manner.

Some of the members of the committee had to be informed about their rights and duties, and about the manner in which they were expected to deal with the people, their colleagues, officers and me. Within a few days of their joining the council and becoming members of the committees, they picked up the skills needed to perform their duties.

At times, some of them could not grasp the laws and rules that were required to be followed in doing their duties and helping their voters, and sometimes they were cross with their colleagues, officers and with me, also. But that did not create any big problems. We dealt with them, keeping in mind their desire to help their voters, the welfare facilities to be provided to the citizens of the town, and legal provisions which were required to be followed. The understanding thus developed did solve many problems and difficulties.

Gibbs, a senior officer who later became the collector of Osmanabad district, was the chief officer of the municipality. He knew how to deal with the people, the elected members, and his subordinate officers, in order to produce the required and desired results. While trying to help everybody who went to him for assistance, he stuck to the provisions of laws and rules and did not allow any deviation from them. With me, he was correct, cooperative and helpful. Generally, I did go by the advice given by him. In matters of policy, I came to my own decisions, according to my inclination and understanding of the demands and aspirations of the people. There was perfect understanding between him and me in all our actions. After expressing his views, he abided by the decisions taken by the elected members, chairpersons and the president of the municipality. Later, we often met as friends, exchanging our views on the policies made at different levels in the country.

▪

Some other officers were students in the government high school at Latur when I had joined it. So, we knew one another and felt comfortable working together. In the municipality, we had opportunities to work together, which we did in a very understanding manner. They kept a certain distance between them and me in order to follow the protocol. In their hearts, they had friendly feelings towards me and desired to see that my tenure was successful. After I left the municipality, they kept meeting me and became my lifelong friends.

The municipality had large numbers of workers and officers doing municipal duties. They cleaned the town every day, supplied drinking water in the morning and evening, collected the octroi and house and water taxes, gave permission to citizens to build their houses and shops, helped in maintaining and building roads, and provided medical help to the needy in municipal hospitals. I understood their difficulties and helped them even before they asked me to solve their problems. At times, they were criticized wrongly by certain persons who had their own axes to grind. In the council, in the office and in the public, I protected them fully for the good work done by them in a correct manner. When I found that some of them had made mistakes, they were warned and, on occasion, punished. This kind of treatment created a firm bond of understanding between them and me. At times, I said that I was in a position to get any difficult job or task done from them, at any time of the day or night, if it were to be done to protect the interest and meet the demands of the people and the town.

The people of Latur did not expect any miracles from the new council and office-bearers. They expected that the good work that was started in the past should be continued. They expected that certain problems that had arisen because of the increase in population should be solved as expeditiously as possible.

After the election results were announced, and when the new office-bearers began to discharge their duties, various associations and bodies of citizens existing in different parts of the town invited the president, the vice president, the chairpersons and other members of the council to felicitate their success. We all accepted their invitations and attended the programmes organized by them. In the felicitation programmes, we were able to hear about and understand their aspirations and demands. Personal contacts thus made helped in the future to cope with difficulties and remove misunderstandings that had developed. We found people had nothing but goodwill for us, which was a great asset for the municipality.

The officers of the state government found that it was very

easy for them to deal with the newly elected members. When they realized that the office-bearers were inclined to do their duties only according to the relevant laws and rules, and did not go against the relevant legal provisions, they were relieved and felt happy. They became quite friendly and cooperative with all the new office-bearers.

At the state level, the government received favourable reports about the activities of the municipality. The ministers and officers in the state government were always willing to help the local government, and never created any problem or obstacle in the ways the municipality functioned. The state government treated Latur municipality as one of the best local governments in the province.

The Latur municipality had enough funds, equipment and manpower, as well as effective leadership provided by its elected representatives, to ensure its efficiency in discharging its duties in the best possible manner. The presidents of the municipality who had preceded me were freedom fighters and educated men with ability and understanding the art of governance. They collected revenue in the correct manner, and used the funds to purchase equipment and build roads and markets in the town. Their work created a tradition that helped administrators to discharge their duties in an acceptable manner, which made the job of the newly elected council and its members easy to perform.

The Standing Committees were expected to solve the problems of the people relating to water supply, cleanliness and healthcare, arising in the wards of the elected councillors. They were given the powers to spend funds required for these purposes, after taking decisions in meetings. They were happy to help their voters and would meet them in the office and outside it. I did not interfere in their duties. The officers were expected to take orders from the committees through the chief officer and act to implement them. I did not try to guide them or restrain them in any manner. As the president of the municipality, I concentrated on pending issues, which were relevant to the entire town and had not been tackled for many years. These issues related to enhancement of taxes, collection of arrears of taxes, taking up the construction of a dam to store and supply sufficient water to the increased number of citizens, to construct an underground drainage system, to lay out parks in many open spaces, to construct libraries, to provide entertainment and other kinds of facilities for groups of four or five constituencies, to set up primary and secondary schools to be run by the local body, to construct houses for scavengers who were the employees of the municipality, to start a society to meet the needs of the workers to get loans, to build new markets and to prepare plans for new markets, and to organize sports and entertainment activities.

The municipal act expected the local body to revise the house tax every five years, but the Latur municipality had not done it for over fifteen years. I thought that it was necessary to do that and discussed the matter in the council. Some members were not in favour of doing it, while others thought that it should be done. I spoke to the members in the meeting of the council and tried to convince them that it would be in the larger interest of the people to do what was required by the law. I explained to them that the taxes could be increased, and a committee could be appointed to hear the objections by the owners of the houses and properties to see if the increase in taxes were just and correct or not. The committee could consist of a few councillors, officers and members of the society. The council agreed to take steps according to the laws. The officers of the municipality made a list of houses and mentioned the increased taxes against them. When the list was published, petitions began to come in. A committee was constituted to hear the objections filed by the owners of the properties, and decisions on the objections were taken. A few citizens filed cases in the courts objecting to the decision taken by the council. However, the cases were decided by the courts in favour of the municipality. In this manner, the matter which was pending for many years was tackled. Initially, people in the town objected to it, but later, appreciated what was done and cooperated with the municipality. Taxing the citizens is not easy. Citizens always oppose such moves and proposals, but when it is explained that the revenue collected would be used to provide more and better facilities to the people, they cooperate and appreciate the steps taken. This we experienced in Latur in a manner that was encouraging.

In big and small cities and towns, the revision of taxes is not done as required by the laws, which then results in insufficient funds to provide civic amenities and facilities to the citizens. With the migration of job-seekers from rural areas who then live in the city slums, the population grows, but the revenue of the local bodies does not increase as it should, according to the laws. If the laws relating to this aspect are implemented, the problems of finding funds for coping with new challenges of urbanization can be handled in a better and easier manner.

In the Latur municipality, there were property owners who paid their taxes regularly. There were also a few who defaulted in paying taxes and had to pay huge arrears of taxes. The local body was not always ready to take the necessary steps to collect the arrears, which consequently grew into crores of rupees which remaining outside the coffers of the local body. Many property owners had not paid property taxes or the water cess. I brought this issue to the notice of the council members and asked for their advice. They said that the arrears should be collected by adopting means and methods such as discontinuing water supply to the defaulters. Even the supply of electricity could be stopped. This was what they said in the meeting, but privately, they asked me not to be too harsh. They advised that those who could pay should be made to pay, and those who could pay in two or three instalments should be given that concession. Those who were very poor and could not pay should not be forced to sell their possessions and properties. I agreed to go by their advice and asked them to voice their opinions openly in the meeting of the council. Some of the members did give that advice in the next meeting, but others refrained from speaking out. They asked the officers of the municipality to dilute their efforts to collect the arrears. They were of the view that governments at all levels should refrain from taxing the people and should concentrate on giving facilities to the people. They did not realize that the majority of the property owners paid their taxes, and were happy when taxes were collected and facilities were given to the people.

When the municipality continued to collect taxes, the officers of the local body faced some difficulties in the initial stages. Those who deserved to be given the time were given the time to make the payments. Those who were in a position to pay the arrears in two-three instalments, did so.

These steps were brought to the notice of the state government, which took these facts into consideration while agreeing to help the municipality to take up projects for supplying enough water, starting schools and constructing the underground drainage system.

There were a few cases filed in the courts against these steps. The courts decided all these cases in favour of the local body, which strengthened its resolve to go ahead with its plan to make the municipality more able to discharge its duties by collecting more funds in its coffers and collecting the revenue.

These steps were difficult to take and did create some opposition. However, they also indicated that the new council was determined to take positive steps.

The council took many other steps to provide better facilities to the people. When the people saw that it was trying its best to help them, they began to slowly forget the increase in taxes and the steps taken to recover the arrears. Some persons openly appreciated what the council had done and was doing.

■

Near Sai Village, which is at a distance of about three kilometres from Latur, a dam was constructed to collect water in the riverbed, to be used for drinking purposes and to supply it to the inhabitants of Latur. The dam could meet the demand for water of nearly thirty thousand people. But the population of Latur had gone up to nearly one lakh. The government decided to construct another dam at Nagajari on the same river. The project was prepared a few years earlier, but the construction of the dam had not begun. I decided to pursue the matter with the state government, and have the construction of the dam started. The council was also of the view that the construction of the dam should not be delayed and that it should be completed in as short a time as possible.

The government agreed to start the construction. It began the work of construction without any fanfare and completed it in a short time. The water from that dam was taken to Latur by a pipeline. At Sai, there was a water-purification plant, but Nagajari did not have one. It was built near the border of the town. The scarcity of drinking water was thus overcome. The people were happy to see that the work was done expeditiously and efficiently.

The water stored at Nagajari was sufficient to meet the demand of nearly one-and-a-half lakh people. Within a decade, the population of the town went up to three lakhs, and again the water scarcity was felt. Latur was a trading town that turned into an industrial one, and an educational and medical centre of great value in the area. These activities also needed more water. Later, the government laid two big pipelines from the major irrigation tank at Dhanegaon to take water to Latur. One pipeline supplies water to the industrial area, and the other supplies water for domestic purposes. In my view, within one decade, these arrangements are also likely to be insufficient to meet the demand of the town fully.

Latur had open drains to take sewage out of the town, which did not help in keeping the town as clean as it should be. So it was felt that an underground sewage system should be built. In the city of Benaras, the underground drainage system was built four hundred years ago. That system is still in existence and helping the city to remain clean. These facilities were built a few hundred years ago. When I asked the government of the state to take up the development of the underground drainage system for Latur, the authorities were not very enthusiastic. It thought that the local body would not be able to share the cost of building and maintaining the system. I made the council agree to the proposal and give about ₹10 lakh at the start of the project, and to pay more funds to share its cost every year, as decided between the government and the local body. When the local body gave that amount of money, the government agreed to take up the project. It was decided that the work should be started from the periphery, and then would be taken to the heart of the town. But it did not gather the momentum required to complete it in the given time, and was done after we had left the council at the end of our term. The system could not be extended to the heart of the town, and since the newly elected council did not take any interest in it, it remained unfinished. As the elected representative of the people from Latur constituency in the Maharashtra legislative assembly, I tried to see that it was fully completed. However, in the absence of willingness of the newly elected body of the local government, the project could not be completed. I was sorry about it. But in democracy, this kind of thing happens and we are required to put up with it. This weakens the democratic system.

■

In one part of Latur, there is a golai, a market which was built during the regime of the nizam, on the model of Connaught Place in Delhi. The market is circular in shape. Only the shops on the ground floor were built, but the shops on the first floor remained unconstructed for many years. Our council decided and built shops on the top of the ground floor. The shops were given on rent to shopkeepers. The construction added to the beauty of the market and earned a lot of revenue for the local body. This achievement was appreciated by the people and the state government.

The Latur municipality had acquired very valuable land in the centre of town. That land was used for running a cotton ginning and pressing factory. On the acquired land a new market was built. A part of the land was given to the State Transport Corporation to build a new bus station. The council got a plan prepared to build shops in the remaining area, and this was published in the media to invite comments and suggestions from the people. Within a short time, the project was completed and the shops were given on rent to shopkeepers. Cars were not allowed to enter the market. Customers had to visit the shops only on foot, leaving their vehicles outside. That made the market different from other ones and attracted customers in large numbers.

There were some open spaces in the town where the council built public gardens. The town became more beautiful and green. The people flocked to the gardens to enjoy the fresh air.

The council decided to build a library, an indoor stadium and a hospital, close to each other at one place, in an open area in the town to meet the demands of the people of four to five wards. It aimed at building about fifteen such centres with facilities for reading, sports and medical care. The council could build only a few centres in the period of five years.

Before the panchayati raj system was brought into existence, primary and secondary schools were run by the state government. After the panchayati raj came into being, schools were given to the district and taluka panchayats to manage. It was also decided that they could be given to local bodies which had the capacity to manage them. In Latur district, there were municipalities which could run them. It was decided that primary and secondary schools should be transferred to the Latur municipality, on the demand made by the local body. The council passed a resolution to that effect and the state government agreed to give the schools to it.

Some people in the town and members of the council were not in favour of that decision. They felt that if the schools were transferred to the local body, the standard of education could decline, because the teachers in the schools would be residents of the town and would spend their time and energy looking after their private activities and properties, instead of teaching the students. On the other hand, others thought that the local body would be in a position to supervise the activities of the schools more regularly and intimately, which would raise the standard of education. The decision taken by the concerned bodies and the government was in tune with the policies made for education in the state.

In Latur, there were a few government hospitals and private doctors who provided medical help to the patients. In the government, as well as private hospitals, modern equipment required to diagnose the diseases were not available because they were too expensive. The council decided to purchase such equipment and keep them in municipal hospitals. It was also decided that the doctors from other hospitals in town could be allowed to use them on payment of fixed charges, a facility that could help doctors and patients on a large scale.

The council decided to help private colleges with financial assistance. This decision helped the colleges to develop with greater speed. Today, Latur is a well-known education centre in the area, where students from different parts of the state seek admission for different courses.

Latur had about three small libraries. The council decided to establish a big library for all the students and citizens living in the town. A new big building was built for that purpose. A committee of principals of all colleges was constituted to purchase books for the library. It was also decided that in future, every year, at least ₹5 lakh should be spent to add new titles to the library. This step was appreciated by many and criticized by a few. Those who criticized it said that the expenditure incurred on the library was of a non-productive nature. Those who favoured the establishment of the library felt that it would help students and other citizens to add to the store of their knowledge. The library was used by many in the town. Initially, it was well managed and maintained. It was neglected in later years, and the decision to add new books every year was not implemented as it was decided. It has, therefore, become less attractive and useful.

The employees of the municipality were in the habit of taking loans from private moneylenders, who charged exorbitant interest on the loan given. Every month on the day the salary was paid, the moneylenders stood in front of the municipal building to collect the interest and get back the money given by them. The council members did not like that, and felt uncomfortable to see that the employees had to give such hefty interest on the loans taken by them. So they decided that a cooperative moneylending society for the employees of the municipality should be started. The council decided to give funds to the society, which was to be given to the employees to pay back their loans to the private moneylenders, and to give the employees loans at a reasonable interest. The loan could be recovered by deducting the agreed amount of money from the salary paid every month. This was a great relief for the employees who could now get the loans they needed on reasonable interest. It lessened their burden. Of course, they could have taken loans from banks, but the formalities required to be fulfilled to get the loan from banks, made them hesitant to approach the banks. This facility helped the employees in the best possible manner.

Unfortunately, scavengers were employed by the council in Latur to carry excreta in buckets carried on their heads. The scavengers were not given houses to live in or on rent in the town, so they had to live in huts outside the town. The council took a decision to build houses for the scavengers and give them on rent. The national and state government helped the local body to build the houses. The system of scavengers carrying buckets of excreta on their heads had continued for a very long time. The country needs to take special steps to do away with this morbid system. Funds needed should be given for this purpose and rules should be made to ensure that all houses have latrines which do not need this system. Private organizations can also help by building these kinds of latrines.

The municipality also helped newly established schools and colleges to develop games and sports activities in the town. For this purpose, the municipality prepared playgrounds and gave funds to organize games and sports competitions every year.

Latur artists who were interested in staging dramas, holding music competitions, painting exhibitions and dance performances were encouraged by the municipality. They also helped to develop the other cultural aspect of Latur. Latur thus became a well-known small centre of cultural activities in the region.

These were some of the activities to which as the president I paid attention. Other activities were looked after by other office-bearers and the councillors.

Problems faced by the Latur municipality were not very different from the problems faced by other municipalities in the state.

The roads in the town were quite wide, and had footpaths. But they were occupied by shopkeepers. The result of this was that the pedestrians had to walk on the roads, which were meant to be used by vehicles. The crowded roads caused accidents. It was necessary for the municipality to see that the footpaths were kept vacant, to be used by the pedestrians and not occupied by the shopkeepers. But this duty was not done by the officers and employees as it should have been done, because members elected from the constituencies in which these encroachments on roads were done were also keen to see that the illegal occupants of the footpaths were not disturbed. The matter was discussed in the council, which could not come to an unambiguous decision about what should be done. If some areas were earmarked for hawkers to do their business, it could have eased the problem. Some steps for this purpose were taken, but did not solve the problem substantially. For a few days, they appeared to give some relief, but after a few days, the situation got back to square one. The councillors pleaded that the poor in the society should be helped and the situation should be allowed to continue as it existed. Even today, it is not very different from what it was in the past.

Some open areas in Latur were illegally occupied by some persons who had built pukka structures on municipal land. The municipality tried to take action against them. But matters were taken to the courts where they were kept pending for many years.

In these cases, the elected representatives were not very helpful. They, in fact, proved to be obstructive. The municipality prepared a plan to shift the trespassers to other places and help them. But the plan proved to be ineffective, as the steps taken to remove the temporary trespassers from municipal land were not allowed to be implemented through the court orders and by the elected councillors. Something drastic was needed to solve the problem, but that was not allowed to be done. If some time is allowed to pass between the initial stages and a later period when it becomes too unwieldy to tackle, it is very unlikely that it can be handled successfully in the future also.

In Latur, there is a labour colony which was built by the government of the nizam. It is very well planned, has wide roads, open spaces and generous gaps between houses. Trees are planted on both sides of the roads and all the houses get fresh air and enough sunlight. In the new areas of Latur, on the borders of the town, new colonies have been coming up. The expensive houses built in these colonies are big, but are so close to one another that there is no space for air or sunlight to enter them. The roads in the colonies are so narrow that only one vehicle can pass through them safely and easily. The houses were required to be built according to approved plans, but the plans were not followed and the construction was done against the designs given to the builders. The municipality has a right and duty to see that the town develops in a planned manner and houses are constructed in accordance with the approved designs. Officers who try to prevent violation of rules are obstructed by some elected members who think that it is their duty to help their voters, even when they do not obey the laws and rules. Cases are initiated against some such builders, but the orders passed in some cases are challenged in courts of law and are stayed for many years, thus frustrating the objectives expected to be achieved. The council did not take any steps different from the steps taken against the trespassers. Even in the period when the council was not in existence, the administrators could not tackle the problem effectively.

The city of Delhi and the new city of Chandigarh are built in conformity with the original plans made for them, but no other cities in India appear to be following the plans made for them in a proper manner. They are coming up in a very haphazard manner. The unplanned developments are bound to cause many difficulties to inhabitants of these towns and cities; yet, this reality is not understood and necessary steps are not taken. In the days to come, the residents of these cities and towns are bound to suffer. Villages do not have big and expensive houses. Villagers live in huts and small houses, but there are ample open spaces for fresh air to circulate through them and sunlight to reach the interiors of their houses. They appear to be more hygienic and comfortable to live in than the houses in ill-planned cities and towns. This aspect of urbanization must be kept in mind to guide the development of new cities and towns, and new areas in the old cities and towns.

It is clear from the above examples that one of the most important problems faced by modern urbanization is the absence of proper planning. All the existing cities and towns should be properly planned. The new cities and towns should be developed as per well-thought-out plans only. In order to handle the problem of urbanization, there is a need for organizations that can plan towns and cities wisely, and build them in such a manner that they are capable of coping with modern challenges. The organizations should be well equipped and manned by experts who have modern ideas and concepts. They should be able to make the plans in given time frames.

Urban planning should take into consideration the demands and needs of many years to come. If it takes demands for short periods of time, the plans may not be able to help. In fact, there should be plans for the short term, medium term and long term developments. Only then can urbanization take place in a perfect manner.

The existing cities and towns attract migrants from rural areas. They settle in cities and towns in the slums, facing many difficulties and living uncomfortable lives. Urban planning should help to see that slums do not develop. This can be done by ensuring that no industry or commercial centre is allowed to come up without making provisions for its workers to have dwelling places and houses. Rooms and facilities for domestic servants should be built in new houses. In Delhi, all the bungalows constructed for government officers have servant quarters, but private houses very rarely do have such facilities. It should be made necessary for owners of factories and trades to take care of those who help them to produce their commodities, goods and services and do the trading and carry on business activities.

The existing cities should not be allowed to develop in a manner which would create new problems for all those who live in them.

In modern times, the law and order problems in cities and towns are going to become more complicated and not easy to handle. They can provide hiding places to criminals. So while developing them, attention should be paid to this aspect. Cities and towns should have underground control rooms, CCTV cameras at many places, mobile police stations, helicopters, and better communication facilities to maintain law and order. All houses should use modern equipment and devices which can help them to communicate with the police if they are attacked or raided.

Rural areas should be developed and made more comfortable for the villagers to continue to live in them. They should have schools, hospitals, entertainment facilities and opportunities for employment in various professions and activities. They should have roads and power supplied to them. Only then villagers would prefer to stay in the rural areas, rather than migrate to urban areas.

In urban areas, industries should not be allowed to be crowded in the cities. They can be built in areas far away from cities. In fact, separate industrial cities can be built where officers and workers should have all the facilities needed.

All large institutions, like hospitals and universities, should be built away from the cities, and provided with modern urban facilities. For this purpose, the country can be surveyed with the help of satellites, and the areas suitable for these purposes identified and marked on the map of the country. With the speedy means of transport available at present, it should not be difficult to adopt such concepts to have systematic urban development. Building these kinds of big institutions and organizations in such areas is going to get easier. What is required in this respect is proper perspective and proper inspiration.

The problems of urbanization can be tackled in a successful and better manner by adopting a multi-pronged approach.

Let us hope that it would be in times to come.

■

Latur was a taluka in district Osmanabad. Osmanabad town had a smaller population and was weaker in industry and trade, education and healthcare facilities than Latur. The people in Latur made a demand that Latur should be turned into a district.

In the 1970s, the State Transport Corporation decided that a bus transport division should be built in every district. The district transport division was expected to build bus-stands, run buses on the roads in the district and other places, and maintain the vehicles. It decided to construct a district bus transport division in Osmanabad, but the people in Latur began an agitation for it to be built in Latur, on the ground that Latur was a bigger place and could provide better facilities for the division to function. The agitation was supported by all parties and students. It became violent and caused much damage to buses and to the properties of government and private persons in the town. One day, the mob burnt four buses and some shops, and tried to attack the police station located at the centre of town. The police did not have enough manpower to control the agitators, and apprehended that the mob could attack the police station and set it on fire. When this was going on, I was at home. When I learnt that the mob had gone out of control and the police had taken positions to fire at it, I proceeded to the place where this was happening.

I met the police officers who had made arrangements and taken positions to fire at the mob to protect the police station, and asked them to refrain from taking any precipitate action, and promised that the mob would be persuaded to disperse. The police were unwilling to believe that the mob could be dispersed, but allowed me to go and talk to them.

When I proceeded towards the mob from the police station, the mob controlled itself and stopped throwing stones. The mob did not want to hurt me, but when I approached them, some of them began to speak in loud, threatening voices. I told them that the police had decided to open fire. If they did not disperse, some casualties would occur. If they continued to agitate and resort to violence, it would not be good for the people of Latur.

Some people at the back of the mob silently left the place and disappeared, but others were not inclined to accept my suggestion. A little later, however, they too disappeared when they saw that many people had gone away, realizing that it was inadvisable to continue the agitation. So they also dispersed and within a few minutes, the mob disappeared. The police went back to the police station and I went home.

In the evening, a meeting of the members of a peace committee convened at the police station to see that the situation was brought under control without using force. I was invited to attend it. All those who were present in the meeting felt happy that the mob had dispersed and the firing was avoided. The police felt relieved and obliged that no uglier incident could take place.

The agitators in Latur had determined to continue the agitation. After a few days, a scene of the same kind occurred in the town. When it happened, I was in the office of the municipality. One police officer came to me and asked me to help them, as I had done last time. I told him that every time I might not be able to control the mob. However, I went with him to the place where the mob was collected. As I had done last time, I proceeded towards the mob and the agitators stopped pelting stones. When I spoke to them, as I had done the last time, I found them more reasonable. They asked me to tell the police to go to the police station and not stand on the road. When I promised that it would be done, the mob dispersed for the second time. I asked the police officer and his men to leave the spot and remain in the police station. They did so and for the second time also the situation was controlled in a peaceful manner.

When the same kind of incident occurred for the third time, I was not the president of the Latur municipality. I had been elected to the Maharashtra legislative assembly and had resigned from the position I held in the local body.

The mob could not be controlled in a peaceful manner the third time. The police fired at it and four persons were killed. When this happened, I was in Mumbai attending the session of the legislature. On hearing about the incident, I left for Latur by train. Next morning, the train arrived at Harangul railway station. The driver and the guard of the train were unwilling to take passengers to Latur, without full information about the law and order situation in the town. They decided to send only the engine to Latur. I went to Latur in the engine with the driver. When the engine came near Latur and stopped, the police met me and gave information about the situation, to me and the driver. The police took me with a police escort to my place. I asked them if I could help them in any way. They said that I would not be able to help them and did not allow me to meet anybody without protection. My friends who had come to receive me at Harangul also concurred with the police. I abided by their advice. I was shocked to see the streets of Latur covered with stones and sticks. Curfew was imposed and strictly implemented. Many citizens were beaten by the police, the market was closed and a few shops and buses were burning.

In the legislature, the matter was raised and discussed. A demand to hold a judicial inquiry was made by some members, and was accepted by the government. For about a week, the town bore a deserted look. A large number of policemen patrolled the roads of the town from corner to corner, and were very strict with persons who came out of their houses.

After about three months, the judicial inquiry was held and a report about the incident was given. The report blamed the agitators, while the police force was not criticized or praised. Many witnesses who gave evidence spoke the truth, and the report was brief and balanced.

After the third incident, the government and the state transport corporation decided to have the division divided into two segments: one, which related to administration, remained at Osmanabad, and the other, which related to maintenance, went to Latur. The people in Latur and Osmanabad were not fully happy with the arrangements, but did not agitate against the compromise.

After a few years, Latur became a district. When that happened, Osmanabad district as well as Latur district got full-fledged state transport divisions.

The agitation was not appreciated by the people in the state. It became violent because from the beginning, nobody was willing to talk about it in clear terms and stop it. The members of the opposition parties were all out to make it effective regardless of violence while the members of the ruling party thought that not opposing it was the correct political strategy. Thus, all the political parties gave tacit strength to the agitation. Some of us felt that if the wise people in the town and ruling party had expressed their views opposing the parochial approach, the agitation could not have crossed the limit of sanity and caused bloodshed. But no one had opposed it. I was not happy with the situation that developed and the stand that I had taken. If I had been a little more frank and forthright, probably what had happened could have been avoided.

The agitation and my role in the dispersal of the mob caused a lot of difficulties to me in my political life. There were many who praised what I had done to ensure that the agitation was controlled and not allowed to cause more damage than it had done. For the third agitation also, no one complained against me. In fact, nobody blamed me for what had happened. However, I kept telling myself that I should have been more bold and correct in expressing my views at the start of the agitation.

■

Once Shankarrao Chavan, a respected minister from Marathwada in the government of Maharashtra, wanted to contact and interact with the senior and junior leaders of the area to learn about what should be done to help the people from the state in all fields. I was given an opportunity to speak on that occasion on behalf of the young generation. I made a brief statement which was liked by the minister and other members in the audience.

I said that the young generation can play a big role in developing the strength of the society and the nation. The young men and women have lot of energy which they should use to perform duties of a positive nature. If it is not used for the right purposes, it can cause damage to the society and interests of the nation. I said they should be given opportunities to participate in all kinds of political activities at all levels. And that would help them to use their energy in a positive manner.

Young men and women are not burdened with old ideas and concepts, and are more ready to adopt new ideas and concepts and to venture into new activities. They need to be given the liberty to do what they want to do in a positive manner. At the same time, they should be familiarized with the ideas and concepts developed by humanity over periods of thousands of years. Thus, if they are made to understand the value of the ethos of the society and the new ideas and concepts developing in the world, and use them by bringing them together properly, they can produce results of a lasting nature.

In politics, they should not be asked to remain isolated and secluded, for a political party without the young men and women does not have a future. It is bound to become weak and suffer if the youngsters are prohibited and not encouraged to play a positive role in their lives, politics and society. The old generation has to yield its place to the new generation. If that is not done in a balanced manner, a vacuum would be created which would weaken the party. In politics, nearly 30 per cent of the posts at all levels should be given to young men and women, 30 per cent to the middle-aged politicians and 30 per cent to experienced people. The remaining 10 per cent should be used to increase the number of young, middle-aged or experienced people, depending upon the availability of able candidates at different levels.

The Congress party had followed the policy of encouraging the young generation to play their role in all fields at all levels. That was why it remained effective, strong and maturely modernized.

I hoped that in the state of Maharashtra, also, that would be done.

That was the second time I was recognized by the state level politicians and leaders. The first time I was recognized by the Maharashtra leaders and politicians was when I had welcomed the defence minister of India, the chief minister and the members of the Maharashtra assembly in Chakur, my native village, when they inaugurated a cooperative oil mill established by the people of the area.

6

MEMBER OF THE MAHARASHTRA LEGISLATIVE ASSEMBLY

The Latur and Ausa constituencies were adjacent to each other. Keshavrao Sonawane, his brothers and their wives and children lived in Latur. Keshavrao Sonawane had contested his election for the Maharashtra legislative assembly from Latur, got elected and was included in the council of ministers of Chief Minister Vasantrao Naik. Keshavrao Sonawane's brother, Manikrao Sonawane, and the other brothers did their business and professional work in the town, and had earned a good name for themselves in the fields in which they functioned. In the first general election Keshavrao Sonawane contested, he got the support of the voters and defeated a well-known freedom fighter. He lost the second election. The fact that he was a cabinet minister did not help him. That was why when he decided to contest the third election, he was not willing to try his luck in the Latur constituency, but he wanted to stand from the Ausa constituency, in which his family had land and his father and uncle lived. All the members of his family were in favour of his contesting the third election from the Ausa constituency. He was the general secretary of the Pradesh Congress Committee of Maharashtra and had many friends in Mumbai and Delhi who could help him to get the ticket from any constituency he chose. He had decided that he should put up a candidate who came from the Ausa taluka in the Latur constituency to give an impression to the voters in the Ausa area that they would have a person from their area in the legislature to look after their interests and help them. This was discussed in the entire district in and around Latur and Ausa. The district Congress party was willing to support the proposal. However, some young friends of mine were unwilling to agree with what was suggested. They asked Keshavrao Sonawane to contest from the Latur constituency, and said that they would give a guarantee to get him elected. In case he was not willing to accept their suggestion, he should put me up as a candidate for the Latur constituency. However, he was not willing to change his plan and contest from Latur, or allow me to contest from there. This he made very clear to my friends.

A few days before the party had to select the candidates, he told me that I would not be given the ticket, and that he had decided to put up Vishwanath Birajdar as a candidate for Latur constituency. At the same time, he asked me to appear before the selection committee in Mumbai. I was surprised to hear that. I asked him, 'If I am not going to get the ticket, why should I go to Mumbai and appear before the selection committee?' He replied, 'I am sure you will not get the ticket and Vishwanath Birajdar will. However, in case the committee wants someone from the Latur area to contest, you could be given the ticket. So you should take the chance and appear before the selection committee.' I did not like what he was trying to do, but I did not want to hurt him either, so I went to Mumbai with him and tried my luck.

The selection committee had two representatives of the All India Congress Committee. One of them was K.D. Malviya and the other one was Dr Shankar Dayal Sharma. Yashwantrao Chavan, Vasantrao Naik, S.K. Wankhede, Nasikrao Tirpude, Keshavrao Sonawane and some others were also members of the committee. All of them were very respected and influential leaders of the Congress party.

When I appeared before the committee, only Wankhede asked me a few questions. Others watched the interview and made some notes on the papers they had before them.

Wankhede asked me, 'In the Latur constituency, Bapusaheb Kaldate will oppose the Congress candidate. If you contest from that constituency, would you be elected?'

I replied, 'Yes, I think I would get elected if I am allowed to contest.'

He said, 'You are young. You appear to be very enthusiastic and over-optimistic. What makes you think that you will win?'

My reply was, 'The Congress party, my friends and I have worked in the constituency for the last five years and created an atmosphere which can be very helpful. Any person who contests from that constituency on a Congress ticket can get elected against any candidate of any party.'

He asked me, 'Does that mean that any other candidate set up by the Congress will be elected?'

I said, 'Yes. I mean that.'

He asked, 'Can you guarantee the success of any other candidate?'

I replied, 'Yes. We would see that any candidate given by the party would be elected.'

All the members of the committee lifted their heads and stared at me. They appeared to be surprised to hear my replies, and liked them.

The questions and answers in the committee were discussed a lot for the next two days by all those who had come there seeking tickets. I knew that I could not be given the ticket. So, I was not surprised when the list of selected candidates mentioned the name of Vishwanath Birajdar as the candidate selected for the Latur constituency.

My friends, specially Amarchand Darda and my maternal uncle Trimbakrao Patil, were very angry and felt disappointed. They complained against Keshavrao Sonawane and other members openly and bluntly. They insisted that I should file an appeal before the high command in Delhi against the order of the selection committee. However, I was not willing to do it. I knew no one in Delhi who could guide and help me.

I preferred to return to Latur along with Keshavrao Sonawane and remain silent—which I did.

■

On 15 August 1972, I attended all the programmes organized by the municipality and the state government to celebrate Independence Day. In the evening, as usual, my friends and Keshavrao Sonawane were at my residence. When we were making light conversation, I received a telephone call from New Delhi. On the other side of the line were Shivajirao Patil Nilangekar and Bhaskarrao Chaluke. Taking turns, they spoke to me and gave me the news that brought about a big change in my life. Their message was: 'The All India Congress Committee has selected you as its candidate to contest the election from the Latur constituency. Congratulations! Prepare now to enter the election fray. Wish you all the best.'

I could not easily believe the news. I had not gone to New Delhi and there was, in my opinion, nobody who could have pleaded my case. I was surprised to know that such a decision had been taken. My friends saw me growing pensive. They asked me, 'Who spoke to you? Why are you looking so perturbed?' I disclosed to them what was told to me. They were amazed, but Keshavrao Sonawane was not surprised. Amarchand Darda congratulated me and asked my other friends to get sweets from the market to celebrate the message. It was only then, when the initial shock subsided, that all of them became vociferous and expressed their views boisterously. Sweets were then brought and distributed to all my friends and neighbours.

■

The new turn of events worried me. My father was not in favour of my contesting the election, and I had not made any preparation to enter the election fray. I did not clearly understand how the change in the selection of the Latur candidate had been made.

Later, I was told that Tulshiram Kamble, the sitting member of Parliament from the area, had put in a word to Mrs Indira Gandhi in my favour. Indiraji had decided to allow young candidates who were educated, had some experience of public life, and had enjoyed a good reputation, to contest the election. In all these criteria, I fitted well. So she preferred to give me the ticket instead of giving it to Vishwanath Birajdar.

•

I decided to contest the election and do my best to win it. Amarchand Darda and Trimbakrao Patil were happy to receive the news. They and many other friends felt that it was not necessary for me to worry because I could win the election easily. The Congress party of the district was not opposed to my candidature, and stood by the general secretary of the Pradesh Congress party because it did not want to go against his wishes.

Most of my friends were optimistic about the outcome. There were a few who were worried and they expressed their apprehensions while talking to me. I told them not to worry about the result and to campaign with confidence. I told them that if others saw them worried, they would lose their confidence, and that would not be good for my election. Later, they threw themselves fully into the election activities, without caring for the result. The voters appeared to favour me. They were not open in expressing their views, but they did indicate in many ways that they were happy with me as their candidate and would elect me as their representative.

The election was fought in a sober, dignified manner. I did not criticize other candidates who opposed me. I did not mention their names or the names of their parties in my speeches, and in response, they also refrained from criticizing me. I spoke about the policies of the Congress party, the governments at the state and national levels, and compared them with those of other parties, without mentioning their names. I talked about the differences in policies and asked the voters to vote for the policies they liked the most; I pointed out that the young voters were in favour of the Congress party, the poor preferred the Congress policies, and women liked it. There were some Congress persons who opposed me openly, in the name of caste and on other grounds. The criticism levelled against me earned the sympathy of the voters and did not affect me. In all, the election was enjoyable, educative and promising. Keshavrao Sonawane and members of his family helped me in the election, contrary to rumours that the Congress party leaders were canvassing against me. However, the majority of voters did not attach any importance to the rumours. The election result showed that almost all the Congress persons and others who did not belong to any party supported me. The result showed that the election was won by the Congress party with a big margin of 22,000 votes, which was very encouraging for all Congress party leaders and workers. It showed that the opinion I had expressed before the selection committee was not an exaggerated statement.

The victory in the election was celebrated in a very sober manner. There were some supporters who wanted to celebrate it on a grand scale, but I agreed with those who thought that a show of jubilation was unnecessary and superfluous. I agreed with the second view, as it reduced the chances of unnecessary acrimony and animosity between the members of the parties supporting the contesting candidates.

My election to the legislature compelled me to reduce my appearances in the courts, and deprived me of the opportunity to lecture to the students of Dayanand College. On the plus side, it gave me the chance to contribute towards law and policymaking, and working with those who were trying to help the people and bring about development of the state and the country. My area of activities widened. I realized that I had to learn a lot, work hard and face many difficulties to meet the level of expectation of the people from their representative.

■

The Maharashtra legislative council and assembly were lodged in a very beautiful building which was close to the Gateway of India, the seashore and the Taj Hotel. In the British regime, the legislature's meetings were held in that building. In the past, the Maharashtra legislative assembly had renowned Indians as its members, such as Dr B.R. Ambedkar and G.V. Mavalankar.

For a few months after I joined it, I generally occupied a seat on the benches in the last row in the House. From my seat I saw other members speaking, ministers replying to the questions, the debates and the presiding officers conducting the proceedings. I was not in a hurry to participate in the proceedings of the House. As a member of the Latur municipal council and as its president, I had learned the rules, procedures and art of participating at discussions in the council. The main principles that were followed when participating in discussions in the council were useful in helping me to understand how to participate in the proceedings in the legislature. I studied the relevant constitutional provisions, the rules of procedure and a few rulings given by the presiding officers, to equip myself to carry out my legislative duties. I was a student of law and the Constitution of India, which was of great value to me to understand and grasp the art of being a good legislator.

I did not ask questions. I selected the subjects on which I wanted to speak, studied them carefully, wrote down on paper what I wanted to say, tried to be brief in my statements to fit into the time limit fixed for my speeches, and decided always to go by the decisions and instructions of the presiding officers. I never interjected or made any statements to object to anything said by the other members in their speeches. Most of the members in the House preferred to speak in Marathi, others in Hindi or English. Generally, I spoke in Marathi. At times, I spoke in Hindi or English, depending upon the topic of the debate.

The speech I had made while participating in the debate on the decision taken to establish the Agriculture University at Parbhani, in the Marathwada region, and three more universities to be established in other regions of the state, was liked by the minister and members of the assembly. Shankarrao Chavan, who was then the minister for agriculture in the state government, had initiated the debate. The people in the Marathwada region wanted one new university to impart agricultural knowledge to students from the region to be established at Parbhani, an area surrounded by very fertile land with good irrigation facilities, provided by the Jaikwadi dam. On finding that their demand was not accepted by the government for many years, the people became angry with the government. They organized an agitation which became very violent. When the government found that it could not control the agitation easily, it announced that it would have one university at Parbhani, and three more universities in the other three regions of the state. That decision was presented to the legislature to obtain its approval.

Most of the members of the legislature supported the establishment of new universities. Those who opposed the decision felt that the existing universities were not doing well and lacked the funds and facilities they needed. They could not impart quality education or develop the research they were expected to do. So, they said, the existing universities should be strengthened and helped with more funds and the wherewithal required by them. If the government did not do this and tried to establish new universities instead, it was not right. There was a grain of truth and rationality in the arguments made by the members opposing the decision of the government.

I was given an opportunity to speak. I argued that what was said by the members opposing the decision could not be rashly brushed aside and not taken into consideration. Steps should be taken to strengthen the existing universities.

However, the number of agriculture universities in the state was very small. The existing universities could not meet the demand of new knowledge required by the farmers and all those who had decided to join agricultural activities. For meeting their demands, it was necessary to have more universities. So, if the government took a decision to have a few more universities, it should be supported and not opposed.

Universities need more funds, more equipment, better facilities to do research and development, and more help to take new knowledge to the doorsteps of the farmers. All these things required by them could not be provided in a short span of time. The government should make all efforts to reduce the time required and provide the facilities in a shorter time. That would be a practical approach. The legislature should allow the executive to handle this matter in a pragmatic manner.

Research and development (R&D) was necessary for the development of agriculture. However, it could not be expected to be achieved in a fixed time frame. In some cases, it could fructify in years, months or days. R&D was a journey into the unknown. It could bring about revolutions. If one new formula was discovered, it could help to recoup all the expenditure incurred in doing research and development. In fact, in some cases, it would pay back in millions of times. So, the government and the people should have a correct perspective about it and encourage it, rather than demoralize the seekers of new knowledge and new technologies.

The minister was in the House when I spoke. He was happy to hear the argument I had advanced, and in his reply to the debate, mentioned some of the points made by me.

The decision taken by the government was endorsed. The debate proved to be enlightening, and my participation in it created an ambience for me in which I could always be allowed to speak, when I wanted to speak. After that debate, I did not have to struggle in any way to get the opportunity to participate in the discussions.

In the first few months of my entry into the House, I spoke on three other topics. They related to the budget presented and on municipal administration. The speeches made on these topics were very short and brief. They did not attract any attention from anybody in the House or create any problems or controversy. But they appeared to have created soft corners for me in the hearts of the ministers and the presiding officers. In the House, I was recognized as a disciplined member, who could be relied upon to speak on serious topics, within the time fixed for the speeches, without emotionally tilting my arguments in favour or against the government.

•

V.S. Page, who was the chairman of the Maharashtra legislative council for many years, was a freedom fighter, a person who had travelled in different parts of the world, and was a very well-read, respected and honoured politician. He was the chairman of the committee constituted to manage a religious trust created to look after the Devasthan of Pandharinath and Rukmani of Pandharpur. He guided the government of Maharashtra in evolving new policies for the development and betterment of the people, and drafted the election manifestos for his party. In the House, he was impartial and helpful to members of all political parties. He was very kind to me from the first day I met him and campaigned for me in my elections. I revered him for helping the poorest amongst the poor, and for the clean life he lived.

He conceived the idea of the Employment Guarantee Scheme and got it approved by the state government. The scheme which he framed is adopted with some minor changes at the national level for all the states of the country. For this scheme and the concept, he will have a special place in the parliamentary history of India, because of its uniqueness and the justice it does to the poorer sections of society. He was of the view that the government of the state had taken steps to develop industry, trade and agriculture, which was the right thing to do. But he felt that enough was not done to give employment to workers in rural areas to help them to sustain their families and lives. There were persons who had no lands, no industries, no shops, no government jobs and no guarantee that they would get employment when they needed the same.

In the periods when they could not get employment, some

desperate workers committed thefts or dacoities, or even committed suicide. So he felt that the government should prepare a scheme to guarantee employment to such unemployed people in rural areas. He was of the view that it should be done through a statute passed by the legislature. To consider this issue, he constituted a committee of legislators and I was included in it. The committee discussed the matter with the chief minister and other members of the state government, with experts in economics, legislators and media persons. The government and ministers were not fully in favour of the scheme, saying that the farming activity in the state would suffer. The committee suggested that the scheme should remain in abeyance during the period in which sowing of seeds, harvesting of crops, and such other agricultural activities were carried on, so that agriculture would not suffer. It was also decided that the scheme could be used only for ninety days in a year. The tehsildars of the talukas were given the responsibility to provide employment to fifty persons when they asked for work within a period of seven days. To be ready to provide employment, they were asked to collect information about the possible number of unemployed people from each village of their area, to have a list of jobs that could be given, to have the information regarding the availability of implements to be used, and to have funds to give the wages when the work was started. The information collected from the blocks and talukas was collected at the district headquarters, and the information collected at the district headquarters was collected at the state level. On the basis of the information, the funds were expected to be provided in the budgets. Thus, all the steps that were required could be taken before the demands for employment were made, which would help in giving the employment without any delay.

Economists were of the view that the scheme would not be implemented efficiently. They said that the ad hoc, not planned, manner of providing employment was bound to make it more expensive.

V.S. Page could not have a law made for the scheme. He agreed to the compromise that it could be implemented under orders issued by the executive. The government was of the view that it could experiment with the scheme, find out how it could work and then decide if a law for the purpose should be made or not. The matter was discussed by all stakeholders, It received a mixed reception about its value and feasibility.

In the first year, the scheme needed ₹40 crore. The question of how to raise that amount was discussed by the committee. I suggested that the revenue collected by imposing the profession tax should be used for this purpose. The profession tax was expected to be imposed and collected by the local bodies. However, almost all local bodies had refrained from imposing and collecting it. I suggested that the state government should impose and collect the profession tax and use it to provide employment to the unemployed. In the meeting, some members asked what should be done to deal with the problem if a few local bodies had begun to collect the tax. I suggested that they should be allowed to collect it and use the funds in their areas to provide amenities and civic facilities to the people. The government should collect the taxes if the local bodies did not do it. The suggestion was accepted and forwarded to the state government, and the state government accepted it.

The committee decided that the projects that were to be started to give employment to the unemployed should be of a productive nature. It prepared a list of projects and schemes which could be started for the purpose. It was also decided that machines should not be used in the projects because that would reduce the employment-giving potential of the projects. The scheme was not very efficiently employed for the first few years. However, later, it was used in a better manner. The defects it suffered from were identified and rectified.

At the places where projects were started, women with their children came to do the jobs. The children were forced to remain in the open in the bright sunlight, unattended by their parents. To remedy these defects, sheds were erected, a few women were employed to look after them and first aid was provided. At some places, fair price shops were started to see that the workers could purchase foodgrains and other essential items at the place where they worked.

In order to ensure that the unemployed were not shown as employed and funds were not embezzled, payment was made in accordance with the work done. This measure reduced the chances of corruption a great deal.

The legislature constituted a committee of legislators to supervise the work done under the Employment Guarantee Scheme. The committee was allowed to visit the sites where the schemes were implemented and give their report to the government and to the legislature. The legislature was allowed to discuss the reports of the committee and the action taken on the reports by the government.

The scheme has remained in existence for all these years from its inception. It is now accepted at the national level in a statutory form. Initially, it was made applicable to nearly 250 districts in the country. Now it has been made applicable in all the districts. With this scheme in existence, the landless labourers get the jobs they need, and the wages that should be justly given to them. The wages given are nearly equal to the minimum wages given to them under the Minimum Wages Act.

There are farmers and others who oppose this scheme and say that they do not get the hands to cultivate their lands. They complain that they are required to give the wages to the workers, which does not allow agriculture to remain an attractive option. There are some farmers who say that the scheme should be used to cultivate their lands, that is, their lands should be cultivated at the cost of the government. The governments are not ready to accept this suggestion fully, although some state governments have allowed this scheme to be used to develop their lands, by digging farm ponds, open wells, and so on. In some states, horticulture in private lands is allowed to be done under this scheme at the cost of the governments.

Small farmers do not need labourers to work in their fields. They are able to cultivate their own land and also to work on projects started by the government to give employment to the unemployed, in order to supplement their income from their lands. Farmers who have bigger pieces of land have now started to use machines to cultivate their land. Thus the scheme has helped to modernize and mechanize agriculture and to see that proper wages are given to workers in rural areas.

When the scheme was presented in the Maharashtra legislative assembly, I sought permission to speak on it from V.S. Page who was responsible for bringing it into existence. He said that I should speak and would be given the permission to do so. When I asked him about the points I should emphasize in my speech, he said I could say anything I liked, and that as a member of the committee, I had attended the discussions which would give me the hints to underline important issues relating to it. When I insisted on getting some points from him, he became emotional. With tears in his eyes, he said he was happy that the scheme was coming into existence. He would have liked it to become a scheme given through a statute and not through an executive order, because the statutory scheme could not be dropped or changed at any time by the executive, without the consent of the legislature. He said he would die a happy man if it became a scheme given by the Constitution of India, but the Constitution does not in specific terms give a fundamental right to employment or work to its citizens. The Supreme Court has said that the right to life means: the rights to a good life, to food, to education, to shelter, to medical help, to work and to employment. He said all the countries which accept the communist ideology have given the right to work to their citizens. Some socialist countries also have given that right to their citizens. There are some capitalist countries which give the right to work to their citizens, and also many capitalist countries which do not give the right to work to their citizens, but they give dole to their citizens who are not employed. All the countries who have given the right to work have enjoined the duty to work on their citizens. In fact, the Constitutions of some countries provide the right and duty to work in one chapter. In some countries, they are given in one article. In the Constitution of Japan, the article which provides the right and duty to work reads as follows:

'The citizen shall have Right and Duty to Work.'

The old Constitution of Egypt provided that:

'The citizen shall have Right, Duty and Honour to Work.'

Thus, the right and duty to work help to make the life of the citizen easier to live. With the duty to work mentioned in the Constitution, the right to work becomes feasible and implementable.

The Indian Constitution avoided giving the right to work because the framers of the Constitution thought that the cost of giving the right to work to all citizens would be economically unbearable to the state. It is not possible for a government to provide all kinds of jobs to its citizens, which is why it has become non-feasible and unimplementable in some countries. But if the Constitution provides that the citizen has a duty to work, he has to accept the work offered to him. If he does not accept the work offered to him, he loses his right to work. If the right and duty to work are mentioned in the Constitution, the citizen has a right to work which can help him to live. For example, if a person has a PhD degree, he cannot ask to be given the job of a professor, unless it is available—he may be given a job of a clerk which can fetch him a small amount of salary to enable him to live. If the duty to work is provided in the Constitution, this way of giving job to unemployed can become possible and feasible.

In India, the Constitution can be amended to provide that the citizen shall have a right and duty to work, and to make this scheme workable and implementable.

V.S. Page wanted that the Constitution should be amended to provide right and duty to work to the citizens of India. He felt that the Employment Guarantee Scheme given by the state was certainly better than the scheme under which the dole is given. The employed person does not get wages without doing and producing something, unlike under the dole system.

I made the speech in the House and was very happy to do it. I did not make all the points that I have mentioned in these pages, but the essence was mentioned.

▪

In my opinion, the Employment Guarantee Scheme should guarantee employment for 365 days of the year to the unemployed. If that is not possible in the near future, it may be made applicable, at least, for all the days of a year in the areas affected by Naxalism and terrorism. If that is also not possible, it should be made available for 200 days in a year in the areas affected by Naxalism and terrorism. Its provisions should be used to develop the land of all smallholders, and not to cultivate the lands of the big farmers.

If it covers the cultivation of land of the farmers, the workers should be given a share in the profit earned by the farmers. The profit can be calculated on the basis of income earned, over and above the cost of cultivation and production of the farm produce.

The Constitution of India has given a right to education to children of certain ages. It should be amended to give the right to work and provide for the duty to work.

The Constitution should make it clear that the citizen shall be bound to accept the employment offered to him, and shall not be allowed to insist on employment that he likes and wants. These provisions are going to be helpful to those who have no land, no shops, no industries, no government jobs, but are able to work and live on an income earned honestly. These provisions are needed to ensure economic, social and political justice to one and all.

The Employment Guarantee Scheme applied in all districts of the country by the Union government is criticized by some in the media. The benefits it gives to the citizens are not specifically mentioned and underlined. This is the result of clashes of interests of different sections of the society. In order to maintain peace and tranquillity in the society and to help those who have no lands, no shops, no industries, no government and private jobs, this scheme should be continued while it is needed. If there are any defects identified in implementing it, they should be rectified. But, if it is given up or diluted in such a manner that the needy suffer and the vocal and more powerful sections of the society get undue and unfair advantages, it would be wrong and unjust. That would make the needy feel that they should help themselves, not through democratic methods but by using force and violent methods. In the interest of democracy and justice to be done to one and all, the help given to the unemployed and needy should be continued.

I feel happy to remember that I was a member of the committee that had drafted and got the Employment Guarantee Scheme adopted by the state government, which has now been made applicable in the entire country.

■

The forty-second amendment to the Constitution of India was introduced in and passed by Parliament, and was discussed by political parties, lawyers and intellectuals in the country on a large scale. I studied the amendment and wrote a small booklet on its provisions. In one of the meetings of the members of the legislature held by the party, I spoke on the amendment. My speech was welcomed by some legislators and opposed by some others. The young legislators were in favour of the amendment, but most of the senior legislators were opposed to it. My booklet explained why the amendments were necessary and what their implications were. My speech attracted the attention of the party members, and included me in the group of legislators who stood by Indiraji. From that time, I was deemed to be the supporter of leaders at the national level and lukewarm towards some state leaders.

■

Vasantrao Naik was the chief minister of Maharashtra for more than twelve years. There were some leaders and ministers who thought that he should resign and one of them should be given the opportunity to head the government of the state, there were some others who supported him. Some of the ministers and legislators on both sides were active and tried to garner support for their friends. One of the ministers from Marathwada prepared a letter addressed to the high command of the party at the national level, alleging that one minister was trying to destabilize the government of the chief minister and that he should be restrained from doing so and punished. The minister supporting the chief minister wanted me to sign that letter, I refused to sign it. I told him that I was not in favour of destabilizing the government, and at the same time, I would not sign the letter accusing the minister against whom it was complaining. The matter was discussed by many legislators, Congress leaders and workers in the state, some of whom approved my stand. Some others criticized it. However, I did not try to explain my stand in favour or against the statements made by others.

Vasantrao Naik learnt about what I had said and done. He did not object to my stand. He continued to behave with me as he used to behave before my stand was made known to him. For this, my respect for him increased. The minister against whom the letter was written did not speak to me about my not signing or signing it. He, too, continued to treat me as he used to do before. Both the leaders indicated that they were above petty things and did not attach great importance to the moves started by some politicians.

■

After Shankarrao Chavan became the chief minister of Maharashtra, he got me elected as a member of the legislative committee on public undertakings of the state. Later on, the committee elected me as its chairman. For nearly one year, I functioned as the chairman of the committee.

The committee consisted of members of almost all the parties in proportion to their strength in the legislature. It was expected to examine the working of public undertakings in the state and send reports to the legislature, as well as to the executive and the undertakings. The executive and the undertakings were expected to take actions on the suggestions given by the committee. Generally, suggestions given by the committee were accepted and acted upon. In some cases, the executive and the undertakings expressed their inability to act upon the recommendations of the committee. The committee could ask them to reconsider their report, expressing their inability to accept the recommendations. If they refused to change their stand and continued to say that they could not implement the recommendations, the matter could be discussed in the legislature, which could give the final decision, either asking them to act on the recommendations, or asking the committee not to insist on getting the suggestions implemented.

The committee could prepare questionnaires and send them to the executive and the undertakings, which were expected to respond to them in writing. The committee could invite the officers of the government and the undertakings to appear before it and reply to the questions put to them. It could visit the undertakings, examine the experts and get the issues technically examined by the expert organizations. The committee could decide upon the undertakings which could be examined by it.

In the period of my chairmanship of the committee, it was decided that it could examine the undertakings producing power, providing transport facilities, the power-loom and handloom corporations.

The committee examined the power corporation first. It visited the hydro- and thermal-power stations—at Koyana, Nasik and at other places. The Koyana power project supplies power to many parts of the state. The water that is used to generate power in the Koyana project flows into the Arabian Sea. It can be collected in dams on the western side of the ghat, and diverted through tunnels to the eastern side to be used for irrigation purposes. Udhavrao Patil, who was the leader of the party of farmers and workers, used to plead that the rainwater which fell on the western ghats, should not be allowed to flow into the ocean. It should be collected in dams and diverted through the tunnels to the eastern side and used for irrigation and other purposes. This suggestion is very valid. But up to this time, no action has been taken to act upon it. If it is used, it can meet the demand of water for irrigation purposes on a large scale.

The Koyana power plant was doing well. The committee did not suggest anything else to be done. The power project in Parbhani was doing well. Its only problem was the non-availability of water in a scanty rainy season. However, the committee did not make any recommendation about this plant.

The thermal power plant at Nasik was kept unused for three to four months when the cleaning of the boilers and machines was done. The committee members wanted to know as to why the undertaking was taking so much time to clean the boilers and other parts of the plant. The officers of the undertaking explained that the boilers had to be cooled down by keeping them unused for some period of time. They had to put scaffolding to clean the insides which took many days. The committee in its report suggested that the undertaking should get the machines and use them to reduce the time taken to clean the boilers and other parts of the plant. This suggestion of the committee was accepted by the executive and the undertaking.

For the development of agricultural industry and transport facilities and for domestic use, energy is needed. The demand for energy is going up. It is produced by using coal, water and oil resources, which are getting depleted. So, producing energy by using these resources is going to be more difficult and expensive in the future. Hence, renewable and new sources of energy are required to be discovered and used. Nuclear, solar, wind, biomass and wave energy can be generated and used. Now the time has come to find new sources of energy by doing research and development for this purpose. Matter is energy and energy is matter. Technologies to turn

Odyssey of My Life ▪ 109

matter into energy and energy into matter should be developed and used. The more we pay attention to the development of new sources of energy and technologies, the better it would be for our present and the future.

The committee examined the State Transport Corporation of Maharashtra. The corporation was doing very well. It had increased the number of vehicles used in different parts of the state. Its declared policy was that it would take its buses to all parts of the state where roads were constructed. It built bus stands, established offices in every district to manage transport activities, and workshops to maintain its vehicles. It had earned profits and could pay handsome salaries to its employees. The committee was happy to see that it was working as it should and gave a favourable report.

The committee examined the working of the power-loom and handloom corporations. They were brought into existence to protect the interests of the power-loom and handloom weavers. The government had reserved certain kinds of cloth to be produced by the power-loom and handloom weavers only, and not by textile mills. The weavers were given tax concessions and help. But unfortunately, they did not reach the weavers. These were grabbed by middlemen. The weavers, who were poor and illiterate, could not get the benefit out of the policy as they were expected to.

The committee gave a report on these issues and the management mistakes and wrongs committed by the corporations. The reports were not easily accepted as the members of the corporations and the executive tried to defend the corporations and those who manned them. The committee decided to see that the weavers were given justice and help was provided by the government for this purpose.

The two corporations were examined at the fag end of the year. The new committee that came into existence later was expected to see that the recommendations of our committee were accepted and implemented. The committee members took a very correct, impartial stand in deciding upon the issues presented before it.

The members of the committee got opportunities to work and

live together for many days. They became lifelong friends with one another.

All the members and officers cooperated in the best possible manner with one another and with me. I carry very happy memories of having worked with them.

7

DEPUTY MINISTER OF LAW AND JUDICIARY, IRRIGATION AND PROTOCOL

In 1975, Shankarrao Chavan expanded his council of ministers and included me in it as a deputy minister of law, irrigation and protocol. B.J. Khatal was the law and irrigation minister and Dr Rafiq Zakaria was the protocol minister. Before inducting me in the ministries, the chief minister had asked me about the ministries in which I liked to work. I had indicated that I preferred to work in the ministry of irrigation and law. He allowed me to work in these ministries. Dr Rafiq Zakaria wanted the chief minister to induct me in the protocol ministry to work with him. The chief minister agreed to allow me to work in the protocol ministry also.

In the law and irrigation ministries, I was allowed to take decisions in certain matters on my own, and in others, with the approval of the cabinet minister. In the protocol ministry, the cabinet minister allowed me to discharge almost all the duties he was required to do. In the legislature, I replied to the questions asked by legislators and took part in the debates relating to ministries with me. Initially, the ministers were not confident that I would be able to manage legislative duties very comfortably. However, after seeing me working in the legislature for a few days, they were inclined to shift their responsibilities to me. They took the floor in the legislature only in matters of very complicated nature. In fact, more than 90 per cent of legislative work was done by me.

My studies to understand the constitutional provisions and rules of procedure helped me to feel equal to the tasks I had to perform in the Houses of legislature and as a member of the executive.

Initially, in Maharashtra, all the members of the council of ministers were not expected to attend every meeting of the cabinet. The ministers of state and the deputy ministers were allowed to be present in the meetings of the cabinet when subjects from their ministries were taken up for discussions and decisions. Later, Shankarrao Chavan, as the chief minister, allowed all the members of his council of ministers to attend cabinet meetings, and allowed them to express their views on the subjects, even those unrelated to their ministries. He did this with a view to train the junior ministers to discharge their duties in a better manner. He thought that if all the members of the council of ministers knew what the government was trying to do, they would be more efficient and effective in discharging their duties.

■

Bills to be introduced and passed by the legislature were drafted by the appropriate ministries, and were refined and corrected by the law ministry. After that, they were approved by the cabinet and then they were introduced in the legislature. The drafting of bills in India follows the models used in the UK. In the US and other countries, drafting is done in a more comprehensive and different manner, which we should follow. The laws made should be easy to understand and read. They should be unambiguous and written in a language understood by the common man also without facing great difficulty.

The law ministry is consulted by other ministries to find out if their legislative work is constitutionally correct or not. When the laws made by ministries are challenged in the courts, the law ministry helps them to argue and put forth their points of view. The law ministry decides how many courts should be established in the states to deal with cases, and appoints lawyers who can deal with government cases in the courts. It prepares budgets and provides funds to the judiciary to discharge its duties.

•

Judges and lawyers at the national, state and other levels, have discussed how justice could be provided to all citizens in the country at a cost affordable by them, and in time, acceptable to them.

Justice P.N. Bhagwati who was then a Supreme Court judge, Ramakant Goswami who later became the law minister of India, Rajni Patil and many others discussed the pertinent issues at the national level, and travelled to various states to discuss them with judges, lawyers and law ministers. As Mumbai High Court was one of the reputed High Courts in the country with many eminent lawyers, they came to Maharashtra to discuss these issues with their counterparts.

The judges and lawyers thought that lok adalats should be held at different places in the states to hear the smaller cases and dispose them off on the spot, without getting bogged down in the procedural complications. They decided that in each state, there should be a legal aid scheme started and funded by the government to provide legal help to poor litigants. In Maharashtra, at some places, lok adalats were held and cases in large numbers were disposed off, and a legal aid scheme was begun. The state government helped in both these matters. Along with judges and lawyers, I attended a few lok adalats. I drafted a legal aid scheme and presented it to the cabinet which approved it and gave funds to run it in all courts in all districts. Initially, a small amount of money was given for this purpose. The state government promised to give more funds, if required, to run the scheme.

At present also, the scheme is in existence in all courts in all districts. Under the scheme, a list of lawyers is prepared and kept ready. When a poor client approaches the lawyer heading the scheme, a lawyer from the list is asked to help him. The fees of the lawyer and court fees are given out of the funds provided for the purpose.

The scheme has helped many, though not all, poor clients to get the justice they seek. If one of the parties in a case is in a position to engage a senior lawyer paying huge amount of money as fees, the other party who is not able to engage a senior lawyer suffers. In criminal cases, no accused is allowed to go undefended in the court. In criminal cases, the courts appoint amicus curiae to help the accused. In civil matters, this kind of provision was not available. Now, with the legal aid scheme in existence, no client goes to court without the help of a lawyer.

The fees that are given to lawyers helping poor clients should be increased. It is said that all citizens are equal in the eye of the law, but not in the court of law, because the legal assistance given to every client is not of the same kind and the same standard.

In India, cases take years to be decided. The procedure followed to decide them is of a complicated nature. The procedure ensures that no mistake is committed in providing justice. But at times, the same procedure is used to delay the dispensation of justice. It has, therefore, become necessary to amend the procedural laws to avoid delays and to do speedy justice. The procedural laws have been amended, but have not been implemented satisfactorily.

The number of people living in the country is big and so is the number of disputes. Every year, many new laws are passed by the Union and state legislatures, but the number of courts to decide cases is not equal to the number of people, the number of laws, and number of cases to be decided in the country. That is why the delays in dispensing justice occur. That is why the number of courts should be increased.

The courts need more judges. Good lawyers are not willing to become judges. That is why the posts created to have more judges remain vacant. That happens because the good lawyers earn a lot which they cannot do by becoming judges. Hence, the salaries of judges should be increased to attract good lawyers to become judges.

In many advanced countries, judges continue to work for many more years than the judges in India do. In India, when judges retire, their posts remain vacant. To solve this problem, the age of retirement of judges should be increased. In America, the judges of the Supreme Court are appointed for life. In some other countries, they continue to function up to the age of seventy-five years. A decision to allow them to work for more years should be taken. If justice is not done without delay and in an inexpensive manner, citizens' faith in the rule of law may be reduced, and maintaining peace and tranquillity in the society may become difficult. Hence, all that is necessary to make the judiciary strong, efficient, and inexpensive should be done.

■

More than 80 per cent of Indians depend upon income from agriculture. The climatic conditions in India are propitious for agriculture. Water from big and small rivers can be used for farming. The Himalayas are covered with snow which melts and feeds water into the rivers. Water in rivers needs to be stored. In many countries around the world, the water from rivers is stored in dams and used to cultivate the land. Over the centuries, rivers have carried fertile soil and spread it in different parts of the country, making it fertile for farming. In the southern part of India, waterbodies were constructed to supply water for farming and other purposes also. During the British period too, attempts were made to build dams and provide water for irrigation purposes. The British had surveyed the land to find sites where dams could be built. They found many sites where dams could be constructed. All the sites identified by them have not been used.

After India became free, steps were taken to develop agriculture. The first five-year plan was devoted to the task of developing agriculture. It was understood in clear terms that to increase the productivity and production of land, irrigation facilities should be provided on a massive scale. Therefore, big dams were begun to be built. This work could not be completed in five years, or in the period of one five-year plan, and it was necessary to continue the task for many more years. Even today, India has not exhausted all the sites on which irrigation dams can be built. For using all available water, many more dams—big, medium, and small—need be built. The work for this purpose must be continued for many years.

In Maharashtra, plans were made to build irrigation dams, funds were provided, and attempts on a large scale were made to use the available water. That was why the ministry of irrigation was treated as a very important ministry. Senior, experienced and efficient ministers were given the charge of it.

B.J. Khatal was supposed to be an efficient minister. All the important executive decisions were taken at his level in the law and irrigation ministries. I had a very limited role to play in the irrigation ministry. In the legislature, I handled almost all the work of the ministry of irrigation. I visited the big dams that were constructed or were being built. I felt very happy to visit the dam sites as the atmosphere around them was very encouraging and inspiring.

In the districts of Osmanabad and Beed, a dam was to be constructed at Dhanegaon. The decision to build a dam at the Dhanegaon site was pending because people in Osmanabad district and Latur taluka wanted the dam to be built at a different site from the one selected by the engineers. If it was built downstream, it could provide water to irrigate about 22,000 hectares of land in Latur district, but if it was built at the site selected by the experts, only about 18,000 hectares of land from Latur taluka and 22,000 hectares of land from Beed district could be irrigated. The people from Beed district objected to changing the site.

Because of this dispute, the work to construct the dam could not be started for more than two decades, and the water in the Manjara river flowed into the ocean, depriving farmers of water for nearly 40,000 hectares of land. Representatives of Beed district invited Vasant Dada Patil, the then irrigation minister, to visit the dam site and take a decision. Representatives of the Latur taluka and Osmanabad district were also invited to meet the minister, so that the decision could be taken after hearing them.

As I was the MLA from Latur taluka, the minister wanted me to express my views on the site to be selected. I told him that he could take any decision he liked and thought proper. He could decide to build it at the site originally suggested or at the site suggested later, but it should be done without further delays. After all, the people living on both banks of the river belonged to one country and should not resent the fact that one or the other area was getting more water. They should not obstruct the work and let the water remain unutilized and flow into the ocean. The minister took the decision to go ahead and the work was started on the same day at the site selected by the experts. When I became the irrigation minister I encouraged the officers and contractors to complete the work in time. That dam is now constructed and is helping the people in the area to irrigate their land and become prosperous.

It is necessary to increase irrigation facilities in a big way. For this purpose, more funds should be provided. Concerted efforts should be made and modern methods used to survey the sites suitable to construct dams, prepare plans and build them. This should be done by the Union and state governments. If there are sites to build big, medium or small dams, they should be used. Many other methods to harvest rainwater should be used. Percolation dams and dams in farms should be built. The would increase the moisture in the soil and help to increase the yield from the land.

All waterbodies, such as percolation, minor, medium and major tanks and dams in which silt is collected should be de-silted. If the capacity to store water in these tanks and dams is increased, their capacity to irrigate more land also can be increased in a cost-effective manner and in a short time.

The land for the projects should be acquired by paying compensation which is just and acceptable to the oustees.

Rainwater should be harvested. It can be done in villages, towns and cities, in agricultural lands, deserts, forests and hilly areas. If the rainwater is absorbed in the soil and not allowed to flow back into the oceans, the irrigation potential can increase enormously and in a cost-effective manner.

Water can be drawn from the waterbodies under the surface of the land and used in farming, as was done in the olden days, on a small scale. These days, electric pumps and motors are used to draw water from the underground reservoirs, depleting the subsoil water storages. To rectify this harmful effect, water stored under the ground should be recouped. Since trees penetrate the soil and their roots spread underground to help rainwater to percolate into subsoil storages. So large numbers of trees should be planted, keeping in mind that they would provide water and food for living creatures.

These days, the water scarcity is discussed on a large scale. In fact, some people think that wars may be fought for water.

Two-thirds of our globe is covered with water and this can be purified and used for any purpose. We have the technologies which can be used for these purposes. Human beings have brainpower which can be used in a more effective manner than other living creatures. Nature helps plants, animals, birds, fish and other creatures to survive. If we use proper methods, and use natural resources, we can have enough food, water, air and energy to meet our demands. The available technologies can be made more sophisticated and cost-effective. If we protect the resources of nature, we can definitely have sufficient food, water, air and energy to meet our demands. If we plan for today and the distant future, we can help protect ourselves, other creatures, plants and non-living things, too.

■

Tourists and guests from abroad visit Delhi, and then want to visit Mumbai, which is supposed to be the financial capital of India. Almost all heads of states and governments, ministers and officers working in high positions in other countries visit Mumbai to see the industrial, trading and other activities that are carried on in the second most important city of India. Private tourists also want to visit Mumbai and see as to how it has developed and is coping

The author's grandfather, Veer Bhagawantrao Patil.

The author's father, Sambhaji, aka Vishwanath Patil.

During the author's brother's marriage, with (L–R) his grandfather, father, brother Rajeshwar and Rajeshwar's mother Gangabai.

The author with former Chief Minister of Maharashtra Shri Yashwantrao Chavan and others.

With former Prime Minister Indira Gandhi.

The author, in his capacity as minister of state for defence, with Chief of Army Staff Gen. Om Prakash Malhotra, Chief of Navy Staff Admiral R.L.Pereira and Chief of Air Staff Idris Hasan Latif.

With Prime Minister Rajiv Gandhi.

With Prime Minister Rajiv Gandhi and Defence Minister K.C. Pant.

The author with his wife Vijaya.

The author and his wife with their son and daughter.

With son-in-law Basava Prabhu Patil (centre), daughter Swapna (third from the right) and wife Vijaya (third from the left) during Swapna's marriage reception.

With son-in-law Basava Prabhu Patil and daughter Swapna.

With his granddaughters Rudrali and Arushi.

With his daughter-in-law and granddaughters.

The author with Gurumayi.

The author, his wife, his son and friends with Sri Sathya Sai Baba.

The author during a visit to the US, with US President Ronald Reagan and Prime Minister Rajiv Gandhi.

With Boris N. Yeltsin, president of the Russian Federation, and Prime Minister P.V. Narasimha Rao.

Prime Minister P.V. Narasimha Rao (left) and the author with the former speaker, House of Commons, UK.

with the problems of the new age.

The state of Maharashtra has a strong protocol organization, headed by a cabinet minister who is assisted by other state and deputy ministers. However, generally, the cabinet minister is given some other portfolios also, which means that he pays more attention to other ministries and leaves the duty of protocol to be done by his junior ministers.

Dr Rafiq Zakaria was a well-known literary person, well-versed in the art and science of discharging protocol duties. It was he who wanted me to join his protocol ministry. Dr Aliyar Jang was then the governor of Maharashtra. He was the vice-chancellor of Osmania University and Aligarh Muslim University. He was very keen to see that protocol duties were performed in a perfect manner. After the new cabinet was formed, he invited Dr Zakaria and me to discuss the manner in which the protocol duties should be performed.

For about two hours, he discussed the methods and ways in which protocol should be observed and protocol duties should be performed. First, he asked us as to how the VVIPs visiting Mumbai were received, how their programmes were planned, and how their meetings with VVIPs of the state and other private dignitaries were organized and conducted. Then, he expressed his views on the precautions that were required to be taken and preparations that were needed to be done.

His view was that ministers and officers who received guests at the airport should be properly dressed. They should read and make themselves acquainted with the Constitutions of the countries of their guests, should study the situations prevailing in their countries, should be briefed by officers of the foreign ministry, should listen more and talk less, give correct information to the guests, not criticize other countries of the world while carrying on discussions with the guests, not take party lines that are adopted by the Indian political parties, and organize meetings with respected citizens. They should not say anything that may embarrass the guests, they should try to send back the guests with happy memories, not give or receive expensive gifts, and collect authentic information from the guests about their countries and the regions in which their countries were located.

Most of the ministers and officers did not like the protocol duties they were expected to perform. However, I liked to receive and meet the VVIPs, VIPs and other tourists because in the meetings with them, I could get first-hand information about their countries and regions. I tried to use the suggestions given by the governor, quite meticulously, in doing what was required to be done in a proper manner. I did not encounter any difficulties.

∎

I functioned as a junior minister for nearly one year. Shankarrao Chavan had replaced Vasantrao Naik as the chief minister of Maharashtra, and then Vasant Dada Patil succeeded him. Shankarrao Chavan was supported by the then prime minister of India, Indiraji. After her and her party's defeat in the elections, Shankarrao Chavan was voted out of the chief ministership.

Vasant Dada Patil formed his own council of ministers. Shivajirao Patil Nilangekar from Osmanabad district was included in the council of ministers as the irrigation minister. Shankarrao Chavan formed his own party and Rajaram Bapu Patil left the Congress party, although they both remained as members of the legislature and sat on the opposition benches.

When Vasant Dada Patil and his friends were trying to oust Shankarrao Chavan from the chief ministership, a few meetings of the chief minister's friends and supporters took place in my house. I was asked to contest the election for the chief ministership of Maharashtra by a few friends of Shankarrao Chavan, but I refused. Yashwantrao Mohite was then put up as a candidate to contest against Vasant Dada Patil.

Yashwantrao Mohite could not win the election. However, when the council of ministers was formed by Vasant Dada Patil, Yashwantrao Mohite was included in it. Speaker Wankhade wanted to join the cabinet. So he resigned and in his place, Balasaheb Desai was elected as the speaker. After a few days, I was elected as the deputy speaker.

8

PRESIDING OVER THE MAHARASHTRA LEGISLATIVE ASSEMBLY

The deputy speaker of the Lower House of the legislature has all the powers in the House that the speaker has to discharge legislative duties. In fact, everyone who sits in the chair of the presiding officer enjoys the same powers as the speaker and the deputy speaker.

If the speaker is absent from the House for a long period, his administrative and other duties are discharged by the deputy speaker. According to protocol, the deputy speaker comes after the ministers, and before the state ministers, in the hierarchy and protocol list.

■

A few days after the council of ministers was constituted, on 5 July 1977, I was elected as the deputy speaker. Congress leader Shivajirao Patil Nilangekar suggested my name to the new chief minister who offered me the position. And I accepted it.

Balasaheb Desai, who was elected as the speaker, was more interested in a ministership than in the speakership. He was a senior Congress leader and had earned a lot of prestige in the politics of the state. He had strong views on some issues. I had met him a few times only. So he did not know me intimately, and I did not have a clear idea about the manner in which he liked to conduct the business of the House. So for some days, he did not find it comfortable to depend upon me to carry out the legislative duties. For a few days after he became the speaker, he sat in the House to conduct the business in question hour and to regulate the complicated debates. My duties in that period were light and easily manageable. Later, when he found that I was comfortable conducting any kind of business in the House, he rarely attended the House and asked me to do all the duties he was doing in the House. I was always ready to do any business he wanted me to do, in and outside the House, relating to the legislature. A few days of working together in this manner made us respect each other more than we used to in the initial period.

Within a few months, he resigned from the speakership. When he tendered his resignation, I was in Bhubaneswar attending the conference of presiding officers which was held every year in one of the states of India. I was sorry to receive the news and my heart was full of sympathy for him.

After returning to Mumbai, I was expected to do all the duties of the speaker. As the elections to the legislative assembly were required to be held in a few months, the election to have a new speaker was not held. So, until the next election, I remained the deputy speaker while discharging the duties of the speaker.

■

In 1978, the general election for electing representatives to the Lower House of the Maharashtra legislature took place. That election was quite difficult for me. The mood of the people was opposed to the Congress party, and I had to put in immense effort to get myself elected. In that election also, the young voters voted for and favoured me.

In my first election to the legislature, college students had organized a public meeting for all the candidates who had participated in the election. In the second election also, they organized a similar meeting. They met all the contesting candidates and requested them to address the voters from one platform. The meeting was presided over by one of their representatives. They allowed the candidates to speak, one after the other, after drawing lots for deciding the sequence in which they could speak. Each candidate was given half an hour to speak about the policies and manifestos of his party, and not about other candidates. As in the last election, in the second election also, I had consented to speak from the common platform. The candidate who had secured the second largest number of votes did not agree to share the platform, on the grounds that he was expected to address another public meeting at the same time organized in a village which was far away from Latur. However, at the last moment, he approached students, seeking permission to speak. He asked the students to explain to the other candidates that his meeting at the other village was cancelled at the last moment, and if no objection was taken by other candidates, he should be given permission to speak. The president of the meeting, after consulting his fellow students and the candidates, permitted him to speak. Thus, he became the last speaker to address the gathering. He took the floor at 11.30 p.m. to speak for the allotted half an hour. For making a light remark at the beginning of his speech, he said, 'I will start my speech at 11.30 p.m. and end it at 12 p.m. By the time I conclude my speech, I would have finished all the other candidates. I mean, I would have replied to the points made by the other speakers in a convincing manner.' This remark offended the audience. They felt that it was improper for the occasion, and the manner of making that statement was arrogant. Some of the members in the gathering left the meeting, protesting. I was told that that remark of his enhanced the support of the voters given to me.

Something of this kind had happened in my first election also. In my first election speeches, I had spoken against the policies adopted by the Union government, and my criticism against the policies was discussed by the voters, especially young voters, on a large scale. One national leader who had come to campaign against me was informed about what the young voters were discussing.

In order to nullify the effect of my criticism, the national leader mentioned my name and said aggressively, 'What is the qualification of the candidate who dared to criticize the policies of the national government? Does he understand what is meant by a national policy? Does he understand what is meant by a state policy? If such ignorant and uneducated persons are elected, they would damage our democracy. You, therefore, do not vote for this ignorant and uneducated person.' The people in Latur did not approve of the criticism hurled at me. They knew that the person against whom those remarks were made was not an uneducated and illiterate candidate. The harsh words used by a national leader against the person known to them earned sympathy votes for me. The lesson learnt by candidates was that arrogance did not enhance their capacity to garner enough votes in the elections.

In the second election, my margin of votes was reduced to 3,333 votes from 22,000 votes secured in the first election. The second election was held after the Emergency was withdrawn and the non-Congress party government was formed at the national level.

■

At the time the 1978 elections were held, Vasant Dada Patil was the chief minister of Maharashtra. In those elections, the Congress party won a majority, but not a very comfortable one. That was why the government could not be formed within a reasonable time after the election results were announced. The governor took some time to invite Vasant Dada Patil to form the government. The elected Congress members agitated against the delay, but after judging the mood of the members, Vasant Dada Patil was invited to constitute the government. He became the chief minister of Maharashtra for the second time.

■

The political party leaders had seen me working as the deputy speaker and were convinced that I could be elected as the speaker, and so I was elected as speaker on 17 March 1978, without any difficulty. The new deputy speaker, who belonged to an independent group of members, was less interested in political and legislative activities and more involved in social, cultural, and religious activities. Therefore, for legislative activities and duties, I had to depend upon myself much more than speakers in the past had to do. The deputy speaker was an elderly, good-natured person, so I had no difficulty in working with him.

The chief minister and other ministers cooperated with me in an excellent manner. They always went by the views expressed by me and other members of all parties. They knew that I would allow them to discharge their duties and get the work of the government done, and also allow the members sitting on the opposition bench to express their views freely and do their duties as opposition members were expected to do. That balanced approach satisfied both the sides in the House.

The members in the House knew that I would be correct, just and impartial. They had no difficulty in going by my suggestions and accepting my rulings. They also knew that in discharging their duties, I would help and not obstruct them. I never highlighted any innocent mistake done by any member or punished anyone unfairly. They were sure that in matters of legislative procedures, they would be properly guided and helped.

The media in Mumbai is reputed to be very alert and powerful. They watched the proceedings from the press gallery in the House and commented upon them freely and fearlessly. They wrote positively about the working of the legislature, seeing that the proceedings were just and acceptable to all others concerned.

The general impression of the House, insofar as the public was concerned, was favourable. They knew that the legislature does not always work smoothly, and that at times, some verbal fireworks take place. They were in the habit of assessing the performance of organizations, the government, the legislature and the judiciary on the basis of the sum and total of all their activities, and not on the basis of a few exceptional and separate incidents and acts. They were fair to the legislature, the presiding officers and the members of the assembly.

■

During the question hour in the Maharashtra legislative assembly, the members were required to ask brief questions and the answers had also to be brief. They were discouraged from making long statements while asking questions or while replying to them. The result of this practice was that they could cover more questions than those covered in other legislatures, and in Parliament.

■

Members are allowed to get information by adopting other methods also. They could raise discussions on matters of urgent public importance. They could seek information from the government, and in the process of asking questions, they could also give information to the government. Certain methods could be used to get the information. One of them was called the Calling Attention Motion. The government's attention is drawn to a matter of public importance of specific and urgent nature. Members were allowed to attract the attention of the government to only one specific matter. Members from all sides of the House could use that device. When that was done, the government was asked to explain its stand and how it proposed to deal with the difficulties or problems arising out of the specific issue. A Calling Attention Motion could help members to get relief for their voters and the people at large.

When a notice seeking permission to move was given, the government was asked to explain its stand on it. If the stand taken showed that there was a basis to discuss the matter in the House, it was allowed to be taken up. If the material in the Calling Attention Motion and the statement of the government indicated that it was not fit for discussion, it was not allowed to be raised.

Another recognized device was the Adjournment Motion. It

required that the agenda fixed by the House for the day should be adjourned, and the subjects mentioned in the Adjournment Motion should be taken up for discussion. If the motion was passed, it was supposed that the government was censured, and was expected to resign and go. If it was not passed at the end of the discussion and after taking the vote, one of the items on the agenda was taken up, showing that the fixed item on the agenda was discussed on the same day and not adjourned.

A member could give a notice of adjournment for the presiding officer to decide if the notice should be put up before the House or not. If he decided to bring it to the notice of the members, any member could object to it and request that it should not be allowed to be taken up. If that were done, the presiding officer could put it to the vote of the House. If nearly one-tenth of the members agreed to take it up and discuss it, the motion was allowed to be discussed. The motion had to be on a matter of public importance and of recent occurrence. The device could be used to highlight important issues only, and not only with the consent of the presiding officer but with the consent of at least one-tenth of the members of the House.

Many motions for adjournment were moved, but only a few of them could be admitted and discussed.

A No-Confidence Motion against the government can be moved in the Lower House. Any member can give a notice to have a No-Confidence Motion discussed, and it is not required to be limited to a specific and urgent matter of recent occurrence. It can cover the working of the government in all areas of its activities. When a No-Confidence Motion is moved, the presiding officer has to bring it to the notice of the members. In India, under the Constitution, it cannot be moved in the Upper House of the legislature. Adjournment Motion cannot also be moved in the Upper House, because the executive is supposed to be accountable to the directly elected representatives of the people.

Generally, the device of the No-Confidence Motion is not used frequently or lightly. If the No-Confidence Motion is passed, the chief minister resigns, and his council of ministers ceases to have the power to govern. In Maharashtra, not many No-Confidence Motions were moved.

■

The state legislature is expected to make laws. Bills to make laws are generally prepared and moved by the executive. In some cases, private members can prepare and move bills to make laws. But bills moved by private members are not generally passed. Members can give amendments to bills. Amendments moved are discussed in the legislature, and if they are passed, they become the part of the laws made. Generally, they are not passed unless they are moved by the members of the executive.

Except for finance bills, which are moved only in the Lower House, all other kinds of bills are moved in both the Houses of the legislature. The Upper House does not pass amendments to Finance Bills. It can suggest amendments which can be or cannot be accepted by the Lower House. If they are not accepted by the Lower House, they do not become part of the laws passed.

Bills can be passed by both the Houses and assented to by the governors in the states. If the Lower House passes the bill and the Upper House does not, a joint session of the members of both the Houses is held and the bill is discussed. The joint session may or may not pass the bill. If it is passed, it is sent to the governor for his assent.

The governor can send back the bill which is passed by both the Houses of legislature. The legislature can accept the recommendations made by the governor, or send it back in the same form as it was passed. When it is sent back, it is assented to by the governor.

■

The legislature has to pass the budget every year, which is presented by the executive. The budget indicates the funds needed to carry on the governance, and the revenue that can be collected. It contains the information regarding the income and expenditure of the government. No tax can be levied and collected, and no funds can be used out of the coffers of the government by the executive, without the consent of the legislature. When the budget is passed, it means the legislature has given its consent. The legislature can also pass the Appropriation Bill, which allows the executive to withdraw funds from government coffers.

The finance minister presents the budget. The legislature discusses the principles used in drafting the budget. This is called the general discussion on the budget. After that, the demand for grants of different ministries are discussed as decided by the House. When that is done, members can move cut motions. One kind of cut motion is called the one-rupee cut motion, which is moved to indicate that policies made by the government are not acceptable to the legislature. If a one-rupee cut motion is passed in the Lower House, the government is expected to resign and go. There is a second kind of cut motion which can be moved by a legislator. This indicates the mistakes committed in giving the figures relating to the amount of revenue collected, or expenditure made or to be made. The third kind of cut motion is moved to ask for more funds, or to reduce the funds proposed to be given for a project. If the second and third kind of cut motions are passed, the government is not required to resign.

Legislators can ask for opportunities to discuss other issues. If time is given by the presiding officers, any relevant subject can be discussed; to criticize, to guide, or to suggest improvements in the governance.

The legislature has committees which can consider how the estimates are made, how the expenditure is incurred, how rules can be made, how public sector undertakings are working, and for other purposes. In committees, generally, political parties do not take party stands. They try to take decisions which are helpful to the government and the people.

The proceedings of the Houses in their plenary are open to the media, but the proceedings of the committees are not open to them.

The working of the legislature is done according to the provisions of the Constitution, rules of procedure made by the Houses, and in conformity with the conventions and rulings given by the presiding officers. The working is not simple and cannot be fully explained in a few sentences.

The Maharashtra legislature in the past used to work for more than a hundred days in a year. However, the number of its working days is reduced to less than hundred days. It works now for about fifty days in a year.

■

Jayaprakash Narayan was a respected freedom fighter and leader who did not join the government of independent India. In the 1970s, he had opposed the then national government formed by Indiraji, and started a movement for total revolution. The movement became disturbing and violent at some places. To control it and to see that democracy was not disturbed and weakened, an Emergency was imposed in the country. After it was withdrawn, general elections for sending representatives to the Lok Sabha were held, in which the Congress was defeated. A Congress government at the national level could not be formed, and as a consequence of the results of the elections, a non-Congress government under the premiership of Morarji Bhai Desai was formed. The government of Morarji Bhai Desai was replaced by the government of Chaudhary Charan Singh. Chaudhary Charan Singh was asked by the president of India to get a confidence motion passed by him in the Lok Sabha. He could not move the confidence motion and get it passed. So, the Lok Sabha was dissolved and elections for a new Lok Sabha were held at the fag end of 1979.

In the period when Morarji Bhai Desai was the prime minister, Jayaprakash Narayan was admitted in the Jaslok Hospital for treatment of his illness. One day when the assembly was in session in that period, a minister of state came to the legislative assembly and announced that Jayaprakash Narayan had passed away, and asked that the House be adjourned after passing a condolence motion. He informed the House that Parliament and other legislatures had passed the condolence resolutions and were adjourned. I was sitting in the chair of the presiding officer of the assembly when that information was given and a request to adjourn the House after passing the condolence motion was made.

I asked the minister, 'What is the source of your information?'

He replied, 'A newspaper reporter has given me this information.'

Jaslok Hospital, where Jayaprakash Narayan was admitted, is in Mumbai. According to my understanding, the minister could have asked the registrar of the hospital to confirm the veracity of the news.

So, I pointed out that he could have contacted the hospital to know what had happened. I asked him to get the authenticity of the news checked.

The minister went out of the House. The members in the House were feeling uncomfortable and disturbed, most of them saying that that kind of news could not be unreliable.

The minister came back within a few minutes and said, 'The news is correct. Let us pass the condolence resolution and adjourn the House.'

I asked him, 'Who confirmed the news?'

He said, 'The editor of a reputed newspaper.'

I did not find it easy to accept his way of getting the news confirmed. Again, I asked him, 'Why did you not contact the hospital, its registrar? Some responsible person in the hospital or the registrar is in a better position to tell you what has happened to Jayaprakash Narayanji.'

He said, 'Why not rely upon what the editor has said? We should not refuse to do what Parliament has already done.'

Many members in the House got up and began to shout at

me, 'Do not refuse to pass the necessary resolution and adjourn the House. What you are doing is not correct. Why should the House not rely on the information given by the minister?'

I tried to tell them that it would be better to get the information from the hospital, and not from a newspaper office or its editor. I asked them to wait for a few minutes and requested the secretary general of the House to contact the hospital and get the correct information. The secretary general left the House to get the information from the hospital. In the meanwhile, the members in the House remained standing and making comments that were not very correct or complimentary to me.

I said repeatedly, 'Let us not be in a hurry to accept the sad news. Let us think that Jayaprakash Narayan is alive and pray for his life.'

But the situation in the House became very chaotic, and I had no option but to face it until the secretary general came back, even though I was being hectored. Within five to six minutes, he returned to the House. He said, 'Jayaprakash Narayan is alive and Parliament and other legislatures were wrongly informed about his death by somebody. It could have been done by an irresponsible or mischievous person.'

When that news was given, the members were stunned. They looked confused and the minister was speechless.

I broke the silence and said, 'Thank God, he is alive. Let us pray for his health and long life. It would have been a blunder to have relied upon the rumour. We could have been blamed for not contacting the hospital before passing the condolence resolution and adjourning the House. We could have been blamed more because the House and the hospital are in Mumbai, in one city, at a distance of a few miles from each other.'

What the Maharashtra legislature did became big news in the country. The media spread it on a large scale for many days.

Many asked me why I had refused to accept the news given by the minister, not once, but twice. I had no clear answer to give. I said I really didn't know what made me exercise caution. Probably, I was not psychologically prepared to accept bad news very readily. Moreover, I had read that if the monarch in the UK dies, the protocol to be followed is that the news is not disclosed immediately. The government constitutes a committee of doctors to examine the monarch's body carefully, and then report in writing that the monarch is alive or dead. The government examines the report in the cabinet, passes a condolence resolution, and then discloses the news to the people. This could have been the reason that could have been in my mind and could have made me refuse to adjourn the House.

•

All the legislatures of India are members of the Commonwealth Parliamentary Association, which holds a conference every year in one of the Commonwealth countries. In the period of my speakership of the Maharashtra legislative assembly, I attended the conference of the Commonwealth Parliamentary Association held in Jamaica. In the conference, I was asked to speak on the topic of world peace, and the steps that should be taken to protect it. Voraji was a retired district judge living in Mumbai whom I used to meet many times. I had conducted a few criminal trials in his court when he was the district judge in Osmanabad. When I asked his advice about the points I could make to speak on the topic given to me, he suggested that before going to attend the conference, I should meet Acharya Tulsiji, who was at that time camping at a place called Ganga Nagar, and seek his advice and views on the points to be made in my speech. He used to speak about peace in the world very frequently and feelingly. He promised to take me to him as I had not met him before. I had heard and read a lot about Acharya Tulsiji. I also felt that he could give me some weighty and convincing points, different from the points made by other delegates. Voraji was Acharya Tulsiji's devotee.

So we went to meet him at Ganga Nagar. In the meeting with

him, I was very impressed with the way he received his devotees, and his words of wisdom, spoken in simple, understandable and affectionate language. Voraji informed him of the reason for our visit. He said, 'The birthplace of war and peace is the mind of man. It is in the mind that the ground needs to be prepared to see that war does not take place and peace, is strengthened. The world government can help to achieve, protect and preserve world peace. Countries all over the world can also do that. Weapons are produced to win wars and protect peace. But if this is done by all countries, the danger of war grows and the possibility of peace gets reduced. Weapons can invite wars. Peace needs tranquillity and reasonableness. It needs broad-mindedness. Unless there is peace in the mind, chances of peace in the world are not very bright. So, the societies, governments, wise men, thinkers and philosophers should create an ambience in which the mind of man becomes peaceful. Through it, the world can become peaceful.' He made other suggestions also. But the points mentioned above were bound to be different from the points that could be made by other delegates. I adopted and used them, and I was right; my statement in the conference appeared to be different. It was appreciated and applauded. I was happy that I could meet him before proceeding to the conference and get those important points from him.

■

Jamaica is a small country in the Caribbean with beautiful beaches and tropical scenery. It produces sugar and beer on a large scale. Tourists from countries in North America, South America, and some European countries visit it in quite large numbers. It was trying hard to develop its economy.

Michael Manley was the prime minister of Jamaica. I had occasion to meet him when I visited Jamaica. He appreciated the policies of Pandit Jawaharlal Nehru, Indiraji, and the Indian government. He made inquiries in great detail about Indiraji, who was out of power at that time. When we discussed this, he said, 'She is bound to become the prime minister of India again. The people will elect her, her party and help her to form the government.' I was surprised to hear him speaking with such confidence and clarity. That was the feeling the people in Jamaica appeared to have. This became very clear to me in one of the hotels in which the delegates were put up. In a lift of the hotel, an old lady was going to her room. When she saw me, she asked me, 'Which country are you from?' I told her, 'I am from India.' On hearing my reply she became quite friendly with me and said, 'Oh, you have come from the country of my daughter.' I asked her, 'Who is your daughter? What is her name? Where does she live in India?'

She became a little indignant and replied, 'You do not know my daughter? You ungrateful people have hurt her, you have defeated her, her party and government. How could you do that to her? But take it from me that she is going to regain her old position. She will win. She will form the government. She will become the prime minister again. Indira Gandhi is my daughter. You ungrateful people will not be able to keep her out of the prime ministership which is rightfully hers.'

That was the feeling of most of the people in Jamaica and other developing countries of that region and other parts of the world.

■

On my way to Jamaica, I broke my journey in London and in New York. In London, I visited the British Parliament, saw the House of Commons and the House of Lords, met some of my old friends. Ramjibhai Bhatia's son was living in a town close to London, along with his wife and children, practising medicine with the help of his wife, who was also a doctor. He explained to me that Indians came to the UK to earn money, and since they were sincere in doing their duties, the people who took their help liked them. That helped them to earn lots of money.

In New York, I visited the United Nations, the Security Council and the General Assembly, and met some of my friends. I had meals with them right at the top of one of the World Towers. At the top, the tower appeared to swing from one side to the other, and made the city look different and more impressive and beautiful.

In the UN building, I wanted to see the way in which the Security Council worked, and conducted its proceedings from the viewers' gallery. The meeting of the council did not take place on time and was delayed by nearly three hours. When I asked how such an august body could function like that, I was told that the members of the Security Council functioned behind the curtain, and came to the council meetings many times only to announce the results of their discussions and the consensus arrived at.

■

While returning from Jamaica, I broke my journey in Paris, which is very beautiful, neat and clean. In the city, I saw the National Assembly, the impressive Élysée Palace, the fascinating museums and the Eiffel Tower, and met the Indian ambassador, who was in the process of shifting to Beijing on his transfer from France to China.

As the speaker, I also visited the USSR. I saw Moscow, Odessa and St Petersburg. In Moscow, I visited the USSR Parliament and met the chairman of the Russian legislature, and also explored the museums and the Kremlin. In St Petersburg, I saw museums and palaces, and in Odessa, I visited the seaport.

The cities I visited were very beautiful, very neat and clean and maintained very well. All the cities were less expensive, and their markets and shops did not look the same as those in other countries of Europe. The old buildings, structures, palaces and museums were as beautiful and as attractive as the palaces, structures and museums of other European countries. The people looked healthy. They appeared to be simple in their lifestyle.

■

After the Lok Sabha was dissolved and Chaudhary Charan Singh was asked to function as the caretaker government's prime minister, the elections to constitute the seventh Lok Sabha were held in the last months of 1979. In Maharashtra, Sharad Pawar had replaced Vasant Dada Patil as the chief minister of the state by forming a government with the help of the members of Jana Sangh, the Communist party and other parties, as well as some Congress members. He became chief minister when the national government headed by Indiraji was out of power.

In Maharashtra, Vasant Dada Patil, Shankarrao Chavan, A.R. Antulay, Nasikrao Tirpude, Pratibha Patil, Ramarao Adik and some other leaders declared that they would help the Congress party headed by Indiraji, and not the Congress party headed by Brahmanand Reddy, the Congress leader from Andhra Pradesh, supported by Yashwantrao Chavan and Sharad Pawar. They decided that they would select the candidates to contest the election. They asked Yashwantrao Mohite, MLA from Karad in Maharashtra, and some others to contest the election. I was also asked to contest the election. Initially, I was not willing to accept their suggestion. That was because in the last election to the Maharashtra legislative assembly, I had managed a margin of 3,333 votes to get myself elected. And that election had taken place less than two years earlier. However, the leaders who stood by the Congress party headed by Indiraji were not willing to accept my negative response, and insisted on my becoming a candidate from Latur constituency. They told me that it was not correct for me to say that I appreciated the policies and leadership of Indiraji, and then refuse to contest the election when it was necessary for me to strengthen her stand in the legislature. They tried to convince me with strong words, saying that a real soldier does not refuse to fight in war when it has started.

To decide what I should do, I went to Kashmir and stayed in a secluded dak-bungalow, which was away from the city of Srinagar, for four days. The dak-bungalow and the area around it were covered with snow. In the dak-bungalow, there were only a few caretakers and guests. Sitting alone and thinking about the situation in great detail, I came to the conclusion that I should accept the offer made to me and contest the election. Having made that decision, I returned to Delhi and met Pratibha Patil, who was the leader of the opposition in the Maharashtra legislative assembly, and was supporting the Congress party of Indiraji and Vasant Dada Patil. They took me to meet Indiraji and told her that I had agreed to contest the election after resigning from the speakership of the Maharashtra legislative assembly. For a few minutes, we were with her as she discussed issues relating to the activities of the party with the members of the group who had met her. Then she left us to attend some other meeting. While leaving us, she gave an indication that she appreciated my decision.

In Mumbai, Ramarao Adik met me at my residence and asked me to issue a letter to the media saying that I was going to be a candidate of the Congress party from the Latur constituency. I told him that I would contest the election after resigning from the speakership, which I would do after meeting the chief minister to inform him about my decision. I wrote one letter of resignation and another letter to be issued to the media, and signed both of them. Then I went to meet the chief minister. When I told him what I was going to do, he replied by saying that he knew what my decision was going to be and he was not surprised. He told me that he was happy to know that I was resigning from the speakership, and if I had not resigned, he would have compelled me to do so.

In my letter to the media, I said that the chief minister was very correct in discharging the required legislative duties and behaved with me in a very correct manner in all things I did as the speaker, and thanked him for the same. In reply to my written statement to the media, he thanked me for having discharged my legislative duties according to the procedures and correctly. He added that in the ensuing election, his party would oppose me tooth and nail to prove that my decision to contest the election as a candidate of the Congress party of Indiraji was not correct. In my letter to the media, I explained that the policies and leadership of Indiraji could only help the people of India and strengthen the country, and so I had decided to stand by her and resigned from the speakership.

In my district, some senior Congress leaders joined the party which was formed by Yashwantrao Chavan and Sharad Pawar. Most of the young Congress members supported the Congress party of Indiraji. It was clear that most of the voters stood by her and her party. They appreciated the action she had taken to help the people belonging to weaker sections of the society and to strengthen the nation. They decided to elect her and her party, which they did in a splendid manner.

9

MEMBER OF LOK SABHA

I had visited the Lok Sabha and the Rajya Sabha on some occasions, and watched their proceedings from the visitors' galleries. I had done that when I was a student and when I had joined the Maharashtra legislative assembly and become a junior minister in the Maharashtra government, the deputy speaker and the speaker of the state legislative assembly. What I had seen had created a desire in my mind to join Parliament and work in its Houses. Therefore, on getting the opportunity to work as a member of the Lok Sabha, I felt happy.

Within two days after the result of my election was declared, I left for New Delhi to attend the meeting of the elected members convened to elect the leader of the Congress Parliamentary Party. The meeting was held in the Central Hall of Parliament, and was attended by Indiraji, Kamlapati Tripathi, Bhishma Narain Singh, B. Shankaranand, M. Karunanidhi, and the elected members of the Lok Sabha. Shankaranand proposed and Bhishma Narain Singh seconded the name of Indiraji for the leadership of the Congress Parliamentary Party. The members clapped loudly and approved the proposal. Karunanidhi garlanded the leader. The garland was too big and had to be held around her by four persons. After Karunanidhi spoke, Indiraji made a brief statement. The speech conveyed her and her party's thanks to the voters who had given a majority of two-third members of the Lok Sabha to her party.

She said that the party had made promises to the voters which should be fulfilled. The elected members should work to help the people, to bring about all-round development, and strengthen the nation. The future could have good or bad developments in store, but the party should not worry. It should do its duties in the best possible manner and leave other things to happen as they were likely to happen. There was a tinge of sorrow in her statement and the way in which she spoke. That caused an apprehension in my mind. I did not know the clear nature of my apprehension but it worried me. Later, when the tragedy which ended her life occurred, I asked myself, 'Was she hinting at it in her speech? Did she have a premonition?' I do not know what the others had felt about her speech. But they appeared to be elated and happy. My feelings were mixed; I was happy as well as worried.

•

In Delhi, I stayed in Maharashtra Sadan for a few days. Later, I shifted to bungalow no. 9 on Bishambardas Marg, and lived in it until the time I was included in the council of ministers. Then, I shifted to bungalow no. 4 at Janpath. I lived in that house for nearly two and a half decades. It was in bungalow no. 20, Akbar Road, that I lived as the speaker of the Lok Sabha for nearly five years.

In the Lok Sabha, I was given a seat in the third row of the middle section of the House. On the fourth row of the middle section of the House, Sanjay Gandhi, Jagdish Tytler and Rajesh Pilot were given the seats. Shankar Dayal Sharmaji and M.L. Sukhadia sat in the third row of the House which was closer to the first row. Thus, I had the company of very senior, as well as very junior and active legislators.

I had decided to watch the proceedings and the manner in which members of the Lok Sabha functioned. I was acquainted with the procedures followed in the meetings of the municipal council and in the legislative assembly of Maharashtra. In both these bodies, I had to regulate the debates and discussions as a presiding officer, which had given me an idea about that which could help me to do things in a right manner. The issues which were discussed in Parliament were different, and required lots of understanding and information to tackle them in a proper and correct manner.

■

Mani Ram Bagri, a socialist leader, was a very vocal and friendly member of the House, sitting on the opposition benches. His style of functioning was very peculiar. At times, he appeared to be threatening other members, and at other times, appeared to be joking with members sitting on the benches of the ruling party. Once, some young members sitting on the fourth bench behind me poked fun at him. They shouted at him and appeared to be provoking him to react. Mani Ram Bagri got up from his seat, rolled the sleeves of his shirt up and shouted at Sanjay Gandhi, Rajesh Pilot and Jagdish Tytler. Then he marched towards them in a threatening posture. I felt he and the young members were going to exchange blows. He stood in front of them and suddenly raised his arm. I thought he was going to hit one of his tormentors. They shouted at him and he shouted at them. Then he went to Sanjay Gandhi, stood there for a minute—a tension-filled pause, I must say—and embraced him in his arms in a most friendly manner, laughing at him and the others. Sanjay Gandhi also reciprocated the gesture and soon all of them were laughing loudly. I was surprised and appreciated the little drama that showed that they were not enemies of one another, only friends holding different views. I realized that the elected members knew how to deal with one another in the House.

■

R. Venkataramanji was the finance minister at that time. Later, he was given the defence portfolio, then he became vice president and president of India (1987–92). He liked my way of dealing with parliamentary matters and wanted me to work with him in the finance ministry. However, I could not join his ministry because I was required to work in the ministries which were with the prime minister. In discharging my duties as a member of the Lok Sabha, as member of the Union council of ministers and as the deputy and chief presiding officer of the Lower House of Parliament, he helped me a great deal. He tried to discharge his duties strictly, according to the provisions of the Constitution. In fact, I tried to emulate him in this respect. In whatever place and position he functioned, he left a special mark of his style of working.

He presented the first budget in the seventh Lok Sabha. The leader of the opposition was the first member to speak in the general debate on the budget. He criticized the budget and complained that it did not provide enough funds for rural development, for agriculture, and to provide employment to the unemployed. His charge was that it was a budget which gave funds to the rich and urban people and neglected the poor, the needy and the rural masses. He spoke after the lunch hour when the attendance in the House was not very good. The opposition benches were occupied by many members because the first speech was to be made by a member from the opposition. On the benches of the ruling party, only a few members were found sitting and attending the proceedings. There was no senior member of the ruling party present in the House who could speak after the opposition member.

Bhishma Narain Singh, who was the minister for parliamentary affairs, was forced to look for someone from the ruling benches to reply to the speech of the leader of the opposition. He spotted me sitting in the House and rushed to me. He asked me to get up and speak. 'You have to speak. There is nobody else in the House at present who could be asked to rebut the charges made by the opposition member.'

I was flabbergasted. I pleaded, 'How can you ask me to do this? This is my first term in the House. I have not read or studied the budget speech and the budget proposals fully. What can I say? If I was told in the morning that I would be required to speak, I could have prepared myself. Please do not put me in this awkward position.'

He insisted, '*You* should not put me in this awkward position. If anyone else had been here in the House who could have been asked to speak, I would not have asked you to speak. Please get up and say whatever comes to your mind. But speak. You must speak. You and I have no other option available to us.'

He had learnt that I was a minister in the government of Maharashtra, and also the speaker of the state legislature. So he had come to the conclusion that I would be able to make some sensible points in reply to the charges levelled by the opposition.

Thus, I was forced to make my first speech in the Lok Sabha. I used my common sense to rebut the points made by the leader of the opposition. I did not speak on the points made in the budget statement.

The gist of my speech was as follows: 'Rural development needs many things: schools, hospitals, roads, drinking water, irrigation facilities, electricity, employment, and many other things. The education ministry builds schools and educational institutions. The health ministry establishes hospitals and provides medical facilities. The transport ministry builds roads and the irrigation ministry can provide water for irrigation and drinking purposes. The power ministry can produce and take energy to the villages. And all ministries can generate employment by implementing their plans, and working to complete their projects.

'Likewise, the development of agriculture needs many inputs. It needs dams to store water to irrigate agricultural lands, which is done by the irrigation ministry. Agricultural universities can produce new knowledge useful for farming and new varieties of seeds. The industries ministry can produce chemical fertilizers and insecticides, the power ministry can supply power required for agricultural purposes and the transport ministry can build roads for farmers to take their farm produce to the markets. Banks give loans to the farmers that they need.

'This means that rural development is done not only with the funds provided to the rural development ministry but relies on funds given to many other ministries. In the same manner, agriculture can be developed not only with the funds given to the ministry of agriculture, but with the funds given to many other ministries.

'If we take into consideration the funds given to all the ministries expected to help in rural development and the development of agriculture, the funds made available for these purposes are not small—they are quite substantial. If we take into account only the funds given to the ministry of rural development, they may appear to be small and insufficient, or if we take into account the funds given to the ministry of agriculture only, they may appear to be small and insufficient. But, if we take into account the sum total of all the funds made available for these purposes through different ministries, they may not appear to be small and insufficient. In fact, more than 60 per cent of the budget is used for the development of rural areas and agriculture. In view of this, it is not correct to complain that the budget neglects the poor and the people in the rural areas, and cares only for the rich and the people in the urban areas.'

The points made in my argument were appreciated by most of the members in the House. They applauded my statement, thumping their desks.

The leader of the opposition got up and asked me, 'Where are the funds to provide employment to all the unemployed in the country? Do you think that with ₹300 crore it would be possible to provide employment to all the unemployed?' ₹300 crore was allotted for a special scheme to provide employment. I used the same logic to rebut this point also.

I said, 'All ministries have their plans and projects. When they implement them, they generate employment potential. Moreover, the state governments have their plans and projects which also generate employment. The amount of ₹300 crore is provided for special schemes to generate employment. They, by themselves, are certainly not sufficient. The state governments have their employment schemes. Maharashtra has its Employment Guarantee Scheme which guarantees at least ninety days employment to each and every unemployed who approaches the government to get it. Other states also have some other schemes. All of them can help.'

The leader of the opposition again got up and argued, 'The Employment Guarantee Scheme of Maharashtra does not help the unemployed. It helps those who manage it. Lot of corruption is done by those who are given the authority to manage it. Do not talk about it. It is useless. It is a source of corruption and not of employment. It guarantees corruption and not employment.'

My reply to this was, 'Those who are opposed to the scheme cannot directly attack it. So, they use this method to see that it is attacked in this manner and done away with.'

The leader of the opposition was angry at my statement. He asked me, 'Do you think that I am opposed to the scheme which gives employment to the unemployed in the rural areas?'

I could see the anger oozing out of his eyes, gestures, and the statement. I replied, 'I do not think you are opposed to such schemes. But those who are opposed to them use the arguments which can protect them and which can help them to oppose the schemes.'

It was very clear that on this point, also, the majority of the members in the House were in favour of my argument. They thumped their desks and clapped vigorously.

The finance minister and parliamentary affairs minister were present in the House. Both of them appreciated the rebuttal and the points I made. When the finance minister met me in the corridor of the House, he patted me on my back and said, 'Well done. Keep it up. You made my task a little easier.' After that, he showed me a lot of affection and gave me encouragement whenever occasions to do so arose. In later years, he always encouraged, guided and helped me to do my duties in the correct manner. He was always very kind to me.

In replying to the arguments of the opposition leader, I did not use the information which pertained to the rural development and agriculture ministry only. I used the totality of the budget to rebut the charges. That helped me to make the points I did without even reading the budget material fully and meticulously.

My first speech helped me to get time to speak in the House whenever I wanted to speak. In fact, it helped me to get many invitations to speak on complicated matters. And that projected me in Parliament as a legislator who could be given opportunities to make speeches. I must extend thanks to Bhishma Narain Singh for forcing me to deliver my first speech in Parliament. When we were in Parliament, he always showed me consideration. That created a bond of friendship between us, which remains intact. He was a confidante of Indiraji. He managed Parliament skilfully, and earned the respect of all the Lok Sabha members.

■

The second speech I made was on the demand for grants of the ministry of defence. I had sought time to speak and had no problem in getting it.

Indiraji had retained the defence portfolio with herself. C.P.N. Singh worked as a minister of state in the defence ministry. Both the defence minister and the defence minister of state attended the debate, took notes and spoke in reply to the debate.

The speaker of the Lok Sabha had prepared a list of members who could be asked to preside over the proceedings of the House in the absence of the speaker and the deputy speaker. My name was included in the list because I was the deputy speaker and the speaker in the Maharashtra legislative assembly. On the day I was given the time to speak, I was asked by the speaker to preside over the Lok Sabha proceedings. I was in the chair of the presiding officer until ten minutes before I was supposed to take the floor. I was prepared to speak but I was less confident while making the second speech than when I was making the first one. It was because I was speaking on defence issues for the first time, and because

Indiraji was the defence minister who seemed quite attentive while watching the performance of the members as they spoke.

In my speech, I touched upon the points that were relevant to the army, the navy and the air force, and defence research and development and production. I covered the entire gamut of the defence apparatus.

In my opinion, the Indian army was required to defend the territory and sovereignty of the country in hilly areas in the Himalayas. Hence, all equipment required to make them capable of fighting in that difficult terrain should be given to them.

The army needed modernization. It needed different varieties of guns, tanks, armoured vehicles, small weapons, helicopters, transport and communication facilities, and uniforms, which could help them carry lots of ammunition, food material and communication equipment. Its strength was required to be enhanced. It needed to be trained, in the best possible manner, to discharge its duties in mountainous areas.

I said India had a big economic zone which was equal to two-thirds of its landmass. The economic zone was full of natural resources which could be used exclusively by the country. Oceans had natural resources which could also be used by the country. The Indian navy needed many ships, frigates, submarines and aircraft-carriers. India needed to build more dockyards. More funds, more time and better trained manpower were also needed by the Indian navy to build its strength to help it to protect its interests in the economic zone, in the open seas and coastal areas. The navy needed a lot of time to build ships, submarines and aircraft-carriers. The funds allotted to it were not in proportion to its needs and demands.

The air force of India was its youngest defence force. It had aircraft from different countries, but needed more aircraft, more manpower and more funds.

The Defence Research and Development Organization was created to help the defence forces to opt for weapons and technologies which were modern and which could make the forces quite capable. The organization was doing well in the frontier areas, but in the areas at the second and third level, it was depending upon foreign countries. It deserved all the help and cooperation from all the other research and development organizations in the country.

India should form the correct kind of threat perceptions. It should make its forces strong and capable of meeting all the challenges in the present and the future. It should see that it was so prepared that if war was inflicted upon it, it would be able to win victories within a short period of time and with minimum losses caused to the country.

I said the defence forces have done their duties in the best possible manner. The country salutes their dedication and preparedness to make all kinds of sacrifices for its independence and sovereignty. They should always be respected and supported, so that they could do their duties in the best possible manner.

I made these points in a shorter time and spoke for less time during my second speech than I had taken to make my first speech. My speech was received soberly, not in the flamboyant manner as my first one.

Indiraji replied to the debate without contradicting the points I had made. In her speech, she was quite correct and encouraging.

■

The third speech I made was on the demand for grants of the foreign ministry. P.V. Narasimha Rao was the foreign minister. Earlier, he held the post of chief minister of Andhra Pradesh and then became a Union minister, heading successively the education, foreign and home ministries, and finally becoming the prime minister of India. He was the president of the Congress party too. He was known as the wise man of the Congress party. A polyglot, he used to speak to me in Marathi. Since the time I joined Parliament and the Union council of ministers, I had many opportunities to meet and work with him. He always behaved like an elder in the family and guided me in many ways as I discharged my duties as a member of the executive and the legislature. He had a philosophical bent of mind and behaved in a stoical manner in all situations.

On the day of my third speech, he called all the members who wanted to speak on the demand for grants of his ministry to his chamber and briefed them on the points on which they could speak. That he did to make the debate more accurate and meaningful. In his briefing, some of the points made by him were as follows:

The foreign ministry had to deal with a large number of countries and large number of international organizations in matters which were of political, economic, cultural and international nature. It needed a huge amount of funds and trained manpower, which was unfortunately not available to it in proportion to its needs and demands. It was, therefore, necessary for the government to make more funds and manpower and other wherewithal available to it. Other countries made ample amounts of money available to their embassies and offices working in different parts of the world. They managed their activities in a manner which was acceptable at the international level. India had developed the Non-aligned Policy for itself and other countries in the world which had achieved independence from colonial domination. The Non-aligned Movement had become quite acceptable to a large number of countries. It helped the non-aligned countries to take decisions in international matters to protect their interests and independence, to decide what they should do and what they should not do. Some countries which were powerful did not like the Non-aligned Policy. Some of them thought that it was immoral. However, there were other countries which had no objection of any kind to the Non-aligned Policy and supported it wholeheartedly.

The world had faced two mega wars and had become tired of fighting. It wanted peace and tranquillity to be established in all parts of the world. The League of Nations was created for this purpose, but it could not prevent the Second World War. After the First World War, the countries of the world created the United Nations to prevent wars taking place in any part of the world, and to protect and preserve the peace and tranquillity everywhere. It could not stop small conflicts and wars taking place between some countries. But it could prevent big wars and provide a forum where differences between countries could be solved through dialogues and discussions, rather than through armed conflicts.

The United Nations was not a world government. No world government could be formed without countries reducing their independence and sovereignty, to take decisions as they liked. However, the organization could be made more effective and powerful to prevent armed conflicts, and bring about better cooperation between different parts of the world and countries. For this purpose, the charter of the United Nations should be amended, but to do that, the consent and cooperation of the powerful and not-so-powerful countries were required. And that was not available.

These were some of the points members kept in mind when they spoke.

In my speech, I said that in the present-day world, economic diplomacy was acquiring greater value and importance. India's foreign ministry was well equipped to carry on with political and international diplomacy. It should train and equip itself and practise economic diplomacy with the same skill and finesse.

Friendly political relations between countries help them to cooperate with one another. Good economic relations can also help them. In fact, good economic relations have the capacity to last longer than good political relations.

Good cultural relations cannot be easily developed. Once they are developed they can exist for long periods of time. In fact, they can last for centuries. They can help to protect peace and tranquillity and reduce the angularities in approaches adopted by different countries while dealing with one another. They have a soothing effect and should, therefore, be generated and nourished carefully. They can help human beings to see that, in fact, in their basic nature they are not different from one another. They may live in different parts of the world, yet, they have many things in common. Outwardly, they may appear to be different, but inwardly, they are similar in many respects. India can share its culture with other countries, and can partake in the development of modern culture acceptable internationally. This kind of give and take can enrich the cultures of all countries, and that of the world. India should pay more attention to this aspect of diplomacy.

I took less time to make my third speech than I had taken to make my second speech.

The minister of foreign affairs appeared to be inclined to agree with the points in my speech. He indicated his appreciation by nodding pleasantly at me at the conclusion of my speech.

■

The fourth speech I made related to science and technology in India, and this speech was even shorter than the third one.

I said that India should put in a lot of effort to develop modern science and technology, as other developed countries were doing. Without doing it, it would not be easy for it to march with developed parts of the world in many fields. The developed countries were developed because they were developing and using modern science and technology to use natural resources available to them. India had natural resources, but it needed modern methods and systems to use them. In that field, it should not lag behind other countries of the world.

India had manpower capable of doing research and development. Indian scientists and technologists could be provided with more funds, modern equipment and better facilities to discover scientific truths and develop new technologies. That should be given to them by the Union and state governments, by the public and private sector industries, and by individuals and international organizations.

In the past, many truths were discovered and given to human beings by learned Indians following the method of intuition. What they had done was treated as a part of religion and spirituality. What they had discovered was also found out by modern scientists and technologists who followed laboratory and modern methods. India should use its ancient knowledge, along with modern methods, to discover truths and technologies in the cosmos.

In some cases, scientific truths, discoveries, and new technologies could be found out with small efforts and within small periods of time. We had to keep in mind that it might not always happen. Delays or drawbacks should not discourage efforts to discover the mysteries of nature. Perseverance and determination could give glorious dividends. India, and Indians, should march boldly on the path of discovery of new knowledge, new technologies, and the truth.

In my speeches, I did not use harsh words or bitter arguments to say what I wanted to convey. My style and method fitted well with the norms of parliamentary decorum and debate.

▪

I made some more small speeches on some other subjects as well. I did not ask questions. Once or twice, I put supplementary questions on the replies given to questions asked by other members.

My intention was not to find fault with the government. My intention was to contribute towards better government and speedier all-round development. My intention was also not to show that I knew a lot. In a polite and gentlemanly manner, I endeavoured to share my views with other members of the legislature and members of the executive.

My method was sober and responsible, and could have been adopted by any member of the government to explain the nature of difficulties, and to suggest solutions that could be adopted to overcome them. It was not partisan. It did not hurl unwanted arguments at members of other parties and at their approaches. That made my speeches less impressive but more acceptable. That helped me to form friendships with members of all sections of the House, and created no problems for me and the government.

What I was doing might have been watched by the minister

of parliamentary affairs and other ministers. Those who had heard me speaking and seen me dealing with situations in the House might have formed their own views about my style of working, that might have helped to take decisions about me when the occasion to do so arose.

■

There is a committee of Parliament which considers issues relating to the salaries and allowances of the members. First, I was appointed as a member of that committee in 1980. Then, I was appointed as its chairman in the same year. In that committee, I worked for only five months, and ceased to be the chairman and member when I was inducted into the council of ministers as the defence minister of state. The committee had met two to three times to consider some issues which were simple and it was easy to take decisions on them. I feel my tenure in the committee was of no great significance.

10

VISITS TO VIETNAM, CAMBODIA, LAOS AND NORTH KOREA

The Indian Parliament sends some of its members in delegations to other countries to attend international conferences relating to parliamentary matters, or to visit other countries in response to their invitations. Political parties also send their members to visit other countries when they receive invitations to attend programmes and conferences organized by the political parties of inviting countries.

I went to Vietnam, Cambodia and Laos in a delegation that consisted of members of Parliament and others. I was sent to North Korea by my party in a delegation of two members to attend the fifth congress of the political party of that country. The delegation which visited the first three countries consisted of Chandrajeet Yadav, Indrajit Gupta, one member of the Rajya Sabha and two other members who were not MPs.

For one night, the delegation stayed in Bangkok. The Bangkok airport was very well kept and impressive. Some members of the delegation were impressed by it and praised it to the skies, lamenting that Indian airports were not well maintained or magnificent. One of the delegates tried to explain to them that Thailand had never been a colony of any country, and its priorities were different from those of India. But the members praising it were not willing to accept the explanation given by other members.

The next day, the delegation flew to Hanoi. The airport at

Hanoi was not very big and provided facilities to only a few aircraft which would land there. It was not as good as the airports in India and Bangkok. From the airport, the delegates were taken to a place where they were lodged for the next three days, in the heart of the city. The place where they stayed was very modestly furnished. But it was neat and clean and had all the normal facilities. The quality of service was very prompt, and the food was wholesome and tasty. The delegates were provided with single bedrooms.

The delegates were then taken to see the place where Ho Chi Minh, the Vietnamese communist leader who was president of the Democratic Republic of Vietnam, used to live. The house in which he resided was at the centre of a garden, very small and very frugally furnished. It did not look like a house in which the head of a state could live.

The delegates met a few intellectuals who taught in the educational institutions and universities. They explained how their government functioned, the difficulties that were faced by the people, the ways in which their country tried to solve the problems of the people, and the relations their country had with other countries of the world. They were quite elaborate in their statements and it was not necessary for the delegates to ask any questions. It appeared that they had anticipated the questions and tried to give the replies to them.

Pham Van Dong, the prime minister of Vietnam, met the delegation. He was lean, alert and intelligent. A very good friend of India, his statement was quite friendly and less diplomatic. He explained the economic difficulties of his country and wanted to know if India could give his country rice, notebooks and medicine. He said within three years, his country would become self-sufficient in foodgrains and would have enough food that could be exported to other countries. He asked if it would be possible for his country and India to cooperate in research and development and in science and technology. He remembered the manner in which India, under the premiership of Jawaharlal Nehru, cooperated with his country in all fields, and said that the people of his country respected Indians and their leaders, and approved of the policies India was following in different fields.

On behalf of the delegation, the response given to his statement was quite promising. He was told that his views would be presented to the government and leaders of India, and they would be responded to in a positive manner.

The meeting with him was very encouraging. All the delegates were happy to meet and hear what he wanted to convey.

In one of the programmes, the delegation met General Võ Nguyên Giáp who was the commander of the Vietnam People's Army in the Vietnam War. General Giáp was short, well-built, alert and prompt in his replies to the questions put to him. One of the delegates asked him how Vietnam could fight the might of the strongest country in the world, win the war and unite the two Vietnams, North and South. His reply was very short and precise. He said his country did not have the strength and wherewithal to fight the war against the mightiest country in the world. According to him, in the war, the forces fighting against Vietnam bombarded the Vietnamese forces and the people. When they came, the Vietnamese tried to disappear from the battlefield and hide in the forests. In the process, many of them were killed. But when they went back, the Vietnamese reoccupied their original positions. That was not a war fought with weapons. One side fought it with weapons, while the other side fought it with their willpower and determination. And ultimately, the weapons failed to win, giving willpower the victory. The public opinion in all the countries of the world, including the mightiest country, helped Vietnam to win the struggle and unite. He did not take the credit for the military strategy of Vietnam. He did not give credit to the forces that fought in the battlefields. He gave credit to the people, to their willpower and determination.

The delegation was then taken to a few villages to see how the villagers lived, and how they practised agriculture and did other activities. They were taken to the borders too, where clashes with the country's neighbour had taken place.

After three days, the delegation was expected to fly to Ho Chi Minh city, now called Saigon. The delegates were taken to the airport in the morning. For the whole day, they waited to take the flight to Saigon. However, it was not possible that day. So, they were brought back to the place where they had stayed for three days. On the next day, they were flown to Saigon in a special plane.

In Saigon, the delegates met with the mayor of the city, some party leaders, and professors in the university. The delegates were shown the places which the previous government occupied when the city was bombarded and attacked. They explained how both the government at that time and the new government functioned and how the people lived.

The delegates were told that South Vietnam's economic policies were more liberal than the economic policies in North Vietnam. The strict communist ideology was not forced on the people in the south. The delegates were told that the policy adopted by the new government was like the policy adopted by Prophet Mohammad Paigambar after the agreement made at Badar between the forces and the people who lived in the area around Mecca and those who lived in the area around Medina. That agreement was made to bring about change in the minds and hearts of the people in Mecca, and to avoid using force to introduce the change. The delegates could see that the markets and the people in Saigon looked different from the markets and the people in Hanoi. The people in Hanoi were robust and strong, but wore less fashionable and less expensive clothes than the people in Saigon. The buildings and shops in Saigon looked more like those in Western countries. Saigon was less influenced by the communist ideology than Hanoi. The delegates were told that the people in the rural areas in both parts of Vietnam did not look very different from one another.

■

The delegates were taken by a helicopter to Phnom Penh, the capital of Cambodia. They stayed there for two days in the lodge of the French governor which had been lying vacant and unused for many years. A few rooms of the governor's house were cleaned for the guests.

On the first day, the delegates were taken to the office of the prime minister. The prime minister explained what was done by Pol Pot, the Cambodian dictator, to the people, to the old government, to the currency and how he tried to enforce the communist ideology on the people. The prime minister was happy to receive the Indian delegation. He was happy that his government was recognized by India. He took pains to explain how his government was trying to solve the problems of the people and help them to overcome their difficulties. The prime minister was responsible for seeing that the people of Cambodia and the armed forces acted against Pol Pot, and brought his regime to an end.

The delegation was taken to see the city and a museum in which a mountain of skulls and bones was exhibited in a room. The guide explained that in the regime of Pol Pot, those who disagreed with his ideology and way of thinking and governance were done to death, and that the dead victims' skulls and bones were kept in a room to show how cruel his regime was. He explained that Pol Pot had done away with currency and forced the people to exchange commodities and goods and use the barter system. The villagers were asked to come to the cities, live in big buildings and work in offices, shops, and industries, and the people living in urban areas were forced to live in rural areas and cultivate lands and do manual labour. The people from urban areas and from rural areas were not happy with the lives they were compelled to live, and the work they were asked to do, as they were not accustomed to do those kinds of duties. Under Pol Pot's regime, the economy was ruined and the people had to face scarcity of all essential goods. Therefore, they opposed Pol Pot and his regime and supported the armed forces when they revolted against him. He was forced out of Cambodia and after some time, died in a neighbouring country.

The streets, shops and houses in the capital city were in a very bad shape. The guide told the delegation that the new government had tried to see that they were maintained in a better manner.

The delegation was taken to the palace where King Norodom Sihanouk used to live. The king had left Cambodia and was living in a neighbouring country. In the palace, they visited a museum in which the images and idols of Rama, Krishna, Mahadeva, Saraswati, Ganpati, Maruti, and other Indian gods were kept. The guide explained that King Norodom Sihanouk actually meant Narotam Sinha Naik. He explained that in his country, too, marriages were solemnized by going around a fire seven times. The people in Cambodia greeted one another by raising their folded hands, as the people in India do. All these aspects showed that Cambodia was influenced by Indian culture as much as India was influenced by their culture, as some Cambodians thought.

Next day, the Indian delegation was taken by helicopter to the place where the Angkor Wat temples were built. The temples were built by the side of a big natural lake. The helicopter flew over it for nearly fifteen minutes. There were many temples. All of them were very big. They were bigger than the biggest temples in India. Some were intact, others were in a dilapidated condition. The United Nations, India and other countries had contributed funds to maintain some of them, as they were treated as world heritage structures. Built of stones, the temples were like forts. Both sides of the temple walls were covered with carvings that depicted the wars mentioned in the Ramayana and the Mahabharata, the lives of the heroes of the two epics, and ordinary people who were supposed to have lived in those periods. The carvings were beautiful and artistic, indicating the high standard of art that must have existed when they were built. On the tops of the temples there were images of Brahma, Vishnu and Mahesha. In the sanctum sanctorum of the temples, they could see the lower parts of Shivalingas, and at the centre of the Shivalingas was the idol of the Buddha. That showed that the temples were built by those who practised a religion like the religion practised by the Hindus in India and later, the temples were used by the people who adopted Buddhism. That could have happened when Buddhism became more powerful and replaced Hinduism.

The delegates were told that Pol Pot's forces lived in that area, and it was supposed to be a stronghold of Pol Pot. That is why they were taken to the temples from the helipad in armoured vehicles, to provide extra security, as explained by the security persons who accompanied them. The delegates asked some Cambodians standing near the temples, through interpreters, if supporters of Pol Pot still lived in the area. They replied, 'No. They left long back. And now they are living in the area bordering the neighbouring country. However, now they are very weak, and not in a position to cause harm as they had done in the past.' The people who met the delegates appeared poverty-stricken. Physically also, they appeared weak and sick.

Cambodia had water, fertile land, thick forests and rich natural sources, but had not used them properly. That was the reason why the people were poor and lived difficult lives.

■

From Cambodia, the delegation went to Laos. For two days, they lived in a hotel in Vientiane, the capital. In those two days, they met the head of state, who was the youngest son of the monarch, some politicians, and villagers. Young boys were seen standing with modern weapons in their hands in the city and villages. The people were poor and lived on produce from the agricultural lands and forests. They had no industries or trade which could give them economic strength. The only valuable resource was the energy produced by using the water in the Mekong river, which they did not use in their country but sold to the neighbouring country to earn foreign exchange and money. The land was fertile, the forest was thick. However, the land and the forest were not used efficiently.

The country appeared to face instability. The government was trying to provide law and order, develop its economy, use its natural resources, and have friendly foreign relations with its neighbours. The delegates were taken to a few villages to see how the people there lived. In one village, they had lunch in a farmer's house. They squatted on the floor and ate food on big leaves, as we do in India. Each delegate had a young girl sitting in front of him to serve the food, and take care of him.

■

The delegation returned to India via Thailand. In India, they gave a report to the prime minister about their visits and discussions with the leaders of the countries visited, and informed the government that Vietnam wanted some assistance from India. The government of India took the necessary steps to help Vietnam and took note of the report given to it.

■

North Korea organized a national congress of its party every five years, and invited the leaders of political parties of different countries to attend it. It invited the leaders of its own party from different parts of the country and explained what their government had done for them in the last five years, and what it wanted to do for them in the next five years. It also explained how it proposed to unite the two Koreas, and what kind of policies it wanted to formulate and use for the advancement of the country.

The congress continued for nearly a week and was attended by thousands of delegates from Korea and other countries. The head of state addressed the conference. Other delegates also spoke. Everything was done in a most disciplined manner and on a very grand scale. The congress organized cultural programmes and a march past. People in millions joined the march past and the head of state, Kim Il-sung, took the salute. He was elderly and respected, and had fought for the freedom of his country against a foreign country. He had come to power at a very young age and remained in power for more than three decades. He made long speeches, wrote many books, and evolved a policy was called the 'Juche idea'.

In the fifth congress of the communist party of North Korea, he came to the dais on the first day at 10 a.m. and began his speech, which continued for three hours in the forenoon and three hours in the afternoon on the first day and for three hours in the forenoon and three hours in the afternoon on the second day with an interval of one hour between the two speeches each day. Thus, he spoke for twelve hours in total. In the first three hours, he spoke about what his government had done in the first five years, and in the second three hours, he spoke about what his plans were for his country in the next five years. In the third three hours, he spoke about the efforts made to unite the two Koreas and what his government wanted to do, and in the fourth three hours, he spoke about the manner in which he wanted to build the party. For the next two days, the discussions continued in the congress. On the fourth day, a grand march past took place in which more than half a million persons participated. On the sixth day, the head of state met the delegates who attended the congress.

The Congress party of India was invited to attend the fifth congress. The party decided to send its chairman of the committee on foreign affairs and one more member to attend it. I was the second Congress party member who was included in the delegation.

The Indian delegation went first to Hong Kong and from there to Beijing and then, finally, to Pyongyang. We stayed in one of the bungalows built for the guests, situated outside the capital in a thick, beautiful forest. For six days, we had breakfasts, lunches and dinners in the guest house. On the seventh day, we had lunch with Kim Il-sung, organized specially by the government for the Indian delegation. It was attended by the speaker of the Korean legislature and the president. The speaker of the Korean legislature had visited India at the invitation of the speaker of the Lok Sabha only two weeks before the fifth congress was held in Korea.

President Kim Il-sung behaved in a very correct manner with the members of the Indian delegation. He spoke and listened to what other members sitting around the lunch table had to say. He behaved like an elder member of a family. He said, 'I have been inviting Mrs Indira Gandhi to visit my country. She has not said no, but she has also not visited. Please tell her that we are very eager to have her in our country. We want her to see what we are doing here. I want to receive her, the people want to see her in our country.'

The head of the Indian delegation asked him, 'How big would the reception given to her be?' In reply, without taking a single second to respond, he said, 'As big as the reception organized for all the delegates to this congress.'

The leader of the Indian delegation asked him, 'You mean, it would have as many people as were there in the procession yesterday?'

The questions asked were very sincerely replied to. They might have sounded a little undiplomatic. But they were friendly. The conversation established beyond doubt that he was indeed quite keen to receive Mrs Gandhi in his country.

In the congress, the foreign delegates were given front seats in a corner. All the delegates who were in the hall observed the discipline to the hilt. None of the delegates was found leaving his seat and going out of the hall. The hall accommodated more than twenty thousand delegates.

We, the members of the Indian delegation, were given a guide. We were allowed to go to any place in the city and talk to anybody. The marketplaces in the city were not as attractive as those in advanced countries. The roads were neat and clean. There were no boards advertising commodities or goods put up at any place. The people looked healthy and wore simple clothes. None of them appeared to be poor or very wealthy. There were very few vehicles on the road. None of the people we met complained against anybody or the government. When they were asked if they were happy, they replied, 'We have all that we need. We do not have fancy and expensive goods. But what is needed to live a reasonably comfortable life is available to us.'

In our guest house, there were wine bottles on the dining tables. Invariably, on each and every table, was a bottle containing snake wine, with dead poisonous snakes inside it. It was not a comfortable sight for the members of the Indian delegation who asked the wine bottle to be removed from the table. The guide who was with the delegation waxed eloquent on the medicinal qualities of the snake wine, but failed to convince the Indian delegates to accept the praise showered by him on the snake wine.

■

The Indian delegation returned to India via Moscow. I.K. Gujral was the Indian ambassador in Moscow. He organized a dinner for the delegates. At the dinner table, he whispered in my ear that he had received a message from India asking him to send me back to New Delhi without any delay.

The next day, 17 October 1980, the Indian delegation reached New Delhi.

11

UNION MINISTER OF STATE FOR DEFENCE

On 18 October 1980, I received a message from the office of the prime minister saying that my appointment with the prime minister, Mrs Gandhi, was fixed at 11 a.m.

When I met her at her residence at the time of appointment, she informed me that she had decided to include me in her ministry, that is, the defence ministry, as a minister of state. She said I would be required to see that the defence ministry and the chiefs of the defence forces functioned in harmony with one another. She thought that all the chiefs and defence officers should also work in a harmonious manner with one another.

I had not expected to receive that kind of information. I was very happy to hear it, I could not express my feelings and thanks in words. She must have understood how I felt because she smiled and permitted me to leave her office. The next day, on 19 October 1980, I was sworn in and became a member of the Union council of ministers.

The additional defence secretary was present in Rashtrapati Bhawan at the time the swearing-in ceremony took place, as the defence secretary was out of station. The additional defence secretary asked me if I would be able to go to the office on the same day and meet the chiefs of the defence forces and other officers. I said I would go to the office and meet all those who wanted to meet me.

All the chiefs of the defence forces met me in the office. They expressed that it would be possible for them, other defence officers and me to work in a manner which would strengthen its forces and enhance the capability of the country to protect its sovereignty, territory and borders. I agreed with their views and feelings. That meeting made me feel that it would be possible for all concerned in the defence ministry to work in a harmonious and understanding manner, and contribute in achieving the objectives of the defence ministry.

The meeting with the senior officers of the ministry was equally promising. Prime Minister Indiraji had retained the defence portfolio with herself. With her as the defence minister, my job in the ministry was easy to perform and quite prestigious and enjoyable. I was expected to deal with all matters relating to the defence ministry. I had to deal with matters relating to personnel, production, procurement, defence research and development, ex-servicemen, and defence agreements with foreign countries. As the defence minister of state, I was expected to deal with parliamentary matters. Matters which were to be decided in the cabinet were sent to it after consulting the defence minister.

Within four days of my joining the defence ministry, I received two sets of information relating to the 'dos and don'ts' framed for the ministers. One set came from the office of the cabinet secretary and the other from the office of the prime minister. The first set of information was sent to all the ministers, explaining how a minister was expected to conduct himself as a member of the executive, as a member of Parliament, and as a member of society. It expected the minister to dispose of files without delay and in expected time frames, to meet people who wanted to call on him, to meet ambassadors and other foreign persons and dignitaries after getting information from foreign ministry about them, and reasons for which they wanted to meet him from the ministry of foreign affairs. The government expected the ministers to see that no chance or opportunity was given to the people to criticize his conduct or give any room for anybody to doubt his probity. It expected him not to attend parties and functions at the houses and places of persons who were not their relatives or friends. The information was very useful to the new and junior minister.

The prime minister expected certain matters to be dealt with at the level of the minister of state. A list of these subjects was sent to the minister. Some matters were to be decided at the level of the prime minister, while other subjects could be sent to the prime minister for the approval of the decisions taken by the minister before the orders were issued.

In the ministry, the files were not kept pending, but were disposed of well within the expected period of time. When files were sent for the approval of the prime minister, they were returned within one or two days. Except for two files relating to the construction of roads in the islands of Andaman and Nicobar, all the files which were sent to the prime minister were returned with her approval without any delay.

In some complicated cases and the case in which long-term policy decisions were required to be taken, I preferred to have her guidance and advice. She gave it in one or two words or one or two sentences. However, she expected the minister of state to take decisions in accordance with his understanding and without delay. Once she told me, 'Ministers should be quick and prompt in taking decisions. In doing that, if they commit mistakes of bonafide nature, they should not worry. If the malafide mistakes were committed, they should be prepared to face the consequences.'

She was fully informed about the administration carried on by different ministries and ministers. At times, I went to her to seek her advice and guidance, without writing about the issue in a file or informing her in any other manner or speaking about it to any other person, and received her advice, without opening my mouth to speak. I felt that she was able to read my mind. However, that could have happened because everything relating to governance was at her fingertips, and so, intuitively, she could know what kind of advice was required and gave it without waiting for a request for it.

In Parliament, she allowed me to reply to the questions and discussions. Except for four or five times, she did not rise in the House to add to anything I had said. At no time did she have to rise to correct my replies. In briefing meetings, she allowed me to ask questions and get the necessary information, or to inform the officers to take some steps to correct the situation. In consultative committee meetings, she expected me to hear the issues raised, to note the points made, and also to reply to some queries made by the members.

It was a pleasure to work in the ministry under her stewardship. She did not offer advice too frequently, she encouraged me to work on my own. Because she was the minister, everything in the ministry was done in time and without facing any difficulties.

▪

One day, in the Rajya Sabha, a member complained that the prime minister had appointed her relatives as the directors in a public sector unit. He gave the name of the public sector unit. The prime minister was in the House when the allegation was made.

She got up and said, 'Nonsense,' and sat down.

All the members of the Congress party in the House got up and objected to the allegation vociferously. All the members sitting on the opposition benches also got up and began to shout at the Congress members. This continued for more them forty minutes. The chairman of the House, M. Hidayatullah, tried his best to restore order and see that the reply to the point made was given by me. In fact, I was on my legs and struggling to explain the position and dispel the doubt created. But the members did not allow me to reply and created more din and noise. When the House became less noisy, I said, 'I will read out the names of the directors. Please let the House know who amongst them are related to the prime minister.' I read out the names. None of them was related to her—all of them were from Tamil Nadu, Karnataka and Kerala. When it became clear that the point made was raised to embarrass Indiraji and was not based on fact, again the members of the ruling party got up and shouted at the member who had raised it. In the question hour that day, the House could not do any other business.

However, unfortunately, next day, one of the important newspapers reported that the Defence Minister of State Shivraj Patil stated in the Rajya Sabha that a few directors of the defence sector public undertaking were related to the prime minister. The prime minister was in the House and she had heard what I had said. My impression was that she was happy to hear the reply given, which was very brief and did not leave any scope for ambiguity. The entire House knew that the allegation made was of a mischievous nature and false. Therefore, I did not have to give any explanation to the prime minister. I gave a notice to the newspaper asking it to correct the report given by it, otherwise, proceedings of breach of privilege for falsely reporting the proceedings of the House would be started against it. The incorrect report was made quite prominently and with a bold headline. The next day the newspaper corrected the wrong report, but cleverly, it ensured that it would not attract the attention of readers easily because it was given in a corner, not in a bold headline, and in a few words only.

On the day after the noisy question-answer hour, Mrs Gandhi visited Anand Bhawan in Allahabad to inaugurate a TV relay station. I was with her on that visit. At two places she found V.P. Singh, who had resigned from the chief ministership of UP, sitting with the public in front of the dais. She asked me to get him on the dais and gave him the chair beside her. It was very clear that she liked V.P. Singh. After about one and a half years, she got him included in the Union cabinet as a minister of foreign trade. At that time, I was holding that portfolio as a minister of state with independent charge. I vacated that position for him, and shifted to the science ministries and departments, where I continued to work for more than three years.

■

The navy had organized a demonstration of missile firing from the frigates in the Arabian Sea close to Mumbai. Indiraji, Rajiv Gandhi, I and some other ministers were invited to watch the firing. The demonstration was impressive. The missiles fired accurately. On the board of one ship, Rajiv Gandhi met the officers and discussed many naval technical matters and missiles and their usefulness. Indiraji was also on the same ship. However, she kept herself aloof from the others and remained silent in a very pensive mood. I asked her if her visit to Lakshadweep would take place on the fixed day or if any change was proposed. She said the visit would take place on the day fixed. She was expected to go by frigate from Trivandrum (Thiruvananthapuram) to Lakshadweep and stay on board the ship at night. I was expected to stay in a separate frigate. The chief of the southern naval command was to stay in a third frigate. There were other frigates anchored around the frigates of the VIPs. In the daytime, the prime minister and others accompanying her were flown to the islands by helicopters. On the islands, public meetings were organized and the prime minister visited the houses of a few islanders. The houses of the inhabitants were very neat and clean, and the ladies wore a lot of gold jewellery. The male members of their families were generally on the ships and boats sailing in the economic zone of India and in the open, fishing, and returning to their houses once or twice in a few days.

Public meetings were organized on the islands for the prime minister to speak to the islanders. I was asked to speak at a few public meetings. I spoke in English and made short speeches. In one of the speeches, I said, 'India is too big, too vast, and has people who enjoy different kinds of cultural aspects of life.' Pandit Jawaharlal Nehru wrote in his *Discovery of India* that it was very difficult to discover India, to understand the culture and the people fully and so he could not be presumptuous to feel that it was possible for him to discover India. If that was what he felt, how could a person like me say that he was able to understand Indians and their culture? Even to understand a bit of their culture, we need to travel a lot and to visit different parts of the country. Only then would we be able to say that we could have some idea of India. To understand Indians and their culture fully is beyond the ingenuity of ordinary human beings.

After finishing that speech, when I sat in the chair beside Mrs Gandhi, she leaned towards me and asked, 'Why did you use the word "ingenuity"? Could you not find a simpler word to convey what you wanted to say?'

I was confused for a few seconds. Then I said, 'Sorry ma'am, I committed a mistake in using that word. I should have used a simple word which is generally used and easily understood. I will keep this in mind when I speak at public meetings.'

That was how she trained those who worked with her.

▪

The district collector of the islands had organized a lunch in honour of the prime minister. His wife cooked some items and made the arrangements. When the invitees were eating, she moved from person to person trying to serve the food. Indiraji saw her doing that and said, 'Let us help her by picking up the items we need from the tables where they are kept.' She got up from her chair, went to the tables and served the items she liked on to her plate with her own hands. That was how she treated other human beings and tried to help them even in small things.

These were the two things I learnt from her on my trip to Lakshadweep.

▪

Indiraji visited the islands of Andaman and Nicobar too. I was not able to go with her because of some other duties I had to perform. After returning from her trip, she asked me to visit the distant islands and meet the islanders, hear what they had to say and try to help them. On the Great Nicobar, ex-servicemen from the mainland, who had settled and were doing farming, had some problems. She asked me to help them fully.

I went to Andaman and Nicobar, travelling to different islands by frigate and met the inhabitants of the islands in public and small meetings. They had different problems which needed to be solved. In Great Nicobar, the ex-servicemen asked the government to send bullocks to cultivate their lands, and see that their agricultural produce was sent to the mainland to be sold in the market. They wanted the ships and boats to sail between the islands to facilitate their travels and contacts with one another. Orders for this purpose were given and steps to solve their problems were taken.

Rich in genetic wealth, the islands had forests with different varieties of plants, birds and animals. Medicinal plants were in great demand in many places in the world. The culture of the people was close to nature, very rich and attractive. On some islands there were some human beings who did not wear clothes. When some of them were brought to one of my meetings, I asked them through an interpreter if they would like to wear clothes as the others did, if they were given to them. They said 'Yes.' But in their yes, there appeared a big reluctance to wear clothes. I asked the officers to give them clothes and food. They were very uncomfortable in the clothes they wore.

The islands are at a long distance from the mainland of India and are of strategic value. Many ships pass by Great Nicobar while crossing from the Indian Ocean into the Pacific Ocean. The islands had men and officers from the three forces under one joint command, providing them security.

After returning to Delhi, I gave a report to Indiraji. Then she asked me to visit the states in the north-eastern region of India, the international borders, and the actual line of control, and talk to the officers and jawans serving in those areas and on the borders. She thought that the ministers and officers of the government of India should visit them as often as possible. She said much more should be done to protect their culture, develop the economy of the region and try to encourage the people to go to other parts of the country for educational, trading, industrial and other purposes.

In the period when she was the prime minister of India, as in Pandit Jawaharlal Nehru's time, the demand for grants by the defence and foreign ministries was discussed in every budget session, which unfortunately, was not done in later periods. The demand for grants by the defence ministry were discussed in the Lok Sabha when she was the defence minister. She replied to the debate and I was asked to intervene. In a meeting which she had with the officers and me, she indicated the points on which she would reply and the points on which I would intervene.

The issues relating to the sovereignty, national security and foreign policy of the country need the attention of the elected members of Parliament, and are issues which should never be neglected. They have long-term implications and need long-term policies and adequate preparations to be correctly handled and dealt with. The state legislatures are not in a position to deal with and consider them fully. If they are not discussed in Parliament, the country and its representatives remain uninformed, and lose the opportunities to contribute towards making correct policies and taking timely steps to rectify mistakes, or to modify the policies to suit the current period and the future requirements. Hence, every year, at least in the budget session, they should be discussed.

■

After India achieved independence, it was felt for some years that it would be possible in the near future to protect its sovereignty and territory through diplomatic steps and by ensuring an ambience in which it would not be required to face any great difficulty. Hence, the finance ministry did not always agree to provide the budget required by the defence ministry. However, later, the finance ministry gave the funds required and demanded by the defence ministry. This approach helped the country to be well prepared to face any eventuality. Later, it was felt that to defend the country, the economy of the country should be strong, the society should be harmonious and the politics conducted in a manner that provides stability and sound policies. Hence, the demands of the defence ministry were not granted as they were made. They were examined very carefully, and only the most essential and pressing demands were approved and granted. It is necessary to see that this policy needs to be implemented very carefully.

The country needs to form a correct threat perception. The threat may occur in the immediate or in the distant future. It may depend upon the specific situations in the neighbourhood, in the world, in politics, economics, in science and technology and culture in different parts of the world. The world situation may create danger of war, or may control the possibility of war.

India is separated from other countries by the Himalayas on its northern border, and by oceans on its southern borders. The Himalayas and oceans provided it protection in the past, but in present times, countries need protection from attacks from the skies also. Wars are fought not only in battlefields; they are fought in laboratories and markets, agricultural fields and forests. Therefore, countries have to be prepared to protect themselves from such attacks. So, those who are working in different fields are in a position to contribute to preparations for protecting their interests. It is for this reason that the issues relating to war and peace should not remain neglected.

All creatures need peace and tranquility to enjoy existence. They try to create these conditions and at times, fight to create them. Some people feel that fighting can give them joy, prestige and status and so they should not shun fighting, conflicts and wars.

Human beings have tried to create peaceful conditions for an enjoyable existence. They have also fought wars in all times of history. Religious leaders have tried to avoid wars, conflicts, injustice and inequality, but religion has also been used by some human beings to perpetrate injustice and inequality, and unleash wars and conflicts. Thinkers have thought about the issues of war and peace, and have tried to give answers to the question why wars are fought. Some say they are fought for land, women, wealth, power or to dominate others. These days, there are some who think that they can be fought for markets. There are others who think that wars occur in the minds of men and they should be stopped right there, which means they think that men should be made to think in a particular manner. If they care for others, there may not be wars fought. Some human beings are noble, others are less so and willing to cause harm to others. So there is a conflict between the two elements, one of them prompting goodness, and the other succumbing to greed, selfishness and narrow-mindedness. This conflict has been there since time immemorial. At times, one element becomes more powerful than the other. When the noble aspect of human nature becomes powerful, peace prevails, but wars are fought when the opposite kind of element becomes dominant.

It is said that to avoid wars, countries should remain prepared to face them, and should collect the wherewithal to fight and win them if inflicted on them by their enemies. This gives rise to fierce competition between many countries, and in the process, they keep collecting weapons. When weapons are collected, they may also unleash wars.

These days, people say that atomic weapons may destroy the entire humanity. This may or may not happen. But there is no doubt that if nuclear weapons are used in wars, immense damage can be caused to human beings, animals, plants and property collected by human beings to build new kinds of societies and existence. Hence, some people have begun to say that nuclear weapons have proved to be a deterrent to wars, which may have happened in their absence. To some extent, this may be true. But if people with control over nuclear arms do not have control over themselves, and use them, tremendous damage can be caused. The fault does not lie in the weapons. It lies in the minds of human beings who use them. Hence, the only solution lies in training the minds of people and making them just and peace-loving.

There are some philosophies and philosophers who think that

wars should not be shunned. According to them, in order to do justice and avoid injustice done to weaker sections of the society, they should fight. If the concepts and persons who are opposed to justice and goodwill are not controlled from perpetrating injustice, they may prove to be destructive.

The countries and the people have to take decisions which can avoid wars, and solve the problems by adopting peaceful methods. They are also required to be prepared to protect themselves by having things that are required for this purpose. But at the same time, they should be able to control themselves. If they fail to do that, destruction can be caused. If they succeed in doing what is needed in this respect, wars may not occur and peace may be continued.

At times, countries neglect their duty to protect themselves. At times, some countries become too strong and try to dominate others. Such countries may turn out to be losers. If they remain balanced, they may come out of all difficulties with flying colours. There is no scope for complacency. There is also no scope for overambitious, unbalanced activities to dominate others. This restraint has to be practised by the armed forces, the governments and societies. Let us hope that this principle will be followed by India and other countries at all times.

On balance, the cosmos rests. On balance, life exists. On balance, even non-living objects exist. On balance, the energy and life exist. Hence, the balance in existence should never be lost sight of.

This I learnt in my first innings in the defence ministry.

In practical terms, what can be done or needs to be done to avoid conflicts and wars, and to achieve peace and tranquillity? My thoughts on this are:

What is given by nature should be used wisely and not be exploited. These resources should be used carefully.

The resources available should be shared by one and all in an equitable and just manner. The strong should not be allowed to grab more than they need, and the weak should not be denied their due and what is needed by them. Fair distribution of the resources and wealth given by nature should be done.

Ideologies that teach inequality and exploitation, and allow any section of society to look down upon others, should not be encouraged and propagated. No ideology which pronounces that certain kinds of persons are superior, or other kinds of persons are inferior, should be propagated.

People living in all parts of the world should help one another. Only then can there can be peace and tranquillity in the world. Unlimited liberty should be given to one and all to live as they like, provided what they do does not affect, exploit and weaken others.

There should be organizations and governments that can control the unruly and bad elements in society.

The world would become more peaceful if a world government is created to regulate and control its activities.

The world would become a happy place to live in if all human beings realize that in the ultimate analysis, they are chips of the same block and not different from one another.

The world would become a more peaceful place if all creatures are respected and dealt with in a correct and just manner by all human beings.

Wars and conflicts will be avoided if all remain vigilant and determined to be correct and just, and oppose that which is wrong.

These steps are not easy to take. In a short time, they may not produce required results. But with perseverance and determination, the possibilities of war can be reduced, and those of peace can be increased. Most of the human beings have been making these kinds of efforts. That is why life of peace is prolonged, and the strength to perpetrate war is reduced. Let us hope that may be done on an increasing scale.

12

FOREIGN TRADE MINISTER OF STATE WITH INDEPENDENT CHARGE

Indiraji made changes in her council of ministers. She gave up the portfolio of the defence ministry, and shifted R. Venkataraman from the finance ministry to the defence ministry. Pranab Mukherjee was shifted from the foreign trade ministry to the finance ministry, while I was shifted from the defence ministry to the foreign trade ministry as a minister of state with independent charge. Along with the foreign trade ministry, the textile ministry was also put under my charge.

In that period, A.R. Antulay had resigned from the chief ministership of Maharashtra. The leadership at the national level was in search of a person who could be sent or chosen to replace him. My name was mentioned in the newspapers in bold headlines. When I was asked if I was prepared to go to Maharashtra, I indicated my preference to stay in the council of ministers at the national level. I did that because I felt that national level politics and governance could teach me a lot, and national level activities were really quite challenging and more important. Moreover, I thought I fitted better at the national level and was not equipped to cope with state level political activities and demands. Some of my friends and the media said that I was made CM, that is, the commerce minister, and not CM, the chief minister. Some other friends teased me by saying that I was made to hold a balance, instead of a sword, in my hand.

I had developed good relations with all those who were in the defence ministry. Since my young days, I had studied histories and books written on wars and great warriors. I had not paid attention to commercial and trading activities of any kind. Hence, when I was asked to function in the ministry of commerce, I felt a little diffident.

∎

I decided to study the commerce and textile ministries and prepare myself to handle them. I asked the officers of the ministries to brief me on the powers, responsibilities and problems of those ministries, and the solutions that could be used to solve them. The officers in the ministries were very responsible administrators, well informed and prepared to do their duties. They gave me presentations on different points and after hearing them, I felt the commerce ministry had to discharge part of the economic duties of the foreign ministry, as well as part of the duties of the industries and other ministries.

∎

The foreign trade ministry was created to regulate and manage the trading activities of India with foreign countries. Except for a few items, the government did not produce any commodities or goods, or provide services on its own. They were produced by private persons, companies and organizations. The government was expected to make policies to help and regulate imports and exports of commodities, goods, services and technologies. It could decide what should be freely exported or imported. In fact, the country was importing more and exporting less. So, it had to see that it had the foreign exchange to do it. Every year, it prepared a list of items which could be imported without obtaining the permission of the ministry. The list could be changed and the ministry could decide how the list should be made and allowed to be used by those involved in the business of import and export. In some cases, the ministry helped the producers of commodities, goods and services to export to other countries. This was done to ensure that enough foreign exchange was earned for importing items needed by the country. India had raw material and could export the same. It had a big market, and therefore, it could import goods, machines and technologies. It produced foodgrains, but did not produce oil seeds and pulses, which it had to import. It produced tea, coffee, cashewnuts, cotton, jute, iron ore, automobile spare parts, meat, leather, shoe-uppers, and some items of artistic value and exported them to other countries. The ministry examined the situation and demands of the people in India and other countries and decided what should be imported and exported, and the countries involved in the transactions. In order to see that imports and exports to and from other countries were done effectively, the ministry entered into agreements with them, and examined, every year, how these agreements worked, and met representatives of these countries on their own soil in alternate years. For this purpose, ministers and officers of India often travelled to other countries. Before going to other countries, or receiving delegates from other countries the foreign trade minister and foreign minister would hold meetings. At times, the decisions regarding these matters were taken in the Council of Ministers.

■

In India, traders, industrialists and farmers had their associations and federations of associations. Every year, the federations used to meet to discuss their problems and the steps to be taken to solve their difficulties. The foreign trade minister and officers of the foreign trade ministry and some other ministries were invited to attend the deliberations of the federations, with a view to acquaint themselves with the conditions in which they were functioning. The minister and officers generally attended the meetings and made use of the views expressed in them to make policies. In fact, most of the production and trading activities were carried on by private enterprises. Therefore, it was felt useful to have that kind of contact between the government, the other concerned ministries and federations.

■

As the foreign trade minister, I attended the meetings of the joint committees in the UK, Finland, Czechoslovakia, Iran and Bangladesh. In India, I attended meetings attended by delegates of the UK, Iran, Finland and other countries. With all these countries, India's balance of trade was not favourable, because although India produced some commodities, it could not produce enough goods as it was not as industrially advanced as the developed countries were. India's huge market and vast population needed a very large number of goods and items produced by industries. Hence, its imports exceeded its exports and created a trade imbalance with most countries. India had, therefore, to adopt methods to produce goods and items needed in other developed countries. It could produce handicrafts and catch fish and prawns and export them to other countries. It tried to produce iron ore in large quantities which was in great demand in the advanced countries of the world. The foreign trade ministry encouraged the export of tea, coffee and spices. Countries which were close to India, including the USSR, imported these and other items. India had to take many steps to overcome the difficulties created by the adverse trade balance.

■

I visited Ethiopia to meet the ambassadors of India deputed to the African countries. In the meetings, the topic selected for discussion was how the trade of India with African countries could be boosted. The ambassadors opined that the African countries did not have enough funds or foreign exchange to buy commodities, goods and machines from other countries, but were willing to buy them from the countries providing them credit facilities. Moreover, they wanted the credit facilities for long terms. Also they were not in a position to use the new technologies, equipment and machines on their own. They wanted experts from the other countries to live in their countries at least for some years. So, along with sophisticated equipment and machines, they also asked for the services of experts to use them for a sufficient number of years and to train their citizens to use them. These African countries had water resources and wanted to build dams, dig canals and irrigate their lands. They wanted educational institutions to be built and manned by other countries to educate their children. They wanted to start hospitals. For these purposes, they demanded engineers, teachers and doctors to live in their countries. As far as the most sophisticated equipment, machines and technologies were concerned, they preferred to have them from the most advanced countries. But here, they faced one difficulty—they could not easily get experts to man and use them from the most advanced countries. The discussions were very useful. The main points which were made could be used by the foreign trade ministry and the government of India to develop better trading and economic relations with African countries.

China was sending its commodities, goods, machines and experts to African countries, and providing them with long-term credit facilities. They treated it as an investment for enduring and strong relations with the African countries. They attached less importance to profit-making in the near future, and more importance to good and strong diplomatic relations. The policies followed by China in this respect were good and useful. They can be kept in view by other countries also.

■

In Ethiopia, Mengistu Haile Mariam had become the ruler. In my visit to his country, I was expected to meet him and his foreign minister, foreign trade minister and home minister. I met all of them one after the other. In my meeting with him, Mengistu asked me to convey to Indiraji his invitation to her to visit his country.

I was invited to an Ethiopian dinner held in a forest area, where I met other Ethiopian ministers, intellectuals and ambassadors from the other African countries. The dinner organized was very interesting. In it, unusual items, like uncooked leg of lamb, were served. When I said I would not be able to eat it, some of the Ethiopians there told me that I did not know what I was missing.

The Ethiopians looked like Indians. They behaved as Indians did. They admired Indian leaders and policies.

■

In Japan, a conference of industrialists from India and Japan was organized. The conference was attended by nearly 150 industrialists from India and about 400 industrialists from Japan. Abe, who was the minister of industries and trade of Japan, attended the conference. He had met Pandit Jawaharlal Nehru and was a great admirer of Indian policies and leaders. While flying to Tokyo, I met him on the aircraft he had boarded from Singapore, and which had taken off from New Delhi with the Indian delegation and some Indian industrialists and me on board. It was a coincidence which provided me and the Japanese minister the opportunity to discuss certain points in an informal manner.

The conference was well organized and well attended. It was addressed by the ministers of India and Japan. The delegates who spoke made points of an encouraging nature. The industrialists and traders from Japan said that they were willing to increase trade and cooperation in industrial and other activities with the traders, industrialists and government of India. They asked the Indian delegates to bear in mind one point while dealing with Japanese traders and industrialists. They said that the users of machines and equipment in Japan were very choosy and quality conscious, and were willing to take only those products which satisfied fully the standards laid down for maintaining quality. They said they were very keen to import mangoes, mango pulp and prawns from India. They asked that these items should be correctly processed and properly packed. If Indian industrialists or traders wanted any help from them, they were willing to provide it to them. They were ready to establish processing industries and facilities to package these and other items in India. The minister of Japan was quite encouraging in his statements.

Indian traders and industrialists agreed to take all the steps required to provide high-quality commodities, fruit and flowers. They said they would be able to establish industries and facilities for these purposes on their own, but they did not have any objection if the Japanese traders and industrialists were ready to do so themselves in India. They thought that the Japanese should not only import raw material and commodities from India, but goods, machines and other equipment. They should make use of human resources and some technologies developed by Indians. They thought that Indians and Japanese could cooperate in developing new sciences and technologies and share them with Japanese and Indian entrepreneurs.

On behalf of the government, I said that the Indian people and the Indian government were willing to cooperate with the Japanese people and the Japanese government in a manner acceptable to both the countries. India would always be ready to widen its cooperation with Japan in all fields. I wanted to assure the people and the government of Japan that India was willing to do trade and business and cooperate in all kinds of industrial, trading and other kind of activities with Japan. I told the delegates in the conference that India was a big country, had a huge population, raw materials and a big market, which was bound to help both the countries enormously. There were some points raised and discussed to dispel misunderstanding in some areas.

At the conference, we succeeded in achieving the objectives to a great extent. All those who attended it felt happy and satisfied.

■

In Japan, I was taken to see the Suzuki small car manufacturing industry. At that time, India was in the process of entering into a partnership with a well-established automobile manufacturing company to produce small cars in India. Sanjay Gandhi had established an industry for this purpose. But after his death, the industry could not be run by any private person, and was handed over to the government, along with the infrastructure the factory had established for making small cars. There were some companies from foreign countries willing to enter into partnership with India to produce modern cars. Volkswagen and Suzuki of Japan were the two most favoured and well-known companies which were interested in cooperating with Indian car manufacturing factories.

The owner of the Suzuki factory, Shunzo Suzuki, showed me as to how cars were made in the factory. He entered the factory in a uniform which was similar to the one worn by the workers. The factory used machines and computers to assemble the cars, and as we went from one end of the assembly line to the other, we saw the workers doing their job, not distracted by our presence, not even greeting Suzuki. They kept at their jobs in a most disciplined manner. We were given lunch, which we were told came from the cafeteria used by the workers. They told us that there was no separate cafeteria or arrangements for the officers and owners of the factory.

■

Indiraji broke her journey while flying back to India from the US. In Tokyo, she was invited to have an official dinner with the prime minister of Japan. His name was also Suzuki, Senko Suzuki, but he was not related to the owner of the Suzuki factory. I was also invited to the dinner, and was able to see how graciously the Japanese received their guests. The prime minister of Japan was very happy to meet the Indian prime minister, and all the other members of her delegation.

■

In this visit to Japan, a meeting of the Indian ambassadors working in different countries was convened in order to find out what could be done to increase imports and exports to and from India to different markets of that region. This was a good opportunity for me and other members of the delegation to hear from the Japanese delegation what the Indian government, the foreign trade ministry, Indian traders and industrialists could do to achieve the objective.

The ambassadors said that Japan would be interested in importing raw material, iron ore, fruits, flowers, prawns and such other items, but not the equipment, machines and industrial goods required by Japanese trade and industries. They were of the view that they would like to import these items from the advanced countries of Europe and America. Their assessment appeared to be correct. Therefore, it was necessary for India to do better in the areas relevant to machines and industrial goods, to do more research and development and produce indigenous and advanced technologies. In their opinion, in electronics and genetics, India could play an important role.

The officers from the foreign trade ministry and I were happy to hear what the ambassadors had to say and decided to make use of their views. After coming back to India, I gave a report to the prime minister and her government about the conference, and about my visit to the Suzuki factory. After a few months, India entered into a partnership with the Suzuki factory to manufacture small cars in India. The small car was called Maruti Suzuki.

With Suzuki entering the India market with their car, the other car manufacturing companies in India also wanted and entered into partnerships with companies of other countries to make cars in India. This development made the Indian automobile industry strong and modern—and the scarcity of cars in India came to an end. Some cars manufactured in India were exported to other countries also.

■

In Bangkok, a meeting of the United Nations Economic and Social Commission for Asia and the Pacific (ESCAP) was organized. The foreign trade ministers of the countries of the region were invited to attend it. India sent its delegation to participate, which included. Abid Hussain, secretary of the commerce ministry and other senior officers. As the foreign trade minister, I led the delegation.

Shah Abu Muhammad Shamsul Kibria from Bangladesh had been newly appointed as the director-general of ESCAP. He was keen to have a food bank established in the region to meet the demand for foodgrains of some countries of the region that could not produce enough food material for their people, and had to import it from other countries. This was the main issue discussed in the meeting. There were many countries ready to accept the concept and willing to help to form a food bank for the region. The countries which produced more foodgrains than they needed and the countries which could not produce enough food material supported the proposal. But there were a few countries which were reluctant to accept the proposal. A few members of the Indian delegation were averse to the idea. However, a majority of them were in favour of helping ESCAP to have the food bank. I was in favour of the concept. In a meeting of ESCAP members I gave consent to the proposal. The director-general was happy to have India's support to his proposal. When he visited India after a few months after the conference, he met me specially to thank me for the cooperation given to the organization and to him. Unfortunately, after he returned to his country after relinquishing his job, he was assassinated, which was a great loss to his country and the region.

■

When the speaker of the legislature of Iran, Akbar Hashemi Rafsanjani, was invited to visit India by the Indian speaker, he came to India with a large delegation which included the minister of state in the government of Iran who looked after the foreign trade of his country. The Iranian delegation was happy to meet the Indian leaders and ministers. During their visit, I received a telephone call from the Iranian commerce minister of state. He wanted to meet me at my residence. Generally, Indian ministers meet delegates from other countries in their offices. From the talk that I had with him, it became clear to me that he preferred to meet me at my residence, so I agreed to meet him and his officers, along with the officers from the Indian foreign trade ministry.

In our meeting, he asked me to visit Iran and I said I would. He said that I should do it within a month. I replied that I had to see how I was engaged in the next month and that I had to obtain the permission of the prime minister. When he said that true friends could have no difficulties in overcoming such small problems, I promised to give my final reply in the evening. We discussed other small matters along with our officers and then he left.

I consulted Foreign Minister P.V. Narasimha Rao. He said that I should go to Iran and the government and the prime minister would not object to my visit even within a period of one month. The prime minister also allowed me to accept the invitation.

Tehran is a beautiful city. At that time, it was not well maintained because the country was in a state of flux. The revolution against the shah of Iran had taken place and the monarchy had come to an end. Iran and Iraq were at loggerheads and a war was going on between them. At the airport, there were many aircraft sitting on the ground, covered with thick layers of dust. There were no crowds on the road and the marketplaces were deserted. The Indian delegation, including me, was put up in the Hilton hotel. The hotel building was quite big. It was used to lodge the widows of soldiers who were killed in the war with Iraq. The corridors and compound of the hotel were covered with leaves and dust. I was provided a beautiful suite which was cleaned up for me to stay in, while other members of the delegation were lodged in other rooms which were also cleaned temporarily for them.

The next day, the Indian delegation was taken to a big conference room in the hotel to meet its counterparts. The foreign trade minister of Iran was a scholar. He was imprisoned for a few years and kept in jail in the days of the shah's regime. He had read books written by Mahatma Gandhi, Pandit Jawaharlal Nehru and Rabindranath

Tagore. He talked for one hour at the meeting on the foreign trade between India and his country. His attitude towards India, its leaders and our delegation was very friendly, with no artificiality in his talk. Whatever he said was positive and encouraging. I had no difficulty in responding to his points in the same manner. The meeting gave both sides complete satisfaction. Although we did not take any concrete decision on any issue, we expressed our views on the cooperation between our countries.

After the meeting and at lunch, which was organized for the delegation and participants, he spoke and I heard what he had to say. He spoke about the philosophy and policies of Indian leaders. He spoke about the philosophy propounded by Mahatma Gandhi, the policies formulated by Pandit Jawaharlal Nehru and the literary qualities of the books of Rabindranath Tagore. He told me that while in jail, he had the time to read their books and form his opinion about them. He was a revolutionary but he did not criticize non-violence. He said that at times, wars and revolutions were needed to correct the mistakes made by rulers, but that peace was needed for development and justice to be given to one and all. So he appreciated the principle which supported the concept of non-violence propounded by Mahatma Gandhi.

The next day, I was taken to the office of the Iranian prime minister. I was surprised to see that he was a very young man. In fact, most of the Iranian ministers were very young.

The office of the prime minister was guarded by young security officers. The policemen standing at different places in the city were also young. I was taken from the airport to the Hilton Hotel in a big vehicle in which young security officers were sitting. Close to my feet on the floor of the car, one AK-47 was kept. When I asked the minister why it was kept there, he said that I could use it if any occasion to use it arose, to protect myself. From what I saw, I felt that the revolution might have been conceived and planned by older revolutionaries, but it would have been carried out by young Iranians.

The prime minister asked me a few questions about India and the Indian government. Then, for two to three minutes, he explained how the Iranian government was doing and what it wanted to do in future. Then for about fifteen minutes he kept on speaking about the Vedas, Upanishads, the Mahabharata and Ramayana. I was surprised to see that he was interested in talking to me about the Indian scriptures. What he was saying was authentic and based on deep study. I felt that the Iranian leaders were interested in conveying that they appreciated Indian culture and philosophy and that the Iranian people admired Indian thoughts and culture.

The Indian delegation was taken to the palace where the monarch used to live, to the marketplaces, and a wrestling house. The palace remained unoccupied, the market might have done a lot of trade in the past and may do so in the future, while the wrestling house resembled the wrestling houses in India. Iran was famous for wrestling.

The Indian delegates returned to India with satisfaction. They felt that India could have friendly relations with Iran.

▪

An Indian delegation visited Finland to attend a meeting of a joint commission. In Finland, at the time we were there, daylight continued up to 2 a.m. and night existed only for about four hours. Those who wanted to go to bed could do so in the light of the sun, or by pulling the curtains over the windows and doors and creating artificial darkness in their bedrooms. For the first two or three days, the members of the delegation faced difficulties in sleeping when there was sunlight everywhere.

In the meeting of the joint commission, relevant issues and problems were discussed and were solved in a satisfactory manner. The government of Finland fixed my meeting with its prime minister. In a way, it was a courtesy call. The prime minister gave me an assurance that his government would do all that was necessary to increase trade and cooperation between his country and India and I responded to his statement with the same kind of assurance and warmth.

The Indian delegation was taken to see the seaport and a paper mill. At the seaport, the delegation was shown ships and boats which could navigate in the sea where it was covered with thick layers of snow. We were shown these vessels because India was going to hire a ship from Finland to send a team of scientists and sailors to Antarctica, where they were expected to stay for a few months.

At the paper mill, the delegation was shown how trees were grown to meet the demand for raw material. They sowed seeds in paper bags with machines and reared saplings for years in hothouses. They had allotted large areas where the trees would be allowed to grow for some years. Thus, in a systematic manner, trees were grown and the raw material for mills was supplied. Finland exported the trees by air to oil-producing countries to create greenery in their cities and earned much foreign exchange in this manner.

Finland is a very beautiful country. The people of Finland are hard-working and modern in their attitudes toward life. The Indian delegation achieved the objective of increasing interest in trade and cooperation between the two countries.

■

A meeting of a joint commission of Czechoslovakia and India was held in the beautiful city of Prague. The meeting was attended by the foreign trade ministers of the two countries. It was conducted in a very satisfactory manner and the Indian delegation was happy to receive positive responses from the foreign trade minister of Czechoslovakia on all points that were raised in the meeting. India was supplying heavy earth-moving machines to Czechoslovakia which was willing to get more machines from India.

I met the prime minister of the host country. He was positive in his approach to the outstanding issues between the two countries. The offices of the prime minister and other ministers were housed in ancient elegant buildings. However, they were very well equipped with all the modern facilities required to run high offices.

•

The foreign trade minister of the UK came to India and we had a meeting to discuss common issues. He also insisted in meeting me at my place of residence with our officers.

The meeting of the joint commission was held in London. It achieved all the objectives for which it was held. On behalf of the Indian delegation, the high commissioner of India had organized a dinner for the delegates of the two countries. The foreign trade minister of the UK attended the dinner. While we were dining, the UK minister received information about the birth of the first son of Prince Charles. He was asked to attend a special meeting of the British cabinet without fail and immediately. The minister explained that he was required to leave the dinner table to attend the cabinet meeting. He sought the permission of the host and wanted to be excused. This meaningful event was one that the Indian delegation remembered very vividly and discussed on many occasions.

•

The General Agreement on Tariffs and Trade (GATT) took decisions to see that commodities and goods were allowed to flow freely from one country to another, without requiring to cross any hurdles. In the 1980s, it was realized that the services of one country should be allowed to be used in another country, as commodities and goods were allowed. Many meetings for this purpose were held in many countries by the GATT. In 1983, a meeting for this purpose was held in Geneva, and was attended by the foreign trade ministers of all the member countries of the GATT. On behalf of India, an Indian delegation consisting of the foreign trade minister, foreign trade ministry's secretary and other officers attended the meeting. Before attending the meeting, Prime Minister Mrs Gandhi was asked to give her guidance and advice to the delegation. For this purpose, a meeting was organized and attended by the foreign minister, finance minister, foreign trade minister, the cabinet secretary, the principle secretary to the prime minister, the secretaries of the concerned ministries and some other senior officers. The prime minister heard the views of the ministers and secretaries before giving her guidance. She was satisfied with the line planned to be taken by India. She asked the Indian delegation to meet the members and leaders of other delegations at breakfasts, lunches and dinners given by the leaders of the delegations of other countries, and try to find out what they were prepared to say and do at the GATT meeting. She asked the Indian delegation to fine-tune its stand with the stand intended to be taken by other countries, giving liberty to the Indian delegation to adjust India's stand with the stand taken by other countries.

At the meeting, some countries stated that services should be put under the jurisdiction of the GATT without delay. Other countries disagreed. There were some countries which thought that it should be done after ten years.

Developed countries felt it should be done immediately, while developing countries which were doing well wanted it to be done after a decade. The least developed countries opposed the idea. They thought that they would not be able to develop as they wanted if the services were put under the GATT regime. There were some developed countries that were not very comfortable with the concept, but did not want to express their disagreement openly. France was explicit in expressing its views. The French foreign trade minister was quite frank in expressing his disagreement. Japan, Germany, Australia and the UK also had some doubts, but they were very discreet and quite subdued in expressing their views.

India, along with Mexico and Brazil, was of the view that the proposal that services should be put under the jurisdiction of the GATT should be implemented after a few years. It said the less developed countries' interests should be protected by making special provisions for the purpose. The leaders of the less developed countries' delegations were asked by their countries to take the line decided by their governments. They were also allowed to follow the line taken by India on the points which came up without notice and on which they could not obtain the guidance of their countries immediately and fully. The Indian delegation was impressed by the faith expressed by the least and less developed countries of the continents of Africa, Asia and South America, in India, Mexico, Brazil and some other countries.

Some meetings continued up to 4 a.m. The views were expressed by some delegates in a very forceful manner. At times, it was found that delegates of some interested countries tried to misinterpret the rules and laws followed by the GATT to support their stands. This meeting was one of the most difficult meetings I had attended. All the same, the GATT took the decision to bring services under the GATT regime after ten years. The services were brought under the World Trade Organization (WTO) in 1993. GATT had then been replaced by WTO. That was what India had wanted. We were happy to have that kind of decision taken.

•

India was one of the countries that had taken a lead to form the GATT. Pandit Jawaharlal Nehru had supported the concept of creating the GATT and was of the view that, in the future, the countries of the world would be required to cooperate with one another in matters relating to trade, industry, agriculture, science and technology. There were some countries which had not been included in the GATT and were, in fact, not ready to join it in the initial period. However, later they became eager to join it. The Soviet Union of that time and China were not members of the GATT. But later they felt that they should join it and cooperate with other countries. Some countries were of the view that the developed countries may take advantage of the GATT to protect their interests and exploit less developed countries. So they had doubts about its usefulness. There were other countries which were of the view that multilateral agreements were more capable of protecting the interests of the less and least developed countries, which object could not be achieved under bilateral agreements entered into by the developed countries and the less and least developed countries. In agreements made between the advanced and backward countries, the latter may not be able to have terms of agreements which could protect their interests. It is a fact that developed countries want to protect their own interests. When they do so in a manner that can protect the interests of the less or least developed countries, both sides get the benefits for longer periods of time. When that is not done, one side gets the benefit for a short time and when this happens, willingness to accept the concept of globalization lessens. This shows that only the enlightened attitude is conducive to produce beneficial results for longer periods.

Commodities and raw material are needed at some places. But they are produced at other places. If they are allowed to be sold at remunerative prices, they can be produced in ample quantities. But if they are purchased at prices that are not remunerative, they cannot be produced in quantities required. The goods are produced in some places and sold in others. If they are sold at exploitative prices, they can have smaller markets; if they are sold at non-exploitative and just prices, they can have bigger markets. Goods can earn profits by not being easily available in the market. If they are in short supply, they can get more attractive profits. There are some countries willing to produce them in big quantities in order to earn profits. It is a wise step to produce such goods in bigger numbers to meet the demands of all and sell them at just prices. That does not mean that they should be produced beyond the demand because that could harm the environment. On the other hand, producing less number of goods and earning more profit is counter-productive.

Some people think that new, innovative goods should fetch high prices and profits for those who invent and produce them. It is true that unless the producers and inventors of new goods get attractive incentives, they will not be enthusiastic about entering new areas of inventions and discoveries. Moreover, the new areas of inventions and discoveries are areas in which the profit margin should be encouraging. So, if higher prices are demanded and received for new goods, and if they are not of exploitative nature, they should not be unwelcome. However, the percentage of profit to the cost of production of these commodities and goods should not have a huge gap between them. Otherwise, those who produce them may not get just prices and profits, making the concept of globalization less acceptable. Globalization can be acceptable without any problem if it is based on justice and unexploitative transactions.

■

This world is one entity. It does not have boundaries created by nature dividing it into nations. Most of the nations and boundaries are created by human beings. They are based on pragmatic policies and self-interest, and some concepts of governance as well as social and economic philosophies. Globalization in its pure form is more important than nationalism in its pragmatic form. Universalization is more significant and scientific. Cosmic philosophy can be rated even higher than universalization. In ancient India, the entire globe, universe and cosmos were kept in mind while conceptualizing the philosophy of life and relations between human beings, animals and plants. So it can be said that globalization was not a new concept for India. The present-day concept of globalization may appear to be different from the ancient Indian concepts relating to one world, universe and cosmos. In fact, the ancient concepts of universe and cosmos are wider in scope and more inclusive.

If globalization is limited to economic activities—trade, commerce, industry and services—it cannot remain effective. If it allows free flow of commodities, goods and services, but not the free flow of technologies, knowledge and human beings from one country to another, it cannot be very effective in the ultimate analysis. Hence, it should allow raw material to be available at places where it is needed, it should allow goods to be available where they are needed, and it should allow technologies, science and knowledge produced at some places, to be available at all places. Only then can it really achieve positive results of lasting nature.

In the present and in the future, human beings will aspire to reach other planets and discover whether they would be able to live there and use available resources for all creatures in the universe. This can became a reality if human beings from different parts of the globe join hands with one another. Fortunately, this appears to be happening. However, it should happen on a larger scale and in a more scientific and systematic manner and with greater speed.

The cosmos and time are unlimited, without boundaries of any kind. Knowledge is also of the same nature. Probably, it is wider and more powerful than the cosmos and time. It needs to be expanded. This can be done in a joint and cooperative manner with people all over the world, in less time and with less effort. Globalization, universalization and the cosmic approach can help to achieve this.

Looked at from this angle, globalization is not only related to trade and commerce, but is wider and more inclusive. Globalization is smaller than universalization, which in turn, is smaller than the cosmic concept. The cosmic concept can include space, time, knowledge, science and technology, art and culture, and spirituality. Then only can globalization expand and become more effective. When it reaches the heart of the universe and cosmos, it can become more effective, and useful.

■

I enjoyed my tenure as a Union foreign trade minister of state. It widened my vision as I travelled to different countries to have discussions with leaders and sages in different parts of the world. All the officers who worked in the ministry did not hold the views I did, but all the same, the gaps between their views and my views were limited and we could work together harmoniously.

V.P. Singh was the chief minister of UP from 1980 to 1982. He was the deputy minister in the ministry of foreign trade for some time. After resigning from the chief ministership of UP, for some time, he remained outside the state as well as the Union government. Indiraji liked his way of conducting himself as a politician. She wanted him to work in the Union government as a foreign trade minister. So, in 1983, she asked me to vacate that post and join the science ministry, which was with her. I did it with pleasure, because I got the opportunity to work with her again in the ministry which was retained by her.

13

UNION MINISTER OF STATE IN THE TEXTILE MINISTRY WITH INDEPENDENT CHARGE

For some time, the foreign trade ministry and the industries ministry were with one minister. Then, the industries ministry was put under a separate minister and the textile ministry was put under the foreign trade minister. When I was shifted to the foreign trade ministry, the textile ministry was also under my jurisdiction.

India produces cotton on a large scale. In the past, handlooms were used to produce cloth of high quality. The cloth made in Dhaka, now the capital of Bangladesh, was famous in India and other countries also. The weavers had developed the art and skills to produce a very good quality of cloth. That was the story of olden days.

In some countries in the world, handlooms were replaced by textile mills. The handlooms could produce small quantities of cloth. The textile mills could produce large quantities of cloth. The cost of producing cloth by using machines was also more attractive and acceptable. In India also, textile mills were established and used to produce cloth on a large scale.

Textile and jute industries developed in the presidency states when the British ruled the major portion of the country. In the province of Bengal, the jute industry was established and developed on a large scale. Textile industries were established in Mumbai, Ahmedabad, Chennai, Indore, Baroda, Kanpur, Patna and some other cities, as well as in other cities in the state of Tamil Nadu. Initially, they did very well, producing cloth on a large scale and earning huge amounts of money. In fact, the textile and jute industries began the era of industrialization in the country, flourishing during the First and Second World War periods.

Afterwards, India began to establish industries to produce steel, automobiles, medicine, and many other commodities. Industrialists in the textile and jute industry began to enter areas occupied by new industries, which earned more profits. So, the industrialists invested in expanding new industries and establishing newer ones. However, they failed to modernize their old textile and jute industries. The result of that was that they became less profitable and could not meet the demands of the mill-workers. In many mills, the workers went on strike, which also caused difficulties to the less profit-earning industries.

Many of the textile mills were closed down. About one hundred mills were nationalized and given to the National Textile Corporation. The corporation was expected to modernize the mills and make them more profitable and competitive. It did take steps to modernize a few mills, and was able to help the workers to continue in their jobs and get their wages regularly. But it could not modernize the mills to make them as efficient and productive as mills in other countries. The National Textile Corporation's mills also could not compete with the mills of other countries.

In 1983, the textile workers in many mills in India went on strike. The strike continued for months. Dr Datta Samant, who was a sitting MP, led the strike. The mill-owners and workers could not negotiate successfully to end the long-drawn-out strike. The workers wanted their wages to be increased, but the mill-owners said that they were not in a position to enhance their wages. They were inclined to sell the factory land. They were willing to help the workers to have power-looms and handlooms and to continue to earn by making cloth and selling it in the market. They were also willing to give some amount of money if the workers were ready to give up their jobs. On behalf of the government, it was suggested that if they closed down their mills in the cities and if they were ready to establish new mills in the areas where cotton was grown and build houses for all the employees, schools for their children and provide medical, transport and entertainment facilities to the mill-workers and officers, they would be allowed to sell their lands on which the mills were built. That would decongest the cities, and the new mills would be built in the areas where raw material was available. The government wanted the sale proceeds of the land to be kept in banks and operated by the government officers and mill-owners jointly. That condition was put forth in order to see that the funds acquired by selling the lands of the mills could be used for establishing new textile mills and not for other purposes. It was also suggested that after establishing the new mills with new facilities, if any amount of money remained unspent and unrequired, the same could be given to the mill-owners to be shared with the shareholders and themselves. These suggestions were made in order to see that the workers were not thrown out of employment and also to see that new, modern mills could be established. These suggestions were not fully acceptable to the mill-owners and workers. So the strike continued for a long time. As a textile minister of state, I had to deal with it. All the chief ministers of the states were eager to see that the strike came to an end, but they could not suggest any solution to overcome the problem. The media gave wide publicity to the strike. After about six months, the government nationalized a few mills and the workers dispersed to their native places. Afterwards, the mills were allowed to sell their land, and new markets and malls were built on them. If the suggestions given by the government at the initial stages were accepted, new mills could have been established. But unfortunately, that did not happen. The nationalization of mills was done by my successor, V.P. Singh, who became the foreign trade and textile minister after I was shifted to the science ministry.

When I was looking after the defence ministry, the defence

public sector units went on strike for many months. It fizzled out. The government of the time was of the view that in the defence sector and important areas of economic activities, strikes should not be resorted to, to solve the problems of the workers. It felt that their problems should be solved through dialogues and discussions. And if the workers went on strike, they should be persuaded to withdraw their strike and then, their demands should be fully met. In the strike period the only thing that should be done was to persuade them to withdraw the strike. So after the strike was withdrawn the demands of the workers were accepted. Since then, because of the stand taken by the government at that time, no strike has occurred in the defence production units. In the same manner, because of the stand taken by the government when handling the railway strike and the strike in the textile mills, no big strikes have taken place in the country. All the problems of the workers and managements have been solved through dialogues and discussions.

In India, handlooms and power-looms are also used to produce cloth, giving employment to a large number of workers. The number of workers using handlooms and power-looms is quite big, which is why the government has taken steps to help the workers in many ways. Corporations for this purpose have been created. Certain types of cloth are reserved to be made on handlooms and power-looms only, and handloom and power-loom cloth and manufactures are given rebates and tax concessions also. These looms are owned and used by those who are in the textile business, and by the weavers. However, the number of weavers owning them is reducing, and the number of non-weavers taking advantage of the concessions and help given by the government is increasing. Here, the non-weaver middlemen get more benefits than the weavers. The steps taken by the governments have helped the weavers. But some more initiatives need to be taken to see that the weavers and handloom workers get the benefits instead of the others who have very little to do with handloom and power-loom activities and weaving.

India needs to modernize its textile industries. It is a good policy not to export cotton or iron, or cloth alone. It is better to export iron than to export iron ore as it is better to export cloth rather than to export cotton. It is better still to export apparel than cloth. India can, therefore, formulate a textile policy and use it to ensure that finished goods are exported, and not the raw material needed to manufacture them.

India should graduate to producing apparel and develop its capacity to produce new and acceptable designs of garments to be exported to different countries. It needs to have a research and development wing which can develop technologies that can help to produce cloth and garments with ease and of designs that are liked by those who wear them. Unfortunately, these aspects are not paid the attention they deserve. The textile industry is in private hands. The National Textile Corporation has about one hundred units, but these have been taken over by the corporation when they could not be run by private owners. The corporation has tried to modernize them, but has not done so adequately.

Clothes and food are required by human beings at all times and therefore, are constantly in demand. Hence, attention should be paid to all aspects which can help to produce them in required quantities at all times. The quality of goods produced needs to be acceptable to consumers. Keeping these aspects in mind, plans and policies should be formulated by the government and the private sector also. The private sector can have their own policies and plans, and can make suggestions to the government to have its policies and plans in tune with theirs. The government and industrialists should make their policies and plans in consultation with farmers and traders as well. If such comprehensive policies and plans are made and used, the textile industries in India can become very profitable to the country and other countries of the world also. Handlooms and power-looms may be encouraged to give employment to those who need it. But they cannot continue for all time to come. Slowly, they have to yield in favour of textile industries and come up to their level. But this should be done in a very careful and planned manner, and their gradation to higher levels should not create new problems of unemployment.

Cotton is produced in many states in India. Its production and prices have been fluctuating. When it is produced in large quantities, the prices of cotton crash. When it is not produced to meet the demand, the prices skyrocket. In order to avoid fluctuations, a scheme was made and used by the government of Maharashtra for nearly thirty-five years. The scheme provided that cotton produced by farmers would be purchased by the cooperative societies in the state, and not by private traders, at the price fixed by the government. The cooperative societies could then sell the cotton to the textile industries. If it was sold at higher prices, the difference in the prices at which it was purchased and sold could be given to the farmers, after retaining a certain percentage of the profit for the societies to meet the losses incurred by them when the amount paid to purchase it was more than the price at which it was sold to the industries. With this scheme, the interests of the farmers, the industries and consumers could be justly protected, and exploitation by the middlemen, who were not the producers of the raw material, finished goods and consumers was avoided and controlled.

This scheme was liked and approved by the producers of the raw material and goods, as well as the consumers. But it was opposed tooth and nail by those who were affected by it. In fact, this was a scheme which should have been used throughout the country, like the employment guarantee scheme. However, in all states, the cooperative movement is not well developed. The cooperative movement has also developed some defects, which are used by some interested parties for their own benefits and also to see that the cotton monopoly procurement scheme is done away with. The scheme was given up eventually, because the advantages enjoyed by farmers, industrialists and consumers were not highlighted, and the defects were given wide publicity with pressure mounting on the government. After the scheme was given up, the number of suicides by farmers in the cotton-producing areas has gone up. It is essential that fluctuations are avoided and that the interests of the producers, consumers and users are protected. It is essential that the non-producers and non-consumer's interests need not be given undue importance and not allowed to affect the schemes which protect the interests of the producers and consumers. Economic justice should be done. Liberalization should not affect economic justice. It should prevent exploitation. It should help the majority in the society and not only a few interested parties.

■

Jute industries were set up in jute-producing areas. They were established in the province of Bengal during the British Raj. Many of the jute industries are now in Bangladesh. Some of them are in West Bengal. The jute industry made gunny bags, which were used to carry foodgrains, cement and other commodities and goods from one place to another. The jute industry was not modernized. Many of the owners of the textile industries were owners of the jute industries. The policies adopted by the owners of jute industries were not different from the policies adopted by the owners of textile industries.

The profits earned by them were used in other industries and trading activities. No research and development to make them more efficient, cost-effective and modern was done. The new sciences and technologies had begun to produce materials and goods which were more in demand by users, as they were less expensive and preferred by the users of gunny bags. Jute was not used to make curtains, carpets, suitcases, footwear and carry bags. So, industrialists were less enthusiastic about putting in more funds and effort into their jute industries.

Most of the jute industries were owned and run by private entrepreneurs. The government tried to help them but could not produce the desired results. Like the textile industries, they also were responsible for providing large employment. At present, the jute industries in India are not as efficient and profitable as the jute industries in Bangladesh.

The textile ministry, which dealt with jute industries also, tried to establish institutions to carry out research and development relevant to them. They were expected to see that jute was used not only to produce gunny bags, but other goods also. These steps helped them to some extent. But at present, Bangladesh sends its jute goods to India on a large scale in return for what it takes from India. I paid attention to these aspects. As my predecessor, Pranab Mukherjee, had paid a lot of attention to solve the difficulties of jute industries, it made my job easier. Jute is a bio-material and can be used on a large scale and in many other ways. It would be useful if attempts are made to discover its uses in newer fields for different purposes.

14

MINISTER OF STATE IN THE MINISTRY OF SCIENCE AND TECHNOLOGY, NUCLEAR SCIENCE AND TECHNOLOGY, SPACE, ELECTRONICS, OCEAN DEVELOPMENT, GENETIC, NON-CONVENTIONAL ENERGY

In India, there are more than 650 universities and 300 national laboratories where science and technology along with other subjects, are taught. The universities are also expected to do extension and research and development. However, because of the large number of students in science and technology institutions, colleges and universities, it has been impossible for them to perform extensive research and development, as is done in advanced countries. What the universities do in these two areas of activities leaves much to be desired.

In India, the national laboratories perform the task of research and development. The Council of Scientific and Industrial Research, the Indian Council of Medical Research, the Indian Council of Agricultural Research, the Defence Research and Development Organization and other such institutions have national laboratories which work under their supervision, guidance and direction. The Atomic Energy Commission, the Space Commission and the Electronics Commission have their own laboratories in which research and development is done. The science and technology ministry is responsible for making science and technology policies and helping the state governments and other institutions. The departments of atomic energy, space, electronics, ocean development, biotechnology and non-conventional sources of energy are responsible for making and implementing relevant policies.

In advanced countries, research and development is undertaken more by industry, the private sector and in universities than by governments and public sector units. In India, this could not be done by the universities because they have always been overcrowded, leaving no time or energy to the experts to carry on with their duties, which need a different kind of atmosphere. That was why national laboratories were established in large numbers, with the facilities and ambience conducive to research and development.

Pandit Jawaharlal Nehru understood the importance of science and technology for development and was responsible for developing the trend to establish national laboratories. He was also responsible for establishing departments to develop nuclear science and technology. The departments of space and electronics emanated from this department. Then, during the premiership of Indiraji, the departments of ocean development, biotechnology, non-conventional sources of energy, environment and forests were created.

Dr Homi J. Bhabha was a great scientist who was given the responsibility and powers to establish institutions for the development of nuclear science and technology and facilities to use modern science and technology for generating power for agriculture and for providing medical aid to the needy. The people heading these institutions and their colleagues were given considerable autonomy and power. It was not possible for non-scientists to make policies or decide what should be done in these areas. So, the commissions were given autonomy and powers on a scale given to no other institution.

There are some industries in India which pay attention to research and development (R&D). However, most of them are not strong enough to face the uncertainties involved in the odyssey of science and technology into the unknown world of knowledge. The development of technology is uncertain and expensive, while that of science is fraught with greater uncertainty but less expensive. The big multinational companies have the monetary capacity to combat this uncertainty. Weaker industries that do not have the advantage of strong monetary muscles do not venture into activities relevant to R&D. As a result, the government of India has been paying more attention to these activities and finding funds for them. The Union government aids universities and institutions to undertake R&D, and helps industry by providing concessions and tax rebates so that the funds saved are used for R&D. It expects industry and state governments to provide more funds for these purposes. However, so far, industry, universities and state governments have not created visible, tangible and adequate impacts and results. It has, therefore, been necessary for the Union government to provide funds and take steps to boost the R&D activities in India. Let us hope that as the Indian industry becomes stronger and spreads to other parts of the world, it will take greater interest in and spend more funds on R&D. Let us also hope that at the state level, a better appreciation of the importance of R&D develops with the passage of time; let us hope that they pay more attention to and spend more funds on these activities. Let us also hope that the Union government makes larger allocations of funds for R&D.

There are some areas that need funds, manpower and sophisticated equipment, but it is not always possible for all countries to have manpower and other wherewithal for this purpose. Fusion science and technology, biotechnology, nanotechnology, electronics, material sciences, medicine and health, ocean sciences and technologies, space science and technology, all require a great deal of funds, manpower and facilities. In these areas, the countries of the world can join hands and do what is needed to save time and energy and produce acceptable results. It is fortunate that some countries have come together for these purposes. If the United

Nations creates institutions for this purpose and uses them, it would be better. What the UN is doing is not enough and it needs to do much more than what it actually does.

R&D in India can be undertaken in three areas. One area relates to science and technology at the horizon; the second area relates to science and technology at the lowest level, relevant only to Indian conditions; and the third area relates to science and technology used in India and other countries at the middle level. India has done well in areas of advanced and relevant science and technology, but not in the areas at the middle level, where it has always depended on other countries. However, the other countries did not give India their best, but their second or third best. And that did not help India to produce goods of the highest quality that could be sold at prices comparable to those in other countries. Therefore, it has become necessary for India to import technologies from other countries and improve on them to be able to march alongside other countries. If R&D is not done, India cannot compete with other countries. It is also necessary that India establish laboratories and industries which can produce new technologies and use these to build new machines, to help it perform at the same level as other countries. Unfortunately, it has not been possible to march forward in these directions. Indian industry and the government should invest handsome sums of money to achieve these objectives. Middle level technologies are used to produce goods and provide modern services to customers. If weaknesses persist in these areas, the country will not be able to come on par with other countries of the world. In modern times, capital, managerial skills and cooperation of the labour are required to produce quality goods in a cost-effective manner. However, that may not be enough without developing and using new technologies.

A one-time modernization effort may not suffice. The process of modernization has to be ceaseless, if we are to march with other countries and not lag behind. Let us hope that this is done and the desired results are achieved.

■

One of the issues discussed at all levels relates to the so-called brain drain to other countries. India has established a large number of educational and technological institutions which have helped it to cultivate rich human resources. However, bright technologists and scientists are going to advanced countries and earning and learning more than they could in their own country. In some countries, they have earned good reputation and money in abundance for themselves and the country. Because of this, they are not allowed to return to their motherland, even if they wish to. To retain them in the countries where they have migrated, they are given higher salaries and better prospects in their jobs, which makes them stick to their places of work. In India, there are some people who want their talents to be used for the development of their motherland, and stress that they should not, in the first instance, be allowed to go to other countries. Further, if they do go, they should be forced to return as public money has been spent on their education and training in India. However, the government and several others do not favour this approach and are not inclined to disallow bright youngsters from going abroad to benefit themselves and the country other. They say that in other countries they get opportunities to learn in the company of experts at workplaces and places of learning, which they may not be able to do in India. Moreover, they earn and help their relations in India, which reduces the burden on the government and society. The government says they are like fixed deposits kept in the bank, which can be used at any time, when the need arises.

This policy of the government is appreciated by the majority of people, including scientists and technologists in the country and by people in other countries with whom they have been working. In the modern world, this is a correct policy to adopt. The world should be treated as a family and citizens from different parts of the globe as members of one family. They should be allowed to live and work in any country. India proposes to continue with this policy for all time to come.

■

At one of the meetings I had with the prime minister, who held the portfolios of science and technology, the departments of nuclear science and technology, space, electronics, ocean development and non-conventional sources of energy and was the chairperson of Council of Scientific and Industrial Research (CSIR), she advised me to develop a photovoltaic system. The other national laboratories were with other ministries and institutions. Therefore, I studied the issue in great depth and decided that non-conventional sources of energy were to be developed to meet the demands of the people for power, on an increasing scale. Many steps were taken to achieve this objective. Adequate funds were also made available. However, there were some people who did not favour the idea of spending huge amounts of money on developing and using non-conventional sources of energy. On one pretext or the other, they kept creating hurdles and opposing proposals that were put forth for developing and using new methods and technologies for generating energy. Because of this, for some time, the non-conventional sources of energy could not be developed at the required speed. Now it seems the process is being expedited, which is desirable.

Wind, bio-gas and sunrays can be used to produce energy in a decentralized manner and without waiting for many years which is required to produce thermal, hydel and nuclear power units. The energy thus produced can be used for domestic purposes. It may not suffice to run big industries, but could be used to run small industries, pumps for domestic purposes, etc. Moreover, the energy saved by using non-conventional power for domestic purposes can become available for big industries.

The technologies available to produce non-conventional energy were not very sophisticated or advanced. They could be made more sophisticated by investing funds on a large scale. The photovoltaic energy could be used to run vehicles. In fact, in one of the laboratories in Delhi, technologists had produced a three-wheeler which could be run on this energy. They placed a panel of solar cells on top of the vehicle and a battery under the seat, which were used to power the vehicle. The vehicle could be put under sunlight and the batteries charged, even when the vehicle was standing idle. The energy was stored in the battery and could be used even at night. In fact, the silicon cells used to generate solar energy were expensive, but their price could be reduced by enhancing their efficiency and producing them on a large scale. It was for this purpose that it was proposed that a factory be set up, but as some people objected to the proposal, the project had to be given up.

The department of non-conventional sources of energy produced streetlights that could be run on the photovoltaic system. In some industries, factories and villages, these photovoltaic streetlight systems are being used, but it is necessary to ensure that the system is used widely and on a larger scale to reduce the cost of production of the equipment. The cost of pulling electric wires from the place where electricity is generated to the place where it is used is enormous. The cost of maintaining the system supplying energy over wide areas is also huge. Non-conventional sources of energy can reduce the cost of supplying energy and maintaining the system. If this aspect is taken into account while assessing the cost of non-conventional energy production and supply, its use appears to be quite inviting. The non-conventional sources of energy are perennial and inexhaustible. Other sources of energy, like coal and oil, are not perennial and are bound to be exhausted, sooner than later. Therefore, it is wise to use the funds, time and talent available now to develop and make systems of non-conventional energy production more sophisticated and less expensive by using economies of scale. The demand for energy for domestic purposes and transport systems can be easily met by using non-conventional sources on a large scale.

■

Nuclear energy can meet the demands of the modern age on an even larger scale. Fortunately, fusion technology has been tried to be developed and used in many parts of the world to produce energy. In some countries, 60–70 per cent of energy requirements are met by using nuclear technology. If fusion technology is developed and used to produce energy, it would be a big boon to humanity. The energy from the sun is generated through the route of fusion technology. If it becomes possible for us to produce energy using fusion technology, the problem of providing energy would be solved on a large scale. Non-conventional sources of energy can help to cope with the problems of energy requirements in the days to come. Keeping these aspects in mind, steps should be taken to develop technologies for these purposes.

■

The department of space prepared a plan and a timetable to develop launch vehicles and satellites, and achieved their objectives on time. Satellite Launch Vehicle-1 (SLV-1) could not be launched successfully. Satellite Launch Vehicle-2 (SLV-2) also failed. Satellite Launch Vehicle-3 (SLV-3) was launched successfully in the presence of Indiraji and N.T. Rama Rao at Shriharikota.

As minister of state for science and technology and its departments, which were with the prime minister, I was also invited to watch the launch of the satellite vehicle. When it entered orbit successfully, the people who were present at the launching pad congratulated Dr Dhawan, chairman of the space commission and the secretary of the department of space, profusely. However, Dr Dhawan was unwilling to receive their appreciation and thanks until he could see that it revolved around the globe without difficulty. Only after the vehicle completed the orbit was the success in launching it celebrated in an appropriate manner. N.T. Rama Rao was profusely complimentary in his speech. Indiraji was very warm while appreciating the work done by the scientists, technologists and others.

Dr A.P.J. Abdul Kalam, who became the president of India later, was the scientist who led the team responsible for the satellite launch vehicle. I was told that when it first failed to complete orbit, he offered to resign and hand over the task to another scientist. When he handed over his resignation letter to Dr Dhawan, he was told that not he but Dhawan, as the head of the space department, should resign if a resignation was required. When this was brought to the prime minister's notice, I am told that she responded by saying that if anyone was required to resign, it was she and not anyone else because she was the prime minister. She told the scientists that they should continue to develop the vehicle and technologies and should not be dejected if one or two or more attempts failed even when they did their best. What they were doing was an odyssey into the unknown and they were performing their task with limited assistance of scientists from other countries. The stand taken by the prime minister was very encouraging. The scientists put in their best efforts and succeeded in achieving their objective.

INSAT-1A failed to launch, but INSAT-1B and INSAT-1C were launched successfully. However, INSAT-1C encountered some initial difficulties. It was put into the fixed orbit, but the solar panels did not spread out and face the sun. They were stuck inside the body of the INSAT-1C. We were all worried. I telephoned Dr Dhawan to find out if the difficulties could be overcome. He informed me that they were trying to expose the satellite to the sun, to see if its frame could be heated and expanded, so that the panels stuck inside could come out of the frame. I put the telephone down, feeling sad. I remembered a mahatma, a saint whom we called Dev and whom I used to visit for his blessings and guidance. As soon as I thought of him and concluded my prayer, I received a call from Dr Dhawan, informing me that the technique they had used to get the panels out of the frame had succeeded and that the satellite had begun to function and operate according to the design. I was so happy and surprised. The coincidence made me think that science and spirituality could make any project successful.

The satellite was built to perform three tasks. One was to provide wireless telephony; the second was to transmit programmes from relay stations to television sets; and the third was to relay the administration's warnings of disaster to people in areas likely to be affected. In other countries, different satellites were launched to perform these tasks, but India preferred to have one satellite which performed multiple tasks.

The people of India were pleased that the satellites were launched successfully. However, there were a few people in and outside Parliament, who criticized the government for launching the satellites. Their complaint was that the satellites were toys launched into space, useless and expensive. They charged that more than ₹1,000 crore was spent on the project and that spending that amount of money was criminal when the same amount could have been used to provide drinking water to people living in rural areas. In fact, I was informed that only ₹60 crore was spent and that the satellites were insured with a foreign company to ensure that the financial burden was reduced if the satellite failed. These facts were explained to the MPs, not once, but several times. However, similar complaints were raised repeatedly for nearly one year. It is because of satellites that it has now become possible to have wireless communication and telephony across the country, to educate the young and the old through television, and adopt distance learning systems. Today, no one complains that the satellites are useless expensive toys.

Whenever new ventures are launched, they are opposed by some people. This is due to ignorance or a negative attitude towards life. When Pandit Jawaharlal Nehru tried to establish national laboratories, some people opposed it on the grounds that the money could be better utilized to help the poor. The argument was not different from the one used to oppose the launching of the satellites. When the Bhakra Nangal dam was being built, several people opposed its construction. After it was built, detractors told farmers not to use the canal water from the dam, because electricity was extracted from it, the water was ineffective and unable to support crops. If such attitudes can be avoided, projects could be used more fruitfully to achieve far-reaching objectives.

■

When Rajiv Gandhi became prime minister, he retained all the science and technology departments held by Indiraji, and I was asked to continue to function as the minister of state of all the departments, as I was asked to do previously. When I, along with some scientists, called on him for the first time after he took office, he asked the space scientists if it could be possible for India to land a man on the moon. The scientists were enthusiastic and said that it could be done, if the prime minister decided to do so and if funds were made available. The scientists were told to go ahead. Now, it is possible for India to reach the moon through its satellite. The dream visualized by Rajiv Gandhi in 1984 could become a reality in 2008. This is how we have to prepare ourselves to march with other countries and approach the future. The country is preparing to live in the twenty-first century. We have been fortunate to have leaders who have prepared us to face our future with fortitude, imagination, courage and a bold new vision.

■

Electronics is responsible for the third industrial revolution in the world and dominates all aspects of life. A country that does not prepare itself to use it fully in all activities is likely to be left behind. India cannot afford to miss this march towards advancement and development. Rajiv Gandhi was very keen to develop electronics, science, technology and industry. He knew that the Indian mind, which is capable of dealing with all subtleties of life, could cope with the challenges posed by electronics. Therefore, he came out very boldly in favour of electronics and supported its all-round development wholeheartedly. He met electronic scientists, technologists, industrialists, traders and users and told them to do everything necessary to develop it fully. The result of this policy was that it was given the attention and importance it needed in educational institutions. With the availability of manpower, it was possible to produce the necessary software and hardware relevant to electronics. The producers and traders of electronic goods knew what was happening in other countries and were inclined to do the same in India. They believed that India should understand its utility and importance and shed its misgivings about electronic goods.

Rajiv Gandhi was keen to give electronics a major boost. His plan included free import of electronic goods into India. He thought that once people understood their utility, their demand would rise and the need to produce them within the country would increase. In the early phase, the components could be imported to assemble the electronic goods. Later, the components could be manufactured within the country. To compete with other countries, new technologies could be invented and used. Thus, the goal could be achieved in stages: starting with import of goods, then import of components, to manufacturing of components and finally, to developing technologies and manufacturing goods that could compete with those produced in other countries. The private sector could be given full freedom and authority to follow this route. The public sector could help to fill the gaps left out by the private sector. There could be no difficulty in collaborating with companies in other countries to achieve these objectives. The government could give them tax concessions and other kinds of relief and succour. Once the people understood its importance fully, it could help in producing employment, foreign trade, earning and saving foreign exchange, enhancing the capabilities of other industries and making India competitive in several of its activities. This policy was followed and gave good dividends. India joined the group of advanced countries in this field. Today, some Indian technologists in the electronic field are in great demand by renowned companies across the world, and several countries take India's assistance for developing software. However, in the area of hardware, India has to improve its performance. In software, it has done well, but it should not rest on its laurels and should continue to improve with every passing year.

There were some people who did not agree with this policy, saying that electronics was bound to reduce employment, which was not good for a country with millions searching for jobs. This argument was supported by some leaders. It was very difficult to convince them that new technologies and scientific knowledge did not reduce, but, in fact, increase employment potential. They heaped ridicule and used abusive language against the leader and protagonists of this policy. Fortunately, they did not succumb to the pressure. And today, we can see the results of the policy with our own eyes.

India is endowed with a huge population. Human beings do not only have bellies which need to be filled with food, but have limbs with which they can work and brains with which they can produce new knowledge, science and technology to produce commodities, goods, services and other vital requirements of modern time and life. By providing them with employment and helping them with new systems, they can learn to help themselves and others. This had to be explained to the people, with perseverance and determination. At public meetings, at meetings with workers and leaders and in private conversations, supporters of the policy explained how new machines and electronic goods could help to produce real wealth and employment. These points were explained to them in their own language and by giving examples which they could understand easily.

The people were told that if their lands were irrigated, not one, not two, but three crops could be produced in a year. But this could only be done if their lands were ploughed and prepared for sowing and harvesting with the help of tractors and other machines. If these operations were performed with bullocks, the lands could not be made ready for sowing and harvesting in time and it would be difficult to grow three crops in a year.

They were told that to prepare plans for building irrigation dams, designs and plans were required and they could be made with the help of computers and such other equipment in much shorter time. If the dams could be built in one year, instead of four or five years, the lands in the command areas could be irrigated for three additional years, thus producing more employment in agriculture and generating increased employment potential.

They were also explained that if one part of a power plant did not function well and if it was not possible to identify the defective part without examining the entire machine, it could take a long time to repair it. If the examination was done with the help of electronic gadgets, it could instantaneously point out the defect. The time taken to repair the plant without using electronic gadgets could be very long and could result in shutting down the power plant for several months, affecting the industries run on the power supplied by the plant. This showed that it was useful not to waste time and to repair the plant as quickly as possible. This would help in retaining workers without discontinuing their services in several industries. These explanations helped in removing some of their apprehensions, but it took time to convince them. More than words, what actually occurred and what they saw and experienced helped to put their doubts and fears to rest.

•

Indiraji was anxious that the environment was not polluted and damaged. So she created a separate ministry to implement measures to avoid this. She retained the environment ministry with herself. She used to say that if a blade of grass was disturbed, the entire universe would be disturbed. In her opinion, new science and technology should be used to protect the land, oceans and space, so they should be used very carefully. If natural resources, which take thousands of years to develop, are over-exploited, the environment can be damaged which is harmful to human beings.

First, she created the department of ocean development. She was keen to have a separate set-up to protect and use the resources of the oceans. India has an economic zone which is equal to two-thirds of its land mass. The oceans are rich in natural resources. On the ocean bed, material which can be used as food by human beings and can provide ores, chemicals and other essentials are found. Beneath the ocean bed, oil and other such resources are also available. The water in oceans contains many valuable things which can be used to develop the global economy. Oceans store energy and contain metals like uranium, gold and titanium. It is believed that oceans are storehouses of wealth—in fact, life originated and was born in water. All these scientific facts were clearly understood by the then prime minister of India, who believed in taking steps that could help future generations. She was, therefore, keen to have a department to study various aspects, prepare plans and formulate policies, in order to use the wealth of the oceans. In the economic zone, the country enjoys economic sovereignty. In the open sea, in specific areas, the resources may be used with the UN's sanction.

I was told that the officers who were asked to prepare the papers to be put up to the cabinet, proposing to create a separate department for using ocean resources, failed to prepare the cabinet paper within the stipulated time frame. The prime minister asked why the paper was not ready and gave a fresh date by which it was to be prepared. When, on the next date, the paper was still not ready, she asked if it would be prepared and submitted after she was gone. That was too strong a message to be neglected. So the paper was put up, the cabinet approved the proposal and the new department of ocean development came into existence. These facts go to show how keen she was to have a separate department, how she looked at the issue of using ocean resources for the country and the world, and how far-sighted her vision was.

The department of ocean development was asked to send an expedition to Antarctica, the southernmost tip of the globe, where other countries had established their permanent stations. Expeditions of scientists and technologists from different parts of India were sent. Later, a permanent station was built by India on Antarctica called 'Dakshin Gangotri'. Indian scientists and technologists have been living for several months there, carrying out their experiments and studying the environment in the area. India has collaborated with other countries also for this purpose.

On the ocean bed, there are polymetallic nodules that can be used to produce ores and metals. Since India experimented with them on a large scale, the UN gave India the status of a pioneering country in this field. As a result, there are certain areas of the ocean where India can continue experimenting without obtaining prior permission from international organizations.

The enthusiasm with which R&D was carried out in the ocean in the 1980s was quite impressive. The same kind of enthusiasm appears to be lacking in present times. India should not lag behind in this field. Land constitutes one-third of the globe, while oceans occupy two-thirds of the globe. The oceans are virgin and their resources are unutilized. It is wrong not to prepare the country to use them. Human beings are in a position to use land, the oceans and space—but they should not exploit them; they should use them wisely without affecting the environment. The countries of the world should be able to do this on their own, separately or jointly or in a cooperative manner, without conflict.

■

Now, the time has come for attempts being made to reach the planets in the sky. Vehicles have taken satellites to other planets and human beings have landed on the moon. These efforts will continue. India is also doing its best in this respect. An Indian satellite has reached the moon, and perhaps Indians will be able to land on its surface in the near future. India should definitely try to do its best to develop space science and technology and reach other planets.

One scientist told me that in the future, human beings can obtain ores and metals from other planets. Once a vehicle is thrust out of the earth's gravitational field, it can keep moving in the direction of any planet, without using any kind of fuel, because of the principle of inertia applied to all things in the cosmos. A moving object can keep moving until it meets resistance by a force and is stopped. Thus, a vehicle needs force to get out of the gravitational field, which spreads over 200 kilometres around the earth. Beyond that it can move easily and without force to reach its destination. If it is pushed from another planet in the direction of the earth, it can reach the earth because of inertia and the gravitation around the earth, without using any kind of fuel to generate power for the purpose. The only thing that needs to be done is to protect the vehicle against the heat generated by friction caused by the atmosphere around the earth and also to ensure that it can land safely. These wonders are in the realm of possibility. A heat-resistant material has been produced by some countries and devices that help the vehicle in landing also have been produced. These can be made more sophisticated. Thus, in the coming times, an inter-planetary transport system can become a reality and it would be possible for ordinary human beings to use it. In this area also, India can do its best on its own, as well as in cooperation and partnership with other countries. It has the manpower, talents and some wherewithal which is needed for the purpose. It should invest more and more as time passes, to remain on par with the other countries of the world.

■

Science and technology relating to matter is being developed on a large scale, which is as it should be. Science and technology—so relevant to life—is also being developed, but what is being done in this field, though laudable, is not sufficient. More funds and attention should be paid to this area and for this activity. Biotechnology has begun to attract the attention of human beings across the world. Genetic technology is also being developed. It is thought that it will be treated as the most important area of science and technology. In the womb of nature, on earth and perhaps on other planets also, life comes into existence, continues and disappears in cycles. India is alive to this reality and is trying to pay sufficient attention to it. Indiraji wanted a separate department for genetic technology to be established. Eventually, it was created during the premiership of Rajiv Gandhi. The department is in the process of strengthening itself. Let us hope that it develops to produce the results expected of it.

India has genetic and biological wealth. However, it does not have the requisite technology and knowledge to use it fully. It is said that in the world, there are countries that do not have the genetic and bio-wealth, but have the required technology. On the other hand, there are countries, which are less developed and less exploited to meet the demands of modern times, that have an abundance of genetic and bio-wealth, but lack technology of a high order. It is, therefore, necessary to ensure that the countries of the world join hands to use genetic and bio-wealth by pooling their powers and strengths.

The UN wanted to establish an institution to study, use and develop genetic wealth, science and technology. Pakistan, India, Cuba, Italy and Thailand were the countries that claimed to have the facilities and wherewithal required for the purpose. The UN decided to split the institution into two parts between India and Italy. The part relevant to agriculture and medicine is with India and the part relevant to industry is with Italy. These institutions are going to be helpful, but more of them are needed. They should be set up in the public and private sectors and also in partnership with the two. The twenty-first century will be dominated by discoveries in biotechnology, genetics and nanotechnology. No stone should be left unturned in India to achieve the objective of marching forward in these fields, along with other countries.

■

Often, some politicians, industrialists and academicians say that wars may be fought in the future between countries on sharing potable water and that as fossil sources for energy are limited, there is a point beyond which energy cannot be generated and made available for the unlimited economic advancement of the world. In my opinion, these statements do not take into account the ground reality. Two-thirds of our earth is covered by oceans and one-third by land. The ocean water may not be potable, but the heat of the sun turns it into vapour and clouds, which later changes into potable water. And this cycle is continuous. This means that it is possible to convert ocean water into potable, useful water to meet the demands of all plants, animals and human beings. Technologies and sciences have been developed to achieve these objectives. They can be made more sophisticated, easily usable and cost-effective. What is needed is the desire to do this, plans, funds and machinery. It is not beyond the reach of the present generation of human beings to use these sciences and technologies, as well as to make them more efficient and sophisticated.

We know that matter is energy and energy is matter, that matter can be changed into energy and energy can be changed into matter. In the ultimate analysis, existence is part of the cosmic energy. If that is so, why should we think that we cannot generate and have enough energy? It should be clear to us that we can generate any amount of energy we need. What is required is knowledge and technology—and they are also available. They only need to be made more efficient and sophisticated, which can also be done. Therefore, we should not adopt a pessimistic and negative approach and come to the conclusion that there will be a dearth of energy, meaning that development cannot be achieved beyond a point. To think in this negative manner is to ignore the reality—and this should not be permitted.

Beyond matter and energy, there is the realm of ideas and beyond the realm of ideas, there is the realm of spirituality, which is not fully understood and perceived. It is necessary to develop our capabilities in the realms of ideas and spirituality. Once, Dr Dhawan, while briefing MPs at a consultative meeting attended by

Indiraji, said that there is nothing bigger than space. But, in the same breath, he said, 'Probably man's mind is.'

When we think of matter, energy, space, time, ideas and spirituality, we will come closer to reality. Science and technology that deal with matter, energy, space and time are important, but science and technology that deal with ideas and spirituality are probably more significant in the long run. If the first is science and technology, the second is super science and technology. The two together are the reality. Our endeavours should be to adopt a holistic approach, as a partial approach will only give partial success.

Indiraji's approach was closer to the holistic approach. It made working in the ministries and the government headed by her enjoyable and rewarding, and I had the great fortune of working in them for nearly three and a half of the last years of her life. This left an indelible mark on my thinking and approach. While working with her in the ministries and government, I followed the philosophy and policies highlighted in what I have discussed earlier. That is a treasure I value the most.

She gave me full liberty to take decisions and actions. She was always very well informed about what was happening in the country. At times, I approached her for guidance in some complicated matters and she always gave it to me without my explaining to her my problem. At times, I felt that she was able to read the minds of the persons who worked with her. That ability gave her the skill to govern the country as she did. She could do this because she devoted her time, energy and thoughts to administration, public relations and matters of public interest. She treated me like a family member. I felt she had a motherly affection and consideration for me. I tried to keep a very respectable distance from her and spoke to her only when absolutely necessary to perform my duties. She encouraged me to behave without any kind of pressure on my mind.

With her death, I felt that I had lost my mother the third time: once, when I lost the mother who gave birth to me, the second time when I lost my grandmother and the third time when

Indiraji passed away. India is not going to see the likes of her in the near future.

■

The work required in these departments and the ministry, did not burden me with details. The commissions and departments dealt with them. The ministers and the government were expected to lay down the broad outlines of policies and plans. India has the natural resources and if it develops new knowledge, sciences and technologies, a holistic approach, and a vision for the present and the future, for our planet and for other planets as well as the universe on the basis of cosmic realities, what will be done in our country will be of a lasting character, useful to us and to others in the entire world. We should aim at achieving these objectives and not be afraid of thinking big and in a holistic manner. This is what I tried to do, to the best of my abilities in these and other areas of my responsibilities.

15

MINISTER OF STATE IN THE DEFENCE MINISTRY FOR DEFENCE PRODUCTION AND SUPPLIES

V.P. Singh was shifted from the finance ministry to the defence ministry. Arun Singh was then the minister of state in the defence ministry, looking after matters relating to military personnel and other important issues. Both of them were close to the prime minister, Rajiv Gandhi. I was also shifted to the defence ministry as a minister of state, and asked to look after defence production and supplies. Later, Santosh Mohan Dev was inducted in the same ministry as a minister of state.

In that period, two issues were discussed in Parliament, within the political circles of the opposition parties and in the media. The government had entered into a contract with the Bofors Company of Sweden to acquire howitzer 155-mm guns for the army. A charge was levelled that the gun was useless and that a huge amount of money was given as a commission by the Bofors Company to get the contract signed in its favour. The second issue was related to German submarines, where the government had entered into a contract with a German company to buy four submarines, and to assemble another four in India with the components supplied by the German company. In this case also, an allegation was levelled that the German company had given a hefty commission to win the contract. V.P. Singh, the defence minister, put this issue on the floor of the Lok Sabha on his own initiative. Later, he tendered his resignation and separated from the Congress party. The Bofors gun issue was highlighted on Swedish radio, and the submarine issue was also raised in Germany. These two issues were taken up by the media in India on an unprecedented scale, and the government was criticized incessantly for many months. In fact, matters were kept alive for several years. At that time, the elections were drawing near, and the opposition parties thought that they could take advantage of these issues to lower the prestige and strength of the ruling Congress party, and boost their chances of getting more seats in the Lok Sabha and other legislatures. The issues were taken up in both Houses of Parliament.

The members of the opposition parties wanted the matter related to the Bofors guns to be inquired into by a joint parliamentary committee. The government was ready to have it examined by a judge of the Supreme Court and act upon the report given by him. The opposition parties insisted on having the joint parliamentary committee, and the government agreed to the proposal. The opposition parties then changed their strategy and demanded that the chairman of the committee should be a member of an opposition party. According to the rules of procedure, the chairman of such a committee had to belong to the ruling party. On behalf of the government, it was argued that if a member of the ruling party could not be relied upon to give a correct report, it would be difficult to rely on a member of the opposition to give an unbiased view. So the government did not concede to this demand. It appointed a committee and B. Shankaranand was made its chairman. B. Shankaranand was a serving minister, and so he resigned from his post to chair the committee. After going through the evidence produced before it, the committee gave a report which absolved the government of the charge of doing anything illegal and unethical in giving the contract to Bofors' company. The members of the opposition parties who attended the proceedings of the committee added dissenting notes to the report. Many of the opposition party members who had asked for the constitution of the committee did not attend the proceedings of the committee.

The matter was taken to court. The court, too, gave a judgement which did not support the allegations. It was also considered in one of the courts in Malaysia, which again, did not give a verdict in favour of the complainant. It was then considered in a court in Algeria. It also did not rule in favour of the complainant. All the same, for political reasons, the matter was discussed in public meetings and in the media by the opposition parties and kept alive, in spite of the fact that the courts in three different countries had given judgements that did not support the allegations.

Some politicians alleged that the Bofors gun was useless and had no firing capability. They tried to incite people against it by saying that the farmers' sons who were in the defence forces faced danger to their lives because of the gun. Some MPs, who were retired high-ranking officers in the armed forces and other knowledgeable people, were asked to examine the gun and observe the test firing in the field. On doing so, they came to the conclusion that the gun was of very high quality and one of the most effective weapons in mountainous terrains. They said so, openly, in Parliament and outside. The criticism on this ground was reduced to some extent after the MPs stated their views about the quality of the gun. However, some members continued to express their opinions against it, with the intention of maligning the government.

In the Lok Sabha and in the Rajya Sabha, marathon debates took place on this issue. K.C. Pant, who was appointed the defence minister after V.P. Singh tendered his resignation, replied to the debate in the Lok Sabha and I replied to the same in the Rajya Sabha. My reply was quite lengthy. I explained the nature of the contract, India's advantage in entering into it, the quality of the gun and the rules and procedures that could and should be followed in such matters.

The contract provided that Bofors would give the technologies to produce the guns and ammunition to India, free of cost, along with the guns. India could use these technologies to produce the guns and ammunition, and Sweden could buy them from India. It would buy the same number of guns as India had purchased from it. In case India failed to produce the guns, Sweden would buy other goods from India, using half of the total cost of the guns sold by Sweden. It was also agreed that India and Sweden could sell the guns to other countries in partnership. That was the contract and the kind of buy-back arrangement provided.

I repeated these points several times. But, unfortunately, none of these points were mentioned in clear terms by the media. When the buy-back arrangement and the transfer of technology, free of cost, were explained to the people, some of them asked why this was not brought to the notice of the people. This goes to show that the allegations were made with the intention of putting the government in the wrong box. It is also suspected that the intention of raising the issue with such intensity was to ensure that the defence preparedness of the country remained weak. Later, when the Kargil war was fought, the Bofors guns were used in the mountains. If they were not there, the tally of the lives of Indian soldiers lost in the war could have been much higher, and the war could not have been won in the short time it was. If the guns were useless, they would not have produced such good results.

Unfortunately, most important political people took the wrong stand and made the lives of members of the government and officers most miserable. In doing so, they satisfied their ill will and ego and played into the hands, directly or indirectly, of those people who wanted to keep the defence preparedness of India at a low level. India had to get the ammunition for the guns from Sweden. It also had to get the technology, free of cost, to manufacture the ammunition. But because the contract was nullified by the government that came into power after the general elections to the Lok Sabha were held, the ammunition was not available when the Kargil war began, and so, for some time, the soldiers had to suffer. The ammunition for the guns bought for the Kargil war cost a lot, causing a great loss to the coffers of the Union government. If decisions in such matters are taken keeping in mind the whims and fancies of the decision-makers, the country, at crucial moments, is likely to suffer setbacks and losses. Therefore, it is most important that such decisions are taken only with a view to help the country. Those who are in power should face the situation correctly and boldly, without caring for their own prestige or reputation, in order to see that the interest and sovereignty of the country is fully protected and preserved. However, it is not possible for us to imagine the agony they might have suffered silently and without complaining. In fact, they also sacrificed their prestige and reputation in order to ensure that the country did not remain weak and was capable of facing any eventuality with strength and confidence.

■

The army wanted armoured vehicles and tanks. They were imported from the then Soviet Union, along with the technologies with which they were produced. With the technologies thus acquired, factories were established to make armoured vehicles and tanks in the Medak district of Andhra Pradesh on sites selected in consultation with the government of Andhra Pradesh. Indiraji laid the foundation stones for the factories.

■

India wanted to develop a design of its own to manufacture tanks for the army. The prototype was called Arjun—it took a long time to produce the design and build a prototype. This caused some difficulties. Every year, new gadgets were added to the tanks manufactured by other countries, making them superior to the old tanks, and the Indian army wanted to procure systems and weapons that were as good as those available to their opponents. In this dilemma, it was not easy to make them and have the army accept them with enthusiasm and readiness. It appears that the Arjun tank is now going to be added to the army's fleet of tanks.

■

In the defence dockyards, ships, frigates and submarines and sundry equipment needed by other ministries, like oil rigs, were manufactured. The Mazagaon dockyard was better equipped and stronger than the other dockyards, to meet the demands of the navy. In the Mazagaon dockyard, submarines were being assembled. However, because of the allegations raised by some people, only two submarines could be made and the contract to make more was cancelled. In this case also, it became very obvious that because of the dispute, the plan to strengthen the navy could not be completed and the navy remained weak while the project was incomplete. Building ships, frigates and aircraft-carriers takes many years. The plan to build and strengthen the navy needs a long-term approach and a clear vision. It is, therefore, necessary to pay adequate attention to it.

■

The Indian air force has aircraft in its fleet that were acquired from the then Soviet Union, the UK and France. They are assembled in India at Hindustan Aeronautics Ltd. The technologies to make them are procured from the countries of their origin.

India had taken up projects to build helicopters and light combat aircraft. Indian engineers and experts worked on them for several years and have now succeeded in producing the designs. Helicopters and light combat aircraft are presently being manufactured in the country.

It has not been possible for India to establish an industry that can manufacture aircraft needed by the defence forces or for civilian purposes. For a country like India which is very vast, aircraft are needed to cover long distances to transport passengers and goods. The developed countries of the world have established aircraft industries to meet their demands. It is, therefore, wrong to hold that travel and transport by air is a luxury and need not be resorted to for years to come. Air travel saves time, helps to cope with emergencies, enhances the efficiency of the administration and helps in the dispersal of industries and goods to all parts of the country, thus reducing disparities between the states in industrial and economic development. Therefore, in India, aircraft industries should be started in the private and public sectors or on a partnership basis between private and public sectors and foreign entrepreneurs. The sooner we succeed in doing this, the better it would be for the country. Unfortunately, signs of such progress are not visible on the horizon.

■

The ordnance factories produce arms and ammunition and other equipment for the defence forces. They are controlled and managed through a board. Some of the factories were established in the distant past and have not been modernized with up-to-date technologies. It is necessary to take steps to upgrade their capabilities and bring them on par with other factories in the country. Some factories produce the same goods and equipment as those produced by factories run by private entrepreneurs. The goods produced by the private factories are more cost-effective and sophisticated. There are two routes available to deal with these issues. The government ordnance factories can be modernized and allowed to produce and sell their goods in the market, or they can be closed down and the goods be procured by the private sector. Defence forces need vehicles—big, medium and small. Produced by some private companies and of reasonably good quality, they can be procured from them. It is good that the defence forces are allowed to get them from private factories to meet some of their demands. Some government ordnance factories produce goods and equipment needed by the defence forces, so instead of closing them down, the factories can be relied upon and used in a judicious manner. The defence forces and the defence ministry can take appropriate decisions in this respect, taking into consideration the conditions that prevail in the present and will prevail in the future.

■

The public sector undertakings with the defence ministry generally produce goods and equipment requiring advanced technologies. Most of them manufacture electronic goods and equipment; they face very tough competition from other countries. They need to be managed professionally and to keep modernizing themselves to march with time and other countries. Let us hope that this is done without a break.

The workload in the department of defence production was not very heavy. The defence minister, K.C. Pant, was a seasoned politician. It was a pleasure to work with him for he was always friendly, cooperative and inspiring.

■

The capability of a country to defend itself depends greatly on its armed forces. The capability of the defence forces depends on the economic strength, social harmony, modernizing skills and appropriate attitudes towards things scientific, technological, managerial and spiritual of the people of the country.

I was told that V.K. Krishna Menon, the defence minister of independent India, was responsible to a very great extent for building the defence production capabilities of the country. He worked hard to ensure that new enterprises were established for the purpose. As these enterprises take time to start production and also need continuous modernization. So they need to be set up with proper plans and designs and an ethos which can make them march ahead with others on equal terms. There is great scope for bringing about an improvement in this respect in the defence production units of the country.

■

Shankarrao Chavan was the chief minister of Maharashtra when it was decided that he should be inducted into the Union cabinet as the finance minister and Sharad Pawar should be sent to the state as the new chief minister. In 1988 I was asked to take charge of the ministry of civil aviation and tourism as a minister of state with independent charge, after relinquishing the post of the minister of state for defence production. Thus, I got the opportunity of working in a new ministry, which delighted me.

16

UNION MINISTER OF STATE FOR CIVIL AVIATION WITH INDEPENDENT CHARGE

When India became independent, civil aviation in India was not very strong. It was started by some private companies on a very small scale. Pandit Jawaharlal Nehru wanted it to be developed on a larger scale, knowing that India, which is a vast country, needed speedy means of transport that could be provided through aviation activities. He asked the private company owners to strengthen their activities in proportion to the needs of the country. However, the company owners were unwilling to invest in aviation activities, for they were not profitable at that time. So, he decided to nationalize the companies and asked J.R.D. Tata, who had a passion for aviation, to preside over, strengthen and bring them on par with other countries. The government decided to invest more funds in strengthening the Indian aviation, and to fly within and outside the country. The eight existing aviation companies were the first companies to be nationalized by the government after the country became independent. The intention was to strengthen the civil aviation sector.

J.R.D. Tata was a perfectionist. He ensured that Air India, which was expected to fly to different countries, provided facilities that were as good as the facilities provided by other countries. Indian Airlines, for domestic purposes, would connect the mega cities in the country. The standard fixed for it was also very high. In short, whatever was required to strengthen the civil aviation activities was done. For many years, while J.R.D. Tata was the chairman of these companies, aviation in India maintained very high standards. After he left, the standards slowly declined, because those who managed the companies did not have the vision and zeal of the first chairman. Their approach was bureaucratic and mechanical, not visionary and inspiring. It was not the non-availability of funds which caused the decline, but the absence of zeal and vision that was responsible for the downward trend.

This trend continued till Rajiv Gandhi became the prime minister of India and took a special interest in developing civil aviation in the country. He was a pilot and loved flying. He knew what was needed to make it up-to-date and efficient. His vision was wide and far-sighted. He wanted to prepare civil aviation for the next century, which was at the doorstep. He identified the deficiencies, discovered the solutions and took decisions to implement them.

The first deficiency was related to an inadequate number of aircraft, so he took the decision to acquire them. The A-320, one of the most advanced aircrafts produced in the world, was selected for this purpose. However, this decision was wrongly criticized and opposed.

The second deficiency was related to the small number of airports. The International Airports Authority of India was doing well, but it was not possible for it to build and maintain a large number of airports in different parts of the country. So, he decided to establish the National Airports Authority (NAA) to construct new airports at different places. During the Second World War, some airports were constructed, but they were not properly maintained and became unusable.

Former royal rulers of the princely states had built airports in their states, but these were not properly maintained and were no longer usable. It was, therefore, decided that at the district levels and other important places, new airports should be built. The NAA was created for this purpose. But it lacked funds. After

Rajiv Gandhi left the national scene, the NAA was closed down and the International Airport Authority was asked to perform the same duties. However, that could not be done.

In India, civil aviation was developing, but it lacked pilots. As there were no training facilities to produce the requisite number of pilots, the Indira Gandhi Udhan Academy was established. During the premiership of Rajiv Gandhi, the academy was developed and allowed to function efficiently. However, later, the academy could not produce the results it was expected to because it did not get the requisite assistance. Some steps are being taken to help it with the assistance of foreign companies and institutions, which function in India in the same manner as they do in their own countries. The number of aircraft needed in the days to come is expected to increase by leaps and bounds and so the lack of pilots is bound to be felt. It is, therefore, wise to take up the task seriously and provide proper facilities to train enough pilots every year. Let us see if it becomes possible in the years to come. The civil aviation is denationalized and operated by private companies; the private operators should cooperate in strengthening these institutions and establishing new ones. Only then the adequate number of pilots would become available. The Union and state governments should spend funds and provide assistance for this purpose.

∎

The Oil and Natural Gas Commission (ONGC) officers and workers reached its rigs in the sea with the help of helicopters. However, the supply of helicopter service was inadequate. Therefore, Rajiv Gandhi decided to create a public sector company to operate helicopters. It was called Pawan Hans. It acquired several new helicopters and did well. It did its duties in a manner which was liked by the users. It was admired by some, and criticized by some others. Pawan Hans could have done much better. However, it was not encouraged to fly freely, and although it still exists, it needs to be strengthened. Private companies can come into existence and compete with one another, as well as with public enterprises. But they should not obstruct activities of public sector companies. At times, one gets a feeling that the relations between public-private companies in some areas are heading in the wrong direction.

■

Rajiv Gandhi knew that the states in the northeastern region were surrounded by forests and hilly terrain, and did not have railways and roads in sufficient numbers for transporting goods and passengers. Therefore, it was decided to start a public sector unit to fly small aircraft to help sick people reach places where medical facilities can be provided, or to help citizens affected by natural or man-made disasters. The unit was called Vayudoot. It was created mainly to help the people in the northeastern region. But the demand for its services increased and it had to fly to places in other states too. It expanded its activities by nearly 30 per cent every year and did very well. It is true that, initially, it could not earn profit. But it provided facilities to people living in far-flung areas of the country, which were difficult to reach by other means of transport. The unit should have been allowed to operate and function, but unfortunately, it was closed down. Closing the unit because it was not earning good profit was a wrong political decision, which did not help to create a feeling of oneness in the minds of the people living in these difficult areas. In fact, it was thought that flying to all the districts in the country would help to provide better governance and medical facilities to the people. It would help disperse industries in the backward areas in order to use the available natural resources in the best possible manner and to bring about equitable development in all parts of the country, so that backward areas were able to develop on par with advanced areas and rural areas on par with urban areas. Steps were being taken for this purpose, but before a final decision could be taken, the elections to the Lok Sabha were announced. After the elections, a new government came to power, which did not pay attention to the civil aviation activities, and hence, effective steps in that direction could not be taken. And the unit lost its existence.

■

Rajiv Gandhi laid the foundation for the development of civil aviation on very firm ground. If the edifice of aviation had been built on that foundation, Indian aviation could have competed with any other country's civil aviation activities. However, two factors appeared to obstruct these plans and efforts. One was that those who came to power after the Lok Sabha elections appeared to prefer demolishing everything that was built by Rajiv Gandhi. The second was that the new government was of a view that civil aviation was a luxury not needed in the country and therefore, it was considered wise to restrict its development. It was not realized or perceived that it could help the country and the people in many ways, not the least being that it could help to establish industries in backward, undeveloped areas and assist the unemployed, the poor and the needy.

These attitudes became very obvious when the entire fleet of A-320s was grounded after one A-320 met with an accident at Bangalore for more than one year, incurring a loss of about ₹1 crore every day. The entire fleet is usually grounded only when a design fault in the aircraft is detected. The accident at Bangalore did not disclose that a design defect was responsible for the accident. Yet, the government of the time took that disastrous decision, which pushed Indian Airlines into the red, causing loss of about a thousand crore of rupees. Nobody was asked to account for that decision, nobody was blamed for that decision, but people knew that the decision was wrong and uncalled-for. If any decision can be treated as a politically motivated one and not a decision in the interest of the country, it was the grounding of the A-320s. If that decision had not been taken, aviation activity in India would definitely have found itself in a better position today.

■

During my tenure in the civil aviation ministry, steps were taken to ensure that all the new plans and projects, started under the guidance of Rajiv Gandhi, were continued with the spirit and speed with which they were expected to be implemented. During that period, the Indian Airlines and the International Airports Authority of India earned profits. Air India did not do well, although the chairman of Air India did his best, but others who assisted him did not always see eye to eye with him. Some officers were interested in disposing of the profitable properties that Air India had acquired in countries like the US, UK, Australia and Singapore. But these acts caused losses to the unit. However, they escaped the net of responsibility in a very clever manner. Vayudoot did not earn profit. But it was handsomely welcomed by the people in difficult areas. Pawan Hans did well. The National Airports Authority could not get the help it needed. The Indira Gandhi Udhan Academy did better than in the past. In all, the civil aviation ministry made a net profit of nearly ₹300 crore in a year. It did not receive any budgetary help, though, the government helped it to take loans from financial institutions by providing a guarantee for repayment. The demand for aviation facilities was rising. Air India and Indian Airlines stretched themselves to the maximum to meet the rising demands with their available means, but it was becoming increasingly clear that without investing on a large scale in all areas of its activities, it was going to be difficult to fulfil the expectations of the people. A committee was appointed to consider if the private sector could be allowed to enter civil aviation activities. The committee report supported the concept of privatization of civil aviation, and it became clear that it would take place in the near or distant future.

Madhavrao Scindia became the civil aviation minister in the government headed by P.V. Narasimha Rao. He opened the door to private entrepreneurs in the aviation industry. Even though the law prohibited private participation in civil aviation, Madhavrao Scindia took the decision to invite private companies, even without amending the existing law. The decision was supported by the people. So it was not criticized but was tolerated. Later, the law was amended and the decision was legalized ex-post-facto. Since then, private companies have taken a great interest in civil aviation. The government encouraged and supported them. The result was an increase in capacity to provide facilities of civil aviation to the people. Today, it is easy to fly and get tickets for flights because of the availability of a large number of aircraft owned by the public and private sector units. There are no delays, for the aircraft have to fly only to the places they can cover easily and as per the norms. Before privatization, aircraft did not fly on time, and then flights were invariably delayed. Now, they fly to fewer places only and not to large number of places. That has made it possible to avoid delays in flights. Today, difficulties are encountered in landing on time because of the large number of aircraft, which means the airports of all important cities have to be strengthened and expanded, and new airports need to be built. This is being done by private companies, and not only by public sector companies.

A large number of companies have come into existence and are flying their aircraft to different parts of the country and abroad. All of them are not doing well, are likely to disappear, while the remaining companies may do well. In fact, in future, aviation is going to be a very important activity and part of the country's infrastructure. It is a step in the right direction that public and private sectors are trying to do their best. In the past, the private sector was not allowed to play its role. Now that it is allowed to do so. Now the public sector does not enjoy a monopoly and has to face competition. In no way should it be discouraged or disadvantaged from competing to raise its standards. It is better to be fair to both the public and private sector units.

To develop civil aviation in the country, the following steps can be taken:

- Industry to produce aircraft can be established.
- This can be done by the public or private sector or in cooperation between the two and/or foreign companies.

- Old airports should be refurbished and new airports constructed.
- Training facilities to produce enough pilots should be strengthened and new facilities built.
- Small aircraft and helicopters should be produced in large numbers.
- R&D for developing aviation technologies, such as production of aircraft which can take off vertically, should be strengthened and should be produced.
- Existing technologies used for this purpose can be improved upon.
- Aircraft which can land on water should also be produced in large numbers.
- Maintenance facilities should be strengthened.
- Development of aviation activity should be undertaken by public, private and foreign companies, separately or in cooperation with each other.

The capability to travel on land is different from travelling in the ocean. Travelling in space is going to be completely different and is going to be increasingly important in the future. It will dominate our future and would help to use time more efficiently. India should do its best to master it. It is not doing what other countries are doing. If it lags behind other countries, it would take a long time to catch up with them. India should develop the capability to manufacture aircraft. The private sector can take a lead in this, but if it does not, the public sector should provide the lead. In future, if the private sector wishes to take it over, there should be no difficulty in handing over. But the area which covers aircraft manufacturing should not be left unattended. In fact, later, travel to outer space can be approached with greater care, confidence and ease. India should not lag behind in travelling into outer space. The progress in developing the capacity to undertake an odyssey into outer space will take us even further than the capacity to manufacture aircraft for civil aviation.

With Indian President Shankar Dayal Sharma and South African President Nelson Mandela.

With (L–R) former PM Chandra Sekhar, the XIVth Dalai Lama, President Giani Zail Singh, PM P.V. Narasimha Rao and Vice President K.R. Narayanan.

The author with the Indian delegation in Beijing, China. Also seen are Renuka Choudhary, I.K. Gujral, Rabi Ray, R.K. Dhawan and Atal Bihari Vajpayee.

With the British parliamentary delegation to India, 30 November–1 December 1992, while the author was the Lok Sabha speaker.

With Leader of Opposition Atal Bihari Vajpayee and others.

With Prime Minister P.V. Narasimha Rao (left) and Leader of Opposition A.B. Vajpayee (right).

During a procession with President S.D. Sharma, Vice President K.R. Narayanan, Prime Minister P.V. Narasimha Rao, the parliamentary affairs minister and the secretary general of the Lok Sabha.

Procession going to the central hall comprising (back–front) PM P.V. Narasimha Rao, the author, President Shankar Dayal Sharma and the secretaries of both Houses of Parliament.

The author and his wife with Mrs Sonia Gandhi.

Mrs Sonia Gandhi addressing a gathering at Siradi. Seated behind the podium are (L–R) the author and Maharashtra CM Vilasrao Deshmukh (front); Margaret Alva and V.K. Patil (back).

On a river-rafting trip.

The author with officials of the ministry, members of his family and personal staff.

(L–R) Mrs Shamim Deb Azad, Mrs Narayanan and Vice President K.R. Narayanan, Mrs Vijaya Patil and the author and Minister for Parliamentary Affairs Ghulam Nabi Azad.

With Vice President K.R. Narayanan (left) and former Prime Minister Chandra Sekhar (right).

With Shri V.S. Page, chairman, legislative council of Maharashtra.

The author trying his hand at an AK-47.

An accomplished equestrian.

■

Once, during Diwali at Ahmedabad, an accident involving an Indian Airlines' aircraft occurred, killing a large number of passengers on board. At a place in Assam, within one day of the accident at Ahmedabad, another accident involving a civil aviation aircraft occurred. I visited both places. The accident at Ahmedabad was caused due to pilot error, but the cause of the accident in Assam could not be established conclusively. Aircraft accidents occur mainly due to human error. Aircraft fly very fast and if the minds of those who pilot the aircraft do not act as fast as the craft, a mismatch in time and machine management occurs, causing accidents. Rajiv Gandhi knew the causes of accidents. On my return to Delhi, Rajiv Gandhi asked me to meet him and Shankarrao Chavan in his office. I gave him the available details of the accidents. Then he offered me tea and some soothing words, which reduced my tension. It shed light on his nature and sterling human qualities. It made him seem different from other leaders.

17

UNION MINISTER OF STATE FOR TOURISM WITH INDEPENDENT CHARGE

Snow-clad mountains, forests, deserts, large rivers, plains, a long coastline, forts, temples, mosques, churches, palaces and caves and other things—India has it all. Indians speak different languages, dress differently, eat amazing varieties of food. Their dances are thrilling, their music is melodious. They play different kinds of games and are skilful. They have their own ways to travel from one part of the country to another. When they travel, they depend on themselves and do not ask for assistance from governments or others. They are ready to face difficulties and do not complain because their travels purify their inner selves. When they return home, they find that they are different human beings. Their journeys and living in the lap of nature elevate them. They call their tourism pilgrimages. The religious structures and monuments are located on the tops of mountains, in forests, on the coasts and in the most beautiful places, and the beauty of nature and purity in the heart produces bliss, which gives new hope and strength to those who want meaningful lives, capable of coping with the ups and downs of existence.

Tourism in India is managed and developed by the private sector. The states have the liberty and authority to develop it in any manner they like. The centre helps the states to plan tourism, giving the states some funds, ideas and plans to develop tourism. It also helps the private sector to develop facilities needed for tourism with concessional finance.

International tourism needs particular facilities and attitudes, which are not readily available in the country. The Indian psyche does not approve of certain attitudes prevalent in foreign countries thriving on tourism. It may not be possible to change these attitudes easily. So the people as a whole may not like the changes needed to bring tourism on par with that of other countries.

The funds provided for tourism by the centre and state governments are limited. Therefore, it is necessary to increase the allocation of funds for tourism in annual budgets and plans. Tourists from other countries should be encouraged to visit India, and Indian tourists should be given all facilities to visit different parts of the country. The private sector should spend more funds to develop plans for both kinds of tourism.

Tourism is not only entertainment. It is also education. When tourists travel to different places, their fund of knowledge about the geography, history and culture of the people increases. They can become broad-minded by accepting other cultures and their misunderstanding about others can be dispelled, spreading globalization and bringing unity of the peoples of the world. In present times, tourism's potential to create employment opportunities is enormous and should be used. Modern means of transport and communication are helping tourism to thrive.

The civil aviation and tourism ministries were kept under the control of one minister, although at times, they were looked after by different ministers. When they were under one minister, it was felt that civil aviation would help international tourism and it did help. It may help in the future too. But there are many things which should be done. Tourism is a hospitality industry that earns money and goodwill. But there should be manpower available to manage it in a manner that is appreciated by tourists. In India, a guest is treated as a god, but eventually, the facilities provided are of the utmost importance. They should be scientific and up to date.

It is, therefore, necessary to establish training centres for guides. They should know different languages, the history and culture of the areas from which the tourists come, as well as the places where tourists wish to go.

When I was the civil aviation minister, representatives of China, Malaysia and Singapore visited India. They wanted India to help them build their airports and civil aviation. In one or two oil-producing countries, India had constructed airports and assisted in developing their aviation activities. However, what they wanted was not what India could give them. They did develop their airports and civil aviation, and on a very grand scale. For some years, what they had done was considered the best in the world. Now, India has begun to build airports and develop civil aviation on a larger scale than in the past and may be treated as one of the best in the world.

India attracts tourists from some of the most advanced countries of the world. They do not come to India to see what they have been seeing and to live, as they have been living in their parts of the world. They come to India to see and experience something different. Therefore, India should retain its originality on offer to foreign tourists. If what it offers is pure and unique and the best, it will be valued more and prove to be more attractive. The art and skill lie in offering them what is indigenous and unique in a presentable and acceptable manner. It is very necessary to understand this, because if this happens, the tourists would enjoy the experience they get in India, and will not try to make comparisons with what they see and experience in other countries.

18

DEPUTY SPEAKER, LOK SABHA

In the general election to the Lok Sabha in 1989, the Congress party did not get the required majority, so it did not form the government, which was then formed by the parties opposed to the Congress party. V.P. Singh became the prime minister. Rabi Ray became the speaker, but the ruling parties wanted to give the post of the deputy speaker to the opposition party. That was the convention. The Congress party considered a few names for the post and ultimately, decided to propose my name. The fact that I had worked as the deputy speaker and speaker of the Maharashtra legislative assembly favoured my selection.

The deputy speaker assists the speaker in conducting the proceedings of the House. In the Lok Sabha, the speaker prepares a list of chairpersons who can function as presiding officers in the absence of the speaker or the deputy speaker. The speaker is supposed to belong to no party. In other countries, if a person becomes a speaker, he is allowed to hold the post as long as he wishes and if he refuses to hold the post or dies, another person is elected to the post. If he contests the election to the legislature, other parties do not set up their candidates against him. However, this tradition is not followed in India. The speakers in India have been opposed in the elections to the legislature and for the post of speaker, by opposition parties. The deputy speaker occupies the first seat on the benches given to the opposition parties as a member of one of them.

He speaks in the House on behalf of his party and constituency. He is expected to do it when the speaker is in the chair. When a chairperson of the panel is in the chair, he is not expected to speak. When voting takes place, he can vote, but the speaker does not vote unless there is a tie between the two opposing sides. Any person who occupies the chair of the presiding officer is expected to conduct himself in an impartial manner. A person in the speaker's chair enjoys the speaker's rights and has to perform the speaker's duties in the House. The position of the deputy speaker is that of a constitutional authority. The Constitution of India provides that for the Lok Sabha, a speaker and a deputy speaker shall be elected.

When I entered the Lok Sabha and functioned as a mere MP, I was asked to act as the presiding officer in the absence of the speaker and the deputy speaker. The members knew that I could manage the House and regulate its proceedings. The experience I had acquired as the presiding officer in the Maharashtra legislative assembly helped me to face the House and obtain the cooperation of the members.

The speaker sat in the House during the question hour and when important topics came up for discussion. In the zero hour also, he continued to preside over the House. I was asked to take the chair when the House was in a mood to cooperate. My job was thus easier than that of the speaker.

Only on one occasion, when the bill to amend the Constitution to extend president's rule in Punjab came up for discussion, was I put to the test. An amendment to the Constitution can be made if the majority of the members and two-thirds of the votes cast are in favour of the amendment. After the bill was considered, the motion was put to vote. The ruling parties could not get the requisite number of votes in favour of the motion, so I had to rule that the motion was defeated. The ruling parties found themselves in an awkward position. Some senior members of the ruling parties argued that it was while passing the bill, at the end of the third reading, that the requisite majority was needed, and not while passing the motion for the consideration of the bill. That is, at the end of the first reading. I heard the members express their views very patiently. Then I gave my ruling, which was that the requisite majority was required, even when passing the motion for the consideration of the bill. The government did not know how to overcome this difficulty. The period of president's rule would have come to an end, if the bill were not passed. Therefore, after giving the ruling, I asked the leader of the opposition and the opposition members and parties to cooperate with the government and allow the bill to be passed on the next day, when it could have enough members present in the House. The rule not to consider an issue more than once in a session could be suspended with the consent of the members, to overcome the constitutional imbroglio that could otherwise have occurred. Rajiv Gandhi, the leader of the opposition, understood the difficult situation. He agreed to my suggestion, saying that his party succeeded in showing that the government was not careful enough to ensure that its members were present in the House, even when passing a bill to amend the Constitution to deal with the difficult situation in Punjab. Some members of the ruling parties doubted that on the next day the opposition parties would cooperate. I assured them that they would, because they knew the importance of the issue involved in the amendment. Accordingly, on the following day, by suspending the relevant rule, the amending bill was moved and passed with the cooperation of all the members of the House.

I always tried to help members to raise important and genuine problems of the people. They were sure that they would not be exposed if, by mistake, they said or did something not quite right. They knew that they would be guided to raise such issues according to the rules and procedures. There was a perfect understanding between them and me and other presiding officers. Some members of the House prophesied that I would become the speaker in the next Lok Sabha. And that did happen.

19

SPEAKER, LOK SABHA

In the UK, the monarch and the representatives of the people often could not see eye to eye with each other on many matters. When they did not talk to one another, a senior member took the lead and spoke to them. Because of his seniority and stature, he was able to communicate with both sides, and that was why he was recognized as the speaker.

Later, in the House, the members of the ruling party and those of the opposition party were guided and controlled by the speaker, to ensure that the discussions and deliberations were done in a purposeful manner. On several occasions, the speaker's role was not fully appreciated by the monarch and the representatives of the people, and the members of the ruling party and those of the opposition party. While trying to maintain the balance, he often got irritated and left with both sides dissatisfied. That was why senior members were reluctant to act as mediators between them, or to preside over the proceedings of the House. Some speakers lost their lives because they could not satisfy the monarch, or lost their friendly relations with the parties because they could not get their plans and designs fully accepted by each other. In the UK and even in India, when a member is elected as the speaker, he is dragged to the chair by the leaders of the political parties. He is not supposed to proceed to occupy the chair on his own, willingly, and with happiness in his heart.

This indicates that the speaker's job is not one which can be enjoyed. It is a job which can create many problems for the occupant of the post. On one or two occasions, the presiding officers of the legislatures in India were attacked by unruly members. They were also found shedding tears and expressing their anguish openly in front of the members and the media.

The Constitution of India provides that the legislature shall have a speaker and a deputy speaker in the Lower House and a chairperson and a deputy chairperson in the Upper House to preside over, guide and regulate their proceedings. In India, the president is the head of the nation, the vice president can function as head of the nation in the absence of the president, and is the chairperson of the Rajya Sabha, and the prime minister presides over the cabinet, which exercises real executive power. The speaker presides over the proceedings of the Lok Sabha, which is responsible for making the laws in conjunction with the Rajya Sabha. Protocol-wise, the president occupies the first position and the vice president the second. Outside the House, the prime minister occupies the third position. Inside the House, the speaker occupies the third position, while outside the House, the speaker of the Lok Sabha and the chief justice of the Supreme Court occupy the fourth position. Between the speaker and the chief justice, the position depends on their seniority. The one who is senior gets precedence over the other. Thus, we have an arrangement under which the effective executive is headed by the prime minister, the effective legislature is headed by the speaker, and the apex of the judiciary is headed by the chief justice of the Supreme Court.

All the executive orders of the government are passed in the name of the president, and all the bills passed by the legislature become laws when signed by the president.

These arrangements indicate that the speaker in India occupies a very high constitutional position. The decisions given by him in the House are binding on the government and its members, unless they are set aside by the Lok Sabha. The government can stand or fall, based on the speaker's decision on certain crucial issues. The speaker's decisions are not challenged in the courts of law, on the basis that they are not taken by following rules, laws and procedures. All these aspects make the position of the speaker quite respectable and powerful.

■

The speaker presides over the legislature, which makes laws and approves the budget proposals presented by the executive. Hence, he is expected to take decisions and give rulings of a legal nature, involving the provisions of the Constitution and other laws, rules and conventions followed by the country's legislature. Therefore, if he is well versed with the Constitution of the country and other relevant laws and rules, he finds conducting the proceedings in the House easy. There are officers in the legislature who can help him, but certain occasions and situations arise in which he has to depend on his own understanding. This is why he has to be in a position to meet such contingencies in a successful manner. Many Indian speakers had the legal knowledge needed to discharge their duties. They followed the laws and procedures correctly and meticulously. There were some speakers who were endowed with rich experiences of life and conducting public affairs and matters relevant to governance. They had very strong common sense and an understanding of the ways of governance. They took decisions without referring to laws and procedures, but based on their understanding of the ethos and spirit of managing public affairs. And their decisions were respected and accepted by all concerned and were legally correct.

In the legislatures, matters of a political nature come up for discussions and decisions. The members belong to different political parties and have different political views on several issues. The speaker is expected to guide and regulate the proceedings concerning political issues. If he is well acquainted with the political nuances of the members and their parties, he can discharge his duties in a correct manner. If he fails to appreciate why certain views are expressed and why they are expressed in certain ways, clashes can occur, obstructing the smooth and meaningful conduct of the proceedings. The speaker who has a better understanding of the political nuances of the members and their parties is more successful in achieving the cooperation of all the parties holding contradictory views.

The members of the legislature are representatives of the people. They are pressurized by their voters to present their problems in the House in a forceful manner. They, too, have their own ways of thinking and psychology. In the House, at times, they are controlled by the presiding officers and their parties. If the speaker understands human psychology and deals with such members tactfully, he is able to keep the House in order and make sure that the necessary business is transacted in accordance with the expectations of all concerned. Mere authority, knowledge of laws and procedural niceties or acquaintance with political attitudes of the members do not help. Understanding human nature can come to the succour of the speaker.

The legislatures are used by political parties to express their views forcefully and to show their voters that they and their members fight for the people who suffer and whose demands need to be fulfilled. In the House, therefore, situations difficult to manage frequently arise. If the speaker loses his balance of mind and becomes angry, he finds himself unable to control the situation and the members. If he retains his own balance of mind and remains calm, he can succeed in calming the agitated members. The speaker should have a stoical nature, which means that he should not feel elated when situations go his way and not feel dejected when they do not. Once, I was asked how I controlled unruly members. My reply was, 'I do not control the members. I control myself. And when I control myself, the members get controlled.' And that was no exaggeration. It was the result of my experience in the House.

The speaker can allow to speak or disallow a member from speaking. He can throw out a member who does not abide by his order or decision. The authority of the speaker in the House is subject only to the authority of the entire House, and not to any other person holding any position in the House, in the government or outside. Absolute authority can corrupt absolutely, while authority by itself does not solve problems at all times. A sympathetic attitude of the speaker can solve many problems. If the members are convinced that the speaker will help them, he can persuade them to cooperate with him. In a democracy, this is a very important element, since many demands cannot be met at one and the same time. Those who make demands also know this fact and if they are convinced that the speaker is sympathetic towards them, they are satisfied and cooperate.

The speaker functions in the House in the presence of the members. They observe everything he does and says. If they feel that he conducts himself in an impartial manner, they respect him and cooperate with him. If they feel that he behaves in a partial manner to support his party or the government or a member or a group of members for any reason, they may not cooperate with him and his writ fails to run effectively. He is not expected to be on the lookout to punish any member or a party or go out of the way to help any one of them. He is expected always to function as a friend, philosopher and guide to the members, without bias of any kind towards anybody. Speakers in India have succeeded in creating this kind of impression on the members and winning their confidence in discharging their duties effectively. At times, it is found that the members of the speaker's party expect too much help from him and when their expectations are not fulfilled, they become unhappy and angry. In most cases, the members of the party to which the speaker belongs appear to be more dissatisfied with him than members of other parties. The members of other parties do not expect too much help from him, so when he does pay attention to them according to laws and rules, they feel that the speaker has been correct and just with them. They do not complain too much against him. If the members of the ruling parties are less satisfied and the opposition parties are not dissatisfied with him, it may be held that the speaker has done his duties in an impartial manner.

The speaker in India visits the legislatures of other countries and attends international conferences. When he does that, he represents the dignity, prestige and authority of the Parliament of the country. In fact, it is found that the speaker visits more countries and attends more international conferences than the other ministers. It is, therefore, necessary for him to understand the policies of countries relevant to India and the world. If he commits any mistake in this area of his duties, it affects the country as a whole, which should be avoided. He functions as an ambassador of goodwill to other countries, that is why his skill in diplomacy of a correct nature is of vital importance.

On occasions the speaker expresses his views on important issues discussed in the House. His views are not always binding on the government. Decisions taken on motions passed by the legislature become binding. Even some of these decisions, if taken only by one House, are not binding on the government. All the same, the views expressed by the speaker are respected and implemented by the government. Generally, the speaker is careful while expressing his views and taking decisions. If he makes a mistake while doing so, it becomes quite embarrassing for the government and the speaker himself. So, he is expected to be very circumspect in these matters.

The media is allowed to publish what is said and done in the House. Anything which is not said or done according to the rules, can be expunged, and is not allowed to be brought to the notice of the people. If any person commits a mistake in this respect, he can be proceeded against for breach of privilege of the House or the chair or the member, and if found guilty of the charges, he can be punished. The speaker decides if there is a prima facie case to start proceedings for breach of privilege, or not. He gives notice to the media or its representative to allow him an opportunity to submit his rebuttal. On hearing and examining both sides, he can send the case to the Committee of Privileges for deeper examination and a decision. Generally, a very stringent view is not welcomed in such matters. The speaker tries to be as considerate as is possible. He is expected to be just and lenient. This helps the media to cover the proceedings and keep people informed about what happens in the legislature.

•

I was the speaker of the tenth Lok Sabha for its full term. In that period, S. Mallikarjunaiah was the deputy speaker. The experience I had acquired in working as the presiding officer in the state and Union legislatures helped me to function without difficulty. Many of the members in the House and I knew each other, so they were sure that I would conduct the business of the House correctly. I always tried to follow the Constitution, laws and rules of procedure. I did not go against the conventions that had developed in the last sixty years or more. I tried to establish a few new conventions and adopt new methods of working.

Before going to the chair in the House, I anticipated the issues that could be raised, and decided on the manner in which they could be handled. This practice helped me not to be taken by surprise by events or by the actions of any member and I could deal with difficult situations smoothly.

During question hour, I tried to cover a large number of questions. The members asked questions with long preambles, while the questions themselves were short. I tried to convince the members that they should ask questions and avoid making statements. But I could not succeed fully in that mission. On occasion, the questions were very long without making the points clearly. It was also found that the replies given were too long and intricate. I ventured to explain the gist of the questions and answers very briefly, in one or two words and sentences. Fortunately, this exercise was not misunderstood or objected to. It was my impression that the others who waited for their turn to ask and reply to the questions felt that efforts to facilitate their participation were welcome.

In the Lok Sabha, only three to four questions could be covered in the question hour. All presiding officers had tried their best to increase the number of questions covered, but none of them had fully succeeded in achieving this objective. The cooperation of the members and the ministers is required for this. If question hour is managed properly, it can give more and better opportunities to members to hold the executive accountable for their acts of omission and commission.

On each working day, the number of questions that can be asked is twenty. For every question, a prior notice of a fixed period is given to the concerned ministry. Whether the question is admissible or not, whether the question should be treated as starred or unstarred, is decided by the secretariat of the legislature and the speaker. The ministries collect the information from offices and places which are located in different states. If the questions are not taken up for replies, this exercise is wasted and a potent instrument in the hands of private members is blunted. Therefore, to observe the necessary discipline is in the interest of the system and the members. Efforts are made to bring these aspects to the notice of the members and to obtain their willing cooperation. But the results produced are not very satisfactory. Therefore, efforts should be continued to find a solution to improve on the system that is followed.

In some state legislatures, there is no question hour. Instead, there is a question period, during which these legislatures do not stop the members from asking the questions after one hour is over, but continue till all questions are asked. It is managed in this way to help the members to hold the executive accountable, not to reduce the legislator's power to hold the government responsible for what it does or does not do.

In order to discuss matters of urgent public importance, some devices are provided. A member is permitted to call the attention of the government by giving notice one hour before the House starts functioning. He is also allowed to move an adjournment motion, with a notice one hour before the House starts, as is done in the case of a calling attention motion. The presiding officer can decide if the notice should be admitted or not. If he admits the notice, the matter is presented to the House. If the requisite number of members vote in favour of the notice, a discussion on the adjournment motion is allowed. At the end of the discussion, the motion is put to vote. If the motion secures the majority of votes, it is treated as passed. The motion of adjournment is treated as a censor motion. If it is passed, the government is expected to resign. The adjournment motion is not admitted for discussion, unless it pertains to a very important matter of urgent public importance.

When it was found that these devices could not meet the members' demands to mention important matters, it was decided that a certain number of special mentions could be made by the members in the House by giving notices on the same day, one hour before the House started functioning.

Initially, it was not expected that the ministers would reply to the special mentions thus made. However, they were expected to note what was mentioned and act on the information provided. Later, it was decided that the ministers could keep the members informed on the steps taken on the special mentions made in writing. On some occasions, the members insist that the speaker should direct the ministers to take appropriate action on the special mentions. In the past, the speaker could direct ministers on his own, if he thought it fit to do so. Now, he is forced to do it.

Not fully satisfied with these provisions and devices, the members have invented zero hour. During zero hour, any member can get up and raise any issue, without giving any kind of notice. Members compete with one another to attract the attention of the speaker and make their points. The result of this is chaos. Many members are seen standing and speaking at one and the same time. The scenes are so unruly that parliamentary practice has been defamed because of what happens in zero hour. There are no rules to guide zero hour activities. In fact, what happens during zero hour is a free-for-all. On some occasions, very important issues are also raised, and discussions on the issues are very pointed and effective.

Many members oppose zero hour activities, while others are adamant on continuing with them. The main thing that attracts them is the freedom with which they can indulge in such activities. They are not required to give any kind of notice, but can just stand up and raise issues. Some members suggest that zero hour activities should be allowed during the last hour of the day's proceeding. There are others who apprehend that if they are shifted to the last hour, some members may raise them after the question hour and during the last hour also. That is why the existing procedure is continued.

Once, an MP was asked by a member of the British Parliament how the Union legislature could transact business during zero hour, without following any rules of procedure. The reply given by the Indian MP was that if the UK could govern the country without having a written Constitution, the Indian Parliament could have business transacted during zero hour without having rules of procedure.

I tried to guide and control the business of Parliament during zero hour. I had long discussions with the members to ensure that zero hour activities were performed in an effective and dignified manner. For a few days after the discussions, the proceedings were conducted in a better fashion. But later, they fell back into the same style and became as erratic as they used to be.

After the zero hour discussions, generally, the business of the government starts. It continues till the House rises, as agreed by the parties in the Business Advisory Committee. The period during which government business is transacted is disciplined. In that period, meaningful discussions take place, laws are passed, budget proposals are approved, and important issues discussed. During this period, the members' attendance is low, which ironically helps to have disciplined discussions on important subjects. Usually, the deputy speaker and members on the panels of chairpersons preside over the discussions in the afternoon session and after the zero hour discussions.

I used to preside over the House in the afternoon when very important and complicated subjects were taken up for discussion. There were some members who always prepared themselves on these subjects in the best possible manner. I had identified them. So whenever they asked for time to speak on such topics or for more time on other subjects, I used to concede to their requests.

Every year, the president of India addresses the members of both the Houses of Parliament in a joint meeting. The address is devoted to the achievements, policies and plans of the government. The members are given the opportunity to discuss the points made in the address, and also the points that could have been made on behalf of the government, or any other points. At the end of the discussion, a motion thanking the president for the address is put to the vote. If the motion is passed, it is presumed that the address is approved. If it fails, it is presumed that the government does not enjoy the support of the members and is expected to resign.

To make a law, a bill is prepared by the executive and introduced in the legislature. It is read three times. In the first reading, its principles are discussed. In the second reading, its clauses are discussed. In the third reading, with or without amendments, it is passed or defeated. If a bill is defeated, the government is not expected to resign. Only if the Finance Bill is defeated, the government resigns.

Every year, a budget is prepared by the finance minister, which is approved by the cabinet and presented to the legislature to be discussed and approved. It is only the Lok Sabha which has the right to approve or disapprove the budget presented by the executive. This right is not available to the Rajya Sabha, which can discuss the budget proposals, but cannot vote to approve or disapprove it. It can send recommendations to the Lok Sabha for its approval. If they are approved by the Lower House, they become part of the budget. If they are not approved, the budget is passed as approved by the Lok Sabha. For a few days, fixed by the Business Advisory

Committee, the general principles on the basis of which the budget is prepared are discussed. Then, the demands for grants by a few ministries are discussed and passed. The budget needs to be passed within the days allotted for the purpose. So, on the last day allowed for discussion, the demands for grants of all ministries are put to vote and passed. Then, the Appropriation Bill is passed. Unless the Appropriation Bill is passed, no money can be spent by the government. The Finance Bill is presented and passed. It allows the taxes to be imposed, increased or reduced. No tax can be collected by the government without the approval of the Lok Sabha.

India is a multi-party democracy—and there are a large number of parties which contest elections to the Union and state legislatures. There was a time when parties could get the majority of their members elected and form their governments, without help from other parties. But in the last few elections, it was found that none of them could get the requisite majority to form a government on their own. They had to seek the help of each other to get a majority. For this purpose, they had to compromise on many principles. After the government was formed, some member parties used their strength and position to get their terms accepted by the government. When their demands were not accepted, they defected from one side to the other, which sometimes resulted in pulling down the government and led to forming a new government. The new government also could not continue for long. Thus, governments became unstable and remained in existence for short periods, which were insufficient for them to deal with the long-term and complicated problems of the people. To avoid these kinds of defects, which were recognized as 'Ayaram' and 'Gayaram' activities, demands were made to enact an anti-defection law. The first few attempts to enact the law did not fructify. However, when Rajiv Gandhi became the prime minister, a bill was prepared and moved in Parliament. It was discussed with the leaders and members of different parties, who expressed their views in different ways. In the original bill, it was decided that any number of members defecting from one party to another would lose their membership in the legislature. On behalf of the members, it was stated that if the leaders of the parties, or the parties, went against the promises made in their manifestos, and gave directions to the elected members to follow a line opposed to the promises made in the manifesto, the members should not be compelled to follow the whip. It was then asked if a small number of elected members felt that way, should they be allowed to disobey the whip? Thus, the number of members who thought differently became very relevant. First, it was suggested that if three-fourths of the members held different views, they should be allowed to vote differently. However, that number was held to be too large. So, the second suggestion was that number should be half the total number of members elected. That number was also held to be inadequate. So, it was reduced to one-third of the members. That number was accepted and become part of the law. Therefore, some critics continued to say for many years that retail defection was disallowed, but wholesale defection was allowed.

The political parties used this provision of the law also to see that defections could take place, and governments could be formed and pulled down. The ruling given by Rabi Ray disallowed members leaving their parties and joining other parties, in bits and pieces, with impunity. That was why some parties adopted a method of expelling some disgruntled members who were likely to join other parties. When they sensed that one-third of their members were likely to defect and join another party, they expelled a few to reduce the number to less than one-third, so that they could say that the total number leaving their party was below the requisite level. This was experienced in a case in which a party had four members. One of them was ready to leave his party and join another one—but that could not make up one-third of the members. So, the leader of the party expelled one of the four members and the total number of remaining members became three. If one of the three left the party, he could be one-third of the total number and immune to the anti-defection. When a group of twelve members were deciding to leave their party, the leader of the party expelled four of them from the party. The remaining eight members could not form the one-third of members required. So, when the twelve of them joined another party, a petition was filed that they were liable to be expelled from their membership. The argument advanced on behalf of the group of twelve members of the House was that the Constitution and other electoral laws or rules did not allow elected members to be expelled from their parliamentary parties. If that was allowed to be done, it would affect the right of the members to vote differently as was allowed by the Anti-Defection Law. That kind of exercise of law was colourable and not allowed. The matter was discussed at great length. The petitioners could not cite any legal provision in support of their action. And so, the petition was disallowed. For some time, it was rumoured that the ruling given by Rabi Ray was nullified. It was said that the new decision allowed the members to leave their parties in phases, which was not a fact. When this matter was explained in the House forcefully, the rumours died down.

∎

In every session, the speaker invites the leader of the House, the leader of the opposition, leaders of all important parties, the deputy speaker, concerned ministers and officers for lunch or dinner, with the aim of holding informal discussions on important issues, which can be taken up in the House for discussions and decisions.

At one such luncheon meeting, P.V. Narasimha Rao, the then prime minister, asked me if it would be possible to constitute Departmentally Related Standing Committees consisting of members of both the Houses, in proportion to the number of members of the parties in Parliament. My reply was in the affirmative. The leader of the opposition and leaders of other parties conceded that the idea should be adopted and acted upon, and affirmed that it would be supported by their parties. I told the prime minister that if the scheme was moved in the House and accepted, it would be difficult to withdraw it later, and so, before it was introduced in Parliament, it would be better to consult the members of his Council of Ministers. He was very emphatic in his reply. He said that he would take care of his ministers, and I should take care of the proposal and move it in Parliament as soon as possible. I promised him and others that it would be done within a few days.

I was clear in my mind about the manner in which it could be done. The officers helped in drafting the rules and preparing the scheme. However, some very senior ministers, MPs and former members expressed their opposition to the concept, while some ministers and a majority of the members supported the idea. A few newspapers wrote articles supporting the proposal. I invited the former members of Parliament, ministers and others who were not in favour of the proposal to lunches and dinners. I heard their objections and tried to dispel their doubts while explaining the advantages that would accrue. I explained to them that in the plenary, members were inclined to demonstrate rather than to discuss in detail the bills, budget proposals and other issues. Moreover, the time was not sufficient for all members to speak. If they considered the bills and budget proposals in the committees, they would be able to discuss the details dispassionately and objectively, and in a better ambience that would help to frame laws and approve budget proposals in a better manner. The number of sittings of the Houses was getting reduced. If the members worked more in committees, the deficiency thus created could be recouped. Some people who heard me were convinced of the utility of Standing Committees. Others agreed to support the proposal, give it a chance, and see how it worked. So, the scheme was approved by members of both Houses with enthusiasm. It has remained in existence since its inception, and has been welcomed by all those who have experimented with it. In fact, it has proved to be a very popular and successful scheme.

The committees' chairpersons are nominated by the presiding officers. They are allowed to nominate them to make sure that the right type of members are given the responsibility. The chairpersons nominated to the committees were very senior and experienced members of Parliament, some of whom later became prime ministers and ministers, holding important portfolios in the government.

These committees have functioned very effectively and successfully under the guidance and leadership of their chairpersons. If the chairpersons were not well equipped to discharge their duties, perhaps the committees would have failed to function satisfactorily and correctly. The conventions and ethos that the first few chairpersons developed pushed the committees onto the right tracks, which are now followed without difficulties or obstacles. The Standing Committees have received the support of all sections of society and all political parties. The media has also supported and praised them. They have criticized the system on one point only. They wanted to cover the proceedings of the committees, as they do in the plenary. However, the rules provide that this is not allowed. The reason is that the members of the committees would then conduct themselves as they do in the plenary, where they support their party lines and demonstrate. They are more inclined to criticize the government or one another, rather than to make suggestions to improve upon the existing or proposed situation, policies and plans. So, to keep the proceedings free from party biases, it was agreed that they should function in camera and not expose their work to the glare of the public, which could make them follow party lines. The media keeps demanding that they be allowed to cover the committee proceedings. But, so far, all governments of all parties have not conceded to their demands. The committees give their reports after agreeing on the issues considered by them. Generally, they make unanimous reports. If any member disagrees, he is allowed to file his dissenting note. After they are submitted to Parliament, they acquire the status of public documents and are available to the media also for their comments.

The recommendations of the committees are considered by the concerned ministries and implemented. Over 70 per cent of the recommendations have been accepted and implemented, and some have been rejected. Some are under the consideration of the Union and state governments. The recommendations that need to be implemented by state governments have to be accepted by them. Since the process takes time, the recommendations are often pending with the concerned governments. There are only a very few recommendations which are rejected. The committees are permitted to return the rejected recommendations for reconsideration and acceptance. If the government refuses to accept them the second time also, generally the committees concede to the decision taken by the government. If they do not agree with the second rejection, the recommendations are sent to Parliament for its final decision. And the decisions taken by Parliament become binding on the government and the committees.

Before the Standing Committees came into existence, bills could not be considered in adequate detail in the plenary, and were passed sometimes without full discussions. With the introduction of the Standing Committee system, they are discussed in great detail and then passed. In many cases, the amendments suggested by the committees are accepted by the government. That helps law-making not only in accordance with the views of the members of the executive, but also with the members of the legislature. Earlier, demands for grants of only a few ministries were considered in the plenary, before they were passed. Now, the demands for grants of all ministries are considered by Standing Committees, and only then are they passed by the plenary. This provision has increased the authority of the legislature to control the financial powers of the executive, and make spending on public projects and collection of taxes responsive to the views of the legislators. Democracy should function in accordance with the wishes of the people, which are ascertained through their representatives. If the system does not help this to happen, both the system and democracy are bound to weaken. By introducing the system of departmentally related Standing Committees, parliamentary democracy has been strengthened.

We have created our system on the basis of concepts accepted in many countries in the world. The details of the system and its form are not identical with those in other countries, based as they are on our own ethos and within the broad framework of our democracy and parliamentary system. I was frequently asked if we had emulated any model elsewhere in the world and my reply was that the concept accepted by us was not different from that in other countries, but the form we had adopted was certainly different.

■

One day, an honourable member brought a pistol into the Lok Sabha. He had managed to carry it inside the House without difficulty and exhibited it to all of the members. The member could have been punished for committing a breach of privilege, but was let off because the intention of his was to highlight the need to tighten the security of Parliament. After that incident, steps were taken to provide scanners at entry points and close to the outer doors of Parliament House. However, it became clear later that those steps were not sufficient to keep a watch on people within the premises of Parliament. The officers who were responsible for providing security to Parliament and its members, both within and outside its premises, were told to ponder over the problem and suggest means to raise the level of security. They suggested that at the entry points and within and outside the galleries and corridors, CCTV cameras should be fixed and connected to a control room, where security officers could keep an eye on suspicious visitors and their movements, thereby increasing the level of their vigilance. The suggestions were accepted, but before they could be implemented, the leaders of the parliamentary parties were consulted. In the meeting organized for that purpose, one leader objected to the proposal, saying that it would enable spying on members and cause difficulties in discharging their duties freely and boldly. He was told that the members of Parliament did not mince words or hide anything they did, that they criticized the government boldly and stridently, and that the devices proposed to be used in Parliament were meant to keep a watch on people who aimed at harming the members and damaging Parliament premises. But the member who objected to the proposal did not soften his stand. Then he was told that the proposal would be given up, and the reason for doing so would be mentioned in the minutes of the meeting. Other leaders and members present in the meeting were not in favour of giving up the proposal, and thought that it was necessary to provide the devices suggested by the security experts, and so, they favoured the acceptance of the proposal and implementation of the scheme.

Later, when Parliament was attacked by terrorists, the CCTV cameras and the control room helped the security personnel to protect it. The terrorists tried to enter Parliament through the gates, but the security personnel in the control room saw them on the screen. According to the drill adopted, when a person tried to intrude into the House alone or with others, an alarm bell could be rung and the people standing close to the doors could close all the doors, to prevent them from entering the building. One of the terrorists tried to enter through Gate No. 12 and another, carrying explosives on his body, proceeded towards Gate No. 1. When the terrorist at Gate No. 12 tried to enter the building, the security guards went all out to stop him. The struggle was seen on screen in the control room and the alarm bell was sounded. In response to the alarm, all the gates of Parliament House were closed. Gate No. 1 was also closed, so the suicide bomber could not succeed in his mission of entering Parliament. Other terrorists who had rushed to the other gates also could not get inside the building. They were engaged by security guards in the compound and were 'neutralized' one by one. In the process, nine security personnel lost their lives and all the terrorists were killed. The suicide bomber was killed outside Gate No. 1 and the explosives he carried on his person exploded. If the explosives had gone off inside the building, it could have caused many casualties and immense damage to the building. These facts were not highlighted, but they are relevant to understand how steps have to be taken in advance to avoid attacks by terrorists and prevent them from achieving their nefarious objectives. If, in response to the objections of the member, the CCTV cameras had not been fixed at different places and the control room had not been established, the terrorists could have succeeded in entering the building. Long-term and imaginative planning is necessary to face the menace of terrorism successfully. I am sorry to say that when such steps are planned, considerable resistance is offered on political grounds. If the war against terrorism is fought on politically biased grounds, the results are bound to be unconformable and of serious nature.

The steps taken to protect Parliament are laudable but not sufficient. There are many other steps which need to be taken, and if they are not taken expeditiously, Parliament will remain vulnerable. For better security, it would be advantageous to depend on electronic gadgets. Moreover, security arrangements should continuously be modernized. Depending on human agencies on a larger scale would also be necessary. Steps needed should be taken continuously and in proportion to the increased danger and perception of it. Initiatives must be taken to guard Parliament against attacks launched with the help of biological, chemical and radiological devices, and aircraft.

These matters were discussed after Parliament was attacked. Some steps have been taken, but more measures need to be implemented and taken without delays.

•

The Parliament serves the interests of the people. The people should know how it functions, how the laws are passed, the budgets approved and measures taken to overcome the problems faced by them. In the past, the people were informed through gazettes that were published and newspapers. However, they could not cover all the important issues handled by the executive and the legislature. These days, the electronic media helps to keep the people abreast of what happens in Parliament, especially since it covers events the whole day. Fortunately, the legislatures are in a position to have their own channels. The Lok Sabha has its own channel, which relays its proceedings. In recent years, the Rajya Sabha has also established its own channel and relays its proceedings.

Initially, there was resistance to televising parliamentary proceedings. First, only very important proceedings, such as the president's address to the joint session and question hour, were telecast. Now, all the proceedings of the day are televised. I was always in favour of televising all the proceedings in Parliament. When I was the deputy speaker of the Lok Sabha, I had written a paper and sent it to the speaker and the government, suggesting to start direct telecasting of parliamentary proceedings. However, no steps were taken till I became the speaker. I sent a committee of experts to visit other Parliaments to find out how telecasting of proceedings was done and how the difficulties faced in doing the task were overcome. The committee prepared a report. The suggestions given by the committee were implemented.

I decided to set up a studio in a room to record the statements of ministers, members, officers and foreign visitors and dignitaries. The project has been implemented and Parliament has its own well-equipped studio with a relay station set up in the new library building. Now, the proceedings, such as the presentation of the budget, is watched by people across the world. It helps the people concerned to take decisions in time on matters relating to their business and other activities. This was done in the period of speakership of Mr Somnath Chatterjee.

There were some people who objected to televising parliamentary proceedings. They said that the Houses of Parliament do not always conduct their proceedings in a dignified manner. The disturbance caused by some members do not add to the prestige of the legislature. On the contrary, they earn the ridicule and distrust of the people. If such scenes are watched by the people on television screens, democracy and the parliamentary system are bound to weaken and become the butt of jokes. So, they opined that it was unwise to show the proceedings on television. Fortunately, there were not many opponents. There were others who saw merit in keeping the people informed about what the legislators do. If law-making in the Houses and discussions on the bills are seen by the people, they can grasp the essence of the laws better and may become more responsible and law-abiding citizens. If they watch the presentation of the budget, they would make use of the government's decisions more fruitfully. There were some others who thought that televising helped to make the members more conscious of their image and they dressed and behaved better. I received a few letters containing the essence of this statement. In my replies, I made it clear that they behaved in the same manner as they used to do in the past.

Some MPs in the UK were opposed to televising the proceedings. In one international conference on the topic, one of the British delegates asked, 'Should the circus staged by the members in the House be shown to the people?' Many members in the conference responded by saying that if the members staged a circus, 'Let it be seen by the people.'

Any attempt to introduce something new is always opposed by some people, probably because of fear of the new and unknown. However, in the interest of the advancement of humanity's capabilities, it is wiser not to succumb to such criticism, and to go ahead with what appears to be useful to the majority of human beings and concerned people.

In the Lok Sabha, I had decided that the proceedings during zero hour, which are not supported by the rules of procedure, should not be exposed to the people through electronic media. Any disturbance created by any member or group should also not be shown on the television screen. The camera crews were kept informed that they should shift their cameras from the members causing the disturbance, either to the speaker or to the entire House, thus discouraging the chaos-makers from trying to indicate to their voters and the people outside the House that they were extra active. These rules were not applicable in the Rajya Sabha then, although

I am informed that now they are. My view on this point is that it would be better to have rules of this nature to keep the prestige of Parliament intact and unsullied.

▪

According to the provisions of the Constitution, the MPs who are not ministers are law-makers, but do not enjoy any executive powers. They can question the ministers and the government and hold them accountable for what they do or do not do. But they cannot issue orders, give any jobs to anybody, approve of any project, or help any person in need of assistance, because this is done by or based on the orders of the members of the executive. When the MPs go to their constituencies, they are approached by their constituents with many requests from their voters for the renovation of schools to strengthening roads and such other things. To help them, the MPs need funds, so they demand that some amount be kept at their disposal to help their constituents. The demands at the national level were not accepted for many years, although some states had accepted them. So, at the national level, the legislators increased the pressure on the executive for this purpose. I was not sure if it should be done or not. I apprehended that the legislators would be criticized for not using the funds correctly and they could be defamed and maligned on the allegation that their funds were misused and in some cases, embezzled. At the same time, I knew the pressure exerted on the legislators and the genuine need to help them to assist their constituents. However, I had thought that the government would not accept the demand, because it involved big outflows of funds from the treasury.

One MP from Mumbai raised this issue in every session. The government either did not reply to his query, or replied saying that the matter was under consideration of the government. To the surprise of all the members, the prime minister himself responded one day, saying that the government had decided to concede to the demand and he would request the speaker to prepare a scheme and get it approved, according to the rules, and implement it in the same year. The member thanked the government and the prime minister. I assured the House and the prime minister that necessary steps would be taken to prepare and implement the scheme. The rules for this purpose were drafted and approved by Parliament within a few days.

The rules provided that each MP would have the authority to sanction projects mentioned in their list of works for ₹1 crore every year. The collector of the district would give the works to government or private agencies, on the basis of tenders issued by him. The funds would be kept at the disposal of the collector, who would be responsible for disbursing them and maintaining the accounts. The MP would not be authorized to issue the tender or disburse the funds, and required to maintain the accounts. These arrangements were made to protect the MPs from difficulties involved in performing these tasks in a lawful manner and not to give them a bad name. Later, the amount was raised to ₹2 crore. There was a demand made by some MPs that the amount of ₹2 crore was insufficient and that it should be raised to ₹5 crore. This demand has been accepted by the government.

The scheme continues and, every year, the MPs can sanction works worth ₹5 crore. The MPs are happy to have the scheme to help their constituents. Many good projects are taken up with the funds provided under the scheme. However, on finding fraud committed by some MPs, it was suggested that the scheme be abolished. However, the suggestion did not find favour with the majority of the members and the government.

One difficulty encountered in operating the scheme is that the MPs are flooded with demands for funds, and the funds available are insufficient to meet all the demands. It is, therefore, necessary to use the scheme in a judicious manner. I advised the MPs that they should not give unnecessary publicity to the sanction of projects, in order to avoid inordinate demands.

■

Rajiv Gandhi, as prime minister of India, had encouraged the computerization of administration at all levels in the country. The Union legislature decided to use computers in many of its activities. Some state legislatures also took steps to computerize their administrative and legislative machinery. Initially, computerization moved at a slow speed, but when the pace increased, it helped the legislature in many of its activities. Rajiv Gandhi tried to give it great impetus and bring it on par with computerization in advanced countries.

The minister of state for electronics and some other members thought that providing computers to all the MPs would help them to perform their duties in Parliament and outside in a more efficient manner. The idea was laudable and was accepted. It was discussed with the leaders of other political parties and in the concerned committees. All agreed that the MPs should be provided with computers for their use during their tenure. I decided that the ministry of electronics should procure computers and hand them over to the secretariat of the legislature, to be distributed among the members. The MPs were given training to use the computers. The National Informatic Centre helped Parliament in many ways to make the legislators competent in using them. Now, Parliament gives computers to all the members at the start of their parliamentary terms, which has helped in enhancing the efficiency of the legislators in many ways.

■

In the Central Hall of Parliament, portraits of great leaders and renowned parliamentarians of India are displayed. Some members wanted flowers to be offered to their portraits on their birth anniversaries. The suggestion was discussed with the leaders of the parliamentary parties who approved and adopted it. Members and leaders of all the important parties now offer their respects, together with the speaker, the deputy speaker, the deputy chairperson and senior officers of both the Houses. These occasions give the political leaders opportunities to meet one another informally to exchange views.

▪

Many MPs wanted a statue of Mahatma Gandhi to be installed in or outside the building of the national legislature. This suggestion was accepted by members of the General Purposes Committee of Parliament. Mrs Kaul, the Union minister for urban development, informed the members that the government had a statue of the father of the nation, made by a well-known artist, which was to be put on Rajpath. The statue was made about five years ago, but it could not be installed because some citizens opposed its installation on Rajpath. The government did not want to install the statue with a controversy, for fear that it could be vandalized. Therefore, Mrs Kaul proposed that if Parliament was willing to put the statue up in its premises, the government could donate it. The proposal was accepted by the committee, and the prime minister was glad to know of the committee's decision when it was discussed with him.

The artist had made a model in fibre glass before the statue was cast in bronze. The fibre glass version was brought to Parliament and placed in front of Gate No. 1. The leaders of all the political parties could see it and the site where it could be installed, and approve what the Parliament secretariat had proposed to do. The statue was installed within a few days and was unveiled by Dr Shankar Dayal Sharma, the president of India. The respected Dalai Lama sent a message to Parliament saying that he would like to be present at the unveiling ceremony. All the members of Parliament were very happy to know that the Dalai Lama revered the memory of Mahatma Gandhi. The members of Parliament, the government and all of us in Parliament felt very happy to welcome him in the installation ceremony and treated him as the guest of honour.

Everybody who visits Parliament is impressed by the magnificent statue of Mahatma Gandhi. Statues of other great leaders—Pandit Motilal Nehru, Dr Babasaheb Ambedkar, Aurobindo Ghosh,

Chandragupta Maurya and Gopal Krishna Gokhale—were installed in the courtyards and gardens of Parliament in the initial years of India's independence. Several more statues were installed in the Parliament building, in the last one and a half decades, which include those of Pandit Jawaharlal Nehru, Vallabhbhai Patel, Abul Kalam Azad, Jayaprakash Narayan, Indiraji, Netaji Subhash Chandra Bose, Yashwantrao Chavan, Jagjivan Ram, Pandit Ravi Shankar Shukla, Shaheed Bhagat Singh, Shaheed Hemu Kalani, Shaheed Durga Malla, K. Kamaraj, S. Satyamurti, C.N. Annadurai, M.G. Ramachandran, Murasoli Maran, P. Muthuramalinga Thevar, Andhra Kesari Tanguturi Prakasam, Prof. N.G. Ranga, Comrade A.K. Gopalan, S.A. Dange, Indrajit Gupta, Bhupesh Gupta, Acharya Narendra Dev and Gopinath Bardoloi. The statues of Rana Pratap, Chhatrapati Shivaji Maharaj, Ranjit Singh, Mahatma Bashweshwar, Mahatma Jyotirao Phule, Chowdhury Devi Lal, Sahu Maharaj and Birsa Munda can be seen in the gardens. The statue of Rabindranath Tagore is installed in the new library building and was made from Parliament funds. The statue of Vithalbhai Patel, who was the presiding officer in the central legislature is expected to be installed in Parliament. It is expected to be paid for by the Union legislature. All the other statues were paid for by organizations and donated to Parliament. It was also decided that they could be made by any artist approved by the donor and Parliament. The artists had to prepare the models and show them to the speaker, and a committee was constituted to approve the models. Only after the models were approved were the statues allowed to be made. The statues which did not tally with the approved models could be rejected by Parliament. Later, these precautions were not fully implemented, which is why the statues made in the initial period are more artistic and authentic than those made in subsequent years.

Initially, there were no objections to the installation of the statues. Later, many objections were raised by members. Their first criticism was that the statues were of varying sizes and width and did not fit in the architectural design of the building. The second point was that Parliament would look like a museum of statues. Some people objected on the basis of their political biases also. The Parliament building is a magnificent and beautiful structure, with its own aesthetic ethos. That aesthetic ethos should not be disrupted by the different kinds of statues which would create disharmony with the existing building. It appears that this aspect was not always kept in mind when statues of different sizes and shapes, made by ordinary artists, were put up at different places, inside and outside the building. Let us hope that, in future, care is taken to install statues that blend in with the beauty of the Parliament building.

In Parliaments of many European countries, many statues are installed. In the Capitol hill in America, and Parliament of UK, statues of great leaders and parliamentarians are put up. They add to the beauty of the parliaments and make the histories of them more poignant.

■

A suggestion was made that, every year, a parliamentarian who is adjudged the best in his performance should be given an award. It was discussed with the leaders of political parties and in the appropriate committees, and was approved.

There were many good parliamentarians in the Lok Sabha and Rajya Sabha, and it was not very easy to select one for the award. For making the selection carefully, a committee consisting of the presiding officers, a retired chief justice of the Supreme Court, the minister for parliamentary affairs, and some others was constituted.

The first award was given to Indrajit Gupta. He did not take the floor of the House every day or too often. But when he spoke, he made brilliant, thought-provoking and relevant points in a very inspiring, impressive style. Members belonging to all parties respected and admired him and his performance as a parliamentarian. The second award was given to Atal Bihari Vajpayee, a seasoned politician who understood Indian politics and its ethos, with a wonderful command over the Hindi language. He was respected and admired by parliamentarians and politicians of all hues.

The others who received the awards included Chandra Shekhar (1995), Somnath Chatterjee (1996), Pranab Mukherjee (1997), S. Jaipal Reddy (1998), Lal Krishna Advani (1999), Arjun Singh (2000), Jaswant Singh (2001), Dr Manmohan Singh (2002), Sharad Pawar (2003), Mrs Sushma Swaraj (2004), P. Chidambaram (2005) and Mani Shankar Aiyar (2006).

Some members suggested that one of the young members should be chosen for a different annual award for his performance in Parliament. This suggestion is awaiting a final decision.

■

The Parliament library has a vast collection of books, journals, documents and reports. The space allotted for them was insufficient. The books, journals and reports were kept at several places on the premises of Parliament, as well as in other buildings and godowns. Every year, new books and reports are added to the existing stock, creating greater scarcity of space. So, it was decided that a new library building should be built. In fact, once, the foundation stone for a new library building was laid in the compound of the annexe, but the project was abandoned. It was discussed periodically, but no final decision was taken for many years. I knew the history and difficulties the project faced. After I took over as the speaker, I discussed the issue with the prime minister, who agreed to support the idea that a new library building should be constructed. I discussed the matter with the minister for urban development and told him that Parliament would decide on the design and plan of the building, his ministry would build the structure, and Parliament would not interfere in the matter, except to ascertain that the construction was done in accordance with the design and plans. He agreed to get the building constructed by his ministry. He suggested that, every month, a progress report on the construction would be given to me and Parliament. With this understanding, after getting the approval of the government, the construction work was started. I decided not to have an ostentatious foundation stone-laying ceremony. The building was to be constructed in the compound where the old Parliament building stood.

The original design prepared by the architect provided for a star-shaped building. He had followed the designs used in building temples in some parts of India, but I thought that the new building should harmonize with the old one and should also be circular like the old Parliament building. These suggestions were incorporated in the plan.

The old building is a magnificent structure. It was decided that its view should not be obstructed by the new building. So, it was decided that one storey should be above ground and two storeys should be underground. Thus, the major portion of the building was to be underground.

When the actual excavation to construct the underground portion of the building was started, it was found that there were large, hard stones below a certain level that could not be easily removed. The construction company asked for permission to blast the stones with explosives, so that the work could be done on time. I refused to grant the permission, and everyone in Parliament also agreed that the blasting operation could damage the structure of the old Parliament building and should not be allowed. Instead, the builders got special equipment to drill holes in the stones and break them with pressure put through them.

The builders stuck to the plans and built the library according to the design given to them. The building has an auditorium, several committee rooms, rooms to store reading material, rooms for readers to read and study, a studio and offices. The books in the library at that time were counted in the millions, and in the future, their number was going to increase. It was felt that the building should have enough space to store and keep them properly for the next fifty years at least. Designed and planned to have the most modern equipment and gadgets in order to store, retrieve and use reading material, video and audio tapes, the library was also meant to be able to communicate with all the libraries of the state legislatures in and outside the country, as well as international organizations. It was expected to remain ultra-modern for a long time, and have the most convenient facilities to study and rest at intervals. Though the building was built according to the original design and plans, it could not have the modern facilities of libraries which are available in other advanced countries. The furniture did not harmonize with the building and its ethos. The speakers and officers, who took over the supervision of the construction later, had their own views and concepts which were not totally in line with the original ideas. This is the reason why the ultimate product is a little different from what was originally planned. All the same, the building received international appreciation for its architectural magnificence and beauty.

A major part of the building was constructed while I was the speaker. It was inaugurated when the government which had sanctioned the project was not in power. It is a national project of the people and for the people of the country. It is a storehouse of information and a temple of knowledge. Anybody who had anything to do with its construction could feel satisfied and proud that it was completed in time and in the best possible manner.

The day it was inaugurated, I was not in Delhi. On that day, I had lost my daughter and I was with her mortal remains in Bangalore. In life, probably, there is an arrangement for the sum total of loss and gain, happiness and sorrow, to be kept at the same level at all times. It is not easy to know why these things happen and who is responsible for them. A human being needs to put up with them with a balanced and stoical mind, which I did.

■

Some people think that the Indian Parliament does not function in an orderly manner. There are others who think that it functions like the legislature in other countries and at times it gets disturbed. Therefore, it need not be criticized beyond a point and people need not be disenchanted with its method of functioning. They also think that only a few members create the noise and chaos, while the majority of them conduct their activities in line with the rules of procedure and conventions and in a dignified and sober manner.

Parliamentary proceedings should certainly not be disrupted. Parliament is meant to make laws and pass budgets. If it is disturbed, it is likely to commit mistakes. As it is an institution at the apex, it should work flawlessly. Of course, it may commit mistakes. If the mistakes are committed with design, they are objectionable, but if they occur because of oversight or any other bonafide reason, they can be corrected and tolerated. In my opinion, the Indian Parliament functions as legislatures in India and other countries function. However, there is scope for improving upon its working. So efforts should be made to make it function better, and in a more effective and disciplined manner.

∎

What can be done to see that Parliament functions in a better and more effective manner?

The departmentally related Parliamentary Standing Committees should continue to regulate parliamentary proceedings. Information relating to Parliament's legislative and parliamentary activities should be computerized. The proceedings in Parliament should be televised, as is done now.

Parliament should function for more days and hours than it is doing now. If the time available for a discussion is limited, members compete for opportunities to speak, and in the process, disturbances occur. In some countries, Parliaments work throughout the year, except for holidays. In India, which is a very big country, it should function for a larger number of days than it does currently, if not for all the working days of the year. It is better if it functions throughout the year.

In India, the committee system can be strengthened. If committees carry more loads, the load on the plenary can be reduced. If the committees examine the executive functioning in greater detail, it may become less necessary to do so in the plenary. And that would reduce the chances of disturbances in the plenary.

Often, members who join Parliament are not fully acquainted with parliamentary procedures. When they do not clearly know what should and can be done, and what should not and cannot be done, and how business should be transacted, they are unlikely to use the available time and opportunities correctly, and are likely to quarrel with other members or the presiding officers to get opportunities to make their speeches and points.

Parliament trains the new members for a few days, but this kind of training is insufficient. Audio and video tapes can be prepared for training purposes, which is bound to make them more proficient in using the system in the best possible manner.

In India, members are prohibited from making written speeches. If they read out their speeches, as is done in other countries, they can make more points in a shorter time, and make them more cogently and precisely. In the US and some other countries, members are asked to read out their speeches. They speak for three or four minutes. Within the given time, they convey the gist of their views and perform their task efficiently. The logic which is put forward for banning written speeches in India and other countries is that the speeches may be given to the members by some interested parties from outside the legislature, which should not be permitted. This logic does not take into account the fact that the outside people who want to express their views through MPs can ask the members to do so, even without written speeches.

In the US, the members of the Senate and the House of Representatives, and the legislatures in Europe and many other countries, can speak only from the podium. In Parliament and legislatures of the states in India, in the Parliaments of UK and countries following the Westminster model, the members are permitted to speak from their seats. When speaking is allowed only from the podium, order in the legislature is maintained in a better manner. Where it is allowed from the seat, the legislature is likely to be disturbed. So in India also, the system of allowing members to speak only from the podium should be introduced, to make the proceedings more orderly and disciplined.

The Constitution provides on what subjects and topics laws should be made by Parliament and what subjects and laws should be made by the state legislature. This is made clear by giving the Union, state and concurrent lists and in other articles. The district, taluka and local bodies are not allowed to make laws. They are permitted to make rules and take decisions on subjects allotted to them by the Constitution and the laws made by the legislatures. If members know what can be exclusively discussed in Parliament, the state legislature or other bodies, the time can be better managed to deliberate on relevant topics. However, it is often seen that members attempt to raise, discuss and decide matters that cannot be done in Parliament. Therefore, members of the legislatures should know the constitutional provisions in clear terms. But as that does not happen, the proceedings are burdened and disturbed unnecessarily. To think that without understanding the Constitution, it would be easy to function in Parliament is incorrect. This deficiency should be removed through lectures and training organized for the benefit of new members.

The speaker is expected to maintain order in the House. He can use the authority given to him and punish any member who violates his orders. In some cases, he has to obtain the consent of the House to punish an erring legislator. He can ask an unruly member to leave the House, suspend such a member and disallow him from attending the House for any number of days decided by him and the House. In some cases, his membership can be terminated with the consent of the House. The presiding officers have used these powers very carefully and sparingly. They always tolerate mistakes committed by mischief-mongers and try to discipline them through persuasive methods.

When the golden jubilee of Parliament under the Indian Constitution was celebrated, the Lok Sabha decided that in many grave cases, the speaker could take action against erring members, without obtaining the consent of the House. However, even now, the speaker does not freely use the powers given to him. He refrains from doing so because once action is taken against a member, obtaining his cooperation for smooth functioning of the House later becomes more difficult.

Once, the members of the opposition decided not to allow discussions on the annual budget presented to the Lok Sabha to take place. They obstructed the discussion on all the days allotted for discussion. The government was worried, and I was asked if the budget would be passed or not, because if it was not passed, the government would face problems. I assured the government that I would see that the budget would be passed. When the members wanted to know how that could be done, I told them that they should leave it to me and not worry.

In my mind, I had decided to give a long rope to the members of the opposition. My plan was to disallow them from coming to the House one day before the budget was to be passed, and in their absence, get it passed. The members of the opposition were expecting me to try this strategy. I then decided not to disallow them from coming to the House one day before the budget was to be passed. I preferred to disallow them from coming to the House in the morning session on the date on which it was expected to be passed, i.e. 31 March, and pass it in their absence. The members of the opposition party felt that if that happened, it would create an adverse public opinion against them. So, they took the decision to allow the budget to be passed on the last day in the morning session and conveyed it to me.

It suited me also because I did not really want to impose my harsh decision on them. Thus, on the last day in the morning session, the budget was passed unopposed in the presence of the members of the opposition in the House.

What I did was practical. I could have solved the problem by adopting a legal position, but it could have hampered the smooth functioning of the House. So my authority and tactics were based on law and pragmatism in the future at least to some extent and that helped. It only goes to show that the parliamentary system of democracy needs to be dealt with in a sagacious manner.

■

Another time, a member made a very rabid and unparliamentary remark in the House. Immediately, there was a hue and cry in the House, demanding that he should be punished. I could have put the matter to the House and got a resolution passed to punish the member, since the members present in the House would have had no difficulty in voting in favour of the resolution. I wanted the member to apologize, but he was unwilling to do so. The members in the House insisted on passing a resolution in the House, but I ruled that the matter would be sent to the Committee of Privileges. On getting its report, it would be put to the House, and the member would be dealt with according to law and as per the decision of the Privileges Committee. The leader of the member's party explained to him that he would be punished by the committee, and advised him to apologize. The member also realized the seriousness of the issue, and felt that tendering an apology was better, for him. He apologized and the case was closed. Later, he was very careful not to make any wrong statements.

■

The executive in India consists of selected members of the legislature. A person who is not a member of the legislature can be a minister only for six months. If he does not get elected to the legislature within six months, he ceases to be a member of the executive.

In other words, the executive and the legislature are not fully separated from each other. The executive can initiate policies, prepare bills and budgets, and get them passed by the legislature. The legislature can refuse to approve the policies, bills or budgets, and hold the executive accountable for what it does or does not do.

The executive can remain in existence only if it enjoys the support of the legislature.

The members of the executive can attend the sittings of the legislature, and are allowed to express their views in the Houses of Parliament. It is only they who can address the legislature, and not the government officials. In some countries, the members of the legislature cannot be members of the executive. If a member of the legislature joins the executive, he has to resign from his membership of legislature. In other countries, members of the executive cannot enter the Houses of legislature and address their members. Thus, there are countries, such as France, where the separation between the executive and the legislature is more pronounced than in India. In some other countries, like the US, it is complete.

In India and the US, the judiciary is fully separated from the executive and the legislature. In the US, a person becomes a judge of the Supreme Court after his appointment is endorsed by the Senate. In India, the appointment of a judge does not need the approval of the legislature. Thus, in India, the executive appoints the members of the judiciary and the legislature does not have any say in their appointments.

In some countries, like France, constitutional matters are decided by a group of judges and a few members of the executive and the legislature. In France, other matters are decided by judges who have nothing to do with executive or legislative duties and are not members of either body. In UK, all kinds of matters can be decided by the members of the executive, the legislature and the judiciary working together. Here the concept of separation of powers is not in vogue as it is in USA, France, India and a few other countries. In India, constitutional matters are heard and decided by the higher judiciary, that is, only the High Courts and the Supreme Court. The members of the executive and/or the legislature cannot hear and decide the issues brought up and pronounce judgements on any matter, except as provided by law.

The principle of separation of powers ensures that powers are not concentrated in one authority, to avoid absolute power corrupting the authority absolutely. The executive has to perform the task of execution, while the legislature has to perform the task of legislation, and the judiciary has to dispense justice and interpret laws. These tasks need different kinds of capabilities and experiences. They cannot be performed well if they are performed by one authority, lacking the high level of abilities required for each of these duties to be performed in time and in the best possible manner, which is acceptable to the people. Each of these wings of government has vast duties to perform. Hence, in modern times, the theories of separation and decentralization of powers are accepted and used.

Separation of powers helps in governance in diverse ways, but it also creates some difficulties. When things are done in compartments, a holistic approach is given a go-by. In many countries following this theory, the executive, legislature and judiciary have developed contradictions and misunderstandings in their relations and working with one another. They have functioned in a manner which indicates that they are not a part of the whole but are completely separate from one another. This has happened more in countries where the separation of power is more pronounced, as in the US.

The three wings of government are parts of the state, which is an organic whole. The brains, the eyes, the ears, the hands, the legs, the heart, and the digestive system of the human body discharge different duties and perform different functions. But they are all dependent on one another, and cannot function efficiently if they become fully disconnected from one another. They function in a manner useful to one another, and to the body. The executive, the legislature and the judiciary have to function in the same manner. They are separate from each other and function on their own, but what one does impacts on the other. If they become completely disconnected, unaware and oblivious of the impacts they create on one another, they would create problems similar to those created if the heart, the brain and the digestive system in the body functioned in a totally unconnected manner.

In India, the executive, the legislature and the judiciary have functioned in accordance with the provisions of the Constitution, which has helped the state to govern. On occasions problems did occur between their approaches when dealing with their relations with one another and in performing their duties. But, very wisely, they were solved by those who headed these wings, at times, on their own, without consulting one another, at times, in consultation with each other and in accordance with the words and true spirit of the Constitution.

The executive remains accountable to the legislature, and submits to the final decisions of the judiciary. The legislature helps the executive to make policies and laws, and also holds it accountable. The legislature is not subject to decisions pronounced by the judiciary in relation to what it does in the Houses on matters generally of procedural nature, as is made clear in the Constitution. Yet, on some occasions, the judiciary tried to pronounce judgements on what the legislature did, while following the procedure laid down for its functioning. That was when conflicts arose. Yet, they were not allowed to escalate and become a hurdle in the smooth functioning of the government, as a whole. In those matters, the wisdom and holistic vision of those who headed them helped. The same kind of approach is visible today also. Generally, they see that a cooperative ambience prevails in their efforts to discharge their duties.

■

In the ninth Lok Sabha, two complaints were filed before the speaker. One was against a judge of the Supreme Court and the other one was against the chief election commissioner. The procedure for impeaching the election commissioner is the same as that followed for impeaching a judge of a High Court or the Supreme Court.

In the first case, the speaker admitted the notice given to him, signed by more than a hundred members. A committee was constituted to hear the parties, record the evidence and give a report, which could be discussed in the Houses of Parliament. However, the Lok Sabha did not pass the motion by the requisite number of votes. So, the matter ended without impeaching the judge. The voting on the impeachment was done in the tenth Lok Sabha.

That case was the first to be considered by the Lok Sabha. It was handled very carefully. Information regarding such matters from other countries and the procedures followed by them was collected. The judge was allowed to present his case through his lawyer, who argued the case for over four hours. Members who were lawyers also took an interest in making their arguments, supporting as well as opposing the case. Some members of the legislature, the judiciary, the media and the society thought that the decision taken by the House was just and correct, while others disagreed. Those who held the first view thought that the charges levelled against the judge were not of serious nature requiring his impeachment, and that the evidence produced was not sufficient to prove the charges. Those who held the second view thought that judges need to be above board in every respect, and if a judge is found to have committed a wrong, he does not deserve to continue in the post and should be impeached and punished.

In the second case of impeachment, the notice was not admitted. Those who had given the notice were asked to appear before the speaker and prove that there was a prima facie case to be taken up and examined fully, according to the provisions of the law. They did not care to respond and appear before the authority to support their stand, even after several notices were served on them. So a final notice was issued, stating that if they failed to support their case with evidence and their arguments, it would be presumed that they had nothing to say. When they refrained from making their points as required by law, the notice was rejected and the case was closed.

The chief election commissioner is given this kind of immunity and protection to ensure that he is not pressurized while deciding election matters. That is why he is also given the same protection under the law as a judge of the High Court or the Supreme Court.

In UP, the legislative assembly found a journalist guilty of having committed a breach of privilege, and punished him with imprisonment for a certain period. The journalist approached the High Court and obtained an order which stayed the implementation of the decision by the assembly. The legislative assembly issued a notice to the judge, asking why he should not be proceeded against for having interfered in the proceedings of the House, and for having committed a breach of privilege of the legislature. The High Court issued a notice of contempt of court against the speaker for not following the order of the court, and against these notices, appeals were filed in the Supreme Court. The matter attracted the attention of the people, media, politicians and jurists. It was discussed at the highest level of the country, with a view to see that a confrontation between the legislature and the judiciary was avoided. The legislature was of the opinion that courts could not interfere in the proceedings of the legislature, while the judiciary was of the view that the court could interfere, if it was found that a patent wrong was committed and the wrong was clearly visible. The judiciary went to the extent of saying that even if the Constitution specifically disallowed non-interference by the judiciary, the courts could use their inherent powers to dispense justice, even against the specific provisions, and interfere in matters with the legislature, in order to see that no injustice was perpetrated. The Supreme Court, however, dismissed the contempt case and closed the matter. Thus, the powers of the legislature to punish wrongdoers, and interfering in legislative proceedings were reduced to some extent through this ruling.

In one case in Malta, the legislature of the country punished a person for breach of privilege of the House. The matter was taken to the highest court in the country, and it also decided that the legislature had the authority to discipline and punish the wrongdoers, in the interest of the orderly conduct of business in the House. The country then became a member of the European

Court of Criminal Justice. The case was taken to that court, which decided that the legislature was not a court that could dispense criminal justice. It had a duty to make laws and policies and pass budgets. For this purpose, it needed discipline in the House, which it could secure by taking disciplinary action against a wrongdoer, not amounting to punishment. It went on to say that the legislature could discipline the members, but could not punish him as though he had committed a crime. This matter was discussed in international conferences of the Commonwealth Parliamentary Association and members of the Inter Parliamentary Union (IPU), privately and officially, in an oblique manner.

There are two objectives to be achieved. One is to ensure that the proceedings of the House are conducted in a disciplined manner. The other is that matters discussed in the House are brought to the notice of the people at large, without fear or favour shown to anyone. When it is held that discipline in the House is required and important, one stand can be taken. When it is held that the right to information should be freely enjoyed by the people, the other stand can be taken. It is not easy to lay down rigid rules to achieve these objectives. Much depends on the facts of the case and the intentions behind the actions. It is better to be balanced and restrained, and try to be as correct as possible, taking a holistic view of the matter.

In India, the members of the executive, legislature and judiciary have been circumspect, and have tried to be holistic and correct in the stands they have taken. That was why, on many occasions, tricky situations could be tackled in a tactful, correct and just way, without creating unnecessary tension.

Two such cases occurred during the tenth Lok Sabha. In one case, the speaker of a legislative assembly terminated the membership of a few members for violating the Anti-Defection Law. The members who lost their seats approached the High Court of the state and obtained an order permitting them to attend the sittings of the House, without exercising the right to vote. They attended the

House, according to the court order. The secretary of the legislature was instructed to throw them out of the House, which he did not do, so his services were terminated for not implementing the orders of his superior. He appealed to the High Court against his dismissal. The court asked his superior to undo the injustice done to the secretary, but the superior did not implement the court order to reinstate the secretary. A notice for contempt of court was issued against the superior, who then counter-attacked by issuing a notice of breach of privilege against the judge, for interfering in the proceedings of the House and the exercise of the authority of the head of the legislature. Under these circumstances, the Supreme Court was approached. The Supreme Court issued notices to the concerned parties, but the head of the legislature did not respond to the notice of the Supreme Court and avoided appearing, personally or through his lawyer, in the court. The Supreme Court issued a notice of contempt of court, but that notice was also not heeded, even when the Supreme Court asked the state executive to produce the person against whom the notice was issued. The Union executive was asked to help the court to discharge its duty and to produce the required person in the court, and it was only then that the head of the legislature was compelled to appear in the Supreme Court.

The speakers of the state legislatures complained against the Supreme Court order issuing the notice and telling the speaker to appear in court. They did not want the dignity of the presiding officers to be trifled with, and wanted a resolution to be passed, criticizing the actions taken by the court. However, after due deliberation on the issue, they refrained from insisting on passing the resolution.

The Supreme Court knew about the situation that was developing. The court was also of the view that there should be no confrontation between the legislature and the judiciary. It wanted to assert its authority, but did not want to create a conflict between the two wings of the government. So, when the head of the legislature appeared in the court hall, the presiding judge declared that it was not necessary to proceed with the contempt case—and the matter was closed. It is true that certain aspects of the case could have been tackled in a different manner to avoid this unnecessary acrimony. Yet, it is also true that those who took the final decision conducted the proceedings in a way that did not widen the divide between the two wings of the state. Here lay true sagacity and an enlightened approach, which should be cultivated and practised.

In one case pending in a court in Delhi against a politician, all the politicians were criticized. When the judgement was pronounced, Parliament was in session. Senior members raised the issue in the Lok Sabha and argued that while deciding a case against a particular politician, who was also a parliamentarian, it was wrong to criticize all the politicians and parliamentarians. The members of the Lok Sabha demanded that a notice of breach of privilege of the House and Parliament should be issued against the judge who had passed the judgement. Almost all members of the House felt hurt and insulted, believing that judgements of that nature obstructed the exercise of the member's right to function freely. The House insisted on sending a notice to the judge. I persuaded the members to agree to allow me to read the judgement first, to decide if a notice should or should not be issued. I went through the judgement, which included the judge's alleged pronouncements against the parliamentarians. The matter might have been brought to the notice of the chief justice of the Delhi High Court and that of the Supreme Court. Suo moto, the judgement was examined by the chief justice of the High Court. The portion against which the objection was taken was deleted and the judge of the lower court was advised not to pass such remarks against those who were not present before him to defend themselves. The next day, the matter of issuing the notice was again taken up in the House. I informed the House about the High Court's action and told the members that in view of those facts, it was not necessary to issue a notice. Initially, the members thought that the notice should be issued. However, they too, realized the correctness of the logic behind my stand and agreed to desist from pressing for the stringent step, which was no longer needed.

What the Supreme Court, the High Court and the legislature did was wise, correct and just. With the wisdom and maturity of all concerned, the matter was handled with circumspection. It is this kind of approach which helped the three wings of the state to function, without letting the situation escalate into unnecessary confrontation. Laws can help, and human beings can ensure the laws are made effective and useful. At times, human beings make mistakes, but if the mistakes are tackled in a sagacious manner, they do not create insurmountable problems.

There have been occasions when laws are made, decisions are taken, and judgements are pronounced which have not been fully approved by the people, professionals and intellectuals. Yet, those who have manned the three wings of the government have conducted their duties in such a manner that laws, executive decisions and judgements have not created problems. On the contrary, they have limited their adverse impact and helped in taking governance in the right direction. The spirit and letter of the law, the spirit and design of executive decisions, and the wisdom and vision found in judgements have been followed to a very great extent in the governance of the country, and to protect the interests of the people, the country and our system.

■

Some feel that parliamentary debates during the first few Lok Sabhas were of a very high order, while those during the last few years were not of the same standard. After independence was achieved, the freedom fighters joined Parliament. They were successful lawyers, doctors, academicians and experts in their fields of work. They were fired by ideologies followed in the struggle for independence. They knew the people of the country from close quarters and had travelled widely in different parts of the world. They were well read, erudite leaders who had thought about many aspects of governance and life. Whatever they said in and outside Parliament was heard with respect. They spoke in chaste and pristine language. Their speeches could be compared with the best in the world. Their speeches related to the philosophies, ideologies and policies they desired to adopt for the country and they did not have personal biases and narrow approaches where issues of national importance were concerned.

In the periods after the first few Lok Sabhas, the government's attention was concentrated on plans and projects. The speeches of the legislators of those times emphasized development and were related to actions taken by the government rather than to ideas and concepts. They did not waste time criticizing the government, but concentrated on the contours of plans and projects. They were accepted and admired by the people and those who were interested in developmental activities. During that period, the number of freedom fighters, lawyers and academicians in Parliament was reduced and were replaced by people who were successful in various fields. Even at that time, it was felt that the standard of debates was better in the earlier times.

Recently, the emphasis has not been on ideas and policies, or on plans and projects. It has been on discovering mistakes committed in implementing policies, plans and projects. The speeches contribute less towards the making of policies, plans and projects and more towards criticizing the executive and finding fault with them. They are politically motivated and often biased in favour of or against particular members belonging to particular political folds. These speeches do not compare well with those made soon after independence was achieved or a little later.

During all the three periods after independence, there were a few members who were erudite and respected, and whose statements were heard with rapt attention. The performances of the most articulate members of these periods are not always compared with each other. Instead, the performances of the most learned members of the earlier periods are compared with the performances of all members of the present times. Therein lies the mistake. It is true that the average performance of members of the earlier periods was better than the average performance of the periods that followed. But in the performances of the best members of the past and the present, there is very little difference. Moreover, we need to look at the aspects of life and development that are being discussed. There is bound to be a difference between a speech on ideologies, policies, plans and projects and a speech made to criticize without suggesting improvements. In all the periods, policies and plans were made and implemented, but the emphasis has not been the same. And that is why we feel the speeches of all the periods have not been of the same standard.

Some members' speeches are appreciated for the high standard of the language used. Others are appreciated for their contents, which may be relevant to the present situation or may be of a futuristic nature. They may provide facts and figures or speak about directions to be taken. They may depend on theoretical knowledge or experiences of life. They may be prepared by burning the midnight oil or made extempore, on the basis of an understanding developed by living a full-fledged life. They may be made by using the faculties of understanding or aspirations of the heart or through spiritual inspiration. They may make the audience laugh, think or act.

I had the pleasure of listening to all kinds of speeches. I appreciated those which emanated from the heart and reached other hearts. And I realized that in every Lok Sabha, there were members whose speeches compared well with the best made by the members of different countries. The current MPs are in tune with the realities of their times. And so, in my view, their standards and speeches are of a high order.

■

The Inter Parliamentary Union (IPU) is a body of parliamentarians of different countries. It meets twice a year, in countries selected by the Union. The Commonwealth Parliamentary Union (CPU) is a body consisting of MPs of Commonwealth countries and meets once in a year. The concept relating to the IPU developed in France, and it is said that the concept of the League of Nations emanated from that of the IPU. Later, the United Nations was brought into existence on the basis of the concept of the League of Nations. Every two years, a conference of the speakers of the countries of the CPU takes place. Conferences of the speakers of countries of the regions of the IPU take place every year in different countries. An association of parliamentarians of South Asian countries was also created, and although it was expected to meet every year, it meets as and when the members decide. The conferences take place in countries willing to host them. Thus, every year, the presiding officers and a few MPs travel to different countries to attend the international conferences of legislators. Delegations of MPs and the presiding officers of different Parliaments are invited to visit each other. The presiding officers and the Parliament of India invite the presiding officers and MPs of other countries to visit India, and every year, Indian parliamentary delegations visit other countries on several occasions. The speaker visits several countries, making almost as many visits as the foreign minister does.

The members of the different Parliaments contribute to policymaking in their own countries. In the international conferences, they deliberate on several issues and learn how the representatives of different countries think about issues of international importance. Sometimes, they influence each other. Through their deliberations, the angularities in their concepts are rounded, their visions are widened and they become far-sighted. The results of the deliberations may not be visible immediately, but they remain in their subconscious minds, and are often expressed when they are expected to take a stand in their policymaking forums. International conferences and organizations help in creating a unity of approach between the countries of the world. They prove useful in globalization, which is beneficial to everyone, avoid misunderstanding between countries holding different views, and bring about harmony and a cooperative ambience among different parts of the world.

India supports the idea of making our world integrated. It has been in favour of the League of Nations, the United Nations, the IPU, the CPU, SAARC and other such organizations. It always attends international and regional conferences and believes in bilateral interactions between India and other countries. Therefore, I attended almost all the international and regional conferences and participated in bilateral interactions with other countries.

Most delegations that attend conferences and visit other countries include the leader of the opposition, leaders of various parliamentary political parties and other important members. While travelling abroad, the members of the delegations had opportunities to discuss several matters of national and international importance in a friendly and unbiased manner. It was a pleasure to interact and exchange views with them. The members of the delegations often became good friends, and in some cases, their friendships were so strong that they lasted their whole lives.

The IPU conference held in Delhi was attended by delegations from almost all the member countries. The conferences of non-aligned countries and of the heads of states and governments of the Commonwealth countries were held successfully in India, organized under the guidance and presidentship of Indiraji. At those conferences, certain standards were fixed and achieved, which became the guiding principles for other conferences held in India. The IPU and CPU conferences also followed the procedures and principles followed in the non-aligned and Commonwealth countries' conferences. The Parliament of India followed them very meticulously. After the conclusion of the conference, the members of the delegations were taken to various parts of the country, according to their choice, to see how India was developing and how fascinating Indian culture, architecture, flora and fauna, and the mountains and rivers are.

In the IPU conference, it was suggested that the CPU conference should also be held in India. Therefore, the CPU conference was also held in Delhi and was as impressive and meaningful as the IPU conference was. After the conference, the delegates were taken to different cities and areas of India. The IPU decided that the regional conference of Southeast Asia and South Asia should be organized in India, and so it was. After the SAARC Union of Parliamentarians was created, it was decided that its first conference should be held in Pakistan. However, Pakistan expressed its reluctance to organize it, which is why India agreed to host it. Thus, in five years, from 1991 to 1996, four international conferences of parliamentarians were held in India. These conferences helped to dispel several wrong impressions held by members of some countries, encouraged tourism and created conditions for better cooperation between different countries of the world.

During those five years, I attended international conferences and bilateral meetings as the head of the Indian delegation in Chile, Australia, Sri Lanka, Cyprus, Nepal, the Bahamas, China, Cyprus, Bulgaria, Romania, France, Germany, Ireland, Israel, the US, Egypt, Austria, Hungary, Mongolia, Canada, Kuwait, Syria, the UK and Bangladesh.

At the IPU conference held in Santiago, Chile, the president of the IPU had to be elected. The speaker of Pakistan was one of the candidates for the post and was opposed by a candidate from UK. The delegation from Pakistan asked the Indian delegation to help its candidate with its vote, which was done. India helped its neighbour with the hope that the gesture could help both countries to better their relations and understanding. However, the candidate from the UK won the election.

The president of Sri Lanka, Ranasinghe Premadasa, was the president of SAARC. He was keen that SAARC should establish unions of parliamentarians, members of the judiciary and members of the industry, to allow them to function and to create greater opportunities for the people of South Asia to interact with each other. The prime minister of India, P.V. Narasimha Rao, was also of the view that such unions should be brought into existence.

Barring one or two countries, leaders of most countries were also in favour of creating them.

The first meeting of the speakers of the Parliaments of SAARC countries was held in Colombo, Sri Lanka. A decision to create the union was taken at that meeting. The second meeting was held in Nepal, where the rules for the union were drafted. The rules mentioned that bilateral and contentious issues would not be taken up for discussion at the union's meetings. The reason for such a provision was to ensure that the union became a forum for cooperation in matters of mutual interest and benefit, and not for discussing controversial and contentious issues. Pakistan offered some resistance to the idea of not taking up contentious issues for discussion in the meetings of the union, but because this provision was exactly in line with one of the provisions of the charter creating SAARC, it was ultimately accepted by all countries. The third meeting to accept the rules was held in Dhaka. The rules were approved, and it was also decided that the first meeting of the member countries of the union should be held in Pakistan. However, that meeting could not take place. It was then decided to hold it in India. And so, it was held in Delhi.

When the issue to create the union was discussed, it was suggested by some intellectuals that it should be created on the lines of the European Union. However, that concept was not accepted.

Parliamentary delegations from the European Union, China, Japan, Surinam, Nepal, Canada, Australia, the Maldives, Seychelles, Cyprus, Turkey, Jordan, Syria, Iran, Afghanistan, Kuwait, Bahrain, Trinidad and Tobago, Russia, Uzbekistan, Kazakhstan, Poland, the UK, Mexico, Botswana, Romania, Germany, Switzerland, Bulgaria, Morocco, Tanzania, Egypt, Namibia, Botswana, Thailand, Korea, Vietnam, Cuba, Brazil and South Africa have visited India in the last few years.

The Indian Parliament welcomed these visits, considering them important. Thorough preparations were made to ensure that all the visits produced good understanding and results. The officers of the ministry of external affairs and other concerned ministries prepared papers and provided documents on the subjects that were fixed, or likely to come up, for discussions. On all the meetings held between the Indian and foreign delegates, comprehensive reports were prepared for the government and Parliament. The reports contained the points on which actions were needed to be taken immediately, or within a reasonable period of time. They were dispatched to give information to the prime minister, external affairs minister and other concerned ministers. During the visits to foreign countries, the Indian delegations called on the heads of states and governments of the countries visited. That gave the delegates opportunities to obtain authentic views on issues important to India and other countries from those who were in a position to speak with authority.

The Indian delegation headed by the speaker visited Australia at the invitation of the speaker of the Lower House of the Australian Parliament. The delegation visited Melbourne, Sydney, the capital Canberra and Perth, the four important cities of the country. Melbourne is a beautiful city. Sydney is like New York and Mumbai, the financial and industrial capital of Australia. Perth, located in the western part of Australia is, in my opinion, one of the most beautiful cities in the world.

In Canberra, the delegation met the prime minister, the presiding officers of both Houses and other MPs. In the meetings, matters of mutual interest between the two countries and those relating to international issues were discussed. Australia is a continent and a large country, but sparsely populated. Australians pay considerable attention to agriculture, and since they produce more food than required by its people, they export it. They discussed various matters with the Indian delegation, including why it was necessary for India to strengthen its navy. They thought that to maintain peace in the oceans, naval forces of different countries should be developed in such a manner that they do not threaten one another. It was quite clear that Australia was keen to have cordial relations with China and India. Of course, it is closer to China in geographical terms, and does trade and business with it and other countries of Southeast Asia. Recently, several diamond mines have been discovered in some parts of Australia. The government is keen to export rough and unpolished diamonds to other countries, including India. Internationally, Australia always sides with the countries of the West. However, it does not interfere much in conflicts that arise between the countries of the world. The visit definitely created goodwill and better understanding between the Parliaments of India and Australia.

At the invitation of the speaker of the Canadian Parliament, I led a delegation to that country and visited the National Parliament and the legislature of the state. The Parliament of Canada follows the Westminster model and it was interesting to discuss matters relevant to Parliament and other subjects with the presiding officers and members. The Indian delegation met Canadians of Indian origin who showed great interest in the economic development of India and wanted to know if they could invest in the industry and other economic activities of their country. They were told that they were welcome to invest in India and would be given all the help needed for that purpose. The Canadian speaker wanted books written by Mahatma Gandhi for the Canadian Parliament library. They were sent to him within a month. The Canadian Parliament library is beautiful and very well equipped. Canada is a vast country with a very small population and is one of the richest countries in the world. It has always been in favour of democracy and inclined towards the ideologies of the West. I met the governor-general and the prime minister of Canada. The prime minister informed me that he had visited China with a hundred Canadian industrialists and traders and that he was proposing a visit to India in the near future with nearly three hundred Canadian industrialists and traders. I told him that he and other members of his delegation would be welcome in India and we, in India, appreciated the interest they were showing in Indian matters.

The parliamentary delegation that visited China comprised senior parliamentarians. Atal Bihari Vajpayee and I.K. Gujral, who later became prime ministers of India, Rabi Ray, former speaker of the Lok Sabha, R.K. Dhawan, an important member of the Congress party, Renuka Choudhary, who was then an important member of the opposition party, and some other members were asked to join the delegation, which they did with pleasure. The delegation visited Beijing and Shanghai and called on the then prime minister of China, Li Ping, and the presiding officer of their Parliament. The discussions with the prime minister were fruitful and interesting. He expressed his country's desire to have friendly relations with India and other countries of the world. He said that the existing problems between the two countries could be solved through dialogue and discussions. He spoke about comments made by some countries on the human rights of the Chinese people. He stated that China attached greater importance to food, clothing, health and education, facilities needed by the people, rather than to agitations on the negative aspects of life. He was very forthright in saying that those who criticized China did not really understand what the people in his country wanted. He thought that China protected the human rights of its people in the best possible manner. Li Ping became the speaker of the Chinese Parliament and visited India later.

The city of Beijing looked more modern, neat, clean and impressive than it had one and a half decades ago. Shanghai can be compared with the city of New York or Mumbai with its highrise, modern buildings. In Shanghai, they took the delegation to an industrial estate being built on the outskirts of the city, which was planned as one of the biggest industrial centres in their country.

We were taken to places of historical importance. At the mausoleum of the first emperor of China, we saw an army of terracotta soldiers that had been unearthed from the ground. They looked very impressive and indicated how wars were planned and fought in ancient times. At another place, we saw a temple constructed by a Buddhist monk, which had scriptures on the philosophy of Buddha. In one city, the delegation was invited for lunch by the presiding officer and members of the provincial legislature, and it was there that one of the members of the Chinese legislature asked me a surprising question, 'How many gods are there in India?' The other members of the Indian delegation waited in bewilderment to hear my reply. I thought that the Chinese member was trying to poke fun at the Indian delegation. I told him, 'In India, nearly 900 million gods are there and worshipped.' He expressed his surprise and asked, 'Where are their temples located and built? Do you have enough temples in your country for them?' My reply was, 'In India, each human being is treated as a god and his body is supposed to be his temple.' The Chinese member looked at me for some time, then rose from his seat, came up to me, caught hold of my hand and shook it for quite some time, repeating that he was happy to hear what I had said. I asked him, 'What part of my reply made you happy?' He said, 'Mao Tse Tung used to tell us the same thing. He said that unless you treat others as gods, you are not going to treat them as equals and do justice to them. And this is exactly what you say you do in your country. And so, I was happy to hear that part.' I was surprised to hear what Mao Tse Tung used to say to convince the people about the importance of equality between the members of the society. A communist concept appeared to be quite close to a spiritual concept. Thoughts flow from different directions, but ultimately, they merge into each other. This is how we can understand one another and realize that all human beings are alike in their thoughts and views, in the ultimate analysis, and there is no scope for quarrelling, harming and killing one another.

The delegation's visits to different countries enlightened the members of Parliament about the way the world was developing and progressing. To build our country, it is necessary to help the needy, the weak and the poor in India. At the same time, it is essential to increase its productive capacity and adopt new means and methods to achieve these objectives. Remaining bogged down in one kind of activity and neglecting others are bound to bring about lopsided development and delay political, economic and social justice. Seeing how other countries manage their affairs helps to form our own policies in order to cope with our own problems in a better manner. The visits educated the delegates on an enormous scale.

In a political life of nearly five decades, I spent more time performing the duties of a presiding officer than duties of any other kind. For nearly nine years, I worked as the deputy and full-fledged presiding officer in the Union and the state legislatures. I was the deputy speaker for nearly one and a half years, and the speaker in the Maharashtra legislative assembly for one and a half years. For nearly one year, I was the deputy speaker in the Lok Sabha and the speaker for five years. During this period, I spoke as little as I could, and guided the members more than I did at any other time. I tried to be just, helpful and understanding with everyone who came in contact with me. My work gave me full satisfaction. My experience as a member of the executive helped me to provide better facilities to the legislatures and members to perform their duties and I was able to introduce new schemes and provide better facilities to the legislatures with ease and speed.

■

Our legislatures are the forums where laws and policies are made, budgets are passed and the executive is held accountable for what it does. Today, policy- and law-making appear less glamorous and attractive than criticizing the government. Therefore, more attention is paid to holding the government accountable and less to policy- and law-making. In fact, policies and laws apply to everyone in the country and remain in existence for years to come. Any mistake in making them is bound to affect large numbers of people. Policy- and law-making have to take into account their implications to different sections of society at different places in the country and at different times. They should therefore be made very carefully and without delays. If they are made in a hurry and wrongly, we should be worried. This fact should be impressed on the minds of the members, and they should be prepared to pay more attention to their main duties rather than to their subsidiary ones.

Principles that are totally valid and useful to small states may not be so valid and useful to larger states. In the same way, principles which are valid and useful to a country with a population of, say, sixty or seventy million, are not valid to a country which has a population of, say, 200 or 300 million. Certainly, on the same principle, it can be said that the principles and procedures valid for a country with 200 to 300 million people cannot prove to be of full use to a country with a population of, say, 1,000 to 1,050 million. So, for example, what works for the city state of Singapore or UK, a small country, would not have any full efficacy for big countries like India and China. They need principles, procedures and Constitutions of a different nature, which suit their conditions. What is followed in UK is different from that in Singapore. What is followed in UK, Canada, Australia and India is based on a set of principles which are by and large identical in nature.

The legislatures in UK, Canada, Australia and India attach great importance to the accountability of the executive, which can be pulled down and dissolved at any time and has to be reconstituted by fresh elections. The legislature as well as the executive in USA, Russia and China are more stable, and this helps in paying more attention to policy- and law-making. In France, the executive is quite stable. In India, Canada, UK and Australia, neither the executive nor the legislature is stable—some of them have survived, at times for a few months or one or two years only. Instability of this nature has made governments less effective and less productive. The time has come for these deficiencies to be done away with. What is adopted need not be thrown to the wind and given up totally; only modification in some principles and procedures are needed. The legislature should not be dissolved easily, and the executive should not be dissolved by a simple majority. It is elected by the people, who cannot dissolve it, so a special majority should be required to dissolve it. Such a decision should not be taken by only one House. If there are two Houses, they should be involved in taking the decision to dissolve the House of the People with a special majority.

Two issues are considered while deciding the position of the legislature. One pertains to accountability, the other to stability. The question is: is accountability more important than stability? In fact, both are needed. Therefore, one cannot be jettisoned to save the other. A balance should be struck between the requirements of the two.

At present, the concept of stability occupies a subsidiary position, and that of accountability occupies the primary position. But if the balance tilts more against stability, some steps need to be taken to avoid its ill effects and to restore the balance. Otherwise, the system would become less effective, more maligned and would, finally, become very weak and ineffective.

20

SITTING ON THE OPPOSITION BENCHES

For nearly eight years, the Congress party was not in power. During that period, H.D. Deve Gowda, I.K. Gujral and Atal Bihari Vajpayee were prime ministers. During this period, three general elections to the Lok Sabha were held. The elections were fought fiercely and were tough. However, I could win them with reduced margins. During this period, P.V. Narasimha Rao resigned from the presidentship of the Congress party, and Sitaram Kesari became the president. Later, he too resigned, and Mrs Sonia Gandhi became the president.

•

Soniaji appointed me as the chairman of the media committee of the party. The committee was chaired by V.N. Gadgil for a few years. Later, it was chaired by Varma. The committee briefed the media every day on important and relevant issues, and the stand of the party on them. On special occasions, the committee held press briefings. It was given the responsibility of ensuring that members of the media were facilitated to attend and cover meetings of the Congress president and other leaders of the party. During elections, it received the manifesto and other printed material, and distributed them to the Congress candidates and leaders. The chairman of the committee was assisted by a few other members. On some important occasions, the chairman had to brief the press, while in day-to-day briefings, other members spoke to the media. After becoming the chairman, I tried to refurbish the room where briefings were held, and to get the library on the premises reorganized and properly run. The party decided that besides talking to the media in Delhi, it was necessary to brief the media in all the state capitals and even at the district levels in all parts of the country. The state units were asked to constitute media cells and activate them. Meetings of the chairpersons of the State Media Committees were also held. In some states, the committees were quite active and effective.

Elections to the legislative assemblies of four states—Delhi, Rajasthan, Madhya Pradesh and Gujarat—were held while I was the chairman of the committee. The Congress party was elected in all the states. In the elections, the points raised related to good governance, inflation and secularism. The stand of the Congress party was that it knew how to govern. Therefore, when it was in power, people got the help they needed and the states were able to develop. The Congress party had learnt the art of governance from its experience of many years, and knew the intricacies of governance, whereas the other parties knew how to criticize, find fault with others and highlight negative aspects, which was why they could not produce the desired results when they got an opportunity to govern in some states. About inflation, the stand it took was that it could and should be controlled by the governments in power in the states, by anticipating the situation and taking steps to overcome the problems in time. On behalf of the party, it was explained that the Congress governments in the past had found out which commodities were not available or were unlikely to be produced in sufficient quantities and imported them to make good the shortfalls. They took steps to ensure that hoarding of scarce commodities and goods was not permitted, through measures taken by the finance ministries or through the supply ministries.

On secularism, the Congress party tried to convince the people that during its governance, miscreants knew that they would be handled strictly if they misbehaved and created communal violence.

And so, they refrained from creating communal problems, whereas while other parties ruled, they knew that their mischief would be overlooked and excused. So, communal hatred and violence spread and affected the secular nature of the society. The points made by the Congress party were convincing. When the results were announced, the Congress president asked the media committee to conduct itself in a manner that was not arrogant or insulting to parties that had lost the elections. It did conduct itself in a very responsible way, which enhanced the prestige of the party.

During that period, my wife suffered from cancer of the liver. I was asked by the doctors to take her to a foreign country for treatment and, if possible, a liver transplant. I took her to Singapore, where she was operated upon to remove the malignant part of the liver. After returning from Singapore, I took her to my village where she breathed her last. During her treatment, my daughter, son-in-law, son and daughter-in-law helped me a lot. But the ailment could not be cured and all of us were saddened. We had to submit to the design of providence, which we did with fortitude.

■

Soniaji appointed Pranab Mukherjee as the chairman of the media committee and asked me to chair the committee to draft the manifesto for the ensuing election. Mani Shankar Aiyar, Kapil Sibal, Jairam Ramesh were other members of the drafting committee. Once, during Rajiv Gandhi's premiership, I was asked to chair a committee to prepare a draft manifesto. I knew how drafting was done. The committee collected past manifestos of the Congress and other parties in India, and several important political parties in other countries. The topics hotly discussed at that time were listed. The views expressed in the All India Congress Committee (AICC) sessions were also collected. The committee invited important organizations and experts for discussion and a draft was prepared on each point, after which discussions were held by the committee. When all the points were covered, the entire draft was discussed again. As the manifesto related to political, economic, social and cultural issues and those relating to the security, defence and foreign policy of the country, senior ministers who had dealt with these subjects were also consulted. The draft was considered by the working committee of the party and was approved. One point discussed in the working committee related to nationalized banks. Some members of the working committee suggested that nationalized banks should be slowly privatized. However, that suggestion was not approved. Some other members suggested that more private banks could be established, but the executive committee did not change the manifesto. It was allowed to remain as it was, without accepting the suggestions made by either side. I was happy to participate in drafting the manifesto, because the exercise gave me and the other members the opportunity to examine important aspects of the lives of people, and important policies and issues faced by the country, and to understand them in clearer terms. The manifesto was translated into the state languages and circulated to the people. It was well received by everyone as it was a balanced document, and it considered the problems of all sections of society in every respect, and was comprehensive, looking into problems and their solutions.

■

After the election of 1998, Atal Bihari Vajpayee of the Bharatiya Janata Party became the prime minister. His government did not have the support of the majority of the members of the Lok Sabha. So, in the House, when voting on the motion to prove that he had the support of the majority of members was taken up, a question arose whether a member of the House, who had become the chief minister of a state, could vote or not. Giridhar Gomango, a member of the Lok Sabha, had become the chief minister of Orissa. On the day of voting, he was in the House to cast his vote against the motion, as on that day, he was a member of the Lok Sabha. The members of the ruling party argued that as he had become the chief minister, he should not be allowed to vote, while the members of the opposition parties argued that as he was a member of the House at the time of voting, he had a right to vote and should not be denied that right. A member ceases to be a member of the House if he resigns or if his membership is terminated by the speaker because of his absence from the House for many days without permission, or if he has violated the Anti-Defection Law or for any other valid reason. As long as he was a member, he could vote. Since that was permitted in the past, the speaker accepted the arguments of the opposition and allowed Giridhar Gomango to vote. The motion moved by the ruling party was defeated by one vote and Vajpayee resigned. He was asked to continue as a caretaker prime minister, which he did. And elections to constitute a new Lok Sabha were held. After the elections, Vajpayee became the prime minister again and this time, he could prove that he had the requisite support of the members. He continued to be the head of government for five years. During that time, the Congress party conducted itself as a responsible opposition party. It criticized or supported the government when it was necessary to do so, in the interests of the nation. It was not out to pull down the government, by hook or by crook. It was prepared to wait and play the role of the opposition in a perfectly constitutional manner, even when some major and intolerable incidents occurred. And that strengthened the system the country followed.

▪

Soniaji was declared the leader of the opposition in the Lok Sabha, and Dr Manmohan Singh was made the leader of the opposition in the Rajya Sabha. In the Lok Sabha, Madhavrao Scindia became the deputy leader of the Congress Parliamentary Party, and in the Rajya Sabha, Pranab Mukherjee became the deputy leader. I was asked to function as the chairman of the Departmentally Related Parliamentary Standing Committee on Finance, which examines budget proposals, bills and other issues relating to the financial activities of the country. One of the bills it considered was the Fiscal Responsibility and Management of Budget Bill, related to budget management and controlling the financial deficit and provided that the government of India and state governments should control their expenditure and reduce the deficit, keeping it at a level mentioned in the law. The governments were asked not to borrow from the Reserve Bank, but from the open market. They were, in some cases, allowed to spend more to meet extraordinary contingencies. Many experts were invited to depose before the committee on the provisions of the bill. According to some, the bill was necessary, but others felt it could obstruct developmental activities and cause problems for the weaker and needy sections of society. Some others suggested that the limitations put on government expenditure should not be done by having a provision in the statute, but in provisions for the same in the rules. That suggestion was made for the first time by Suresh Keswani, a member of the committee from the Rajya Sabha. It was accepted and the committee asked that the bill be modified and passed, which was done. This law is now in vogue. One of the arguments opposing the bill was that deficit financing is not always bad. If more funds are spent on productive activities or building the requisite infrastructure, development can be expedited. If the conservative view of funding is accepted, and enough funds are denied for speedy development, the economy can also suffer. In recent times, the world has been facing a downturn in the economy and it is suggested that more funds should be made available to reverse it. The law made in India and some other countries may help to reduce spending, but it may also contribute towards a dip in the economy. So, swinging from spending too much to spending too little is bound to create problems. While making such laws, we should not lose sight of these contingencies.

If, in the law made, these limiting provisions were in the statute, the governments could have found it difficult to induct more governmental funds in the economic activities of the country, to overcome the present difficulties caused by the downswing in the world economy. With the limiting factor provided in the rules, the difficulty could be overcome by amending the rules. If that were not so, the law would have required an amendment by Parliament and that would have taken a long time. This is why laws should not only try to help overcome the present difficulties, but should visualize different situations and be able to deal with the problems and difficulties when they arise.

21

DEPUTY OPPOSITION LEADER OF THE CONGRESS PARTY IN THE LOK SABHA

After the demise of Madhavrao Scindia in an aircraft accident, I was asked to function as the deputy leader of the Congress party in the Lok Sabha. Soniaji attended the Lok Sabha sittings very regularly. When Parliament was in session, she presided over the meetings held at the party office, attended by the leader of the opposition in the Rajya Sabha, the deputy leaders and other senior members of the party from both Houses. In these meetings, decisions on the stand to be taken by the Congress party on different issues were made. These decisions were followed meticulously. The party decided on the names of members who could be asked or allowed to speak on different subjects. As the deputy leader of the party, I was expected to be present in the House and ensure that these decisions were followed and also to take decisions on issues that were not considered at the meetings and were thrown up during discussions, while supporting and guiding the members. Priya Ranjan Dasmunsi was the chief whip of the party. He was very active and took a tremendous load on his shoulders to make sure that the Congress party performed in the best possible manner. He spoke in the House on several occasions. I spoke only on some important topics and when it was absolutely necessary to speak. Discussions on the motion thanking the president for his address to both the Houses covers very wide areas of activities of the government, and its present and future policies. Discussions on the budget also cover almost all important developmental and financial activities of the government. These two discussions are considered very important. Bills are also discussed and given more time for deliberations on them by the members.

In the first year that the Congress party sat on the opposition benches, I spoke on the motion to thank the president for his address to both the Houses of Parliament. In my speech, I touched on the points made by the president and also the points which were not mentioned in his address. While speaking on the presidential address, according to the rules of procedure and conventions, I made the points included in the party's manifesto also. My speech was a marathon one and quite comprehensive. It touched on topics which were relevant to long-term planning and the future.

■

Parliament was attacked by terrorists. When that happened, both Houses were adjourned, and almost all members were sitting in the Central Hall. The prime minister had not come to the House that day, and the leader of the opposition had left the premises only a few minutes before the attack began. The home minister and the speaker were in their chambers, while I was in the party office. When the police and terrorists fired at each other, the doors of the Parliament House were closed. From inside, we could only hear the sound of bullets fired.

The terrorists had come in a car. They had procured a false label and stuck it on the windshield of their car to enter the compound of Parliament. They alighted at a place close to Gate No. 12, through which one of them tried to enter the Parliament building. Others moved towards other gates, through which they had planned to enter Parliament.

The attempt by a terrorist to enter the building through Gate No. 12 was seen in the control room by the security men, whose duties included watching the gates on CCTV cameras. They rang the alarm bell, all the outer doors of the building were immediately closed, and the terrorists were stopped from entering the building. The security personnel took their positions and attacked the terrorists. In the crossfire, the terrorists and nine security personnel were killed. At Gate No. 1, one of the terrorists who carried explosives on his body was fired at and killed. The explosive material on his body exploded and injured and killed some people. If the security personnel in the control room had not sounded the alarm, and if the gates were not closed in time, the terrorists could have entered the Parliament building, the Central Hall and other parts of the building, and could have taken the insiders as hostages, or even killed them. They could have bargained with the government for anything, or could have caused damage to the building. The CCTV cameras, the control room and the alarm bell had helped. The sacrifices of the security personnel saved Parliament. If the terrorists had succeeded in their nefarious designs, the country could have suffered a loss of immense dimensions. What also saved Parliament was the vision to ensure security preparations to counter terrorism. Yet, as described in an earlier chapter, some members of the House had objected to the CCTV cameras being put up.

■

In Kargil, the Bofors howitzer guns were used. These guns fire into the sky and the shells hit the targets. They were useful in the mountains, where the enemy forces could operate from behind hillocks, providing shelter to them. With the howitzer guns, they could be attacked and repulsed. If, in the Kargil war, the howitzer guns were not there, the number of lives lost could have gone up by many times. The opposition parties had objected to the acquisition of the guns on the ground that they were not effective machines, and that money was given as commission for entering into the contract for purchasing the guns. The enemy could spend big amounts of money to spread rumours to see that the country remained without modern weapons or the deals were unduly delayed, depriving the forces of necessary weapon systems. The enemy could plan to win a war by adopting such tactics and plans. Eventually, the Bofors guns were acquired, but the technology to make them, which was being given free of cost, could not be acquired. Technology for producing the ammunition was also not acquired. The country had to spend a large sum of money to acquire the ammunition, when it was actually needed.

Therefore, political parties should not take pleasure in hurling accusations at one another in such matters. If there is truth in what they say, they should be bold enough to state their objections openly and prove what they say. If they are not careful enough in such matters, they are likely to jeopardize the interests of the country.

In the home ministry, I had seen some people trying to adopt policies similar to those they had adopted to criticize the Bofors guns. They had objected to the acquisition of AK-47 guns to be given to, and used by, the paramilitary forces and state police forces. They used the same tactics with regard to acquiring bulletproof jackets.

Similar tactics were also adopted when a submarine was acquired from Germany. The funds made available to the armed forces and police for their modernization remains unspent, because of the fear created by interested parties. Therefore, it has become necessary to find some solution to handle such matters in a correct manner.

When the attack on Parliament was taken up for discussion, I was the first MP to speak on behalf of the Congress party. In my statement, I said that Parliament was very close to my heart. Probably, nobody was as close to it as I was, as I had been in Parliament for nearly two decades and was the presiding officer of the Lok Sabha. So, when bullets were fired at its wall, I felt they were fired at my body. While defending Parliament, nine people died. I felt I lost nine of my family members. Nobody could refrain from condemning the terrorist attack. If the attack had succeeded, they say it could have changed the history of India. The government was saying that they would fight an 'aar-paar-ki-ladai' fight to the finish and had mobilized its forces. They were sent to the border to execute the orders of the government. It was but natural for all of us to feel angry and agitated about the attack and its audacity. But a war should not be started without preparation, because if it is started at the spur of the moment, it can inflict enormous tragedy on the country. They should know what kind of preparation for starting and fighting a war should be made, how many casualties were likely to occur, what kind of damage would be caused. Therefore, the government should be careful and cautious in taking such decisions. If wrong decisions were taken, they could prove very costly and dangerous.

When I spoke, the leader of the opposition was in the House. I had not consulted her before I spoke. However, I felt that my views were not disapproved by her or other members of the Congress party.

The forces that were moved closer to the border of Pakistan remained there for many months. Whenever big terrorist attacks took place, the reaction of some people in the country became very difficult to ignore and brush aside. At the same time, if some strong action was taken in response to the attacks, the purpose for which the terrorists attacked got fulfilled, at least to some extent. Therefore, it became necessary to take action before the attack took place. A balanced and effective policy should be evolved and used to counter and control terrorism.

In Jammu and Kashmir and Manipur, the legislative assemblies were attacked. In Gujarat, after the Godhra incident, riots took place in which many valuable lives were lost and properties worth hundreds of crores of rupees were damaged. The incidents in Gujarat were highlighted in the media and attracted the attention of the people in the country. These and many other incidents were discussed in Parliament. The stand taken by the Government of India was that the state governments would be helped to see that such incidents did not recur. The opposition party asked the government to be vigilant, careful and diligent in taking necessary action, and asked the government to be sure that it would be helped by all parties in times of national difficulties.

In the tenth five-year plan, the Government of India had decided to produce 48,000 megawatts of electricity in five years. It had also decided that the private sector would be allowed to set up plants and produce, transmit and distribute electricity. However, the target was reduced twice. It was brought down to 30,000 and then 20,000 megawatts. The government had declared that the private sector would be allowed to generate electricity; a decision that was good. But the steps required to encourage the private sector to enter the power generation industry were not taken. If 1,000 megawatts of electricity were to be produced, an investment of nearly ₹6,000 crore was required. To put up a power plant, a period of about five to seven years was required, and the investor would have to wait for nearly two decades to get the returns on the investment. After the plant was put up, the investor would have to wait at least ten years just to get back the funds put up. Therefore, the private sector was not very enthusiastic about entering this field and no investment that could give full satisfaction was made by it. The government was not willing to invest funds, expecting that it would be done by private entrepreneurs. The result of this policy was that power could not be produced as planned, the targets were reduced from 48,000 megawatts of electricity to 20,000 megawatts and the actual electricity that could be produced was about 18,000 megawatts. The demand for power was going up in the villages, towns and cities for domestic purposes, and for industry, agriculture and transport activities. Therefore, a scarcity of electricity was experienced, which is still ongoing. In such matters, if the policies that are made go in the wrong direction, the ill effects are felt throughout the country, for decades, and this was exactly the reason why the scarcity of power was felt everywhere.

In Rajasthan, the state government decided to allow two units of power plants to be established by the private sector. For nearly fifteen years, the two units could not be established and not one unit of electricity was added to the total power generated. The government headed by Ashok Gehlot decided to establish two plants through the state public sector undertaking. It also decided that if any private company came forth to take up the responsibility of putting up power plants, it would be given permission to do so, over and above what the government had done—and adequate power began to be produced for the people. Rajasthan then became a power surplus state because of the correct decisions taken, and the mistakes committed by the previous government was thus rectified.

The government of the UPA believes that power should be produced in abundance and new methods should be adopted for the purpose. It knows that depending on fossil fuel for all time to come will cause difficulties and that new fuel resources are needed to generate power. It, therefore, decided to generate power through nuclear technology and new kinds of fuel. When I visited France, I was told that the country had decided to produce power using nuclear technology on a large scale. It, therefore, established a mechanism that helped it to produce 70 per cent of the power it needed by using nuclear technology. I was told that France was willing to help India to establish nuclear power plants, in which one reactor could produce more than 2,000 megawatts of electricity. I conveyed this information to the NDA government, and asked why India should not accept the offer and start producing power using nuclear technology. I was told that France was willing to help, if it were given the right to inspect the plants in India to check if they were being used to produce weapon-grade nuclear fuel, which is the reason why India was unwilling to accept the offer. At that time, it was also suggested that some plants in India could be inspected and could be used to produce energy for civilian purposes and other plants could be kept out of the ambit of inspection by the International Nuclear Energy Commission. This is exactly what the UPA government has done in it present term in office. If the NDA government had gone ahead with it then, we could have saved some time and have begun to use nuclear fuel and technology to generate more power needed by the people. It was a question of vision. If the vision is far-sighted, it is beneficial. If it is short-sighted and limited, it does not help to overcome problems faced by the people. I made these points in my statements to the House and in conversations with the concerned ministers and authorities in the government. However, it was clear to me and others that the government had its own views, policies and plans and could not assess and accept the importance of such suggestions given by others.

■

I used to sit in the House for nearly the whole day of its working hours. In fact, I used to be present in the House for a longer time than most other members. In the evening, the attendance of members was very low in the House, and on occasion, I had to speak on subjects raised in the absence of other members of the Congress party. In the morning, the House was full of members and the galleries were occupied by media persons. In the afternoon, only members who had to speak or were interested in the topics of discussion remained present, which helped to give the members enough time to speak. On Fridays, private members' business is taken up and bills and resolutions moved by them are discussed in the afternoon. I remained present in the House and participated in the discussions, and enjoyed doing it. At times, I felt that I was speaking to a nearly empty House. Yet, the absence of several members helped me to make my points in a serene and undisturbed atmosphere. Whatever I said was recorded, and I thought that at some time in the future, my statements may be examined and used to take correct decisions of national and international importance. I spoke on the relations between the Union and the states, on using foodgrains lying unconsumed in godowns, on establishing infrastructure in villages, towns and cities, and on giving employment to the unemployed. The ministers who replied to the debate were good enough to appreciate the points made and to put forth their points of view. All the ministers, the presiding officers and almost all the members were quite cooperative and correct in every respect with me.

•

The Congress party, sitting on the opposition benches, wanted to perform its duties in an effective and constitutional manner. The members sitting on the benches of the ruling parties did not fully grasp how they should conduct themselves in the House. They appeared to behave more like opposition members and less like members of the ruling parties. The mistakes thus committed by them, at times, created awkward situations for their government and ministers. Some members of the Congress party were also at a loss to know as to how they should behave as members sitting on opposition benches. They behaved as if they were the members sitting on the benches of the ruling parties. Some of them thought that they could call the attention of the government on all topics of importance, or move adjournment motions and raise different kinds of discussions to hold the government accountable. When their notices were not admitted by the presiding officers, they got agitated and angry with the government and the presiding officers. Once, they wanted to obstruct the discussion on the budget proposal and not allow the budget to be passed easily. They wanted to force the presiding officer to get the budget passed amidst the din and noise in the House, and then the opposition members crowded the well of the House. As a former speaker of the Lok Sabha, and as a presiding officer who had dealt with such situations in the House and tactfully avoided getting the budget passed in chaos and confusion, I was not in favour of allowing the Congress members to act in that manner. Dr Manmohan Singh, who was then the leader of the opposition in the Rajya Sabha, was the finance minister in the government of the Congress party. His budget was threatened and obstructed from getting passed. He held the same views as I did. Soniaji appreciated the points made to ensure that the budget was passed in a quiet and correct atmosphere and asked the members to refrain from obstructive behaviour.

Some members of the ruling parties, at times, behave as if they are going to remain in the government for all time to come. Some members of the opposition parties also, on several occasions, conduct themselves as if they are going to occupy only the opposition benches forever. Therefore, they take extreme positions and create problems, which causes chaos in the House. When they got the opportunity to exchange their seats and benches, they realized who were right and who were wrong. When such occasions arose, they felt embarrassed to act as they had done while on the other side. On some occasions, I had to remind my friends that they were not going to sit on the opposition benches for long, and should speak and act as if they were sitting in the ruling benches.

The Congress party did not intend to topple the government. It favoured its continuation, if it behaved responsibly. However, it did not overlook the mistakes the government committed.

▪

A terrorist was released from jail and sent to Kabul in a government aircraft, escorted by the foreign minister. It was done to save the lives of the passengers on a plane hijacked by a terrorist group. It was not difficult for the Congress party to understand the dilemma in which the government had found itself. But it could not understand why it was necessary for the foreign minister to escort him, so the government was criticized for what it did.

▪

When the prime minister went to Pakistan in a bus, he was received in the neighbouring country by dignitaries in a proper manner. However, it was also clear that some officers in that country behaved in a manner not in keeping with the expected protocol. Some people in India were happy that the prime minister had gone out of his way to convey to and convince the neighbouring country that India wanted to have friendly, peaceful and cooperative relations with it. But some others were not able to appreciate how such gestures could create the desired results. They felt that the manner in which the visit was organized reduced the efficacy of the visit and appeared to ridicule it. They thought that it would have been better for the country if it were organized in a different manner. The Congress party thought that it would have done the same thing, but in a different manner, which would not have reduced the chances of creating goodwill between the two countries. So we criticized it.

■

Kargil was attacked shortly after the prime minister visited Pakistan, which indicated that India was not vigilant and had not studied the situation carefully. The attack was repulsed, but it was done at the cost of many lives and a lot of damage to properties of Indian citizens. The Congress party supported the government for defending the country's sovereignty and territory, but criticized the fact that the attack on Kargil took the country by surprise.

■

The president of Pakistan was invited to India. The representatives and leaders of the two countries tried to prepare the ground to build better relations between the two countries. They discussed matters, but could not arrive at any acceptable conclusions. The members of the ruling party made statements of a contradictory nature, and the president of the neighbouring country returned without even signing a document of any importance. It was a failure of diplomacy, showed that the visit was arranged without preparing the ground to ensure its success. Before such meetings are held, diplomats at the lower level meet and discuss what can and what cannot be done, and decide to have high-level meetings only when absolutely necessary; otherwise, they delay or avoid such meetings. In this case, it is clear that nothing of that kind was done and the visit ended in a fiasco, which should have been avoided.

■

During the general elections to the Lok Sabha, the government issued advertisements and statements saying India was 'shining'. It desired to tell the people that it had governed the country very successfully and the government had done some things which were appreciated by some people. It was quite legitimate for the government to take credit for the positive steps it had taken and commendable results it had produced. But to say that India, as a whole, was shining and happy was not acceptable to the people. There were many sections of society which had not received their due and were unhappy because their difficulties continued to trouble them. They could not agree fully that India was shining. The Congress party criticized the 'India Shining' advertisement of the ruling party.

■

The ruling party had declared that it was in favour of linking the rivers of India, so that the water of the rivers did not flow into the ocean, and, instead, could be used to irrigate the lands in the north, east, west and south. During the premiership of Indiraji, the manifesto of one of the elections mentioned that the rivers in India would be connected. That idea was welcomed by the people. However, there were some leaders of other parties who did not agree with the concept. They opposed it on the ground that the project would take a lot of time and funds to be completed and would also disturb the ecology. They opposed it saying that the water in the rivers should be used fully in the areas through which they passed. And, if excess water remained, then it could be diverted into other rivers through connecting links. As the idea was becoming controversial, it was not acted upon immediately. When the ruling party proposed to implement the idea, the Congress party did not oppose it. However, it knew the complications involved in acting on the project. Once, in the House, the ruling party asked the Congress party to approve the project. Since Soniaji was in the House, the government appealed to her to agree to it in the House itself. I was also present in the House and I requested her to give her consent to the project. She herself did not say anything and I thought that I was expected to express the views of the Congress party. I, therefore, stood up and said that the concept should be examined carefully and implemented. However, as the government also knew the complications involved in such a project, it created a committee to look into the views expressed by the experts, and suggest to the government how the matter should be handled in its totality. The committee worked for some time, but could not come up with any valid suggestions, which could help the project to be taken up and completed. The matter was not difficult from the point of view of the ecology or economy. It was difficult because of the politics involved in it and parochial feelings were responsible for creating the obstacles in implementing it. Unless the people develop a national perspective and wider view, these difficulties are going to continue. It is easier for the national parties to entertain ideas, which cover the nation as a whole. The state or regional parties do not find such concepts useful to them for their survival and success.

■

Indiraji, as prime minister of India, permitted the explosion of nuclear devices in Pokhran. The work done by the Indian scientists was appreciated by the Indian people. However, some countries criticized India and declared that they would not cooperate with it in matters relating to nuclear technology and fuel. Congress governments had consistently said that they were for a world without war and nuclear weapons. They had said that they were willing to accept an agreement, which was applicable in an identical and non-discriminatory manner to all the countries of the world. Rajiv Gandhi was of the same view. In his speech to the General Assembly of the United Nations, he advocated the cause of peace. He said that the world should be freed from the scourge of war and nuclear weapons, and the countries with nuclear weapons should dismantle them. They should refrain from developing technologies for producing nuclear weapons. And that should be done in a non-discriminatory manner over a period of twenty years. However, some countries were not willing to accept such a proposal.

The NDA government also carried out an explosion of nuclear bombs at Pokhran. Some countries objected to this. Pakistan also exploded some nuclear bombs within days of India's experiment. The Congress party stuck to its policy on this issue. It said that it was for peace and a world without nuclear weapons and wanted all countries in the world to be treated in the same manner in that matter. Some Congressmen opposed the explosion.

■

The CPI(M) and other parties which stood for secularism in the country cooperated with the Congress party. On important issues, they evolved common strategies and followed them in the Houses. The leaders of like-minded parties consulted the leaders of the Congress party on several occasions. Somnath Chatterjee organized a dinner, attended by the leaders of the Congress party, the CPI(M) and other parties, to exchange views on cooperation in conducting business in Parliament, before and after the general elections. It was attended by all the senior leaders of the parties. The meeting, in my opinion, was responsible for developing a better understanding to form the government after the elections. In the Houses of Parliament, the ethos created in the meeting helped all concerned parties to discharge their duties in a responsible manner. Thus, the Congress party and other parties did help the democratic and parliamentary system to operate without major difficulties, although what they did in Parliament did not always appear very edifying. However, the sum total of their thinking and activities were helpful to uphold the democratic and parliamentary system. They helped the system to work, but there was scope for improvement.

22

HOME MINISTER

The Union home ministry has three main functions to perform. It deals with the relationship between the Union and the states; it helps the states to maintain law and order; and in recent times, it has been given the duty to help state governments to manage disasters perpetrated by man or nature. The general impression that it is a ministry responsible only for law and order is not correct.

■

India has the Union government for the country as a whole, state governments for their states, district bodies for their districts, taluka bodies for their talukas and local bodies for their cities, towns and villages. This arrangement is provided in the Constitution and other laws and is made to govern the country properly and to meet the demands of the people efficiently and in time. It incorporates the principles of federalism and decentralization. The word 'federal' is not used in the Indian Constitution, yet, the constitutional provisions do indicate that they have the elements of federalism.

In this arrangement, the Union government has exclusive powers over certain subjects, the state governments have similar powers with respect to other specific subjects, and the Union and states have concurrent powers over some other subjects. The Constitution has three lists. The first list which is recognized as a Union list mentions the subjects which fall within the exclusive jurisdiction of the Union, the second list recognized as State list mentions the subjects which fall within the exclusive jurisdiction of the state governments, and the third list recognized as concurrent list mentions the subjects over which Union and the state governments have concurrent jurisdiction. In addition the Union has jurisdiction over subjects which are not mentioned in the three lists.

The Union and state governments can use the powers given to them independently and do not have to seek the permission of one another to use them. They expect that they should not be obstructed in using their powers.

The powers that are given to the Union need to be used carefully. They have to produce good results, and ensure that the principles of federalism are protected and preserved. They have to be used to facilitate the functioning of the state governments, and to help them discharge their duties, according to the expectations of the people. The Union and the states do have exclusive rights and powers in certain areas. The Union has the power and authority to make sure that governance is done in accordance with the provisions of the Constitution, and the states have to govern as per the provisions of the Constitution. If the states fail to govern properly, the Union can advise and direct them to adhere to constitutional norms. If a state does not mend its ways of governing, or fails to follow the provisions of the Constitution and the directions and advice given by the Union, the Union can take over governance in the state, after suspending the legislature and removing the state government. The states are expected not to allow such situations to develop. The Union should suspend the legislatures and remove the governments only if it is absolutely necessary. The country suffers if there is a lack of cooperation and coordination between the Union and the states. The states should feel inspired and happy to work according to the provisions of the Constitution to protect the interests of the people. They should not feel alienated from the Union. If that happens, the country cannot be governed well. The Union should feel confident that without using coercive measures, it can obtain the full cooperation of the states. The skill lies in creating a cooperative atmosphere between the Union and the states.

How can this be achieved? How was it achieved?

India is a multi-party democracy. In the initial years of its independence, at the centre and at the state levels, one party—the Indian National Congress—could form the governments, which helped them to understand one another without difficulties, and function in a coordinated manner. Later, governments were formed at the national and state levels by different parties, following different ideologies. Seeing eye to eye with one another was, therefore, not very easy for them. Sometimes, they functioned in a coordinated manner. At other times, clashes occurred, retarding the process of development. However, by and large, they functioned with understanding and cooperated with one another in a proper manner and on the right scale. That happened mainly because of the sagacity of the leaders at the national and state levels.

During the UPA regime, the Union and states understood in clear terms what they were expected to do and what they were not expected to do. They worked within their jurisdictions according to the Constitution, laws and conventions. The Union was confident of getting the cooperation of the states, which it did. The states knew that they would be helped to the hilt by the Union, in their difficulties. They had no doubt about the attitude of the Union and could cooperate with one another in an exceptional manner, where there were no disputes and clashes between them. This helped the principles of federalism to be upheld and used in the best possible manner. In my opinion, this is the most important duty of the Union. In this, the home ministry helps the Union government, and fortunately, it has been able to perform this duty without difficulties, in a smooth and understanding manner.

All the same, it was suggested by some people in the states and some at the national level that the gamut of centre–state relations should be re-examined to create an ambience more favourable for federalism. So, necessary steps in this respect were taken.

On behalf of some states and politicians, demands were made that they should be given more powers. They asked for more executive, legislative and financial powers. While drafting the Constitution, it was felt by some members that the states should be endowed with more powers, and by some others it was felt that in order to keep the country united and to counter fissiparous and divisive tendencies, the Union should be given more powers. At the time of drafting the Constitution, these views were expressed by the members of the drafting committee and those of the Constituent Assembly. By taking their views, the constitutional provisions which regulate the relations between the Union and the states, were drafted and made part of the Constitution. These provisions struck a balance between their different views. In order to consider if there was any scope for rearranging the balance between the Union and the state powers, a commission under the chairmanship of Justice Sarkaria was constituted. The commission considered the views of politicians, jurists, intellectuals and other learned people and examined the facilities provided for governance through the Union and the states, and the difficulties faced by them, and gave a comprehensive report. The suggestions in the report were considered by the Inter-State Council and the cabinet. Most of them were accepted and implemented.

Again, a demand was made that the total ambit of centre–state relations should be considered by a body of experts. The parties which joined hands to form the government after the elections for the thirteenth Lok Sabha (2004–2005) were held, decided in their common minimum programme that one more commission for this purpose should be constituted. The commission was expected to consider the issues related to the executive, legislative and judicial powers of the Union and the states. It was expected that the commission would consider how the executive, legislative, financial and other powers should be shared by the Union and the states.

There were some who thought that the matter was too

complicated and difficult to handle and should not be tampered with. There were others who thought that it should be considered in a patient and careful manner. As the common minimum programme suggested that a commission for the purpose should be constituted, steps were taken to implement it. The commission was brought into existence and worked for nearly three years to give the report.

When the Constitution came into existence, the bodies at the district, taluka and local levels did not have clear constitutional provisions to guide their activities. They existed under the laws made by the states, which provided the required details. However, when it was found that after the first two decades, they were not created by holding elections regularly in some states, the Constitution was amended to make elections mandatory, and to provide funds to them regularly and adequately, on the basis of the recommendations given by the State Finance Commissions, which were expected to be created as per the amended provisions of the Constitution. The district taluka and local bodies were given more powers in some areas, and the constitutional status.

In the world, the concept of globalization is accepted and implemented on a grand scale. In the changed situations, the Union and states have to play their role and discharge their duties, which requires the rearrangement of the balance of powers between the Union and the states.

In recent times, the private sector has become stronger, bolder and more active. It is trying to discharge the duties which were expected to be done by the government and public sector units. This also needs a change in the power structure regulating relations between the governments at different levels.

The people have become more conscious of their rights. Their demands for more liberty and rights are also increasing. They are helped in their demands by the media and non-governmental organizations (NGOs).

In the last six decades, science and technologies have developed in such a manner that the legal concepts relating to the sovereignty of the country and the relations between countries of the world and provinces within countries have changed a lot, requiring a different constitutional approach to govern properly, effectively and efficiently. The provinces and countries depend on one another more than they used to in the past. In the light of these changes, it was felt that the provisions of the Constitution should also be modified.

All these and such other changes are making the thinking masses feel that the relations between the Union, the states, the bodies at district, taluka and local levels, private organizations and individuals should be changed so as to facilitate smooth working, interaction and production of a more satisfying and better nature.

In some states, after the elections to the legislature, the governments were formed according to the rules and laws. In some states, that could not be done, and the governments that were formed could not be stable and function efficiently or properly. The Union could do nothing to achieve the objectives set out in the Constitution. When the states were pulled down or became dysfunctional, the Union had to intervene and impose president's rule to govern the states for the people.

When governments cannot continue according to the provisions of the Constitution, when law and order in the entire state breaks down or the financial situation becomes unviable, president's rule is imposed under Article 356 of the Constitution. In the first few years after independence, it was held that a decision by the executive to impose president's rule could not be challenged in a court of law, and was not justiciable. However, later, under decisions given by the Supreme Court, it could be looked into by the court to decide if the decision was unbiased or not. In fact, the executive decision is considered by Parliament. On the approval of Parliament, it is acted upon, and if it is disapproved, it is not implemented. Parliament checks and balances the authority of the executive to impose president's rule in a state. Therefore, it was not subjected to the scrutiny of the judiciary. But now, even after the legislature approves the exercise of its authority to impose president's rule, the court can examine it to ensure that it is done in a proper manner, and can pass orders nullifying the action of the executive. By some parties, a demand is made that Article 356, which provides for president's rule, should be removed from the Constitution, and in no case should president's rule be imposed. The logic advanced for this demand is that the members of the state legislatures and executive are elected by the people, and so, the two wings of the state should not be denied the right to continue for the full term.

The demand for abolishing the concept of president's rule was not accepted. It was rejected by the Sarkaria Commission and by many political parties. It is felt that in order to make sure that every part of the country is properly governed in accordance with the Constitution, and to maintain the unity of the country, Article 356 is needed and should never be deleted from the Constitution.

In some cases, only a few districts of a state are affected. In such cases, it becomes very difficult to impose president's rule on the entire state. If the Union government finds that the state government does not follow its directions and advice, it becomes difficult to take corrective action in the affected districts. It is, therefore, suggested that in such cases, the Union should be allowed to take over the administration of the affected districts, by following the same procedure used to impose president's rule. In other words, the Union can advise the state to govern the affected districts in a proper manner and in line with the directions given by it and the provisions of the Constitution of India. If the state fails to follow the directions, the Union can take over the entire administration of the affected districts, with the approval of Parliament, when in session. If it is not in session, the Union can take over the administration and then seek the approval of Parliament in the ensuing session. If it succeeds in obtaining the approval, it can continue to administer the affected districts. If it fails, the administration is returned to the state.

The Union gives funds to the states every year in accordance with the norms laid down by the Finance Commission. The Constitution gives powers to the Union and states to raise revenue according to the existing laws. However, the demand made by the states is that they should be given more financial powers, as they think that the powers given to them in this respect are inadequate.

Some people think that the powers given to the states to raise revenue and impose taxes are not used. Even if more powers are given, they are not likely to be used. The funds given to them are not properly utilized. There are no provisions in the Constitution under which the states can be asked to account for non-utilization and misuse of funds. Therefore, they feel that a legal mechanism should be created to ensure that the states use the funds properly for the purposes for which they are given and that they use the powers given to them to collect revenue and taxes and should not avoid to do that.

Five-year plans are drafted and accepted by the Union. Under the Constitution, there is no forum in which the draft can be considered and accepted by the representatives of the Union and the states. The Planning Commission is created by the executive order of the Union and is not a constitutional or statutory body. It also does not have constitutional and statutory powers to see how funds provided to the states are used. Every year, the Planning Commission approves the annual plans of the states. While doing so, it examines how the funds given in the previous year were spent. But according to some, this method is not very useful and effective and some other method, which can give better results, should be invented and adopted.

To overcome this difficulty, Pandit Jawaharlal Nehru created the National Development Council (NDC), in which the draft plan is discussed and approved. However, the NDC is also not capable of meeting all the demands in this respect. It should be given at least a statutory position, otherwise, it is not likely to be as effective as it should be.

In a country like India, which is so large and complicated, there should be an executive body in which representatives of the

Union and the state governments can take decisions applicable throughout the country. The Inter-State Council is a constitutional body which is expected to resolve disputes between the states and the Union, and between the states. In fact, it was suggested during the drafting of the provisions that it should be made into a forum for representatives of the Union and state governments to take decisions of long-term implications and applicable throughout the country. Although that concept was not fully accepted, some practical steps have been taken to see that it discharges some of the duties, which some members of the Constituent Assembly wanted it to do.

To consider these and some other issues, one more commission was set up. The commission has given its report. We have to see which recommendations given by it can be accepted and made part of the Indian Constitution and other laws.

■

By and large, the Union and the states conduct themselves in a correct and constitutional manner. On some occasions when it was found that mistakes were committed, they were corrected without delays. The remedial measures taken prove that the government tries its best to act constitutionally, and has thus laid the foundation for trust and cooperation between the Union and the states. The Union did not apply different criteria while dealing with states governed by the same political parties as those governing at the national level and those governed by parties with different ideologies. To the states of all hues and colours, it was quite clear that they would be helped without any reservation, and would not be allowed to govern in an unconstitutional and wrong manner. The Union did its best to care for the people and to ensure that no undue advantage was reaped by any government belonging to any political party. This was true when law and order situations, disasters or financial matters were managed by the states with the help of the Union.

At times, leaders from some states complained against the Union when their excessive demands could not be met. Legal and appropriate demands were met and this fact was known to the complaining leaders, but they voiced their dissent and dissatisfaction for political reasons. If such situations are ignored by the state, it is possible to say that they were more than satisfied with the manner in which they were assisted.

The home ministry or the other ministries of the Union government, at no time, tried to take undue advantage of difficulties faced by the states for political reasons. The Union always endeavoured to understand their difficulties and help them, rather than to expose them to criticism. This attitude was very useful to bring about a cooperative atmosphere and understanding between them. It helped to overcome the difficulties and hurdles in assisting the states and the people.

Thus, it can be said that the Union and the home ministry did their best to protect and preserve the spirit and character of federalism enshrined in the Constitution.

■

Parts of India governed by the British were returned to the representatives of the Indian people, who had fought for the freedom of the country. The princely states were allowed to decide if they would like to join the Union or not. When people were fighting for India's freedom, they were fighting to establish the democratic system also, as seen in the princely states where the people were in favour of governments by their representatives instead of the monarchs. Mahatma Gandhi, Pandit Jawaharlal Nehru, Sardar Vallabhbhai Patel and other leaders tried their best to create unity between the people living in different parts of the country and to establish democratic and republican rule in all parts of the country. And they succeeded in achieving this objective. When the British left India, most of the rulers of the princely states found that it was appropriate for them to join the Union. The states of Hyderabad, Jammu and Kashmir (J&K) and Junagarh delayed in joining the Union. However, they too, later, joined the Union as all the other states had done.

All the states joined the Union and the credit for this should go to the people, the representatives of the people, the makers of the Indian Constitution and the leaders of the country. To continue to have conditions conducive for this purpose is a major achievement. The country has been successful in attaining it. Constant vigilance and care are needed to work for unity, which the governments have tried to provide. Except in two-three states, no voices in other states were raised at any time against the unity of the country, and against joining the Union. Even in the two-three states also, only a few misguided individuals were responsible for speaking against the unity of the county. Now such voices are not heard and the unity of the country has become more strong and stable.

In India, many languages were and are spoken, which is why there was a demand for the reorganization of states on a linguistic basis. Some leaders were in favour of the demand, and some were opposed. In accordance with the wishes of the majority, the states were reorganized on the basis of the languages spoken, but now there is a demand that some of them should be divided into smaller states to facilitate faster and better development. Gujarat and Maharashtra were one state. Punjab, Haryana and Himachal Pradesh were parts of one state. They were divided into different states. The division created the separate states of Maharashtra and Gujarat. Punjab was also divided into the states of Himachal Pradesh, Punjab and Haryana. This was done on the basis of the languages spoken in the different parts of the state. Uttar Pradesh, a large state consisting of Hindi-speaking people, was divided to create the states of Uttar Pradesh and Uttarakhand. Bihar was split into the states of Bihar and Jharkhand. Madhya Pradesh was divided into Chhattisgarh and Madhya Pradesh. In Andhra Pradesh, a new state of Telengana is on the anvil. This matter of the division of states has been handled in a careful manner and is not allowed to acquire unhelpful dimensions.

■

Different religions are practised by the people of India. The Hindus have followed the caste system, though this system has been tainted by the obnoxious concept of untouchability. People belonging to different religions, castes and communities have not seen eye to eye with one another, and for political and other reasons, some people have tried to create bitterness between them. Fortunately, the majority of the people in India do not subscribe to these narrow and divisive tendencies, which is why it has been possible to maintain harmony and amity between the people belonging to different religions, communities and castes. However, on some occasions, some mischief-mongers have been successful in creating problems and shedding the blood of innocent victims. It has, therefore, been necessary to keep a constant vigil on the activities of the enemies of social harmony and amity. To achieve this objective, a National Integration Council was created by Pandit Jawaharlal Nehru, consisting of politicians and other influential members of society. In the last many years, it had not met and had not been active. So a decision to reactivate it was taken to enable it to deal with problematic social issues. It is, like the Planning Commission, a body created by an executive order, with no constitutional or statutory backing.

There are some forces in the country and outside that want to make use of the differences between religions, communities and castes to create problems for the country. In some cases, they were able to succeed beyond their expectations. However, during the UPA government, they could not create big problems. They were controlled in time, tragedies were avoided and miscreants were brought to book.

■

A human being can be attacked by another human being or a group of persons, or he can be exposed to danger generated by man-made or natural disasters. In such cases, he tries to protect himself on his own or takes the help of others. Today, the state and society protect him. Those who attack him may have small or large groups of people to help them, which can include all people in the society or country. They can be well equipped and trained. When such situations arise, the individual, or his kith and kin, friends or fellow citizens may help him.

Thus, tribes came into existence. Thus, also, city states were born. And later, the states that we find in the present day world came into existence. The main reason for the genesis and evolution of governments was the security of individuals and groups. Monarchs and heads of tribes tried to provide security, but this responsibility is now shouldered by governments which are formed by representatives of the people.

A country can be invaded by a neighbouring or any other country. It is then that the question of providing national security arises. Wars have been fought to invade a country or to defend it. Fortunately, today, wars are no longer fought to acquire land. They are fought to gain control over sources of raw materials, energy or markets. Major wars were fought in the past, in which millions of people were killed. Wars were also fought for reasons of religious or other kinds of considerations. In order to see that wars are avoided, some organizations consisting of the representatives of countries were created, and were able to avoid wars on several occasions. The United Nations is such an organization. It tries to avoid wars and establish peace and tranquillity.

When such things happen, the question of national security arises. Wars are fought by armed forces that may consist of military personnel, the police and other voluntary organizations. The burden of war is shouldered by the entire country and people. In the ancient days, wars were fought between the members of families to expand the boundaries of their influence and create new states or to usurp existing states. Some people conquered lands thousands of miles away from their countries. They established their rule over the conquered areas and exploited their resources. The ruled opposed the rule by the people living hundreds and thousands of miles away from their countries, and fought for freedom to acquire the authority to rule their own countries. In some wars, groups of countries joined hands against each other. In the twentieth century, two world wars were fought. During this period, wars were also fought by people of different countries to gain their own freedom from the rule of other countries.

The history of the world shows that in some countries, such as America, France, Russia, China, people rebelled against their rulers. The rebellions were widespread and changed the systems of governance. In France, the monarchy was abolished and rule by elected representatives of the people was established. Unfortunately, the situation in that country changed soon after, and monarchy was established again. But later, the monarchy came to an end and rule by the representatives of the people was re-established. When these changes occurred, the question of providing security to the people came up; the kind of security recognized as internal security, which can be disturbed by people from within or outside the country for religious, political, economic, social or cultural reasons. Neighbouring countries may add fuel to the fire. It is said that a country may not fight an open and direct war with its enemy; it may fight a surreptitious war, using cunning methods to weaken the enemy. It may give funds, arms and training to the people trying to rebel against the established government, to create misunderstanding and bad blood between different sections of the society. Rulers, officers and others can be bribed and incited to create problems. In this kind of activity, the advantage lies in the fact that the inciters can deny responsibility for the damage caused to the lives and properties of the victims. The cost, in terms of human lives and money, is also comparatively less than that incurred in open wars. The country planning to do this can choose the time, date and place to harm its enemy. In many cases, arms are not used to harass the enemy country. In some cases, means which appear quite legal and acceptable can be used. If, for example, strikes in transport systems are incited and organized to continue for a long time, they can affect the production units in the country, power generation, supply of foodgrains and drinking water. This kind of situation can create unemployment and resentment in the minds of the suffering masses, inciting them to cause disturbances in the society. Religious feelings can be roused and clashes can be perpetrated. Important installations in the country can be made non-functional. All these methods can disturb the internal security of a country, and are far more dangerous than war, and can continue over longer periods of time. When such a situation occurs, it becomes necessary for the country to take steps to remedy the situation and establish normalcy. In Russia and China, the communist revolutions changed the existing systems. The First World War contributed to the creation of the communist regime in the Soviet Union, while the Second World War helped to create the communist regime in China. The inefficient, insensitive and unjust rulers were also responsible for the rebellion. If governance was just and acceptable to the people, they would not have rebelled, and other factors would not have succeeded in spreading unrest, affecting the internal security scenario. Therefore, to control internal disturbances, it is necessary to understand the main causes and do away with them in ways acceptable to the people. If political, economic, social and cultural justice is ensured to one and all, chances of disturbing internal security recede and disappear. If only force is used to control them, it may prove effective, but may not be able to control the situation for a long time. Such a matter is of national importance. So the nation, as a whole, is expected to deal with it. If it is dealt with in a lukewarm manner, by some people in some parts of the country or state, it does not help. In a country like India which is big and widespread, disturbances have to be dealt with by the Union and the state governments. It should be understood that internal security is different from national security, and is different from terrorism and ordinary crimes. It is necessary to understand the distinction in clear terms to know what their implications are. The Union and states should carefully choose the methods used to deal with them.

Terrorism is a crime committed by an individual, or group of individuals, to frighten people to achieve the terrorists' objectives, which may be to support a religious ideology, a political cause, an economic philosophy or any other issue. Terrorists depend on the fear psychosis they create and on the surprise element, which is in their control. Terrorists can choose a place, date or time that suits them to attack their victims or targets. They strike and disappear. They are interested in combating members of the forces that have a duty to protect law and order and the lives and properties of innocent people. They may attack members of armed forces, to spread fear or to overcome the difficulties and hurdles created by them, on their way to achieving their objectives. They are not as strong as the members of the governmental armed forces are, but they take them by surprise to achieve their objectives. In their actions, innocent people become victims. They aim at perpetrating incidents that give them publicity and help them create terror.

In the present-day world, there are terrorists who are creating chaos to establish and strengthen their religious ideology. They are working in different parts of the world. Supported by rich countries with funds, weapons and other facilities at their disposal, they secure shelter in such countries before and after they strike. They lie in hibernation in the countries where they want to strike, watching the activities of the people and waiting for opportunities to act for years. Those who are involved in such terrorism think that they have the sanction of their religion to perpetrate these kinds of acts. They are indoctrinated to die for the cause dear to them. Those who select such terrorists are careful in choosing only those who are mentally prepared to take risks and die. They are generally from the poorer sections of society, who need money to support their family members. The number of such members is far greater than the number of affluent members, who are well educated and motivated by their ideologies and principles. Their views of the world are not very comprehensive—they are not aware of the concepts and ideologies followed in different parts of the world. They are not influenced by modern ideas that value cooperation, compassion and understanding, and allow other people to follow their own ideologies. In fact, such cruelty is caused by ignorance and not by enlightenment. Anybody who is really enlightened, who knows the world and the meaning of existence and the oneness of humanity, is not likely to inflict terrorism on others. Those who think that they know very little, and there is much more to know, are not likely to inflict terror on others. This kind of terror can be combated not only with force, but ideas and skills to persuade them to move in correct and just direction. At present, religious terrorism appears to cause more harm than any other kind of terrorism.

In the past, terrorism was used to change the systems followed in some countries. It was used as a weapon by the people against the forces of governments and rulers. It succeeded in achieving its objectives in some countries, but not in all. It could succeed where the rulers were not sensitive to the wishes and demands of the ruled. It could not succeed in countries where the rulers were willing to do political, economic, social and cultural justice. It could not succeed in countries where modern concepts to help people were adopted, where science and technology were used for production of goods and to distribute the produce fairly. In some parts of the world, even today, attempts are made by terrorists and disgruntled people to create disturbances and cause damages. But their attempts are not likely to succeed, because the rulers are ready to take steps to help the ruled, and because enough can be produced and shared in a just and appropriate manner.

Terrorism perpetrated for achieving political and economic objectives is not likely to succeed. Yet, it may cause anxiety and concern and can create difficulties for ordinary people. Hence it should be combated, controlled and eliminated with perseverance, vigilance and force, and justice done to one and all.

In the past, some rulers used terrorism to protect their countries and weaken other countries which had unfriendly relations with them. A country could try to fake friendly relations with an enemy country. But if it were strong, it could wage wars against enemy countries, or use the weapon of terrorism to harass and weaken them. It could bribe the officers of the enemy country, destroy its sources of income, spread discontent in the minds of the citizens of the enemy country against its ruler, or kill innocent persons to create a fear psychosis. It would attack the enemy country after it was weakened and harassed, sabotage its projects and plans, and create total chaos. Today, also, some countries use these tactics. They fund terrorism. They train terrorists, provide them with weapons and nefarious plans, and provide them shelter before and after the acts of terrorism are committed. They provide everything needed by the miscreants. They cause difficulties to their neighbours and to countries which do not want to take action against them, to avoid the death and destruction of innocent people and their properties. Unfortunately, this kind of humane consideration is treated as a sign of weakness by terrorists and countries that support them.

Terrorists use modern weapons, transport, communication facilities and lethal technologies. They are likely to use nuclear, biological, chemical and psychological devices and methods in the future. If that happens, fighting terrorism is likely to become more onerous and difficult than it is at present.

The number of terrorists in the world is not very large. But they are highly motivated, well trained and well equipped. They have the element of surprise in their favour. Ninety-nine per cent of people in the world do not favour terrorism, and most governments have enough strength, armed forces, personnel, funds, transport and communication facilities, and well-equipped intelligence agencies to combat it effectively. Therefore, it is better not to feel frightened of terrorism and fight it instead. If that is not done, terrorists would be happy and feel that they have achieved their objectives.

The most effective method to control and combat terrorism is not to allow its seed to be sown and grown into a menacing organization, and not to provide it with funds or a safe haven.

Otherwise, terrorists can attack not only other countries, but the people and systems of the same country in which they are created, thrive and are supported. To prevent wars being fought, organizations like the United Nations were created. Terrorism needs to be fought in the countries where it becomes visible. If it is allowed in a country that thinks that it would not harm it, it would be a big mistake. The countries of the world have to unite to combat terrorism. The war against terrorism must be fought not only in the field, but also in the minds and hearts of human beings who are likely to get affected by it, not only with weapons, but with ideas and thoughts as well. Let us hope that this would be done and would happen.

In a society, when an individual commits a crime against any other individual, the government punishes the criminal. It becomes necessary to do so to see that all citizens, weak or strong, are allowed to live in peace. Police forces ensure that no citizen is subjected to criminal activities by any other person. A nation is defended by its military mainly when attacked by another country. Internal security is provided by the police. When a country suffers from terrorism, the police or the armed forces combat it. When ordinary crimes occur, they are dealt with by the police. The number of crimes in the world is increasing in proportion to the number of laws made. It is increasing in proportion to the multiplication of material desires generated in the minds of men and women of the modern world.

Criminal intent, which is the soul of crime, is born in the mind. It is said that wars occur in the minds of men and they need to be fought and won in the same places.

India has been through six wars and won five of them. All the wars were fought by the Indian armed forces. In the first few years after independence, the military had difficulties in getting the funds it needed, but later, it could get all the funds it demanded. Initially, it was thought that sanity would prevail and the goodwill that India had in the world could defend its sovereignty and territory. Later, the government realized that India should prepare its armed forces to face any eventuality. It should also have a well-developed economy and social harmony to protect its interests against any attack from any corner of the world. In the process, an attempt is being made to use available funds for economic development, social harmony and the security of the country in a balanced manner. Deciding what is balanced and appropriate is not very easy. In the process of balancing demand and supply, it has to be carefully seen that what is required in any area urgently is not denied. By and large, decisions taken so far have proved to be acceptable and appropriate.

Fortunately for India, the problem of internal security was not allowed to disturb the country. On one pretext or the other, some forces from inside and outside the country tried to disturb some areas of the country. But they could be tackled and dealt with by using persuasion, political sagacity and the skill and might of the armed forces. To provide internal security, military or paramilitary forces have been used, but where they did not actually threaten internal security, they were managed in most cases by the state police forces.

In some parts of the country, terrorism was in existence. Punjab suffered for some years, but the situation was tackled by using political sagacity and the armed forces of the states and Union carefully.

In Jammu and Kashmir, terrorism caused some concern, mainly because it was supported by the neighbouring country. Political, economic, social and cultural steps were taken to thwart terrorism. The state police, paramilitary and military personnel were used to control infiltration from the neighbouring country and terrorist activities. The futility of shedding the blood of innocent persons was realized by many. The situation improved by nearly 70 per cent. In the state, elections to all bodies were held, giving power to the people to govern themselves, along the lines of the basic laws of the country. In J&K, the army guarded the actual line of control, while the paramilitary forces guarded the international borders and helped the state police to maintain law and order and combat terrorism, guided by the unified command under the chief minister of the state. The state was disturbed by external forces, but the constant vigil of the forces and the appropriate decisions taken by the state and Union governments helped to overcome the problems created by terrorists. Terrorism or wars were not allowed to affect the unity of the country in any manner.

The northeastern region of the country touches the boundaries of three neighbouring countries. The region is rich in natural and human resources. It has the potential to become one of the richest parts of the country, by using modern technologies. In some parts of the region, terrorist movements were started by some persons demanding that it should be given independence. They were persuaded through dialogues and also by using force to give up their demands, and join the mainstream of the country to do their best to bring about economic, social and cultural development of their areas. These efforts improved the situation to a great extent in some parts of the region. The situation in Mizoram, Meghalaya, Tripura, Manipur and Nagaland showed signs of improvement. Arunachal Pradesh was under control and peaceful. It was, therefore, possible to say that these states did not suffer from deteriorating situations. The Government of India spent huge funds in the region to ensure that it became economically strong, and contributed towards its and other states' all-round development, by using its bio and hidden wealth. Terrorism in the region was controlled and combated by the state police forces, with the help of paramilitary and military forces under the guidance of the unified command headed by the chief minister or the chief secretary.

In some parts of the country, terrorism existed in the name of economic justice and changing the system of governance followed in the country. It was called Naxalism. The states where it was visible were Chhattisgarh, Jharkhand, Bihar, West Bengal, Maharashtra, Uttar Pradesh and Tripura. In these states all the districts were not affected, but just one or two districts, and within each of these districts, only a few villages were affected. In fact, two districts in Chhattisgarh and two in Jharkhand were responsible for 70 per cent of the Naxalite activities in the country. In one or two places in other states also, terrorist activities were detected.

The figures relating to the affected states and districts were presented by some in such a manner that they created fear. It was said that ten states and 180 districts in the country are affected, which means one-third of the country was affected, which was not correct. India has about 14,000 police stations, out of which about 300, or 3 per cent, of police stations were affected by Naxalism. If it were held that the numbers given by some persons were correct, they were definitely bound to create a scare. If the number of police stations affected were taken into consideration and held to be correct, they would not have created the scare, and would have assured that the situation could be controlled easily.

The state governments were expected to deal with Naxalism with the help of their police forces. The Union had given more than 75,000 men and officers, armoured vehicles, helicopters, intelligence and modern equipment to the states to deal with it. Those affected by Naxalism were also given funds to bring about economic development in backward districts, which were over and above the funds given to them for normal development as they were given to other states and districts. The states were encouraged to use employment guarantee schemes, schemes to provide help to people living in the forests, to provide midday meals to schoolchildren. The governments were advised to use their plans and schemes to bring about the all-round development of the backward areas of their states. They were also asked to use the forces provided to them to protect public property, and the lives, limbs and properties of private individuals. They were advised to cooperate with one another, in every respect, to control terrorism. Each state was asked to have nodal officers to deal with other states to control terrorism. The situation in all parts of all states were not identical. In some parts, the states enjoyed peace and tranquillity. In others, they faced disturbances. However, the situation was not allowed to deteriorate. In fact, in most of the affected states, such as Andhra Pradesh, Bihar, Mizoram and Tripura, it was improved considerably. In the other states also, Naxalism was not allowed to escalate by dealing with it with determination, imagination, and justly. The graph of the Naxal movement had not gone up, but showed a downward trend. However, because of the wide publicity given to the incidents that occurred, the situation appeared to be going out of control and scary, which was not the case.

Incidents of terrorism have occurred in some places in the hinterland. They occurred in cities like Delhi, Mumbai, Bangalore, Jaipur, Ahmedabad, Surat and Hyderabad, they occurred in places of religious importance at Ayodhya, Varanasi and Ajmer, and in temples, mosques and churches. Some of these incidents were triggered by terrorists, who had come from other countries and lived in some parts of India as sleeper cells. Terrorists joined educational institutions as students and also conducted business activities. They used advanced electronic devices to cause explosions. It was, therefore, necessary to be vigilant and alert.

Terrorism in India was discussed a great deal in Parliament, in the media and society. According to some, it was handled in a soft and in an inappropriate manner. Those who held this view advocated that strong and stringent measures should be adopted to deal with them. They asked that laws required to deal with them in an effective manner should be passed.

There were others who were not in favour of being unduly harsh or soft. They were for adopting a balanced attitude and to deal with Naxalism in a correct, just and effective manner. They asked the government not to be very soft or very strong. In fact, the government in India followed a policy towards this issue in a balanced, correct, just and effective manner.

The problem was, at times, discussed in a manner which had political overtones. At times, the Union was criticized. At times, the states were criticized. At times, other countries were criticized by some. At times, they criticized one another. The problem was asked to be handled by using other methods which contributed towards its genesis. They asked that social, economic, political and cultural justice should be done, employment, proper education should be provided, and they suggested not to use and depend upon force only to deal with it.

The governments took a balanced, correct and legal stand, and tried to handle the problem in a holistic manner. The approach adopted by them helped. It could help in the future also. There were others who were in favour of passing laws like POTA (Prevention of Terrorism Act), MISA (Maintenance of International Security Act) and TADA (Terrorist and Disruptive Activities [Prevention] Act). They felt that they violated the human rights of citizens, and so, they should not be allowed to remain in the statute book. However, it should be accepted that there was scope for improvement. In fact, there is always scope for improvement in all matters. Governments, societies and individuals should cooperate with one another to help solve problems of this nature, without blaming each other, and by offering constructive criticism with a desire to improve the situation, and not to malign anyone, any organization, any party, or any section of the society or country.

New methods and technologies and more manpower can be helpful in handling the problem effectively. That was done, and it helped to achieve better results.

■

Compared to other countries, the crime rate in India is more moderate. This is because the people of India are more contented and peaceful in their attitudes towards their lives. This attitude may not help in bringing about rapid material growth and development, but it certainly gives them more satisfaction. In India, people have learnt to live happily with the little they have. People in materially better-off countries are taught to achieve more and compete. As a result, they are rich in material things, but they are not happy or satisfied like the people who are less demanding and more content. When they compete to do better, they commit mistakes. That is perhaps one of the reasons why more crimes are committed in developed countries than in India. However the attitudes are changing and becoming more like the people in developed countries, and concurrently, the crime rate in India is also rising. If this is to be prevented, policing and coercive force are not enough. The Indian philosophy of detachment should be inculcated in people, so that their lives are guided to become more competent and productive. This can be done not only in police stations and prisons, but in homes and educational institutions. In this respect, the synergy of science and technology and spirituality can help. In fact, both are parts of the same reality. Noble thinkers do not want to punish criminals, but want to reform them. They treat criminal intent as a result of a diseased mindset. Therefore, suspects are not punished and proof beyond the shadow of a doubt is required to punish an accused person, which is why many criminals get acquitted and only a few are punished. This is also the reason why delays occur and procedures become more complicated. These are some of the problems of the criminal justice system, and its frailties. These weaknesses should be removed, though all of them are not likely to be wiped out. As time passes, the system may become more refined.

In Parliament, in the newspapers and on TV screens, problems relating to terrorism are discussed quite frequently. To handle terrorism effectively, it is necessary to understand the root causes responsible for it, the means and methods that should be used, and the funds, equipment, information and cooperation between different forces, agencies and countries that are required. If the issue is considered only to condemn parties or persons, the results cannot be helpful. The subject should be handled scientifically. It needs an unbiased approach and careful planning. It needs an understanding of the history, geography, sociology and the psychology of the people of the area. Sometimes, discussions on terrorism and crimes do not touch the core of the subject. Touching the core may produce conducive results.

India is governed by the provisions of its Constitution. It follows the rule of law. Those who govern have the authority given by the law. The Union and states have certain powers and have to function and discharge their duties within the areas allotted to them. They cannot exercise their rights in areas exclusively given to one or the other. In times of emergency, the Union can take over all the areas that are given to the states and exercise its authority, but only after suspending or dissolving the legislature and dissolving the state executive. In matters relating to law and order and terrorist activities, the states have to use their executive power. The Union is not allowed to use the police or the military, for example, without having been invited by the state or obtaining its permission, or by removing the state government. This legal position is not understood in clear terms by some people. In some countries, terrorism is tackled by the military. In India, terrorism is not tackled by the military, except in states which are in the neighbourhood of other countries, or in exceptional circumstances. In the states affected by Naxalism, the military is not used to control terrorism.

The decision to use the army can be taken by the Union government in almost all cases. In some cases, in order to handle the most difficult situation for a temporary period, the decision is allowed to be taken by the state and its district authorities. The police are trained to control mobs and traffic, and to ensure that law and order is not disturbed by unruly elements in the society. They are not trained or equipped to combat well-trained and well-equipped terrorists. Terrorists have begun to use military tactics, with sophisticated weapons and advanced explosives. Therefore, the military is in a better position to control them in many cases. If the military is not to be used against terrorists who are Indian citizens, the police should be trained and equipped to discharge this duty. In recent times, on a small scale, the police have been given protective gear, sophisticated small weapons, better transport and communication facilities, advanced electronic equipment to collect intelligence, armoured vehicles, helicopters, aeroplanes and unmanned aerial vehicles (UAVs). But they have not been given the training required for this purpose on a large scale, which must be done. These are some of the general points, which should be borne in mind while considering what can and should be done.

■

The Union government has military, paramilitary, reserve police and members of the Central Industrial Security Force (CISF). The military is under the control of the defence ministry and is used to protect and preserve the sovereignty of the country on land, in the economic zone, of and in the oceans and in the air. The army is used on land, the navy in the oceans, and the air force in the skies. The actual line of control between India and other countries is guarded by the military. The international border is guarded by paramilitary forces, that is, the Border Security Force (BSF), the Indo-Tibetan Border Police (ITBP), the Sashashtra Sena Bal (SSB) and the Assam Rifles. The coastline is guarded by the navy and coastguards. Recently, the coastal police was created to protect some areas along the coast and the ocean. The Central Reserve Police Force (CRPF) is maintained by the Union, to be sent to the states, if needed. The CISF was created to protect important installations and public sector units. Now, it is used by the private sector, too, on the same terms and conditions on which it is used by public sector units. Military personnel are allowed to extend help to civil authorities in the states during emergencies. The strength of the paramilitary forces, the CRPF and the CISF need to be increased. India is a vast and heavily populated country with different climatic and geographical zones, with forests, snow-clad mountains and plains. Therefore, it needs more forces trained to discharge different kinds of duties in different geographical conditions. The Union government has taken decisions to increase their strength, but what is done is not sufficient. They have to protect a border of 7,500 kilometres, and a coastline of the same length. In the

Himalayan region, the forces have to discharge their duties at very high altitudes. At some places it has to function at a height of 18,000 feet. If they are not rotated at short intervals, they are likely to suffer permanent injuries. In fact, if a person lives at such a height for one year, he ages by three years. This difficulty can be overcome by increasing their numbers by 50 per cent. The numbers in the coastguard, navy and coastal police should also be increased. Protecting the coastline is more difficult than protecting the land border. Beyond the economic zone, the ocean is open to all. The interests in the oceans are, therefore, difficult to guard. The number of people in the navy, coastguard and coastal police should be increased on a much larger scale than what is done in the paramilitary forces. The strength of the CRPF and CISF should be doubled in five years.

The strength of the state police forces should also be increased. To help the state governments in this respect the concept of the Indian Reserve Police (IRP) has been useful. The states were given ₹15 crore to raise a battalion. This amount was raised to ₹30 crore. The states have to pay the salaries of the personnel of the IR battalions. They can send their IR battalions to different states where they are required and can charge for this duty done by them to earn revenue. In fact, they can be sent on international duties to other countries and earn revenue for their states. The United Nations and other international organizations can also make use of them at an acceptable cost. Some states have made use of this scheme in a splendid manner, while some have failed to use it. All states were asked to raise IRP battalions. States affected by terrorist activities have begun to realize that they should be prompt and efficient to raise and use them.

The states have a primary duty to protect the properties, lives, land and interests of their citizens. The number of people living within their borders is increasing. But in proportion to that, the number of police personnel has not increased. The states, therefore, should increase the strength of their forces by at least 50 per cent.

Vacancies in the forces are not filled in time. In some states, these vacancies extend up to 20 per cent of the strength of their forces, and 40 per cent of the strength of their officers at the higher levels. Steps to fill vacancies are taken after they occur, whereas they should be taken before they arise. For this, the forces should provide for salaries of staff recruited for training to fill the vacancies in time. When the states and paramilitary forces were asked why such a large number of vacancies were unfilled, the reply that was given was that timely steps were not taken by the government to fill the vacancies, to reduce the cost of administration. This approach must be altered. There is no point in preventing vacancies in the security forces from getting filled, merely to implement economy measures and save some money. Orders should be passed to highlight the fact that such economy measures are not applicable to security forces. States that have not raised IRP battalions, not filled the vacancies, and not increased the strength of their forces are the ones in which law and order is not satisfactory, and terrorist activities are causing more concern.

In some states, governments are allowed to employ retired servicemen and police personnel to help the police. They are given a small remuneration for their services. The Union helps to reimburse this expenditure. Such schemes have been adopted in J&K, Bihar and some other states, and have attained good results. The graphs of terrorism in these states show an impressive declining trend.

These schemes should be adopted by other states, as they reduce the time required to increase the strength of the security forces, and help to have experienced manpower at their disposal. The Union government would certainly help the states to reduce their financial burden while accepting the schemes, as it has done to help states which have adopted the scheme.

There are other forces in the country that can extend cooperation and assistance to the security forces. They can be used to control traffic, processions and mobs. Policemen who are meant to discharge these duties can be relieved and diverted to other, more risky, onerous and difficult duties. The National Cadet Corps (NCC), for example, can be used on a larger scale. This arrangement is bound to strengthen the police forces.

In India, there are many private security agencies. A law has been is passed to ensure that these agencies are run by reliable and dependable persons. The number of people engaged in providing security through private agencies, I am told, is over seven million, which is too big. These agencies can be deployed to protect private enterprises, industries, shops, transport systems, properties and individuals. Thus, they can reduce the burden of police personnel working under the authority of the government. A system can be developed to bring about cooperation between private security agencies and government forces. If private individuals can run industries, shops and cultivate lands, they can provide security to needy enterprising units and persons. The number of private security agencies is going to increase. They are run by experienced, retired military and police personnel. They are bound to become more efficient, modern and effective as time passes. They should be encouraged and helped to widen their areas of activities.

These days, owners of industries, shops, malls and theatres spend a considerable amount of money on running their establishments. From the beginning, if they are made aware of the importance of taking care of their security, they are bound to heed the advice for it will only help them to save their enterprises from destruction and losses.

Private individuals have a right and duty to defend their lives and properties. They are not punished if they discharge this duty. They can be trained to defend themselves and their properties. This is necessary because it is not always possible to have the police persons present at all places, in time, or when crimes are actually committed. Young people can be trained to carry out these duties through families and educational institutions, or other agencies. This is being done on a small scale, but much more is needed to be done.

The police–population ratio in India is very poor compared to the ratio in many of our neighbouring and other countries. The sooner this deficiency is removed, the better it would be for the country. The states should take a major lead and the Union should help them. The Union can play an effective and corrective role by helping the states in an appropriate manner.

India has about 650,000 villages, but it has only about 14,000 police stations, which is inadequate. Therefore, efficient and timely policing is not easy to provide. In the past, in nearly each big village, there was a kotwal and a police patil, whose duties were to keep a watch on situations developing in the village and on people visiting it, and to keep police officers informed about the law and order situation prevailing in and around the village. The old system was not as efficient as the modern police stations are, but it was quite widespread and helped to manage and control situations in time. The positions of kotwal and police patil were hereditary. They have since been abolished, but it is now realized that they could be brought back into existence, but without allowing them to be hereditary. These posts can be held by people selected by the government, or those elected by the people and may even be integrated with the local bodies. The villages may also have bodies which perform their private duties, as was done in the past, and also perform duties enjoined by the law. The members of these bodies can be given some remuneration and provided with facilities to travel and communicate with officers in the police machinery. They should be given fast travel and communication facilities, which, in present times, is not very difficult to provide. Cell phones can help splendidly. What is required in a country like India is to marry the two systems, the combination of which is going to be very helpful.

The states have to establish, maintain and support police stations. In the last few decades, no substantial steps were taken to increase the number of police stations in difficult areas. The state governments were persuaded to increase the number of police stations and on their demand, funds were made available to them.

Unfortunately, the funds were not utilized and remain unspent in many states. In fact, the states should actually find funds for these purposes from their own resources; otherwise, policing in the states cannot be improved.

The existing police stations are unable to cater fully to the demands of the people for policing. They are not strong enough to defend themselves when attacked. They do not have the appropriate rooms to keep criminals in safe custody or strong-rooms in which weapons and other equipment can be safely stored. In fact, model plans to construct them should be prepared and used. Each police station should have restrooms and eateries for the police. The home ministry of India had asked for the plans to be prepared to meet these requirements, but the plans prepared were too unsatisfactory to be approved and used. In the nizam's state of Hyderabad, in the olden days, police stations were built according to plans prepared by the government. Police stations in villages, towns and cities, in forests, deserts and plains, need not use the same model. To cater to the needs and demands of particular areas, different plans can be made and used.

All police stations in the country should have computers and electronic equipment to store and communicate information. Funds have been provided by the Union to the states for these purposes, which should be used.

All police stations should be connected to one another and to offices at the higher levels. An attempt has been made to establish a police net called the Polnet. The state governments are connected to the district police offices, but are not yet connected to police stations. Some states object to it on the ground that the proposed technologies are obsolete and should be discarded in favour of new technologies. Adopting new technologies needs time and funds, and before such decisions are taken, new technologies become old. It is, therefore, necessary to complete the police net scheme, and provide communication facilities to all states and police stations. Having something is better than having nothing. New technologies can be examined, adopted and used. The police machinery can have redundancies also in these areas. It is better to have more than one system in place to ensure that communication is possible through one or the other scheme, if any of them fail in some areas. This is the principle followed in several other activities. It is followed in wars. Policing is nothing but fighting for peace in different ways. Therefore, police machinery should have alternate facilities and redundancies.

In the villages, small, strong fort-like structures were used by those whose duty it was to protect the villagers from external onslaughts. The structures themselves provided protection to the villagers and their protectors. It may not be necessary to have such structures in present times, but police stations with the strength to withstand attacks are necessary. Police stations affected by terrorist activities should be strong enough to protect the police and the machinery used by them.

Attention should be paid to equipping the police forces with better transport facilities, so that it is possible for it to discharge their duties with fewer personnel. Even if the number of police stations is limited, they can be more effective with better transport facilities. If the number of police personnel is not adequate to meet contingencies, the deficiency can be reduced by using speedy means of transport. The police in the past dealt only with crimes committed by individuals; now, the forces need to deal with terrorists, who are adopting and using new technologies, weapons and transport facilities.

The police forces guarding the borders of the country are provided with modern means of transport, such as helicopters, aeroplanes, ships, boats and armoured vehicles. They need facilities which are provided to them at present in big numbers. In the future, terrorists are likely to use nuclear, biological and chemical devices and weapons to perpetrate terror. Therefore, preparations should be made to provide the police forces with vehicles which can withstand attacks from such deadly devices. Such vehicles cannot be provided on the spur of the moment. They may need time to procure; therefore, from now on, steps should be taken to meet these requirements.

The state police forces also need more and better transport facilities. Some police personnel are given motorcycles and jeeps, but none of them have helicopters or aeroplanes at their disposal. Boats are given to those who guard the coasts of India. However, the number of motorcycles, jeeps and boats given is insufficient. They should, therefore, be given to them in big numbers.

In cities, the police work out of their police stations. If they have mobile police stations at vulnerable places, they would be able to reach the scene of crime without loss of time, and can prove more effective in preventing or controlling crimes. In fact, big cities cannot be policed only with the help of vehicles plying on the roads. If they get helicopters, they would be more effective. In many countries in Europe, the airports seaports and important installations are protected by police using armoured vehicles. It is necessary for the Indian police also to use them on a large scale.

Combating terrorists without having adequate transport facilities may not be impossible. But the cost of doing so, in terms of human lives and the efficiency quotient, is going to be very high. Preventing terrorism with better transport facilities will definitely be easier and more cost-effective for the forces. For this purpose, the states should prepare their plans, provide the necessary funds and implement them, without delay. Investments done to provide these facilities are bound to give good dividends. The Union has many forces stationed at different locations. When they are needed at certain places, they cannot reach in time without efficient transport facilities. In some parts of the country, roads are not available. So in such areas helicopters and aeroplanes can be used. The helicopters and aeroplanes used by the defence forces, the civil aviation ministry and other ministries should be made available to the police forces on demand. The BSF has helicopters and aircraft, and it should be possible for other forces also to have such transport facilities.

The Union and state police forces should have modern communication facilities, which need to be more sophisticated. It has become necessary to collect information from all parts of the country and the world and police offices and stations should be connected to one another. The Polnet project and other projects should be used to provide better communication facilities.

Individual police personnel do not have communication facilities. It should not be difficult to provide this facility to them. They can be given cell phones and police stations can be fitted with equipment that can feed them with information, even when they are on an operation against criminals and terrorists. Electronics has brought about a sea change in the area of informatics and communication, and should be fully used by the police forces. The only thing which should be kept in mind is to ensure that modernization is done in a continuous manner. It should have the plans and facilities for the same. The skill lies in providing continuous modernization.

For this purpose, experts' advice and guidance and long-term, visionary planning is required. Those who can help in this may not be people who don uniforms and carry weapons. They may be scientists and experts who sit in laboratories and libraries and function from their offices and training centres. They are going to be very important for policing in the future and are definitely going to prove to be force multipliers.

At the national level, steps have been taken to achieve some of these objectives, but what is done at the state levels needs improvement. The Union and state governments should find more funds, establish new training centres and laboratories and develop a new ethos for this purpose.

Collecting and disseminating information through modern equipment is being done. But more efforts are needed. It would be unwise not to rely on machines and use them on a large scale, but it would be equally unwise not to pay enough attention to human agencies, since no machine can compete with the human brain. In fact, both can be developed and used simultaneously. Psychology can be developed and used, as it would, in some cases, be more useful than machines. Plenty of planning is required for these purposes.

The paramilitary forces have certain duties to discharge on the borders, in the hinterland and in disturbed areas. The nature of their duties is also changing, but their training is not adequate or apt. It has become necessary to train them to function in the snow-clad Himalayas, in forests, in deserts, on the beaches and on the plains, in crowded cities and remote villages, against criminals, dacoits, and well-trained terrorists. There are training institutions run by the Union government through the defence and home ministries. The training standards have to be changed and upgraded, and should include modern equipment and machines. In many places, this is being done. But, the scale has to be upgraded. More training institutions should be established and more modern equipment supplied to them. Experienced trainers are needed, like in other countries, where a great deal of attention is paid to this aspect. India has also done a lot, but definitely, more action is needed.

The state police forces have to discharge duties not entirely identical to those of the Union police forces. Some of their training centres can compare well with those established by the Union government, and in other countries. But they need more attention and modernization than the training centres at the national level. They have to put in more effort to come up to the level of the best training centres in some other countries. Projects for this purpose take a long time to complete and are hampered by lack of funds. So, the states have to adopt new paradigms to do better. Effective training raises the morale of the forces, which is why an investment to improve their morale is worth resorting to. The training institutions in the country should be used to their maximum capacity. For this, they need cooperation between the states, between the states and the Union, and between the Union and other countries. Trainees should be allowed to move from one centre to another, if needed. The equipment in these centres should be used for trainees from any part of the country.

In recent times, it was proposed that police universities should be established in different states. Some states were very enthusiastic about establishing them. The Union was also inclined to start police universities in different parts of the country to train new recruits, both physically and mentally. They could teach them about laws, train them to follow the discipline required by the armed forces, and how to use new weapons, transport and communication systems. Policing is a specialized area which is quite complicated, and needs separate universities. It would be in the interest of security to have police universities.

At present, individuals depend, for their own security and that of their shops, industries and such other activities, on private security agencies. A law has been passed to legalize and streamline them, and also to ensure that they are not misused by undesirable elements. The number of people working in these agencies is, it is said, three times more than those working in the Union and state police forces. They are definitely going to play an important role in providing security. The people working in private agencies would need to know about the laws and training to understand the security scenario, and to use the appropriate means to protect people and their properties. Police universities can prepare young men and women to join this profession. The certificates given by them would be useful to provide employment to those interested in such activities.

The people can also defend themselves and their properties. The police forces, training centres and police universities can play an important role in advising them on what to do. Young men and women at times take pride in helping themselves and others, but this task has to be performed carefully. In some countries and some parts of India, such groups have on occasions misbehaved with weak and unsuspecting citizens. This should be avoided by ensuring that they maintain strict discipline in the tasks they perform.

■

The Union is enjoined to perform its duties according to the provisions of the Constitution and the law. The same applies to the states. There are some areas in which they have exclusive rights and duties, but in others, they can assist one another in performing their duties. The Constitution provides means and methods for cooperation and coordination between them in certain areas. It provides for zonal councils for the five parts of India—eastern, western, northern, southern and central zonal councils. The home minister of India presides over the meetings of these councils, and the chief ministers of states and other ministers attend them. In the zonal council meetings, the exchange of views between the representatives of the state governments and the Union government takes place. Issues relevant to the security and development of the zones are discussed, with a view to ensure that cooperation and coordination between them are generated. Many meetings of the zonal councils were held in the period of four and a half years of my tenure as home minister. The first meeting was held at Guwahati and others were held at Puducherry, Mumbai, Bhopal, Shimla, Delhi, Goa, Raipur, Ranchi and Srinagar. It was heartening to note that the members of the council were willing to cooperate with one another. At one of the meetings, it was decided that each state should have a nodal officer to coordinate its efforts and activities with other states in controlling terrorism and other crimes. It was also highlighted that in almost all states, some posts were vacant which should be filled without delay. In all the states, there was scope for strengthening their forces, having more police stations, bringing about speedy and all-round development, strengthening their intelligence agencies, obtaining the cooperation of private individuals and security agencies and providing more funds in their annual budgets and five-year plans for making law and order and internal security more acceptable and effective. It was felt that the points thus made created the impact and an understanding for providing better security to the people.

In some states, the police was helped by paramilitary forces and the military to control and combat terrorist activities. Therefore, the concept of a unified command and headquarters was accepted. The unified command meetings were chaired in two states by the chief ministers of the concerned states and in one state by the chief secretary. This arrangement helped to avoid delays in taking decisions and effective actions.

The home minister was expected to meet the chief ministers to discuss the issues relating to cooperation and coordination between the Union and the states. Many meetings for this purpose were organized. The Union home secretary was expected to meet the chief secretaries of the states, once in three months. The special secretary (security) met the directors-general of the police of all the states every month, or as and when required, to take stock of the situation in different parts of the country. The states affected by terrorist activities and Naxalism were expected to prepare plans to control them, which were discussed by the Union and state officers. After they were approved, they were acted upon.

The Union home minister, the Union home secretary and the special secretary (security) visited the states where terrorist acts were perpetrated and made on-the-spot inspections to form their views and opinions. They discussed steps required to be taken by the states and the Union to see that incidents did not recur and terrorist activities were controlled.

The Intelligence Bureau (IB) remained in contact with the state authorities and the state police on a regular basis and kept them posted with relevant and useful information, in writing, on the phone and through other methods. The information thus given helped the states to prevent terrorist attacks and incidents in many cases. Success stories were not published and highlighted. The reporting of incidents only gave the impression that preventive actions were not taken, or if taken, were not successful, which was far from the truth.

The law and order duties, and combating and controlling terrorism had to be undertaken by the state authorities and the state police. The Union helped the states when help was asked for and demanded. The Union was not expected to, and nor was it allowed to, take action in these matters on its own, without being asked to help. If that were done, it could create problems of unbalanced centre–state relations. The states were not blamed by the Union if incidents took place. But if a situation was allowed to go out of control, they were held responsible. By and large, the states understood their responsibility and were able to take steps to prevent the deterioration of situations causing death and damage to the lives and properties of citizens.

■

India has a coastline of about 7,500 kilometres. It is guarded by the navy, coastguard and coastal police. The coastal police guard it when miscreants land on the beaches and enter Indian territory. The navy has ships, frigates, aircraft carriers and submarines, which are used to protect India in the open sea. The coastguard was brought into existence in the 1980s. It functions under the control and supervision of the defence ministry. The coastal police was created in the first decade of the twenty-first century, and works under the direction of the state governments. The Union home ministry helps them with concepts, plans, funds and training facilities. The state governments are given funds and other assistance to establish coastal police stations, to acquire vehicles and boats for their forces, and to recruit police personnel. They are given fast boats, which are manufactured in the country and other countries. They are being acquired and inducted into the forces. The numbers of police stations permitted, fast boats and police personnel are very small. It is necessary to spend more funds and strengthen them in a short time and in a planned manner. It is not easy to guard the coastline. It can be done in a better manner by obtaining the help of fishermen. It has become necessary to bring about better cooperation and coordination between the navy, the coastguard, the coastal police and fishermen. The Government of India has given about ₹500 crore to the states to build their coastal police systems. But, for this purpose, more funds are needed. Terrorists and pirates are likely to use the weak links in coastal security to perpetrate mischief against the interests of the country. The issue is under the consideration of the Union government. The state governments should play a more active role in this respect, for it is they who are responsible for providing security and protection to the lives and properties of the people living in the coastal areas. Fishermen and people living close to the coast should also be sensitized, trained and equipped to collect and pass on necessary information to the concerned authorities. It is necessary to prepare short-term, medium-term and long-term plans for the purpose, and to implement them with enthusiasm, funds and vision. In the past, India paid considerable attention to the military, but not to building naval power. The result was that foreigners entered India through sea routes and dominated the country for long periods of time, owing to their supremacy in the sea and on the sea routes. This should not be allowed to be repeated by terrorists or foreigners today.

■

People living in the rural areas are migrating to towns and cities, where they have better opportunities to earn more, get employment and better educational, medical and entertainment facilities. Those who want to lead honest, active lives and earn more are trying to settle in urban areas. At the same time, those who want to exploit people and create problems for others also migrate to towns and cities. Such people take advantage of the heavy population and crowds to hide themselves, and can easily find safe havens. Terrorists have begun to live in towns and cities, incognito. They remain inactive for years, then suddenly strike and disappear. Therefore, it has now become necessary to pay more attention to policing in towns and cities. Unlike in rural areas, it requires special procedures, systems, equipment and methods. In advanced countries, considerable attention is paid to this and special methods are developed and used. In almost all big cities and towns, CCTV cameras keep watch on the activities of people at important places, in big shops and malls, at crossroads, at places where people collect regularly. The CCTV cameras project the information onto screens in control rooms, which are manned twenty-four hours of the day by experts who are trained to read the information. In the control rooms, hundreds of people watch the big screens and receive information from every part of the town or city. The information is passed on to officers in police stations close to the scenes of offence. With the help of the information thus received, the police are in a position to take necessary action without delay, using mobile police vans and buses equipped with communication systems, motorcycles, jeeps and vans. Cities and towns can be observed from the skies from helicopters and satellites. But unfortunately in India, such arrangements are not yet made on the requisite scale. All mega cities should have helicopters and other such equipment. The state governments should take necessary steps soon and the Union government should help them with ideas and funds.

All important buildings and installations should incorporate security measures in their designs and plans and build them into the structures from the start. This requires awareness about the importance of security measures. People using marketplaces and other crowded areas should pay attention to security measures. They can be trained for the purpose and be authorized to take certain actions in accordance with the law.

In future, towns and cities can become more vulnerable. If terrorists resort to using nuclear, chemical and biological devices, they can cause incalculable damage to the lives and properties of the people. The administration in urban areas needs to be sensitized about such attacks and should be trained to tackle such disasters. They need special equipment for the purpose. For all important cities and towns in all states, plans should be prepared and implemented to deal with such disasters. New kinds of ambulances, protective gear and hospitals and trained doctors and nurses would be needed.

All these things cannot be done in a short time. Fortunately, steps have been taken in this direction. All the same, the Union and state governments should take more steps and spend more funds to be better equipped and prepared.

■

Intelligence helps governments to take preventive action, and is one of the most effective instruments to control crime and terrorism. In its absence, the action taken by governments could be less effective and more expensive. Ever since the system of governance came into existence, governments have developed methods and devices to collect intelligence, and taken decisions on the basis of the intelligence available to them.

In India today, intelligence is collected and provided to the governments through the Research and Analysis Wing (R&AW), Intelligence Bureau (IB) and states' intelligence agencies and special branches. R&AW collects intelligence relevant to other countries, while IB collects intelligence from all parts of the country. The states' intelligence agencies are supposed to garner intelligence from all parts of the state. It is expected that the intelligence collected is analysed and reaches the authorities in time. The agencies have relied on human agencies, and even now, they rely on them. However, new machines and technologies are used to collect the intelligence. The machines are becoming more sophisticated, and technology is becoming more useful. So they are used on a larger scale, with every passing moment. The machines can be set up in the sky, space, in outer space, under the ocean and on lands. As the science and technology relevant to electronics develops, the machines are going to be very effective.

Human beings are more effective and complex than the most sophisticated machines. Psychology, understanding the human mind, can be used to collect intelligence. In future, it is going to play a more important role in this respect. R&AW and IB do have trained manpower, but the number of men and officers with them is limited. They need to be trained to use psychology and other such sciences to discharge their duties on a larger scale.

In the past, police personnel were expected to collect information and intelligence during the course of their duties. They no longer do it, as they did in the past. The result is that the police lack timely intelligence and information and are unable to be as effective as they were in the past. It is better to use the old method also.

Our country needs the help of many hands to discharge its duties. People working in government, semi-government and private offices have opportunities to observe people who come in contact with them. If they are sensitized to pass relevant information to the police and other government authorities, they can help in preventing crimes and terrorist activities. For achieving these objectives, plans should be prepared and discussed with leaders of political parties and organizations and after developing a consensus, they should be acted upon. Even the elected members of the bodies at the local, taluka, district, state and national levels can help in the task of collecting necessary intelligence to avoid and control crimes and terrorism. In the past, there used to be kotwals and police patils in villages, who were expected to keep an eye on the happenings in the village, and to inform the police for necessary and timely action. This system has gone out of vogue, with the result that the limited number of police stations and personnel are not in a position to collect timely information. It is better to revive the old system without jettisoning the new one. These two systems can be married and used for obtaining better results. In towns and cities, people can be given the authority and responsibility to collect intelligence and information at the ward level. What is done in other countries and what is good should be adopted. What was done in our country in the past suited our situation. It is not wise to discard such systems and create asymmetry in demand and supply of facilities in this respect. The NCC, scouts and other organizations of this nature can be used to cope with the huge demands made on existing governmental organizations.

We should continue with the old and relevant ideas, adopt and use the new ones, and create even better ones to cope with the problems of the future. Only then would we be able to perform our duties in the required manner.

The state intelligence agencies are very weak. They need to be strengthened with more human resources, funds and research and development. At the national level, there is a greater realization about the importance of intelligence. At the state level also, it should be realized that good intelligence is needed and should be acquired, and the steps for the same should be taken.

In meetings held at the national and zonal levels, attended by ministers, officers and police authorities, these points were discussed. Fortunately, it was found that there was a consensus of opinion, and some steps were taken to implement some of the decisions. However, it is necessary to expedite the implementation and to make everyone concerned realize its importance.

■

The ministry of defence has a research and development organization, which is expected to examine weapon systems that are developed in the world and used by different countries, and new technologies that are becoming visible on the horizon and are likely to be used by the armed forces in the near or distant future. They are expected to develop new technologies, systems which would fit into new strategies and tactics that would be used to protect and preserve peace or fight and win wars, if they are thrust on peace-loving countries. The Defence Research and Development Organization (DRDO) has a large number of scientists, technologists and experts in the art and science of war and peace as well as equipment- and weapon-making. It has a number of laboratories which are given tasks to be completed within fixed time frames. It is helping our military and the country to perform their duties with better confidence and determination. It also projects the needs of the future that the coming generations would be required to deal with. It makes them better prepared to face future contingencies. Similar organizations do not exist to meet the demands of the police forces working under the Union or state governments. In training institutions and other such organizations, some attention is paid to the research and development relevant to policing, such as equipment and instruments to control traffic on roads in crowded towns and cities, to control mobs and their agitations and to detect crimes committed by groups and individuals. But very little attention is paid to the development of concepts, ideas, equipment, weapons and transport and communication facilities, which can be used by the police to control terrorist activities. Therefore, separate organizations like the DRDO and national laboratories should be established on a massive scale to cover all these police activities. Police stations, offices at different levels, housing, jails and strong-rooms all need be constructed on the basis of research and the requirements of the police in rural and urban, forests and coastal areas. The DRDO has acquired its present shape and strength owing to constant efforts over decades. An organization for better policing would also require time to become available and effective. So long-term plans should be made for the purpose. It should be discussed with the members of the armed forces, the paramilitary and the police. Similar institutions existing in other countries can also be visited. Meanwhile, departments, ministries and universities in the country can be asked to help the police in this respect also. Scientists, technologists and experts can be permitted to move from one laboratory to another, and from one organization to another. Private industry also can be made a partner in this effort. New concepts and technologies, developed in the laboratories and universities can be used to produce the required instruments and systems, weapons, vehicles and communication systems. This idea was discussed in the ministry of home affairs, but it remained at a conceptual level. The concept should take the form and design of a plan, and then, the design and the plan should be acted upon.

In future, terrorism may become more deadly, with the use

of radiological, chemical and biological devices and weapons. If that happens, the damage would be of an enormous nature. Before this happens, governments, people and security agencies should be prepared to deal with them. Security agencies would need new kinds of weapons, protective gear, equipment, transport and communication facilities, medicines, hospitals and post hospitalization care. To meet these threats, research and development in the area can be very useful. What is done by DRDO and other laboratories in this respect can also help. But for policing, special systems and equipment would be needed. The proposed organization can prove to be of great help The national government should take a lead and the state governments should cooperate. Other countries and international organizations can also help. What is being done is in bits and pieces and not with a long-term plan in a concerted manner, which is what is really required. Any government which succeeds in achieving this objective would serve the cause of humanity in the country and the world in time to come. The matter can be discussed in Parliament and with the National Development Council and Planning Commission. A nationwide discussion can also take place to secure support for the concept of the plan.

■

The Indian Penal Code is a substantive, comprehensive law which defines different kinds of offences and provides for punishments to be meted out to those who commit crimes. It has remained in force for more than a hundred and fifty years and is likely to continue for a long time to come. It has rarely been amended in all the years of its existence and covers almost all the conceivable crimes that can be committed. The Indian Law of Evidence provides the principles which can be followed to collect, secure and use evidence to prove the perpetration of offences. It is applicable to direct, circumstantial, scientific and technical evidence and presumptions, which can be accepted as evidence. The Criminal Procedure Code (CPC) provides the procedure which can be adopted to investigate incidents of crime, and is used to try criminal cases and pass judgements in criminal matters. It also provides for appeals and reviews that can be filed against judgements given in criminal matters. The original CPC was presumed to be well drafted. However, the procedures that were followed were examined and assessed to determine if they were apt and adequate, by the law commissions, higher courts and various committees and jurists. To make procedures more effective, humane and correct, the CPC was amended many times. The intentions behind amending these laws were to ensure that offences are properly defined, right kinds of judgements are given, punishments are adequate, innocent persons are not wrongly punished and decisions given can be examined by the higher courts of criminal justice. The basic principles that are followed in criminal matters are to ensure that: innocent people are not wrongly punished; the benefit of doubt is given to the accused; the rights given to citizens are not violated; there is no discrimination while judging people against whom criminal cases are filed or in investigations; and to find out if there is adequate evidence to decide whether offences are committed or not. Thus, the law is inclined to see that no innocent person is punished. For this purpose, the procedure to conduct criminal cases is meticulously followed, which is why cases take a long time to be decided. Even when offences take place in broad daylight and in the presence of many witnesses, cases are not disposed of without following the required procedure and getting the evidence on record.

There was a time when a lot of importance was attached to the evidence of eyewitnesses, rather than circumstantial evidence. Then it was held that witnesses could lie, but circumstances did not. The importance of circumstantial evidence is now understood in clear terms and attempts are made to collect it to support allegations when criminal cases are heard. It may not be wrong to say that efforts for this purpose have been made from the start. Yet now, because of the availability of scientific equipment and methods, greater reliance is placed on circumstantial and scientific evidence.

In the present times, scientific evidence is considered more convincing to decide criminal cases. Evidence given by experts is helping the courts to identify the perpetrators of the crime. As time passes, these methods are likely to be increasingly relied upon.

Even after it is ensured that the laws relevant to criminal matters are applied very carefully and real justice is done, it is found that this objective is not fully achieved. Human beings, when they observe the incidents taking place, commit mistakes. When they depose, they make mistakes, intentionally or unintentionally. When the evidence produced is judged, errors that creep in are corrected in higher courts. Sometimes, even higher courts commit mistakes. Therefore, there are many people in the society who advocate caution, preferring to err on the safer side to avoid judicial injustice.

These matters are discussed by law commissions, special committees and the higher courts. They give their views, which are then adopted. At times, they are not readily accepted. The time taken, however, for accepting and adopting them becomes unacceptable.

Several countries have systems which require the prosecutor to prove that the accused is guilty, while in other systems, the burden on the prosecutor to prove guilt is less heavy and shifts to the accused to prove that he is not guilty. There are systems where very severe punishment is awarded to the guilty, while in others, the guilty are not treated harshly, on the principle that they commit crimes because of the circumstances in which they find themselves. It is also held that if criminals are not treated as human beings who are not fully responsible for what they do, society will not be reformed, but will continue to suffer from such people. In some systems, the complainant and accused are allowed to compromise in some matters and compensation is given. In some countries and systems, even in major cases, they are allowed to compromise.

Criminal cases take time to decide. Attempts are made to reduce the time taken by increasing the number of courts and using new systems for recording evidence and investigating cases. The accused are not considered guilty until the time they are judged as offenders. The law relating to arresting the accused is also modified to take care that an innocent person's reputation is not harmed. The courts decide cases on the basis of the evidence produced before them. Whether the evidence is reliable or not is decided by the courts, after studying statements made by witnesses and after they are cross-examined. This makes the role of the defence lawyer very important. It is said that everyone may be equal in the eyes of the law, but not in the courts of law, for that depends on the presentation of the facts and the interpretation of laws by the lawyers appearing for the parties. This has made the dispensation of justice rather uncertain and expensive. At times, it is found that financially weak parties are unable to obtain proper assistance and legal aid. Laws are enacted and attempts are made to help poor clients with legal aid at the cost of the government. The laws are amended to overcome these deficiencies in dispensing fair criminal justice. The government amended the CPC and other laws also, to achieve the laudable objective of reforming the criminal justice system.

There are several other laws that have penal provisions to control crimes in many areas of human activities, professions, trade and industry, and other such matters. The same principles are applicable in these cases also.

Special laws were made to control terrorist activities. They dealt with the recognition of crimes and criminals, investigation of offences by the police, prevention of terrorist and criminal activities, detaining the accused for certain periods to prevent terrorist activities, presumption of the innocence or guilt of the accused, the onus of proof, the disposal of cases by special courts and providing protection to witnesses. MISA was one such law. It was repealed on the grounds that it was misused against a large number of innocent people. TADA was the second law made for the same purpose, but was also repealed. POTA was yet another law—it was passed by Parliament in a joint sitting of the members of both Houses of the Union legislature. Many members of the government which saw that POTA was made objected to TADA and voted to get it repealed. POTA was repealed as a result of the agreement between different parties that joined hands to form the government. There were many who thought that certain provisions in POTA were required to control and combat terrorism and help the security forces to discharge their duties. The provisions required were retained by introducing them in the Prevention of Unlawful Activities Act, after repealing POTA. It is held that, by and large, the existing laws are sufficient to control and contain terrorism, that certain special provisions required for the purpose are present in the Prevention of Unlawful Activities Act, so it was not necessary to keep POTA on the statute book. When some members argue that the government is soft on terror, the repeal of POTA is cited as evidence to substantiate the charge. It is argued that when POTA existed, Parliament was attacked. At many other places too, terrorist attacks were launched, showing that the law by itself was incapable of controlling and containing terrorism. The arguments advanced by the protagonists of POTA acquired a political colour. On behalf of the government, it was explained that some changes in the existing laws to make them more effective could be made, but it was not going to help in controlling terrorism fully, if innocent people were harassed and wrongly imprisoned—if that were to happen, the number of terrorists would increase and terrorists would find justifications to strengthen themselves and carry on with their activities.

The Indian Penal Code provides that a person who is guilty of murdering another person can be punished with imprisonment for life or with death. Imprisonment for life means imprisonment for the entire life of the convicted person, not only for fourteen years. This has been decided by the Supreme Court. It has also decided that in the rarest of rare cases, the death sentence can be awarded. Several countries have abolished the death sentence and there is pressure on India to abolish it too. The apex court has also ruled that ordinarily the death sentence should not be awarded, but if the court approves the death sentence, the guilty person is allowed to petition the president for mercy and to get the sentence reduced to life imprisonment or any other kind of punishment. The matter is then looked into by the state government. The state government sends its views to the Union home ministry, which can give its views based on the report and other factors to the president, who can then decide either to accept or reject the plea in the mercy petition. Some people argue that the death penalty should not be imposed, on the ground that since human beings are not able to give life, they cannot deprive any person of it.

The home ministry amended some laws, repealed some, and made some new ones too. There were some laws on the statute books which were not required, and so, were repealed. A bill for the Assam Rifles Act, a bill to give a new shape to the Sashatra Seema Bal, one on the Central Armed Police Forces, and another to have a new law for the Indo-Tibetan Border Police were introduced and passed. A bill to manage disasters and to create a disaster management authority was passed. A bill to control communal violence and to provide help, relief and compensation to victims of violence was introduced in the Rajya Sabha. It contained provisions under which victims could be given compensation. Under existing criminal laws, the guilty are punished, but the concept of giving compensation to victims was missing. Under the new law, the Communal Harmony Bill, the concept was accepted, but the bill could not be passed because of objections by some persons and organizations. Thus, the home ministry had nearly ten bills passed in a period of five years, which means that two bills were passed each year.

▪

Religion is a uniting force in its true nature. It unites human beings with each other, with plants, with living and non-living things, with totality, which includes space and time, matter, energy, knowledge and the spirit, which may be called God or the Almighty

Force of the cosmos. Its core at one place is identical with the core at any other place in different outer form. Its outer form may appear different, but its essence in all places and at all times is the same. If its real essence is understood, it can help. It cannot cause anything which is not useful and benevolent. Those who know this do not hate anything, any concept or idea. However, at times, its essence is not correctly understood. Those who understand it partially misunderstand it, and use it in a manner which creates divisions and problems. Religion thus misunderstood turns into a divisive force. History has proved that it has been responsible for conflicts, wars, bloodshed and misery of numerous kinds in the world. This is happening in the present times also in many parts of the world, including India. People of several religious faiths are responsible for causing misunderstandings, bloodshed and misery. In some countries, people belonging to certain religions are more responsible than those in others. These misguided souls have damaged temples, churches and mosques and done many things which true religion does not permit. The remedy lies in understanding the true spirit of religion. It lies in widening its vision and including everyone and everything in its ambit. This can be done by the members of the family, educational institutions, media and religious institutions. The most important requirement is to inculcate the concept of inclusivity in society and ensure that nothing limits the vision or allows narrow-mindedness.

In India, people belonging to the majority community, as well as minority communities, have acted in ways that generated hatred in the minds of some sections of society. This weakness is used by neighbouring countries to achieve their own objectives. Some people in countries which are not on friendly terms with India have helped and misguided people with funds, weapons and training. Therefore, it is also necessary that at the international level, decisions are taken not to provide funds and weapons to people not having authority to possess them, and not to provide safe havens to terrorists. Some decisions in this respect have been taken, but the implementation has not been satisfactory. Let us hope that it will be done with full sincerity and without wasting any further time.

Efforts to widen the vision and make it all-inclusive need perseverance. The results may or may not be visible in a short time. But without putting in efforts, with perseverance and determination, results cannot be achieved.

■

Human beings are influenced by economic factors. Greed makes man violent and interested only in his own self. Poverty makes man miserable as well as angry and violent. The level of economic development is not the same in all countries. Within a country, all states, districts and talukas are not equally developed. Unequal development and poverty anger and affect people. When they find that persuasion and legal means do not help them, they prepare to adopt any means they think can help them. Economic inequalities are exploited by people who have ulterior designs to serve.

In India, some states have better agricultural lands and practices, trading activities and industrial development, resulting from better infrastructure and technology along with mindsets willing to adopt new means for all-round development. In other states, there are no transport facilities, developed agriculture, trade, industry or industrial psychology. In the less developed parts of the country, the people suffer and become angry when they find that others are living lavishly. For these reasons, agitations are started to create new states. Those who take to arms for better opportunities and to come on par with others can be temporarily controlled and restrained. But if these problems are to be solved in a better manner, action should be taken against those indulging in illegal activities. Conditions conducive to prosperity should be created, economic disparities should be done away with, and opportunities for economic justice should be made available. Less developed states do not have proper roads, irrigation facilities, trading and industrial activities. The inhabitants of these states depend on forest produce, mining and hunting. They are more inclined towards terrorist activities than people living in the developed states. To deal with them, it is necessary to improve their economic conditions, to construct roads, build irrigation dams, modernize agriculture, establish modern industries like electronic and biotechnology industries, and convince them that their violent methods are counter-productive. We need to convince them that by adopting legal, peaceful and democratic methods, they would be able to overcome their difficulties more easily and quickly. They should be convinced that they would be helped. And, without fail, they should be helped.

The Government of India has plans and projects, schemes and designs to achieve economic development and reasonable equality. Funds are given to the states for these purposes under the five-year and other special plans. They need to be fully understood and implemented with enthusiasm and sincerity. Modern machines and technologies can help a great deal in these matters. The state governments can play a very important role by making their own plans, projects, systems and schemes to help the people. They need to put in tremendous efforts and funds to implement them successfully. They should depend on their own funds also. It is good and necessary to use the funds of the Union government. It is also essential to find funds in their own states for these objectives to be achieved.

The people at large can also help. They can enthuse the unenthusiastic. They can guide those who need guidance. They can cooperate with people whose efforts would prove helpful to the society as a whole. Terrorism arising out of economic causes should be understood fully and dealt with comprehensively. It may not be very useful to rely only on bullets and guns and armed personnel to control and eradicate it. It is only a comprehensive approach that can prove to be effective.

■

Several religions, communities and castes exist in India. At the core of the variety, there is a strand of unity which keeps the country together. However, the different communities, castes and religions are also responsible for discrimination and social injustice perpetrated against the weaker sections of society. This causes anger and violence when they cross the limits of tolerance. Unfortunately, Indian society has practised untouchability for ages. Treatment given to the untouchables was worse than the treatment given to animals. Social and economic injustices have existed in the society in conjunction with each other. Those who suffer from such discrimination find justification in taking up cudgels and arms against those who perpetrate them.

The people living in forests are not treated in the same way as the people living in villages, towns and cities. They are also exploited in many ways. Those who live in the hills and dales without modern facilities and live on hunting and roots and barks of trees also think that if they are cruel and brutal with other human beings who do not care for their welfare, they are justified. Therefore, it is necessary to treat the people living in forest areas with respect and affection. In the last few years, children of the disadvantaged sections of society have been provided with educational facilities. Some of them are bright and doing well in their classes and examinations. They get the opportunity to see how others live in towns, cities and villages and other countries. They compare their lives with those of their relations, who live in tribes, without shelter or medical help when they fall ill, or other civic amenities and facilities. When they return to their parents and relatives and realize how pathetically they live, waves of dissatisfaction, discontent, frustration and anger surge in their minds and hearts. Some people who are mild and prepared to accept the situation in which they find themselves compromise, but others do not. They revolt and take to breaking laws and rules made by the society and governments. They take to arms and shed the blood of those who are or who think they are, responsible for the conditions in which they live.

It is, therefore, necessary to ensure that economic and social justice is provided to them. For this purpose, the mindsets of many people in society have to be changed, and principles taught and followed in society have to be altered. Educational institutions have to contribute towards creating new attitudes and approaches towards life. Laws have to be changed and the justice system has to dispense the correct kind of justice without delay. The executive must also implement laws and decisions taken by them and the judiciary in a sincere and just manner and promptly.

Society takes years to develop conventions and systems. It takes a long time to change its principles and philosophy. The entire society takes part in making, modifying and using social customs and principles. Therefore, efforts have to be made with perseverance. Laws can be made or modified without delay, but social systems and customs which control society and its ethos cannot be changed quickly. Therefore, the task is quite onerous and has to be done with determination, a clear vision and perseverance.

After the Constitution was framed and adopted, laws to change society were framed and attempts were made to adopt them. But it was found that doing that was not as easy as drafting and adopting the Constitution was. The laws which were ultimately framed and adopted did not have the same shape and flavour as the original forms had.

■

In some parts of the country, political issues are raised to create terror and divide the country. This has been happening in the areas adjoining neighbouring countries. They are supported on the basis of cultural variety which is visible in different parts of the country. It is not possible to say that people who follow this path are not encouraged and supported by neighbours. In fact, there is enough evidence to show that some of these neighbouring countries encourage, plan, fund and indirectly or directly instigate terrorism. India has been dealing with those who are involved in such activities, politically, economically, socially and culturally. To achieve these objectives, some provisions of the Constitution are amended to meet the demands of people from troubled areas. The armed forces are used to deal with them when it becomes absolutely necessary to do so. But problems are solved with patience and perseverance and by using political understanding in a better manner. Some problems have been solved, some are controlled, while others remain to be solved although progress in dealing with these issues has not been unsatisfactory.

The division of states into smaller ones has helped to reduce the intensity of the demands and violent activities as have the onset of rapid economic development and induction of modern technologies. The areas where violent activities are visible are those which have natural resources which need to be used for the welfare of the people with the help of modern technologies. Different parts of the country have different capabilities. When they are used to help one another, all states stand to gain and expedite their development. The states are realizing that they should help one another and cooperate in every respect.

•

The countries of the world have begun to realize that they should help one another and that the time has come to cooperate with one another to use natural resources of the land, the oceans, space and outer space and in the areas of development of modern technologies and sciences.

In agriculture, trade and industry, science and technology, culture and spirituality, efforts should be made in understanding the inner and outer universe of man. These efforts would help to avoid wars and to help people. This understanding and ethos is likely to help in avoiding violence and destructive activities and should be encouraged and supported. These steps may not succeed immediately, but are bound to reduce the severity and destructive capability of violence and may ultimately succeed in controlling it completely.

•

Governments came into existence to provide security. Later, it was felt that the welfare of the people was important and governments should help in bringing that about. Now, they are paying more attention to economic development and social justice. They are paying enough attention to providing national security, but are not spending enough funds to deal with ordinary and terrorist crimes. The funds spent on providing security to the people, compared to the funds spent on economic and social development, are not satisfactory, perhaps because the funds spent on providing security are not considered as productive as funds spent on developmental activities. In fact, security is required for development also. Without security, development cannot take place.

In India, the Union spends funds on military and paramilitary forces, which are used to protect important installations and international borders and sovereignty of the nation. The states spend funds on their state police forces, for which they have to allocate funds every year in their budgets. The Union helps them with funds for special projects, but it is understood that the states have to spend funds from their own coffers for this purpose.

Over the last several years, funding for policing by the states has not been adequate, which is why the strengthening and modernization of the state police forces and intelligence agencies have not been satisfactory. This matter is discussed in forums attended by leaders working in the Union and state governments. The states have now begun to realize that they have to be more liberal in providing funds for strengthening their security agencies. Some states have taken concrete steps and shown willingness to accept the proposal, while others have yet to decide if they should spend more on policing.

The means and methods of committing crimes and terrorist acts are multiplying and becoming more complicated and sophisticated. Modern means of transport and exchange of information are also now easily available to criminals and terrorists. All these aspects need to be examined more carefully and need more funds from governments.

Unless positive decisions are taken to provide more funds at all levels, policing cannot be improved, and the increasing tide of crime and terrorism cannot be controlled effectively.

■

It is said that wars begin in the minds of human beings and that they should be controlled and stopped in their minds. Crimes and violence also germinate in the minds of human beings and should be controlled and stopped in their minds. How can this be done? What needs to be done to control, combat and eradicate them in and from minds of human beings?

The mother and other family members influence children and their thought processes. Today, children are taught in educational institutions on a massive scale. The media is becoming very powerful and now impacts on human beings twenty-four hours of every day. The ethos of society also influences the thinking of people. They can make citizens peace-loving, or strife-driven and violent. The philosophies that are propounded can make human beings love and respect one another, or dominate one another through violent and devious means and actions. The eastern hemisphere has been more peace-loving, while the western part of the world has been more prone to conflict, bloodshed and war in the last few centuries. Through these conflicts and wars, it has been able to strengthen its power, and dominate other parts of the world. But these wars have made them realize that they cannot continue to dominate other parts of the world, with the help of force alone. So they have now begun to give up trying to dominate other countries, and to cooperate in what is likely to make the world more peaceful. The scientific and technological capabilities developed in the world are making people strong and capable of using all the resources available, from land, oceans, air and even space, to meet all their demands. They have helped people to use not only land, but have also made it possible for them to use the oceans, skies and other planets. These new realities can make them join hands with one another and become less violent, and more peaceful and cooperative. If the emphasis is laid on these aspects, the desired results to establish perfect law and order, peace and tranquillity in all parts of the world can be achieved. Such efforts should be made by all peoples of the world. That would produce better results in less time.

∎

Some people think that force should be used and relied upon fully to control criminals and terrorists. They advocate that no mercy should be shown to those who kill innocent, unsuspecting and weak people, and stringent laws should be enacted for the purpose and used relentlessly. Any suspected person should be dealt with strongly to protect innocent people. In some cases, actions are taken to achieve these objectives, which may produce good as well as bad results. It is also found that strong actions are resented as they increase the number of wrongdoers, criminals and terrorists. Sometimes, just and correct actions have produced good results. Actions taken to control crimes and terrorism in an imaginative manner have also helped.

Some people advocate the cause of human rights, saying that governments should never violate the human rights of citizens and should follow the principles of the rule of law very strictly. They are unwilling to be harsh towards accused people. They agitate against governments if steps are taken by them to arrest and detain the accused. They believe that the accused should be tried by courts of law and should be punished only in accordance with the provisions of the law, after following the due process laid down for that purpose. They ask for laws that are more humane and less stringent. The laws should punish only those against whom cases beyond a shadow of doubt have been proved. They say that thousands of criminals may be allowed to go free, but not one innocent person should be wrongly punished.

There are others who distinguish between cases involving crimes against individuals and cases in which terrorism is inflicted. They treat terrorists on a different ground. They want to be very correct with ordinary criminals, but plead for strong laws and methods to deal with terrorists. There are others who are not prepared to distinguish between ordinary criminals and terrorists. According to them, the elements which make them appear different are not of very great consequence. Hence, they are for justice, strictly according to the principles of criminal jurisprudence.

Governments have a duty to protect innocent lives and properties and to punish wrongdoers, and to do it on the basis of the existing laws and principles of criminal jurisprudence. In some cases, they appear to be harsh, while in others, they appear lenient and soft. Whether they are lenient or strong can be decided only after examining the facts very meticulously and carefully, but they must be fair and just. They want to be just and correct, not soft or strong. If they are just, they could be strong or they could be lenient. This stand is appreciated by some and criticized by others. Different sections of society look at it on the basis of their backgrounds and experiences in life.

Terrorists make use of all means and methods to create terror and cause destruction and deaths. Terrorists use communal passions to fuel the fire of hatred to cause violence and destruction. Governments, civil societies, organizations and individuals should not allow terrorism to incite communal passions.

In a democracy, the people are sovereign and have power. Guided properly, they can be helpful, but if they are misguided, their sovereignty and strength can be misused. Therefore, the issue should be properly and correctly projected and looked at in a realistic, scientific and pragmatic manner. If wrong pictures are painted to show that situations are bad and uncontrollable, the purpose of the terrorists to create terror would be served. Terrorists want to create a fear psychosis to achieve their objectives, and they do it by attacking people and places. If these incidents are projected in an exaggerated manner, it suits them, because then their objectives are served. Discussions about terrorist attacks should take place in a manner that does not demoralize people, security forces or the governmental machinery. Striking a balance is necessary. The skill lies in controlling the menace and keeping a vigil, ensuring that people have confidence in the government. At present, all those who are concerned are required to pay attention to this aspect and help. These include political parties, the media and the people, the combined efforts of all, would help to reduce terrorism.

■

The Union home ministry has become a nodal ministry for managing disasters caused by nature or humans beings. The management of disasters is done at the local level by local authorities, who are helped by state governments. The states are helped by the Union government with funds, material, manpower, transport and communication facilities, and other things.

In the past, governmental and private agencies did not have the plans, equipment or material to give succour to affected people in a systematic manner. What was needed was decided on the spur of the moment and could not be done speedily. In the past, many disasters were managed and reports were prepared and made available to the government and the people. On the basis of the information and conclusions arrived at, and given in the reports, schemes and plans were prepared and used. But they were not efficient enough. It was necessary to manage disasters in a more scientific manner. The concept of disaster management was discussed in several countries, including India. The Congress party took the lead in supporting the concept of helping disaster-affected people in a more systematic manner, and agreed that a law for the purpose should be passed by Parliament. It was thought that a National Disaster Management Authority should be established to ensure that state and other authorities could be helped with new concepts, plans, projects, equipment, funds and machinery to supervise assistance and help given to the victims. The disaster caused by the tsunami helped to expedite the passing of the bill. In the common minimum programme of the UPA, it was mentioned that the law would be passed and disaster management authorities should be created.

A bill for this purpose was drafted, approved by the cabinet and other political parties and was introduced in Parliament. The Departmentally Related Standing Committee of the Union legislature dealing with the home ministry examined the bill and approved it with minor modifications. It was passed by both the Houses, more or less unanimously. The consent of the president was obtained and it was made into a law.

The National Disaster Management Authority (NDMA) was created after this law was passed. The state governments were asked to establish state, district, taluka and local disaster management authorities. The prime minister heads the NDMA and the vice-chairman of the authority manages its activities with the help of other members. The State Disaster Management Authority is chaired by the chief minister of the state, while the District Disaster Management Authority is chaired by the district collector and the president of the district panchayat co-chairs it. These authorities are expected to prepare plans, collect equipment, train people and help governmental agencies. They have to frame rules and prepare procedures to help victims of disaster.

The NDMA is expected to prepare a plan for the entire country and deal with similar organizations in other countries. The state and district Disaster Management Authorities are expected to prepare plans and stay prepared to help people involved in disasters. The plans are to be based on the principles and plans prepared by the NDMA.

The authorities are expected to visualize the kinds of disasters that can occur in the future, and to have drills to help people when disasters occur. If a disaster should occur due to human activities, such as the use of nuclear, chemical and biological devices and weapons, the task of helping people becomes very complicated and difficult. The authorities are required to train people and to have the necessary wherewithal required for the purpose. They are also expected to carry out research and development through national laboratories and private agencies and to be prepared to face future contingencies.

The authorities need manpower and resources on a large scale and need assistance. They are taking shape and adjusting with other governmental and non-governmental agencies and organizations. The angularities which exist need be rounded off to bring about better coordination. These authorities should be allowed to coordinate their activities with organizations of a similar nature in other countries, as well as international organizations.

The government and Parliament can take credit for passing the necessary law and creating the Disaster Management authorities. What they have done would definitely help disaster victims to get speedy relief, compensation and rehabilitation.

In India, disasters occur due to heavy rains, cyclones, earthquakes, landslides or heavy snowfall. Drought makes the lives of the people miserable. The Union government has helped the states with funds to build temporary shelters and permanent houses. In every disaster, government servants, private organizations and individuals have worked day and night to provide succour to the suffering masses. The defence forces, paramilitary forces and the state police and organizations have spared no effort to make the lives of the victims more comfortable and safer. The main credit for managing disasters successfully should be given to the state and local governments.

What really helped India to manage the disasters in a satisfactory manner?

People were helpful. Victims were less demanding. They understood the difficulties in providing relief and help.

The officers were attentive and never shirked their responsibilities to help victims, working day and night. The state and local governments took bold decisions and were not bogged down by unnecessary red tape or procedures. The standards they adopted in providing assistance were very high. The Union helped the states.

While doing so, it did not care if the states were governed by people belonging to their parties or not. What was borne in mind was that the people needed help, and their government's ideologies did not matter. The Union did not wait to receive demands for assistance. It was rushed to the states for the people. When the states demanded more help, positive action was taken.

The highest authorities in the government, the prime minister, the president of the Congress party and other parties and authorities and ministers have always been present in the affected areas within hours of disasters. Their presence emphasized that help would be made available without any delay. It encouraged people to put in their best efforts, and the affected people felt reassured and confident that they would be helped to overcome the disaster.

Disasters cause damage to property, houses, etc. The houses are repaired and rebuilt to help the affected people. While doing so, attempts are made to use new technologies and designs to build houses, roads, offices and to provide better civic amenities.

■

In 1993, in Latur district, an earthquake occurred which damaged about seventy villages and caused the death of around 10,000 people. The casualties were high, because the earthquake happened at night, when people were sleeping in their houses, which were not strong enough as they were built with stone and mud. The government took steps to compensate the affected families, constructed new houses with earthquake-resistant technologies in areas newly acquired for the purpose, and allowed the dilapidated houses to be retained by their owners. The new houses were given free of cost. The new villages looked like the villages in developed countries. The survivors were given help to earn their subsistence too.

In Gujarat, an earthquake in 2001 killed nearly 30,000 people. The state government, Gujaratis living in other countries and the Government of India helped the earthquake-affected people splendidly. They gave funds to families to build or repair their houses, and compensation to those who lost their near and dear ones. This was appreciated by everyone.

In J&K, heavy snowfall and landslides often occur. When they occurred, the state government, the people of the state, the government of India and people all over the country went all out to help them. They also repaired and rebuilt their houses in the best possible fashion.

Heavy rains affected many parts of the country. The states of Gujarat, Maharashtra, Madhya Pradesh, Bihar, Assam, Kerala and Karnataka were affected by it. Houses were damaged, crops standing in the fields were destroyed, cattle was lost, and transport facilities disrupted owing to damage to bridges and roads. The governments and the people of the states and the country took effective steps to help them. Mumbai was also affected by heavy rains. The Union government gave all the help to the people, the state and the city without waiting for their demands for assistance. The state was confident enough to help the people, but the Union did not allow it to bear the entire burden.

The tsunami of 2004 caused loss of lives and immense destruction in the islands of Andaman and Nicobar, the states of Puducherry, Andhra Pradesh, Orissa, Tamil Nadu and Kerala. The governments and the people of the states and the country did their best to overcome the disaster. India also helped neighbouring countries. The disaster caused by the tsunami united the people of the country and the world. It created confidence in the minds of the people that they could manage and overcome any kind of difficulties caused by disasters.

Humanity suffers during wars, through the violence of terrorist and criminal activities and by natural disasters. The suffering and damages caused by disasters are enormous, and in many cases, more than that caused by minor wars, terrorism or crimes. Disasters caused by human beings can be as dangerous and difficult to manage as those caused by nature. It is, therefore, necessary to take all steps necessary to manage and control them. The steps taken are not adequate and need greater resolve and efforts. What is required for this purpose is an understanding of the dimension of the problem, adequate research and development, and new systems to handle them.

■

India has borders with Pakistan, China, Myanmar, Bangladesh, Nepal and Bhutan. Citizens can cross the borders into Nepal and Bhutan freely; they need to follow certain formalities while crossing into Myanmar. An area of about twenty kilometres on both sides of the border road can be used freely by citizens of both countries to carry on their trade and business and meet their relatives. In this area, no formalities which create difficulties are needed to be followed. This border is manned by men and officers of Assam Rifles. On this border also, at times, it is found that smuggling is done, causing difficulties to both the countries.

It is not easy to cross the borders with Pakistan. A fence has been erected to prevent infiltration by terrorists and other kinds of criminals from Pakistan to India, and exfiltration of persons from India to Pakistan. The government of India has done this to make sure that drugs and weapons are not smuggled into and outside the country very easily. The expenses for erecting the fence was borne by the government of India. Paramilitary forces, mainly the BSF, man the border and patrol the road there. The fence that is erected is good. It need to be modernized to make it more useful.

By the side of the fence on Indian territory there is a constructed road which is used to patrol the area around the fence. Vehicles, horses and camels are used by the forces to patrol the area.

India and Bangladesh have between them an international border of nearly 4,000 kilometres. A fence is being erected on this border also. The work is not fully completed, and every year, repairs to the fence are required, because many rivers flow through the area to join the Bay of Bengal. At some places, the fence is not built, because of differences expressed by Bangladesh about the ownership and sovereignty of some areas. In these areas, on occasions, forces of both countries have exchanged fire to prove their sovereignty and ownership of the area. Some citizens of Bangladesh entered Indian territory to seek employment or to set up shops and trading. At times, objection is taken to their coming to India on the ground that most of them do not return to their country. This issue is discussed hotly in the states of India adjoining the border.

Bangladesh stands between the northeastern region of India and West Bengal. It has borders which are close to Bhutan and other adjoining countries. This fact makes the area strategically very important, requiring constant vigilance by India. The people of Bangladesh and West Bengal speak Bengali and have a cultural affinity, which unites them but creates problems also.

The international border between India and Bangladesh is manned by the BSF.

The international border between India and China is divided into two parts. One part is in the east and the other is in the west. The border between them is not fenced, but is not easy to cross because many formalities have to be followed. At many places on this border, the men of the forces of both the countries stand eyeball to eyeball and face one another. The two countries have a dispute about the border, which they are now trying to solve through dialogues and diplomacy.

India had taken a decision to deploy defence forces on the line of actual control, and to deploy the paramilitary forces on the international borders.

The paramilitary forces are under the control of the home ministry. During peace time, they man the international borders, with the defence forces remaining behind them and not in the first line. In wartime, the defence forces are required to be on the first line and paramilitary forces on the second one. This means that the home ministry shares the responsibility with the defence ministry to provide protection to the sovereignty, territory and border of the country. The defence ministry also shares the responsibility of the home ministry to provide internal security. Looked at from this angle, it can be said that the major responsibility of protecting the international borders in peace time is shouldered by the home ministry.

BIODATA
Shivraj V. Patil

Father's Name	:	Late Vishwanath Patil
Date of Birth	:	12 October 1935
Place of Birth	:	Village Chakur, Dist. Latur, Maharashtra
Marital Status	:	Married in June 1963
Wife	:	Vijaya Patil
Children	:	One Son and One Daughter
Educational Qualifications	:	BSc, LLM. Educated at Osmania University, Hyderabad, and Bombay University, Mumbai
Profession	:	Advocate, Agriculturist and Honorary Prof. of Law
Permanent Address	:	'Deoghar' Sadbhawna Nagar, Latur–413512 (Maharashtra)
Present Address	:	Punjab Raj Bhawan, Sector 6, Chandigarh 0172-2740740 (O), 2741058 (fax) Email: govsrp12@gmail.com

Positions Held

- Professor of Law, Aurangabad and Latur: 1963-64
- President, Municipal Corporation, Latur: 1967-69 and 1971-72
- Honorary Lecturer in Industrial Labour and Commercial Laws, Dayanand College, Latur: 1965-73

- Member, Maharashtra Legislative Assembly (two terms): 1972-79
- Chairman, Public Undertakings Committee, Maharashtra Legislative Assembly: 1974-75
- Deputy Minister, Law and Judiciary, Irrigation and Protocol, Govt of Maharashtra: 1975-76
- Deputy Speaker, Maharashtra Legislative Assembly: 5 July 1977-13 March 1978
- Speaker, Maharashtra Legislative Assembly: 17 March 1978-6 December 1979
- Elected to the Seventh Lok Sabha from Latur Parliamentary Constituency in 1980 and remained a member of the Lok Sabha till 2004, having been elected consecutively seven times
- Member, Joint Committee on Salaries and Allowances of Members of Parliament: May-September 1980
- Chairman, Joint Committee on Salaries and Allowances of Members of Parliament: September-October 1980
- Union Minister of State for Defence: 1980-82
- Union Minister of State for Commerce (independent charge): 1982-83
- Union Minister of State for Science and Technology, Atomic Energy, Electronics, Space and Ocean Development, Non-conventional Sources of Energy, and Vice President, CSIR: 1983-84
- Elected to the Eighth Lok Sabha (second term): 1984-89
- Union Minister of State for Science and Technology, Atomic Energy, Electronics, Space and Ocean Development, Non-conventional Sources of Energy, and Vice President, CSIR: 1984-86
- Union Minister of State for Defence (Production and Supplies): 1986-88
- Union Minister of State for Civil Aviation and Tourism (independent charge): 1988-89
- Elected to the Ninth Lok Sabha (third term): 1989-91

- Deputy Speaker, Lok Sabha: 19 March 1990-13 March 1991
- Chairman, Library Committee; Chairman, Committee on Private Members' Bill and Resolution; Member, General Purpose Committee; and Member, Business Advisory Committee: 1990-91
- Elected to the Tenth Lok Sabha (fourth term): 1991-96
- Unanimously elected Speaker, Lok Sabha: 10 July 1991-21 May 1996
- President, National Press, India: 1992
- Elected to the Eleventh Lok Sabha (fifth term): 1996-1997
- Member, Committee on Defence: 1996-97
- Awarded Anuvrata Award by Tulsi Foundation: 1997
- Doctorate Degree (Honoris Causa) conferred by Marathwada University: 1998
- Elected to the Twelfth Lok Sabha (sixth term): 1998-99
- Member, Committee on External Affairs; Member, Rules Committee; Member, Consultative Committee for the Ministry of External Affairs: 1998-99
- Elected to the Thirteenth Lok Sabha (seventh term): 1999-2004
- Chairman, Standing Committee on Finance: 1999-2000
- Member, Committee of Privileges; Member, Consultative Committee for Ministry of Home Affairs; Member, General Purpose Committee: 1999-2004
- Deputy Leader, Congress Parliamentary Party (Lok Sabha): 2001-2004
- Member, Committee on Security in Parliamentary Complex: 2001-2004
- Member, Congress Working Committee, AICC: 2002-2009
- Chancellor, Tilak Maharashtra University, Pune: 2003-2004
- Union Minister of Home Affairs: May 2004-30 November 2008
- Elected to the Rajya Sabha: July 2004-21 January 2010
- Governor, Punjab, and Administrator, Union Territory of Chandigarh: 22 January 2010

Favourite Pastime

- Reading and Writing

Sports

- Swimming, Shooting and Horse-riding

Countries Visited

- Widely travelled (forty-one countries): Leader, Indian Parliamentary Delegation to:
- 86th Inter-parliamentary Conference, Santiago, Chile, 1991
- 38th Common Parliamentary Conference, Nassau, Bahamas, 1992
- 39th Commonwealth Parliamentary Conference, Cyprus, 1993
- 90th Inter-parliamentary Conference, Canberra, Australia, 1993
- 40th Commonwealth Parliamentary Conference, Banff, Canada, 1994
- 41st Commonwealth Parliamentary Conference, Colombo, Sri Lanka, 1995
- Special Session of the Inter-parliamentary Council on the occasion of the fiftieth anniversary of the United Nations, New York, 1995
- Attended conferences of SAARC speakers, Colombo, Sri Lanka, Nepal, Bangladesh
- Led Indian Parliamentary Delegations to several countries: Singapore, China, North Korea, Vietnam, Laos, Cambodia, Japan, UK, Germany, Bulgaria, Iran, Bangladesh, Nepal, Egypt, Israel, Syria, Soviet Union, Ethiopia and Jordan

Books Written

- *42nd Amendment of the Indian Constitution*

- *Reminiscence and Reflections* (1995)
- *Emerging Vision of India* (1996)
- *Ecstasy and Agony of a Presiding Officer* (1998)
- *Fragrance of the Innerself* (Poetry, 1996)
- *Dialogues 2004*
- *Shrimad Bhagwat Geeta* and *Das Bodh* (translated into English)

ACKNOWLEDGEMENTS

My friends, Shri Motipawale, Shri Pradip Rathi and Shri Baswaraj Patil, had got published some books written by me. They were keen to have my memoirs written and published too. They would ask me to pen my memoirs whenever they had occasion to do so.

There were others too who thought that I should write about my life and experiences of political activities for more than fifty years.

My son Shailesh, my daughter-in-law Dr Archana and my grand-daughters Rudrali, Rushika and Arushi were also of the view that I should write my autobiography.

Mr Kapish Mehra, the publisher of this book, indicated his readiness to get the book printed and published. Their desire and insistence encouraged and inspired me to pen this book.

I would like to express my appreciation and thanks for what they did. But for their insistence and demand, this book would have needed long years to see the light of the day.

INDEX

Achintya, 22
Adik, Ramarao, 59, 138–139
Adjournment Motion, 127–128
Advani, Lal Krishna, 282
Agarwal, Brijmohan, 32, 58, 66
Agarwal High School, 32
agriculture, development of, 97, 115–116
    irrigation facilities for, 117–118
    rainwater harvesting, 117–118
Aiyar, Mani Shankar, 282, 314
Ambedkar, Dr B.R., 95, 279
Andaman and Nicobar, 173–174
Annadurai, C.N., 280
Antulay, A.R., 138, 180
Appropriation Bill, 130
Archana, 20, 21
Arushi, 22
Asaf Jahi dynasty, 3
Assam Rifles Act, 384
Aurangabad, 43, 45
Ausa constituency, 89
Azad, Maulana Abdul Kalam, 23, 280

Bagri, Mani Ram, 143
Bajpai, Chandrashekhar, 63–64
Bardoloi, Gopinath, 280

Bashweshwar, Mahatma, 280
Beed district, 116
Bhabha, Dr Homi J., 210
Bhagirtibai, 15
Bhagwati, Justice P.N., 113
Bhatia, Ramjibhai, 67, 136
bills, passing in legislature, 129
Birajdar, Vishwanath, 89, 91, 93
Bose, Netaji Subhash Chandra, 280

Calling Attention Motion, 127
Chadarghat College, 32
Chakur, 3–5, 23, 27–29, 36, 43, 45
Chaluke, Bhaskarrao, 92
Charles, Prince, 194
Chatterjee, Somnath, 274, 282
Chavan, Shankarrao, 45–46, 87, 96, 106, 111–112, 120, 138, 237
Chavan, Yashwantrao, 45, 47, 90, 140, 280
Chidambaram, P., 282
Chincholi, 17
Choudhary, Renuka, 307
civil aviation ministry, experiences

from, 239–247
Air India, 239, 244
Airport development, 240–241
development of civil aviation, 245–246
grounding of A-320s, 243
Indian Airlines, 239, 243
Pawan Hans, 241–242
Vayudoot, 242
Commonwealth Parliamentary Association, 134
Commonwealth Parliamentary Union (CPU), 300, 302
Communal Harmony Bill, 384
Congress Party, 60, 64, 89–91, 93–94, 164, 312–330
Council of Scientific and Industrial Research (CSIR), 214
CPI(M), 332

Dalai Lama, 279
Dange, S.A., 280
Darda, Amarchand, 58, 91–93
Dasmunsi, Priya Ranjan, 319
Dayanand College, 61–62, 94
defence ministry, experiences from, 230–238
  Bofors issue, 230–233
  with Indian air force, 235–236
  manufacturing of tanks for army, 234–235
  ordnance factories, 236
  public sector undertakings with, 237
deputy speaker, Lok Sabha, career as, 251–253
Desai, Balasaheb, 121–122

Desai, Morarji, 131
Dev, Acharya Narendra, 280
Dhanegaon, 116
Dhawan, Dr, 217, 227
Dhawan, R.K., 307
Dhoki, 45
Discovery of India, 172
Dong, Pham Van, 157

early years
  betrothal ceremony, 14–15
  bike driving, experience of, 13
  grandparents, influence of, 7, 10
  learning of horse-riding, 2
  legal profession, 44, 47–59
  paternal influence, 10–15
  schooling. *see* education
  teaching career, 32, 42–43, 62
Economic and Social Commission for Asia and the Pacific (ESCAP), 188–189
education
  high school, 27–29
  law, 23–24, 27, 32–37
  National Cadet Corps (NCC) training, 31, 47
  perception on, 39–41
  university, 29–31
education policy, 1986, 39
Employment Guarantee Scheme of Maharashtra, 98–105, 147
English language, 61
executive in India, 289–290

family members, 5–6, 9–22
foreign trade ministry, experiences from

with African countries, 183–185
with Bangkok, 188–189
with China, 184
and concept of globalization, 198–199
with Czechoslovakia, 193–194
with Finland, 192–193
with GATT, 194–196
and India's balance of trade, 183
with Iran, 189–192
with Japan, 185–188
with UK, 194

Gadgil, V.N., 312
gadi, 3–4, 28
  houses on, 4
Gandhi, Indira, 93, 135–136, 138–141, 148, 150, 165, 167–168, 171–173, 180, 187, 194, 216, 222, 228, 280, 331
Gandhi, Mahatma, 23, 190–191, 279, 342
Gandhi, Sonia, 312, 314, 316
Gandhi, Rajiv, 172, 219–220, 230, 241–244, 247, 278, 314, 331
Gandhi, Sanjay, 142–143
Gangabai, 15
General Agreement on Tariffs and Trade (GATT), 194–196
general discussion on the budget, 130
Ghosh, Aurobindo, 39, 279
Giáp, General Võ Nguyên, 158
Gibbs, 68
Girijabai, 2
Godhra incident, 323
Gokhale, Gopal Krishna, 280

Gomango, Giridhar, 315–316
Gopalan, Comrade A.K., 280
Goswami, Ramakant, 113
Gowda, H.D. Deve, 312
Gujral, I.K., 166, 307, 312
Gupta, Bhupesh, 280
Gupta, Indrajit, 156, 280–281

Hanumantrao (Anandrao), 3, 9, 17
Hidayatullah, M., 170
hillock of Haquani Baba, 4, 28
Hindi language, 61
Hindu Marriage Act, 54
home minister, career as, 333–402
  coastal police guard, 372–373
  combating terrorism, 348–351, 366
  criminal justice system, 356–359
  criminal laws, 379–384
  Defence Research and Development Organization (DRDO), 377–379
  intelligence agencies, 371, 375–377
  international border issues, 400–402
  management of disasters, 393–399
  military, paramilitary, reserve police, 359–367
  paramilitary forces, 368–371
  surveillance system, 373–375
  TADA and POTA, 356, 382–383
  Union and state police forces, 360–367
Hyderabad High Court, 35

414 • *Shivraj V. Patil*

Hyderabad state, annexation of, 27–28

II-sung, Kim, 164–165
Inter Parliamentary Union (IPU), 300, 302–303
Irani, Professor, 34

Jang, Dr Aliyar, 119

Kaku, Haribai, 16
Kalam, Dr A.P.J. Abdul, 217
Kalani, Shaheed Hemu, 280
Kaldate, Bapusaheb, 59, 63, 91
Kamaraj, K., 280
Kamble, Tulshiram, 93
Kargil war, 321, 329
Karunanidhi, M., 141
Kaul, Mrs, 279
Kawalkhedkar, Madhavrao Patil, 20
Kesari, Sitaram, 312
Keswani, Suresh, 317
Khatal, B.J., 111, 116
Kibria, Shah Abu Muhammad Shamsul, 189
Koyana power project, 107–108
Kulkarni, Panditrao, 14
Kulsumbi, 9

Lal, Chowdhury Devi, 280
Latur, 5, 10, 17, 27, 29, 44, 62, 117, 124
Latur bar association, 57–59
Latur constituency, 89
Latur municipality, experiences as president of, 62–88
cultural aspect, promotion of, 79
dam construction, 73–74
drainage system, establishment of, 74–75
employees of, 77–78
hospitals, construction of, 77
libraries, construction of, 77
mob incident, 84–87
panchayati raj system, 76
public gardens, market, construction of, 75–76
schools and colleges, construction of, 77–78
transportation, development of, 83–84
urban planning, 80–83
law ministry, 112–113
legal profession, 44, 47–55
fees, 50–51
Latur bar association, 57–59
on legal aid schemes, 56–57
matrimonial cases, 53
perception about marriage laws, 54–55
railway station firing incident, 52–53
workmen's compensation cases, 55–56
legal system in India, 114–115
Life Divine, 39
Lok Sabha, functioning of, 142–143, 255–260

Maharaj, Sahu, 280
Maharashtra legislative assembly, 75
Maharashtra legislative council, experiences from
agriculture, development, 97

budget presentation, 97–98
Employment Guarantee Scheme, 98–105
establishment of new universities, 96–97
legislative committee undertakings, 106–110
participating in discussions, 95–96
presiding over council, 122–140
Malla, Shaheed Durga, 280
Mallikarjunaiah, S., 260
Malviya, K.D., 90
Manikchand Pahade (MP) Law College, 42
Manley, Michael, 135
Maran, Murasoli, 280
Marathwada region, reorganization of, 34
Mariam, Mengistu Haile, 184
Maurya, Chandragupta, 280
Mavalankar, G.V., 95
Menon, V.K. Krishna, 237
Mogekar, Shivraj Patil, 48
Mohite, Yashwantrao, 120
MP Law College, 43, 61
Mukherjee, Pranab, 208, 282, 314, 316
Mumbai High Court, 35, 113
Mumbai University, 34, 42
Munda, Birsa, 280
municipal act, 67

Naik, Vasantrao, 45, 59, 89–90, 105–106, 120
Nandapurkar, Ramchanderrao, 35, 59
Narayan, Jayaprakash, 131–133, 280
Naresh, 18
National Textile Corporation, 202, 205
NDA government, 332
Nehru, Pandit Jawaharlal, 23, 135, 157, 175, 190–191, 196, 210, 218, 239, 280, 340. 342
Nehru, Pandit Motilal, 279
Nilangekar, Shivajirao Patil, 92, 120, 122
No-Confidence Motion, 128–129

opposition member, experiences as, 312–332
Osmanabad town, 83, 116, 120
Osmania University, Hyderabad, 29

Page, V.S., 98–99, 103
Pankija, 18
Pant, K.C., 232
Parliament attack, 320–321
Patel, Rajni, 53
Patel, Sardar Vallabhbhai, 23, 280, 342
Patel, Vithalbhai, 280
Patil, Basava Prabhu, 20–22
Patil, Bhavurao, 17
Patil, Bhavurao (Gurunath), 5, 16
Patil, Chandrasekhar, 17
Patil, Harish Chandra, 48–49
Patil, Keshavrao, 17
Patil, Madhavrao, 5, 13, 16
Patil, Pratibha, 138–139
Patil, Rajaram Bapu, 120

416 • *Shivraj V. Patil*

Patil, Rajeshwar, 11, 15, 18
Patil, Rajni, 113
Patil, Sambhaji (Vishwanath), 5, 10
Patil, Shivraj, 20, 44, 171
Patil, Trimbakrao, 17, 91, 93
Patil, Vasant Dada, 120, 125, 138–139
Patil, Veer Bhagwantrao, 1
Pawar, Sharad, 47, 138, 140, 237, 282
Phule, Mahatma Jyotirao, 280
Pilot, Rajesh, 142–143
Ping, Li, 307
Pokhran incident, 332
political career
  civil aviation ministry, as minister of state, 239–247
  defence ministry, as minister of state, 167–179, 230–238
  as a delegate to Vietnam, Cambodia, Laos and North Korea, 156–166
  as a deputy minister of law, irrigation and protocol, 111–121
  as deputy speaker, lok sabha, 251–253
  as foreign trade minister of state with independent charge, 180–200
  as home minister, 333–402
  as member of legislative assembly, 89–110
  as a member of Lok Sabha, 141–155
  as opposition member, 312–332
  as president of Latur municipality, 62–88
  presiding over Maharashtra legislative council, 122–140
  science and technology, as minister of state, 209–229
  as speaker, lok sabha, 254–311
  speeches in the Lok Sabha, 145–154
  tourism ministry, as union minister of state, 248–250
  as union minister of state in textile ministry with independent charge, 201–208
Pot, Pol, 160
Pradesh Congress Committee of Maharashtra, 89
Prakasam, Andhra Kesari Tanguturi, 280
Pratap, Rana, 280
Premadasa, Ranasinghe, 303
proceedings of the Houses, 127–130

Rafsanjani, Akbar Hashemi, 189
Ram, Jagjivan, 280
Ramachandran, M.G., 280
Ramesh, Jairam, 314
Ranga, Prof. N.G., 280
Rao, N.T. Rama, 216
Rao, P.V. Narasimha, 150, 190, 244, 267, 303, 312
Ray, Rabi, 251, 267, 307
Reddy, Brahmanand, 138
Reddy, S. Jaipal, 282
Rudrali, 21–22
Rushika, 21–22

SAARC, 302–304
Samant, Dr Datta, 202
Sangameshwar, 36
Satyamurti, S., 280
science and technology ministry,
  experiences from
  biotechnology, genetics and
    nanotechnology, field of,
    225–226
  'Dakshin Gangotri' expedition,
    224
  dealing of funds, manpower and
    facilities, 211–212
  electronics sector, 219–222
  environment pollution, handling
    of, 222–224
  establishment of institutions for
    R&D, 209–212
  launch of the satellite vehicle,
    216–219
  modernization initiatives,
    212–213
  non-conventional sources of
    energy, development of,
    214–216
  ocean development, department
    of, 222–224
Scindia, Madhavrao, 244, 316, 319
Security Council, 136–137
Shailesh, 19–21
Shankaranand, B., 141, 231
Sharma, Dr Shankar Dayal, 90,
  142, 279
Shekhar, Chandra, 282
Shivaji, Chhatrapati, 280
Shukla, Pandit Ravi Shankar, 280
Sibal, Kapil, 314

Sidiqui, Abubakar, 66
Sihanouk, King Norodom, 161
Singh, Arjun, 282
Singh, Arun, 230
Singh, Bhishma Narain, 141, 144,
  148
Singh, Chaudhary Charan, 131,
  137
Singh, C.P.N., 148
Singh, Dr Manmohan, 282, 316
Singh, Jaswant, 282
Singh, Ranjit, 280
Singh, Shaheed Bhagat, 280
Singh, V.P., 171, 200, 203, 230,
  232, 251
snake wine, 166
Socialist Party, 60
Sonawane, Keshavrao, 45–46,
  59–60, 63–65, 89–92, 94
Sonawane, Manikrao, 46, 61,
  63–64, 89
speaker, Lok Sabha, career as,
  254–311
  awarding parliamentarians,
    281–282
  bills, passing of, 264–267
  budget presentation, 264–265
  establishing statue of Mahatma
    Gandhi, 279–281
  impeachment incidents, 292–298
  luncheon meetings, 267–268
  motion thanking, 264
  MP funds, 276–277
  Parliament library, 282–284
  pistol incident, 271
  question hour, 260–261
  question period, 261–262

separation of powers in governance, 290–292
Standing Committees, 268–271
surveillance system, implementing within Parliament premises, 271–273
training for new members, 285–289
zero hour discussions, 262–264
speaker functions in House, 255–260
State Transport Corporation of Maharashtra, 75, 83, 86, 109
Sukhadia, M.L., 142
Sulalikar, Shivraj Patil, 48
Suzuki, 186–188
Suzuki, Senko, 187
Suzuki, Shunzo, 187
Swami, Mahadev, 13–14, 25
Swapna, 20–22
Swaraj, Sushma, 282

Tagore, Rabindranath, 190–191, 280
Tata, J.R.D., 239–240
textile ministry, experiences from
cotton cultivation, 206–207
jute industry, 207–208
modernization of textile mills, 204–205

Thevar, P. Muthuramalinga, 280
Tilak, Bal Gangadhar, 30
Tirpude, Nasikrao, 90, 138
tourism ministry, experiences from, 248–250
Tripathi, Kamlapati, 141
Tulsiji, Acharya, 134
Tung, Mao Tse, 308
Tytler, Jagdish, 142–143

Udgirkar, Rajabhahu, 32

Vajpayee, Atal Bihari, 281, 307, 312, 315–316
Varma, 312
Velduda, 15
Venkataraman, R., 143, 180
Vijaya, 18
Vikram, 18
Voraji, 134

Wankhade (Speaker), 120
Wankhede, S.K., 90–91
Workmen's Compensation Act, 50
World Trade Organization (WTO), 196

Yadav, Chandrajeet, 156

Zakaria, Dr Rafiq, 111, 119

www.ingramcontent.com/pod-product-compliance
Lightning Source LLC
Chambersburg PA
CBHW030359100426
42812CB00028B/2769/J